An Uncommon Time

THE NORTH'S CIVIL WAR SERIES
Paul A. Cimbala, series editor

An Uncommon Time

THE CIVIL WAR
AND THE NORTHERN HOME FRONT

Edited by
Paul A. Cimbala *and* Randall M. Miller

Fordham University Press
New York
2002

The North's Civil War, No. 20
ISSN 1089–8719

Library of Congress Cataloging-in-Publication Data

An uncommon time : the Civil War and the northern
home front / edited by
Paul A. Cimbala and Randall M. Miller.— 1st ed.
        p.   cm. — (The North's Civil War ; no. 20)
    Includes bibliographical references and index.
    ISBN 0-8232-2195-4
    1. United States—History—Civil War, 1861–1865—
Social aspects.   2. Northeastern   States—History,
Military—19th century. 3. Northeastern States—Social
conditions—19th century.   1. Cimbala, Paul A. (Paul
Alan), 1951–   II. Miller, Randall M.   III. Series.
E468.9 .U38   2002
973.7—dc21   2002003890

Printed in the United States of America
02   03   04   05   06   5   4   3   2   1
First Edition

To Our Colleagues at Fordham University
and Saint Joseph's University

CONTENTS

PREFACE

NOT SO LONG AGO, historian Maris Vinovskis charged students of the American Civil War to write the social history of the war, especially to discover the ways the war affected, and was affected by, the home front. Over the past several years, various historians took up the task of connecting the war fought on the battlefield with the war experienced at home, and in so doing pointed to the many ways war changed society. Much of this work focused on the southern home front, where invading armies, escaping slaves, and social and economic disruption ended a way of life. But the South had no monopoly on a civil war striking the values and lives of people at home, and it ought not to have such a monopoly in histories of what the war meant to American values and lives. Historians have been slow in applying Vinovskis's charge to studies of the northern home front, no doubt because the wartime impact on communities, institutions, and ideas was less traumatic and visible than what southerners experienced. Conventional accounts of the Civil War largely ignored, or discounted, the war's effect on and in the North, save to calibrate economic change and chart the rise of the Republican party. The assumption often was that the story of "the Union" was synonymous with that of "the North." Thus, looking at developments in Washington or in the major counting houses, factories, and mercantile centers supposedly told the tale of the North's Civil War. The social historians marched off to Dixie.

Recent, seminal, overviews of the northern home front by Phillip Shaw Paludan and J. Matthew Gallman suggested that the story of the North's Civil War was not so neat. They invited further study into the variety of home-front experiences in a society as varied and complex as "the North," for the war meant different things to farmers, miners, factory workers, merchants, and others, as it also varied in its effects based on such factors as geography, race, class, gender, generation, and more. If the demands of wartime mobilization and recruitment led to a more "national" identity and stronger federal governmental institutions, they did not erase local permutations. Indeed, in some ways, the two authors suggest, they enhanced them. The North did not emerge from the war completely remade, certainly not so much as did the South. Thus, measuring the trajectory and character of change wrought by the war demanded close attention to the details of everyday life in various kinds of settings. It had to be so. The variegated "North" had no single religious, social, ethnic, or economic template from which to draw conclusions about "the effect" of "the war." In recognizing the complexity and diversity of mid-nineteenth-century, wartime, and postwar northern society, students of the Civil War also recognized the need to conduct in-depth community studies as a first step to provide the comparative scaffolding on which to construct understandings of the "northern home front." They also understood that doing so meant moving beyond, while never neglecting, "traditional" sources to "read" material culture, fiction, folklore, and "memory," among several sources, to get closer to the "mind" of northerners and the cultural, psychological, and social worlds they made and occupied. Such scholars also acknowledged that no single book could yet capture the "northern home front" in one sweep.

The recognition of the complexity, variety, and even intractability of the northern home-front "story" informs the series of which the present volume is a part. In that regard this volume represents a continuation of the first probings into the northern home front begun over a decade ago by Paludan and of the more recent reconstructions of community life in several northern places. It also reflects the emphasis on social history Vinovskis sought to awaken earlier. And it recognizes that the war intruded, however subtly at times, almost everywhere—from life at home, to the study of science, to understandings of what it meant to be a man or a woman. As such, this volume should be read as part of an emerging conversation on what the Civil War, "an uncommon time" to use Paludan's apt phrase, meant to northerners in their own day, and came to mean in their and the nation's memory.

In preparing this volume over the past several years, the editors incurred a number of debts to institutions and to individuals who made their task easier and this book better than they would otherwise have been. We thank the librarians at Fordham University, the New York

Public Library, Saint Joseph's University, the Civil War Library and Museum, Haverford College, the Historical Society of Pennsylvania, the Library Company of Philadelphia, and the University of Pennsylvania for their assistance. Also, we are grateful to Fordham University and Saint Joseph's University for their continued generous support of our work. The extraordinarily patient and talented contributors to *An Uncommon Time* made our editorial work that much easier by providing us with their thoughtful, innovative essays. This volume is our third essay collection published by Fordham University Press, and Saverio Procario, Mary Beatrice Schulte, Anthony Chiffolo, Jacky Philpotts, and Loomis Mayer, all of the Press, once again provided us with the necessary encouragement and support required for completing the project. The editors also wish to thank Linda Patterson Miller and Elizabeth C. Vozzola for living with yet one more volume for much too long a time. Finally, we thank our colleagues at Fordham University and at Saint Joseph's University, to whom this volume is dedicated, for providing us with congenial environments in which to do our work.

INTRODUCTION

Paul A. Cimbala and Randall M. Miller

ONE MIGHT IMAGINE a North hardly touched by war when reading the letters written by Emma Randolph to her soldier friend Walter G. Dunn. During 1864, a dark period for Union arms, she apparently spent most of her time socializing with friends and relatives in Plainfield, New Jersey. For the most part her letters reported nothing more interesting to her correspondent than the weather and the comings and goings of mutual acquaintances.[1] Yet, even at her gayest, Miss Emma could not escape the war as the conflict intruded into her life in various subtle and not-so-subtle ways. The prayer meetings she attended, for example, petitioned the Almighty for peace.[2] She admitted being concerned about Jubal Early's July 1864 raid north of the Potomac lest the rebels capture Walter. And she listened to her father upon returning from a trip to New York City report that place quiet with "No signs of riot," while expressing her own concerns with the exclamation "I hope there won't be any!"[3]

In the end, Emma's cheery missives probably had more to do with her efforts to buck up Walter's morale, and perhaps her own, than with any concern for detailing the effects of the war on the home front. But it becomes clear that Emma Randolph knew enough about the war to look forward to its end. "Oh what glorious times it will be when the cruel war is over," she wrote in September 1864. "We will have or I will have a grand time when the 'Jo[h]nnies come marching home.'" Furthermore, she understood that a Union victory would have its costs. "But I have no doubt I'll feel sad for those who look in

---

[1] Judith A. Bailey and Robert I. Cotton, eds., *After Chancellorsville: Letters from the Heart, the Civil War Letters of Private Walter G. Dunn and Emma Randolph* (Baltimore: Maryland Historical Society, 1998).

[2] Emma Randolph to Walter G. Dunn, July 24, 1864, in ibid., 82.

[3] Emma Randolph to Walter G. Dunn, July 18, 1864, in ibid., 73, 75.

vain for their loved ones," a sobering thought she added to her more joyful expectations. "It will be a dear bought Peace, but I hope never to see another war."[4] Emma's letters here illustrate that sooner or later the war reared up in the narrative of ordinary things, as historian Phillip Shaw Paludan notes, "revealing the dialectic of common life in an uncommon time."[5]

Even if the war failed to work long-lasting changes throughout northern society or only accelerated changes already placed in motion by antebellum forces, on an intimate human level it affected soldiers and their families during and after the crisis in countless ways.[6] Northern communities were most obviously aware of the consequences of Fort Sumter when they witnessed their men muster and march off to war. These men were not just numbers on muster rolls to those who bid them farewell. Soldiers were foremost members of families, but also importantly members of communities. The home folks identified with the military units raised among their neighbors, making it difficult for them not to notice their going, their continued absence, and later the failure of many of them to return.[7] Just as these home folks rallied behind their soldiers, there were recusant communities from neighborhoods in Manhattan to the mountains of Pennsylvania and counties of the Old Northwest states that helped their men resist service in the Union army. These home folks, perhaps already estranged from the northern Republican mainstream in some manner, also had their lives disrupted in ways unimagined before 1861.[8]

---

[4] Emma Randolph to Walter G. Dunn, September 5, 1864, in ibid., 115.

[5] Phillip Shaw Paludan, *"A People's Contest": The Union and the Civil War, 1861–1865,* 2d ed. (Lawrence: University Press of Kansas, 1996), 326.

[6] J. Matthew Gallman notes that "The North did not change more because it did not have to"; *The North Fights the Civil War* (Chicago: Ivan R. Dee, 1994), 194. See especially his final chapter, "Victory and Its Legacy," 178–97.

[7] Phillip Shaw Paludan suggests how much of a community endeavor this war was in his chapter "Communities Go to War" in *A People's Contest,* 3–31. But see also Thomas R. Kemp, "Community and War: The Civil War Experience of Two New Hampshire Towns," in *Toward a Social History of the American Civil War: Exploratory Essays,* ed. Maris A. Vinovskis (Cambridge: Cambridge University Press, 1990), 31–77; and Michael H. Frisch, *Town into City: Springfield, Massachusetts, and the Meaning of Community, 1840–1880* (Cambridge, Mass.: Harvard University Press, 1972), especially 53–113.

[8] For examples of the treatment of northern dissent, see Iver Bernstein, *The New York City Draft Riots: Their Significance for American Society and Politics in the Age of Civil War* (New York: Oxford University Press, 1990); John W. Geary, *We*

The sacrifices of war changed soldiers in unexpected ways, further altering the lives of those individuals who shared their fortunes. Men abandoned peacetime business, while others left school, family, and "fair civil prospects" to serve in the army, leaving their families in uncertain circumstances. The war had touched their lives and, when it left them injured, altered their futures. For battlefield-injured Colonel John Speidel, for example, continued service in the army was the only way that he believed he could continue to support his family. His was a lament repeated by hundreds of other disabled Union officers.[9] Their experiences, and the experiences of thousands of other northern men, rippled through their communities.[10]

As Emma Randolph's letters suggest, the home front was no more quarantined from the battlefield and camp experiences of Union soldiers than the soldiers' wartime experiences were from their own home life.[11] From recruiting to courting, from ideas about manhood, dependency, and marriage to perceptions of black and white veterans, civilians shaped their views of the war as they interacted in any number of ways with the boys in blue.[12] The very fact that Emma was

---

Need Men: The Union Draft in the Civil War (DeKalb: Northern Illinois University Press, 1991); Judith Lee Hallock, "The Role of Community in Civil War Desertion," *Civil War History* 29 (June 1983): 123–34; Frank L. Klement, *The Limits of Dissent: Clement L. Vallandigham and the Civil War* (New York: Fordham University Press, 1998); Peter Levine, "Draft Evasion in the North during the Civil War, 1863–1865," *Journal of American History* 67 (March 1981): 816–35; Mark E. Neely, Jr., *The Fate of Liberty: Abraham Lincoln and Civil Liberties* (New York: Oxford University Press, 1991); Grace Palladino, *Another Civil War: Labor, Capital, and the State in the Anthracite Regions of Pennsylvania, 1840–1868* (Urbana: University of Illinois Press, 1990); Arnold M. Shankman, *The Pennsylvania Antiwar Movement, 1861–1865* (Rutherford, N.J.: Fairleigh Dickinson University Press, 1980); Kenneth H. Wheeler, "Local Autonomy and Civil War Draft Resistance: Holmes County, Ohio," *Civil War History* 45 (June 1999): 147–59; and Hubert H. Wubben, *Civil War Iowa and the Copperhead Movement* (Ames: Iowa State University Press, 1980).

[9] Col. J. Speidel to Col. M. N. Wisewell, July 2, 1864; 2nd Lt. J. A. Yeckley to Brig. Gen. James B. Fry, August 15, 1865, Letters Received, Veterans Reserve Corps, Records of the Provost Marshal General's Office, Record Group 110, National Archives Building, Washington, D.C. Numerous petitions for appointment now filed in the Veteran Reserve Corps records support this statement.

[10] Gallman, *The North Fights the Civil War,* 77–83. For a good summary of the northern veteran experience, see Larry M. Logue, *To Appomattox and Beyond: The Civil War Soldier in War and Peace* (Chicago: Ivan R. Dee, 1996), 82–102.

[11] For the soldiers' connections with home, see Reid Mitchell, *The Vacant Chair: The Northern Soldier Leaves Home* (New York: Oxford University Press, 1993).

[12] For explorations about interaction of the northern home front and its soldiers during and after the war, see Paul A. Cimbala and Randall M. Miller, eds., *Union*

corresponding with a soldier undoubtedly reminded her of why many of the men of Plainfield and its environs were absent from home. And the situation in which Walter found himself could not help but to alert Emma to the toll that war might take on those loved ones. At the Battle of Chancellorsville, a Confederate ball had struck Walter in the neck and lodged in his upper back.[13] With a correspondent such as Walter, Emma and her circle could not ignore the reality that was the war.

The soldier–civilian connection experienced by Emma may have been the most extraordinary, personal connection between the battlefield and home front, but other connections linked soldiers and civilians from the firing on Fort Sumter through the end of the conflict. Letters from correspondents at or near the front to local newspapers reminded readers of the progress of their community's men at arms and, regardless of any immediate personal relations between reader and soldier, hitched the fortunes of the latter to the former. Soldiers, after all, were fighting for "the Union," which meant their communities and their families. Northern men defended their home and hearth even if in a less immediate and more abstract manner than their southern counterparts facing down invaders.[14]

After the formal surrender of Fort Sumter on April 14, 1861, individuals such as a character in Henry Morford's novel *The Days of Shoddy* could not avoid the reminders of the onset of war. They walked down beflagged New York City streets and purchased "Union rosettes, stars, breast-pins, and other trifles of personal adornment"

Soldiers and the Northern Home Front: Wartime Experiences, Postwar Adjustments in Civil War America (New York: Fordham University Press, 2002).

[13] The editors of the correspondence between Emma and Walter also note the toll that campaigning before Chancellorsville and the battle itself exacted from the 11th New Jersey; see Bailey and Cotton, eds., *After Chancellorsville*, xv–xvii.

[14] There are numerous examples of newspapers publishing letters from individuals concerning war matters on a regular basis, but see Stephen W. Sears, ed., *Mr. Dunn Browne's Experiences in the Army: The Civil War Letters of Samuel W. Fiske* (New York: Fordham University Press, 1998), which reprints letters from a member of the 14th Connecticut Volunteer Infantry first published in the *Springfield [Mass.] Republican*; Lois Bryan Adams, *Letters from Washington, 1863–1865*, ed. Evelyn Leasher (Detroit: Wayne State University Press, 1999), which reprints the letters of a special correspondent to the *Detroit Advertiser and Tribune* first printed in that paper; and James Henry Gooding, *On the Altar of Freedom: A Black Soldier's Civil War Letters from the Front*, ed. Virginia M. Adams (Amherst: University of Massachusetts Press, 1991), which reprints letters from a member of the 54th Massachusetts first written for the *New Bedford Mercury*.

to proclaim their loyalty. Such "emblems of fealty to the Union grew more general day by day," Morford described in his novel, "until within a week after the fall of that fort, the man who did not display something of the kind on his breast or his lappel [sic], was very likely to have his loyalty seriously suspected."[15] Poet Walt Whitman captured the martial mood when he described the changes wrought by the outbreak of war on Manhattan, whose "soft opera-music changed and the drum and fife were heard in their stead." Also, for Whitman the sounds of drums and bugles burst "like a ruthless force" across the land into churches and schools, denying bridegroom and farmer their happiness and peace, as the sound rose "Over the traffic of cities—over the rumble of wheels in the streets."[16]

The war-related activities of communities could not escape the attention of those who remained at home. Patriotic assemblies, political speeches, newspapers, sanitary fairs, elections, troop musters, and parades continued to amplify that din until war's end. In March 1864, for example, citizens of Columbus, Ohio, draped their streets with flags, fired cannon, and launched fireworks to welcome home the 45th Ohio Infantry.[17] On February 15, 1864, thousands of individuals turned out in the streets of St. Paul to greet and then feed the returning men of the decimated 1st Minnesota Infantry.[18] Other towns near troop depots or on train lines suffered the antics of drunken or simply exuberant soldiers who destroyed private property as they made their way to the front.[19] Battlefield victories prompted celebrations across the North.[20] Communities grieved for local fallen heroes.[21] And the

---

[15] Henry Morford, *The Days of Shoddy: A Novel of the Great Rebellion in 1861* (Philadelphia: T. B. Peterson & Brothers, 1863), 107.

[16] From "First O Songs for a Prelude" and "Beat! Beat! Drums!" originally published in the 1865 volume *Drum-Taps* and reprinted in *Leaves of Grass*, ed. Sculley Bradley and Harold W. Blodgett (New York: W. W. Norton, 1973), 279–82, 283–84.

[17] Samuel P. Heintzelman Journal, March 12, 1864, Samuel P. Heintzelman Papers, Library of Congress, Washington, D.C.

[18] Richard Moe, *The Last Full Measure: The Life and Death of the First Minnesota Volunteers* (New York: Avon Books, 1993), 302.

[19] Lt. Col. L. Eastman to Lt. Col. Moore, February 25, 1864; A. Meyer to Lt. H. Montgomery, March 3, 1864, Regimental papers, 16th Regiment, Veteran Reserve Corps, Records of the Adjutant General's Office, Record Group 94, National Archives Building, Washington, D.C.; *Elmira [N.Y.] Advertiser,* February 26, 1864, reprinted in *Rochester [N.Y.] Union and Advertiser.*

[20] *Indianapolis Daily Journal,* September 7, 1864, April 4, 1865; and *Augusta [Me.] Kennebec Journal,* April 7, 14, 1865.

[21] *Trenton [N.J.] Daily State Gazette,* June 6, 1864; and *Indianapolis Daily Journal,* September 21, 1864.

president "Fallen cold and dead" sent the nation into collective exhibitions of mourning, adding a solemn, sad note to the joy of victory.[22]

Even those northerners who tried their best to insulate themselves from the realities of the times could not escape them. The flapping of those flags described by novelist Morford or the drumbeat described by poet Whitman everywhere murmured reminders of war and calls to duty, at least providing some sort of background noise to daily routines.[23] Individuals who read newspapers and novels, listened to sermons, spent and invested, engaged in the political process, and simply tried to cope with disrupted lives or minor inconveniences could not help but be reminded that all was not as it had once been. Farmers, for example, could not avoid the rhetoric or the consequences of the war. In the wake of Fort Sumter, the northern farm journal the *American Agriculturalist* urged them on to greater efforts. The following year, the *Cincinnati Gazette* observed that the army was removing thousands of farm laborers from the

---

[22] From Walt Whitman, "O Captain! My Captain!" in Bradley and Blodgett, eds., *Leaves of Grass,* 338. For the national reaction to Abraham Lincoln's assassination, see Merrill D. Peterson, *Lincoln in American Memory* (New York: Oxford University Press, 1994), 3–35.

[23] The North still needs many more of the kind of community studies that some historians have been producing for the Civil War South, but see Frisch, *Town into City;* J. Matthew Gallman, *Mastering Wartime: A Social History of Philadelphia during the Civil War* (Cambridge: Cambridge University Press, 1990); Theodore J. Karamanski, *Rally 'Round the Flag: Chicago and the Civil War* (Chicago: Nelson-Hall Publishers, 1993); Thomas H. O'Connor, *Civil War Boston: Home Front and Battlefield* (Boston: Northeastern University Press, 1997); and Michael P. Gray, *The Business of Captivity: Elmira and Its Civil War Prison* (Kent, Ohio: Kent State University Press, 2001). Several articles and book chapters have addressed aspects of the war's impact on communities and serve as good examples of what other scholars might accomplish. For example, see J. Matthew Gallman with Susan Baker, "Gettysburg's Gettysburg: What the Battle Did to the Borough," in *The Gettysburg Nobody Knows,* ed. Gabor S. Boritt (New York: Oxford University Press, 1997), 144–74; Michael P. Gray, "Elmira, A City on a Prison-Camp Contract," *Civil War History* 45 (December 1999): 322–38; Thomas R. Kemp, "Community and War: The Civil War Experience of Two New Hampshire Towns"; and Robin L. Einhorn, "The Civil War and Municipal Government in Chicago," both in Vinovskis, ed., *Toward a Social History of the American Civil War,* 31–77 and 117–38. There also is a need for modern state studies that are perhaps considered a bit old fashioned these days. For good examples of newer studies of politics over the war years at the state level, see William Gillette, *Jersey Blue: Civil War Politics in New Jersey, 1854–1865* (New Brunswick, N.J.: Rutgers University Press, 1995); and Lex Renda, *Running on the Record: Civil War Era Politics in New Hampshire* (Charlottesville: University Press of Virginia, 1997).

fields. And in 1863, farther west in Davenport, Iowa, the *Daily Ga-zette* reminded readers that agriculture was adapting itself to the new requirements of a society at war.[24]

Of course, most northern civilians did not experience war in the same manner as southerners caught in the way of advancing or re-treating armies. It was a different kind of home-front war in many ways, but as Emma Randolph's letters suggest, it still insinuated itself into various and sundry aspects of northern society. The war, accord-ing to Ralph Waldo Emerson, was able to purge the nation of its sins because of its very enormity; it was a war that "has assumed such huge proportions that it threatens to engulf us all—no preoccupation can exclude it, & no hermitage hide it."[25] And years after Appomat-tox, one Yankee child of the war remembered how she and other youngsters knew in an intuitive way that "there was some struggle going on in the world which touched all life."[26]

Historian Phillip Shaw Paludan most recently pointed to the fact that the North deserves the same attention as that given to the Con-federacy when searching for understanding as to how the war reached individuals and institutions on the home front. His book *"A People's Contest": The Union and Civil War 1861–1865,* the standard work on the topic since its first publication in 1988, still reminds readers in no uncertain terms that the war also happened to the North.[27] Two years after Paludan's book directed scholarly attention to the northern home front, Maris Vinovskis edited a groundbreaking collection of essays, *Toward a Social History of the American Civil War: Exploratory Essays,* that called attention to the need for further

---

[24] Quoted in George Winston Smith and Charles Judah, *Life in the North during the Civil War: A Source History* (Albuquerque: University of New Mexico Press, 1966), 164–67, 170.

[25] Quoted in ibid., 318.

[26] Ruth Huntington Sessions, *Sixty-Odd: A Personal History* (Brattleboro, Vt.: Ste-phen Daye, 1936), 31, quoted in James Marten, *The Children's Civil War* (Chapel Hill: University of North Carolina Press, 1998), 3.

[27] Also see Paludan's essay "What Did the Winners Win? The Social and Eco-nomic History of the North during the Civil War," in *Writing the Civil War: The Quest to Understand,* ed. James M. McPherson and William J. Cooper, Jr. (Colum-bia: University of South Carolina Press, 1998), 174–200. Gallman's book *The North Fights the Civil War* is an excellent short look at the topic, but its purpose is not to surpass Paludan in its scope and depth of coverage. Gallman asks some insightful questions, answers them, and admirably fulfills his purpose of producing a short text worthy of widespread classroom use.

exploration of the American society at war. That collection continues to act as a stimulus to researching the social history of a period dominated by battles and leaders. Both of these important contributions to the Civil War bibliography influenced the genesis of *An Uncommon Time.*

The present volume, while in some ways an extension of this past scholarship, offers fresh perspectives on a society at war. The contributors touch on a variety of topics heretofore hardly noticed in scholarship. Their essays suggest some ways in which northerners experienced the war, some ways in which the war seeped into northern institutions, and some ways in which the war shaped the perceptions of northerners concerning themselves, their politics, and their government. They discuss building support for the war effort, different ways people became involved in that effort, and the ways people came to know the war and shape it in their own minds, as well as responses to northern mobilization and the role of the government in the process. They remind readers that the war entered virtually every aspect of northern consciousness and conscience. It was, indeed, "an uncommon time" when few people at home escaped at least thinking about the various and diverse changes wrought by the war.

Taken as a whole, the essays in this book do not provide readers with one comprehensive thesis about the war and the northern home front. Rather, they reveal several civil wars on the northern home fronts—of Democrats and Republicans, of workers and employers, of blacks and whites, of those families with men who served and those with men who did not, and more. In pointing to the many and sometimes divergent interests and experiences that made up the North's Civil War, the essays also remind us what Lincoln so well understood about war and society—namely, that in saving the Union, the war was also remaking it. Such a process would remain ever unfinished and contested, even as it brought diverse people together for a common purpose and forged a national consciousness.

An Uncommon Time

1

A Terrible Fascination:
The Portrayal of Combat in the
Civil War Media

Earl J. Hess

IN ORDER to sustain a major war effort, every army has to rely on its soldiers to withstand the shock of combat. The experience of battle was so different from their prewar civilian lives that it could destroy their commitment to the cause. Whatever ideological or political issues a soldier might have supported before putting on a uniform could seem irrelevant when he began to realize that he might die or suffer painful wounds or permanent disability from battle. Every soldier had to weigh cost versus benefit. He had to come to a personal choice as to whether his participation in the war was worth the price he paid in emotional and physical suffering, and whether his nation was justified in collectively paying that price as well.[1]

Civilians, in their own way, had to deal with that problem too. Soldiers came to understand the true nature of combat through firsthand experience. How did civilians acquire such knowledge? They relied on personal, or noncommercial, outlets such as letters written

A version of this paper was read at the Southern Historical Association meeting in Houston on November 14, 1985. I wish to thank Reid Mitchell, Harriet Amos Doss, and Phillip Paludan for their comments on it.

[1] The literature on soldier response to combat in the Civil War is growing. See Gerald F. Linderman, *Embattled Courage: The Experience of Combat in the American Civil War* (New York: Free Press, 1987); Reid Mitchell, *Civil War Soldiers: Their Expectations and Their Experiences* (New York: Viking, 1988); Randall C. Jimerson, *The Private Civil War: Popular Thought during the Sectional Conflict* (Baton Rouge: Louisiana State University Press, 1988); Earl J. Hess, *Liberty, Virtue and Progress: Northerners and Their War for the Union* (New York: Fordham University Press, 1997); James I. Robertson, Jr., *Soldiers Blue and Gray* (Columbia: University of South Carolina Press, 1988); and Earl J. Hess, *The Union Soldier in Battle: Enduring the Ordeal of Combat* (Lawrence: University Press of Kansas, 1997).

home by friends and relatives or conversations with returning veterans. They also had a number of commercial media outlets such as newspapers, illustrated weekly papers, and photographs. The relative contribution of each of these two channels of information was unequal. Personal contact with soldiers far outweighed the commercial media in providing authentic information on the nature of combat. The literacy rate was impressive—as high as 93 percent in some northern urban areas—and the army did not censor soldiers' letters. The men were far from home engaged in a dramatic new experience and felt compelled to write about it. When home on leave, they often were besieged by civilians eager to learn of the fighting. In contrast, the technology behind the media and the professional development of newspaper reporters and photographers were still in their infancy. All of these limitations restricted the impact of the commercial media in educating the public about the experience of war. It could not fully bridge the gulf of experience between the veteran and the home front. By itself, the media was not a major factor in forming civilian opinions about the costs and benefits of the Civil War. It did not have the power to persuade the civilian population that the horrors of combat should dictate whether the war ought to be fought.[2] That is not to say the media exercised no significant role in shaping general public perceptions of the war. Rather, the media provided a broad panorama of war and a context for personal accounts, while making the war visible and knowable to those at home who had no regular contact with soldiers through letters or personal associations. But for the "truth" about war and the particulars of adapting to military life, the media could not, and did not, supersede the soldiers' personal accounts.

This essay will attempt to assess the relative significance of newspaper journalism and the visual imagery of illustrated newspapers and photography on the northern public's perception of war. More simply, it will focus on how the nature of combat was portrayed in these media and how the public responded to that portrayal. To be sure, such an approach has pitfalls. It often is difficult to gauge public response to any kind of news source, art form, or entertainment. One

---

[2] Lee Soltow and Edward Stevens, *The Rise of Literacy and the Common School in the United States: A Socioeconomic Analysis to 1870* (Chicago: University of Chicago Press, 1981), 56, 117, 155.

can only examine the letters, diary entries, or published essays that contain someone's reaction to newspapers and photographs and supplement that material with one's own considered evaluation of the same newspapers and photographs. I also have compared the portrayal of combat in these sources with the descriptions of combat written by soldiers in their letters, diaries, and memoirs to see how close they came to telling the home front about the true nature of battle.[3]

It is natural, even necessary, to focus on the northern rather than the southern home front in this study. The channels of information, the popular culture industry, and the level of literacy were all more highly developed in the northern United States during the 1860s. The Confederacy had no significant illustrated newspapers, whereas *Harper's Weekly* and *Frank Leslie's Illustrated,* headquartered in New York, pioneered in visual journalism. With only half the population of the North, southern towns and cities supported many fewer newspapers, and they were plagued by shortages of paper and enemy occupation as the war continued. There is no evidence that the sale of photographs in the South equaled that of the North. The loyal states retained the only fully functioning, well-developed, and broadly spectrumed "media establishment" of the Civil War era.[4]

NEWSPAPERS

The northern newspaper industry had been vibrant and colorful ever since the development of the penny press in the 1830s. Hundreds of papers were published in the North during the Civil War era. In the 1860s New York City alone had seventeen dailies, and public interest in the conflict greatly increased their readership. Yet the ability of these papers to inform the public about the nature of combat was severely hampered by journalistic canons, editorial policies, and commercial restraints. Journalistic battle descriptions were uneven in quality, ranging from authentic depictions of combat to inaccurate, sentimental drivel that reinforced the popular imagination of war as

---

[3] See Hess, *The Union Soldier in Battle,* 1–72, for descriptions of combat as written by soldiers.

[4] W. Fletcher Thompson, *The Image of War: The Pictorial Reporting of the American Civil War* (New York: Thomas Yoseloff, 1960), 10.

a glorious enterprise. The newspaper industry was a business first, a public servant second. The need to sell copies often overrode considerations of accuracy; often the result was blatant sensationalism.[5]

Oliver Wendell Holmes, Sr., a keen observer of the war's impact on northern society, pondered the effect of rapid communications and cheap presses on the public mind. The quick spread of news to the reading populace constituted "our national nervous system," he thought, and the ready availability of fast-breaking intelligence had the effect of increasing the public's eagerness to hear the latest news.[6]

Holmes even described it as a fever that affected the emotions and produced nervous symptoms. An intelligent man once told him "that he would read the same telegraphic dispatches over and over again in different papers, as if they were new, until he felt as if he were an idiot." Another man confessed to taking the side streets on his way to purchase a paper so he could avoid anyone who already had a copy. He did not want to be told the latest news before he read it himself "first on the bulletin-board, and then in the great capitals and leaded type of the newspaper." The medium seems to have had a hypnotic effect on this man, a conclusion reinforced by Holmes's own statement that "When any startling piece of war-news comes, it keeps repeating itself in our minds in spite of all we can do. . . . The newspaper is as imperious as a Russian Ukase; it will be heard, and it will be read. To this all else must give place."[7]

George Haven Putnam, who had spent the first year of the war studying in Germany, fully understood what Holmes meant. Immediately after debarking at New York City from his transatlantic journey home, he joined a crowd gathered around a bulletin board at the *Herald* office to read the latest news of the Battle of Antietam. Putnam remembered "the curious impressiveness of the present tense, of the report of a battle that was actually 'going on.' To one who reads such an announcement, all things seem possible, and as I stood surrounded by men whose pulses were throbbing with the keenest of

---

[5] J. Cutler Andrews, *The North Reports the Civil War* (Pittsburgh: University of Pittsburgh Press, 1955), 9.

[6] Oliver Wendell Holmes, Sr., "Bread and the Newspaper," in *The Complete Writings of Oliver Wendell Holmes*, 13 vols. (Boston: Houghton Mifflin, 1892), 8:7.

[7] Ibid., 1–4, 6.

emotions, I felt with them as if we could almost hear the sound of the cannon on the Potomac."[8]

The Woolsey family of New York City also felt the impact of the newspapers. The young females of the family, in particular, got "into a perfect fever" if their papers were late, and they waited "with great impatience from night till morning, and from morning till night again" for them to arrive. Paperboys bellowed news of First Bull Run through the streets after respectable people had gone to bed, raising "a tremendous howl" that awoke everyone. The tactic was effective, for the next day crowds jammed news offices throughout the city. Many people came to like "the horrible extras" even though they knew the papers contained far too much unsubstantiated news. Tired of accurate but boring reports while on a visit to Washington, D.C., Georgeanna Woolsey longed "now and then for a real living and lying 'Extra' boy, with his mouth full of fearful statements, all disproved by his paper which you imprudently buy."[9]

The lust for sensationalized reporting did not abate as the war continued. A reporter noted the public's "insatiable appetite for horrible news and rumors" as late as 1863. "To satisfy this morbid appetite the flippant newspaper correspondent has but to work up a skirmish into a column of gore, and his efforts are successful; the miserable imposition is greedily swallowed and no questions asked."[10]

All this laid the groundwork for a tremendous increase in newspaper circulation. The big city dailies were the chief beneficiaries, often selling up to five times their normal circulation when a battle occurred. The sale of such papers among soldiers was very high as well, with the *New York Herald, Philadelphia Inquirer,* and *Washington Chronicle* topping the list of sheets sold to the Army of the Potomac in March 1865. As a visiting English journalist put it, "The consump-

---

[8] George Haven Putnam, "The Civil War Fifty Years After: A Veteran's Experiences as Recalled by Battle Field Pictures," *American Review of Reviews* 43 (March 1911): 316.

[9] Mother to Georgeanna and Eliza, July 19, 22, and 23, 1861; Harriet Roosevelt Woolsey to Eliza, July 23, 1861; Abby Howland Woolsey to Georgeanna and Eliza, July 22, 1861; and Georgeanna to Margaret Hodge, July 8, 1861, all in *Letters of a Family during the War for the Union, 1861–1865,* ed. Georgeanna Woolsey Bacon and Eliza Woolsey Howland, 2 vols. (New Haven, Conn.: Tuttle, Morehouse, and Taylor, 1899), 1:116–17, 123, 128, 133, 125, 110.

[10] *Cincinnati Enquirer,* September 28, 1863, quoted in Andrews, *The North Reports the Civil War,* 647.

tion of journalism in the Federal armies is tremendous, and the pe-
rusal of newspapers appears to yield the men unceasing and unfailing
delight."[11]

The dailies prospered at the expense of hometown weekly papers,
for the latter did not have the money to send reporters to the field or
to compete with urban periodicals for large markets. Small towns like
Rutland, Vermont, had been content with local papers before 1861.
Now its residents could no longer "wait from Thursday to Thursday
to find out what was going on at the front." The urban dailies stepped
in to fill the need. Some towns were too remote to be easily reached
by the dailies. The citizens of Buena Vista, Wisconsin, considered a
daily newspaper "an unknown luxury." Residents of Pocahontas, Illinois, located twenty miles from the nearest railroad, relied on weeklies read by someone with a clear voice standing atop a barrel. The
editors of weekly papers often reprinted stories they found in the
dailies in order to hedge their share of the market against urban
intrusion.[12]

Through their widespread circulation, newspapers had an excellent opportunity to inform the public with accurate descriptions of
the nature of combat. But they failed to live up to their promise. It
was partly because of the nature of the business; the effort to sell
issues promoted an emphasis on colorful and imaginative description
over the unpleasant facts of battle. But it also was the fault of journalistic standards. Editors and reporters were supposed to report facts
rather than inform civilians of the nature of combat. These facts, such
as the names of commanders, the casualties, and the movements of
units, so often dominated battle reporting as to crowd out commentary on how it felt to be engaged in combat.

Yet even when covering facts, newspapers often were woefully inadequate. Soldiers clearly saw this. One man believed that even the
most reliable paper was at least half filled with lies, while another

---

[11] Andrews, *The North Reports the Civil War*, 32–33; Sylvanus Cadwallader, *Three
Years with Grant,* ed. Benjamin P. Thomas (New York: Knopf, 1955), 293–94;
George Augustus Sala, *My Diary in the Midst of War,* 2 vols. (London: Tinsley
Brothers, 1865), 1:289.

[12] William Henry Jackson, *Time Exposure: The Autobiography of William Henry
Jackson* (New York: G. P. Putnam's Sons, 1940), 73; Julian Wisner Hinkley, *A Narrative of Service with the Third Wisconsin* (Madison: Wisconsin History Commission,
1912), 1; Charles Beneulyn Johnson, *Muskets and Medicine, or Army Life in the
Sixties* (Philadelphia: F. A. Davis, 1917), 12.

concluded that "together with the *facts,* you get considerable thrown in to embellish those facts." Illinois cavalry officer Robert G. Ingersoll, who later became a famous agnostic, asserted that "ninety-nine hundredths was a regular lie, and the other hundredth stretched like damnation." Newspapers "and other works of fiction" sometimes failed so badly that even veterans of the battle could not recognize the engagement. Ohio soldier Henry Dwight believed much of the "news" was taken from stragglers who ran from the battle, hovered near the field, and fed wild stories to anyone gullible enough to listen. The result was "a wonderful and stupid nonsense" that tended to "lead one more and more into the dark."[13]

Many civilians also recognized that newspaper coverage was suspect even as they eagerly devoured it. Illinois physician William Fithian called battle reports not "interely [sic] reliable," and even when he trusted one it was "meager & unsatisfactory." Engagements were so often announced as "glorious victories" that Anna Ferris of Delaware, who had enough experience with this kind of rhetoric, wisely interpreted it to mean that "we have *not* endured another disgraceful defeat, but have gained some slight advantage over the Rebels at a most enormous cost of life."[14]

Ironically, journalism was saved from a total failure to convey a sense of the physical reality of combat by the fact that it was not fully professionalized. No journalism schools existed to impose a rigid

---

[13] Entry of February 28, 1863, in *A Diary of Battle: The Personal Journals of Colonel Charles B. Wainwright, 1861–1865,* ed. Allan Nevins (New York: Harcourt, Brace and World, 1962), 169; Thrall to wife, June 18, 1863, in "An Iowa Doctor in Blue: The Letters of Seneca B. Thrall, 1862–1864," ed. Mildred Throne, *Iowa Journal of History* 58 (April 1960): 157–58; Ingersoll to brother, May 9, 1862, in *The Letters of Robert G. Ingersoll,* ed. Eva Ingersoll Wakefield (New York: Thomas Yoseloff, 1951), 121; John William De Forest, "The First Time under Fire," in *A Volunteer's Adventures: A Union Captain's Record of the Civil War,* ed. James H. Croushore (New Haven, Conn.: Yale University Press, 1946), 66; William F. Goodhue to mother, August 15, 1862, William F. Goodhue Papers, Illinois State Historical Library, Springfield; Henry Otis Dwight, "How We Fight at Atlanta," *Harper's New Monthly Magazine* 29 (October 1864): 666; entry of May 25, 1862, "Diary of Colonel William Camm, 1861–1865," *Journal of the Illinois State Historical Society* 18 (January 1926): 873; Kircher to "Everybody," March 18, 1863, in *A German in the Yankee Fatherland: The Civil War Letters of Henry A. Kircher,* ed. Earl J. Hess (Kent: Kent State University Press, 1983), 82.

[14] William Fithian to John Charles Black, October 5, 1861, John Charles Black Papers, Illinois State Historical Library, Springfield; entry of September 19, 1862, in "The Civil War Diaries of Anna M. Ferris," ed. Harold B. Hancock, *Delaware History* 9 (April 1961): 240.

sense of reporting style or to indoctrinate correspondents with rules about what type of information was appropriate. This allowed many rogues to enter the business, but it also gave much freedom to scrupulous and sensitive reporters.

According to Sylvanus Cadwallader, correspondents with these latter qualities were in short supply. Those without "the rudimentary qualifications of common honesty, tact, and the ability to discriminate between legitimate and illegitimate news" perpetrated fraud on the public as they reinforced unrealistic conceptions of battle. They did not hesitate to write spurious accounts of combat. A *New York Herald* account of a Federal attack at Port Hudson on June 14, 1863, was written by an "eye-witness" reporter who was actually on his way from New York to New Orleans when the assault occurred. Even reporters who were near the scene of action often did not risk life to see, hear, or smell battle. According to Whitelaw Reid, most reporters covering the Vicksburg siege remained safely quartered on a steamboat and relied on "Dame Rumor" to supply them with information. Reporters who did not witness battle sometimes interviewed officers who had in order to "get a miscellaneous collection of isolated particulars, fill up the gaps from the imagination, and weave the whole into a 'graphic and thrilling account of the great battles.'"[15]

But there were many good reporters who struck out for the front lines, witnessed combat, withstood enemy fire, and worked long, hard hours to gather information that they reported in a straightforward, informative manner. Bradley Sillick Osbon even accepted a commission in the navy so he could more easily move about and gather news from the scene of action. Conscientious journalists employed a methodology described by Whitelaw Reid, one of the premier Civil War reporters. Noting the confusing nature of combat, Reid outlined his coverage of Shiloh: "But what one man, diligently using all his powers of observation through those two days, might see, I saw, and that I *can* faithfully set down. For the rest, after riding carefully over and over the ground, asking questions innumerable of those who knew, and sifting consistent truth from the multiplicity of replies with what-

---

[15] Cadwallader, *Three Years with Grant*, 12; Andrews, *The North Reports the Civil War*, 403, 645; Reid dispatch to *Cincinnati Gazette*, September 2, 1862, in *A Radical View: The "Agate" Dispatches of Whitelaw Reid, 1861–1865*, ed. James G. Smart, 2 vols. (Memphis: Memphis State University Press, 1976), 1:220–21.

ever still some experience may have taught, I can only give the con-current testimony of the actors."[16]

These men produced the best journalistic battle descriptions of the war, accounts characterized by the absence of purple prose, mor-alization, and sensationalism. Phrases such as "volleys of musketry, which rattled and crackled like a canebrake on fire," rivaled the evoc-ative descriptions of battle to be found in the private letters of sol-diers. J. Cutler Andrews, the foremost historian of Civil War journalism, astutely observed that the use of purple prose was more common among reporters who did not witness battle, that distancing oneself from the experience of combat led one to rely on imagination while dealing with it. He also makes the case that the best correspon-dents gave their reading public "a very real picture of what this terri-ble war was like."[17]

But even among the best journalists the need to inform the public of mere facts balanced if not overrode the desire to tell them of emotions and sensory perceptions evoked by battle. One reporter admitted that the sounds, smells, and sights of combat were the chief impressions left on his consciousness. "The master of the art, how-ever, never allows these minor delineations to become the chief fea-tures of his correspondence. . . . He weaves them into his account as bits of coloring, to set off stupendous facts. He remembers that the chief interest will always center on the heroic deeds of those en-gaged, the responsibility of each for failure or success and the para-mount question of whether the field was lost or won."[18]

---

[16] Bradley Sillick Osbon, *A Sailor of Fortune: Personal Memoirs of Captain B. S. Osbon*, ed. Albert Bigelow Paine (New York: McClure, Phillips, 1906), 131–32; Reid dispatch to *Cincinnati Gazette*, April 9, 1862, in *A Radical View*, 1:120.

[17] Andrews, *The North Reports the Civil War*, 644, 646–47. For examples of good battle coverage, see Charles A. Page dispatches on the Wilderness, in *Letters of a War Correspondent*, ed. James R. Gilmore (Boston: L. C. Page, 1899), 46–63; Reid dispatch to *Cincinnati Gazette*, April 9, 1862, in *A Radical View*, 1:119–71; Henry Villard, *Memoirs of Henry Villard, Journalist and Financier, 1835–1900* (New York: Da Capo, 1969), 251–52, 327–28; Tom Cook dispatch to *New York Herald*, May 7, 1863, quoted in Andrews, *The North Reports the Civil War*, 363; Bernard A. Weis-berger, *Reporters for the Union* (Boston: Little Brown, 1953), 294–95, 297–98. Weisberger also gives an example of Charles Coffin's very unrealistic and sentimen-tal style of battle coverage (pp. 293–94). The influence of journalists on the style of combat fiction of the war decade is noted in Jan Cohn, "The Civil War in Magazine Fiction of the 1860s," *Journal of Popular Culture* 4 (fall 1970): 381n.

[18] Unidentified correspondent writing in *Washington Evening Star*, October 16, 1896, quoted in Andrews, *The North Reports the Civil War*, 651.

　　The contrast between bad and good battle coverage was contained in a comparison of Junius Henri Browne of the *New York Daily Tribune* and William Fayel of the *St. Louis Daily Missouri Democrat.* Both reported the Battle of Pea Ridge, Arkansas, in March 1862. Browne was an interesting product of the journalistic enterprise—a young, idealistic man at war's beginning who quickly learned from experience that combat was "the most prosaic and unattractive of actualities. No spirit of poesy, no breath of sentiment enters into War; no aesthetic principle animates it. War bristles with facts—is terribly real, repulsively practical." For these reasons he believed war should have been abolished, yet he also realized that his "duty was to write of, not against War." The demands of the marketplace dictated his work. "I proceeded to discharge my journalistic obligations as best I could, reserving my sentimental opinions about War for private ears."[19]

　　Browne did an excellent job of subjugating this knowledge to popular conceptions of battle. He wrote a thrilling but unrealistic account of Pea Ridge despite the fact that he was 280 miles away in Kentucky when it occurred. He avoided specific mention of terrain, sounds, sights, or smells and concentrated on high-flown rhetoric about the glorious nature of combat. Ostensibly describing a retreat through surrounding Confederate cavalry by Brigadier General Franz Sigel, Browne let his patriotic imagination roam freely: "Sigel was at last cut off; but his energy and that of his men mowed a passage through the serried ranks of the Rebels. . . . The cavalry charged and re-charged upon the little band at Sigel's back, but each time the Union bayonets gleamed in their eyes, and the light drove them back." According to Browne the ground became "stained and slippery with human gore. Every loyal soldier kept his eye fixed upon his fearless leader, as did the followers of Murat or Henry of Navarre. Wherever they saw his streaming hair and his flashing sword, they knew all was safe."[20]

---

　　[19] Junius Henri Browne, *Four Years in Secessia* (Hartford, Conn.: O. D. Case, 1865), 30.

　　[20] *New York Daily Tribune*, March 20, 1862. Browne simply reprinted this piece in his memoirs as if, even in that book, he felt compelled to give the public what he thought it wanted to read. Along with such drivel, he included some very moving descriptions of his experience as a prisoner of the Confederates. The result is an interesting book that reflects a consciousness torn between the demands of the marketplace and the contradictory impulses of a thoughtful and sensitive nature.

Such a description could only reinforce romantic conceptions of battle and help to prevent civilians from realizing what combat truly was like. William Fayel, on the other hand, accompanied the Union army to Pea Ridge. He witnessed as much of the battle as possible and spent hours interviewing participants of high and low rank to piece together a coherent view of the engagement. No generalized account here, Fayel cited specific units, times of the day at which significant moments occurred, and numbers of casualties. Rather than purple prose, Fayel wrote in a plain style that vividly described such things as the appearance of the vegetation after a severe artillery bombardment. Fayel and reporters like him produced battle narratives that a soldier would not have found unrealistic. They served as a counterweight to the Junius Henri Brownes.[21]

Public response to these two different kinds of journalism is difficult to assess. As already noted, many journalists firmly believed the public preferred the romanticized view of war that they consistently wrote. If a large number of readers actually preferred the more realistic view, they certainly gave little indication of it. The persistence of romanticized views of war in American culture after the Civil War would seem to indicate that journalism had little impact on altering the public's perception of the nature of combat. And journalists continued to give that reading public what it wanted.[22]

The uneven quality of battle coverage helped to prevent journalists from assuming a preeminent role in conveying an understanding of combat to the public. Only periodically could they rival the authors of personal letters for accurate descriptions of battle. Soldiers had no editors breathing down their necks or a desire to shine in the public arena when they wrote to their wives or parents about the traumatic experience of combat. Shocked by that experience, they often had no inclination to perpetuate romantic conceptions of war. To a greater or lesser degree, newspapers filled the public demand for facts about fast-breaking battles, but they too rarely gave readers an authentic impression of the nature of combat.

---

[21] *St. Louis Daily Missouri Democrat*, March 18, 1862.

[22] See Thomas C. Leonard, *Above the Battle: War-Making in America from Appomattox to Versailles* (New York: Oxford University Press, 1978), for a discussion of American attitudes toward war after the Civil War.

ILLUSTRATED WEEKLIES

The visual media, although still in its infancy, also had mixed success in bringing the war home to civilians. Illustrated weekly publications began in the 1850s in the big eastern cities and had firmly established themselves in the journalistic marketplace by 1861. They reached a considerable audience during the war. Their publishers estimated that ten people saw each copy of an issue and that 100,000 copies were circulated each week. Although one million people did not comprise an overwhelming part of the northern population of about twenty-two million, their numbers were sufficient to give the illustrated papers some prominence in public consciousness. Because of problems inherent to army movements, soldiers were less exposed to this visual journalism than were civilians. In March 1865, only two thousand copies of the two leading illustrated papers were distributed to the Army of the Potomac each week, an army of about eighty thousand men. Although not all northerners were able to view the pictures printed in them, illustrated periodicals were a major component of journalistic coverage of the war.[23]

As with newspapers, the demands of the marketplace worked against a full portrayal of war's reality in the illustrated weeklies. The limits of technology also played a large role in this. No one, however, could blame the quality of reporting, for a remarkable group of artists worked for the illustrated papers. Henri Lovie, Theodore Davis, Alfred Waud, and Edwin Forbes all sent evocative sketches to their publishers. Field artists lived and worked among the troops, witnessed battles, came under fire, and sometimes were wounded or captured. Their working methods were much the same as that described by Whitelaw Reid for newspaper reporters: witness as much as was possible, get information from participants, and strive to stitch together a visual scene of a confused, disorderly experience. One has merely to look at their original sketches to see that the field artists achieved their goals of realism, vividness, and accuracy to a remarkable degree.[24]

---

[23] Thompson, *Image of War*, 137, 204n.

[24] Theodore R. Davis, "'How a Battle Is Sketched,'" *Civil War Times Illustrated* 1 (May 1962): 21. See reproductions of battle and death scenes in Frederic E. Ray, "Alfred R. Waud," *Civil War Times Illustrated* 2 (December 1963): 18–23; Thomas Rice, "Fredericksburg under Fire: All the Imps of Hell Let Loose," *Civil War Times Illustrated* 22 (June 1983): 8–15.

The engraved versions of their sketches only occasionally reproduced these qualities. Because photoengraving technology did not exist, these valuable depictions of battle and death had to be transferred onto wooden blocks by engravers in order to be printed on paper. The quality of the resulting woodcut depended entirely on the skill of the engraver. Several engravers worked on a single illustration, and the transfer usually took three to four weeks. Although some woodcuts came close to reproducing faithfully the field sketch, most represented only a faint echo of it, "taking on a crude and stilted appearance and losing all resemblance to the artists' individual styles." The quality of transfer was generally better at *Frank Leslie's Illustrated Newspaper* because Leslie himself supervised the process. The engravers at *Harper's Weekly,* however, often altered the conception of the field artist. At the publisher's direction they injected propagandistic elements into the sketches, despite the field artist's avoidance of editorial comment.[25]

The resulting product left several impressions. The most common scene was a grand panorama with large numbers of men grouped in ranks and files. Except for depictions of skirmishing, where there existed the opportunity for portraying outnumbered soldiers in desperate circumstances, there were few scenes of small groups. Dead bodies existed only in the midst of battle excitement, with little detail, and relatively few dead at that. The larger framework of battle largely overshadowed them so that it was difficult to notice their presence. These were set pieces designed to illustrate prevailing conceptions of battle, not to document the reality of Civil War fighting in terms described by soldiers. The enemy usually was visible and often was depicted toe to toe with the Federals. Battle smoke decorated but did not obscure the scene, and the connection between the dead and injured with the hail of enemy fire was not made clear. They simply lay about in polite contrast to the orderly ranks of living men.[26]

In all this the weeklies illustrated what the public thought they

[25] Thompson, *Image of War,* 83–84, 89; Frederic E. Ray, *Alfred R. Waud, Civil War Artist* (New York: Viking, 1974), 28. For more on propaganda in the illustrated weeklies, see Thompson, *Image of War,* 86–88, 97, and chapter 7; Horace M. Brown, "A Small Boy's Recollections of the War Time," in *War Papers Read before the Commandery of the State of Wisconsin, Military Order of the Loyal Legion of the United States,* 4 vols. (Milwaukee: Armitage, and Allen, 1903), 3:201.

[26] These conclusions are based on an analysis of the illustrations in *Frank Leslie's* and *Harper's* during the four years of the war.

knew about the nature of battle, and too often the remarkable achievement of the field artist was submerged or obliterated by the imagination of the engraver. An example was a depiction of the battle of Dranesville, Virginia, in the *Leslie's* issue of January 11, 1862. No dead bodies appeared, officers assumed heroic and stylish poses, and the soldiers advanced in perfectly formed ranks. Order and discipline permeated this image of one of the most disordered and confusing experiences northerners were called on to endure.

Historian W. Fletcher Thompson argued that a more realistic style emerged in illustrations of the grisly campaigns in Virginia and Georgia in the spring of 1864, but there seems to be no clear transition between these and earlier images.[27] *Leslie's* tended to depict less rigid ranks and lines in its 1863–65 issues, and the enemy was more often seen in less clearly defined images, obscured by distance and by musket smoke. In addition, *Leslie's* published a few stark views of battlefield dead but still retained the panoramic perspective that imposed a sense of order on the scene of combat. Yet *Leslie's* also had published such scenes on March 1 and May 17, 1862, which were views of dismembered dead at Fort Henry and a Lovie sketch of Shiloh. These illustrations were outnumbered by the unrealistic images that crowded the pages of almost all other early issues.

This more realistic trend was evident in *Harper's* from the beginning of the war, despite the editorial tendency of that publication to insert propaganda into its images. Throughout the conflict *Harper's* engravers employed less order and discipline in depicting men at war and emphasized the emotion of battle. Yet they also concentrated on panoramic scenes. Although more emotion-laden, the experience of battle in *Harper's* was still a controlled experience. Soldiers appeared as individuals with facial expressions when they were depicted as part of a larger group. Coverage of Chickamauga in the October 31, 1863, issue was an example. One end of a Federal battle line was in the foreground with individual soldiers realistically depicted, while the rest of the line stretched into the background and into faceless depictions of abstract soldiers. There were touches of individuality in this large, machine-like army.

In its October 18, 1862, and July 9, 1864, issues, *Harper's* published engravings of Alexander Gardner and Timothy O'Sullivan pho-

---

[27] Thompson, *Image of War*, 7, 146–47, 185.

tographs of battlefield dead. Little was altered in the transfers to woodblock, but the stark reality was considerably softened by the different texture of the engraving. Details of the landscape, articles on the ground, and the appearance of bodies were eliminated because of the nature of woodcut technology. It was a medium whose strength lay in bold, simplified delineation, not in subtle shadings of fine detail. Thus much of the impact of these realistic depictions of death was neutralized. The tendency toward more realism in woodcuts was not adequate to convey the experience of battle as described by participants. It still presented, even in images of death, a vision of battle as essentially an environment where order prevailed.

The limitations of the woodcut medium in conveying a sense of battle to the population were contained in the story of Alfred Waud. Probably the best field artist of the war, he did an excellent job of representing the physical experience of combat in his sketches. But Waud's sketches were subtly changed in the transfer to woodblocks. They often depicted the enemy as shadowy and indistinct, which was consistent with soldiers' descriptions of combat. This was evocative of the confusion of battle, yet the woodcut could not reproduce it. Fuzziness in reality and sketch became distinct lines in the final version readers saw.[28]

Waud's depiction of Humphreys's division at Fredericksburg illustrated this problem. He offered the reader a rear view of the division. Its last rank, the one closest to the viewer, was sketched in the barest outline of individual soldiers with little if any detail. The forward rank, in the midground, was not delineated at all but represented by dabs of pencil shading to form the barest resemblance to a man's trunk. The distinction receded as the viewer scanned from foreground to background until the Rebels were rendered only by a line of smoke in the distance. The engraving that appeared in *Harper's*, however, firmly delineated all ranks of Humphreys's men. There was no shading; even facial expressions appeared on members of the last rank. The sense of awe, confusion, and disorientation that delicate shading, fuzziness, and faceless men could convey was eliminated by the distortions of the medium.[29]

---

[28] Compare the sketches of First Bull Run and Kernstown with the woodcuts that appeared in the *New York Illustrated News* and *Harper's* as conveniently displayed for the reader in Ray, *Alfred R. Waud,* 81, 91.

[29] Ray, *Alfred R. Waud,* 120–21.

Editorial decisions based on a perception of what was proper to show the public also played a role in softening the impact of Waud's sketches. His view of a field hospital at Antietam depicted a man on the operating table, the stump of his recently amputated leg clearly visible. The engraving that appeared in *Harper's* reversed the man's position on the table so that his head, not his stump, was visible to the viewer. The perceived demands of the marketplace dictated more genteel images of battlefield suffering than this editor saw in Waud's work.[30]

The reaction of soldiers to these images ranged from derision to qualified acceptance. Thomas Wentworth Higginson described as "highly imaginative" a *Leslie's* illustration of a skirmish by his unit, and Henry Dwight of Ohio complained of unrealistic battle scenes. He saw in them soldiers with neatly packed knapsacks and "officers leading the charge in full dress uniform, with their sabres waving in the most approved style. Now this makes a pretty picture; but let me tell you that soldiers don't put on their well-packed knapsacks to doublequick over a half mile of open ground in the hot sun at the *pas du charge*." Even the positive reactions to the engravings were quite guarded. Frederick Hitchcock's comrades fought near the Sunken Road at Antietam and had ample opportunity to examine this bloody area immediately after the battle. "We afterwards saw pictures of this road in the illustrated papers, which partially portrayed the horrible scene."[31]

There is every indication that editorial stance on war issues, not the quality of engravings, was the key to the success or failure of illustrated papers. W. Fletcher Thompson indicated that *Harper's* came to outsell *Leslie's* as the war progressed because it took a stronger prowar stand. His comment suggests that visual representation of battle in the illustrated weeklies may have had less impact on the public than one would suspect. Editorial policy, expressed in a vigorous support of the cause, apparently was the basis of *Harper's* success, not its visual appeal.[32]

---

[30] Ibid., 112–13.

[31] Thomas Wentworth Higginson, *Army Life in a Black Regiment* (New York: Da Capo, 1970), 27; Henry Otis Dwight, "How We Fight at Atlanta," 663; Thompson, *Image of War*, 137–38; Frederick L. Hitchcock, *War from the Inside* (Philadelphia: J. B. Lippincott, 1904), 70.

[32] Thompson, *Image of War*, 110.

This hypothesis is supported by the fact that illustrated papers were not the only objects of pictorial interest in the North. As William Henry Jackson indicated, the art trade was booming in the 1860s. After his unit disbanded in July 1863, Jackson returned to Rutland, Vermont, and made a very good living by painting for the local market. He touched up photographic portraits by hand, painted portraits of local families on commission, and reproduced dozens of portraits of military and political heroes of the war, such as Grant, Lincoln, and Custer. When we consider the great number of portraits and nonbattle scenes published in the illustrated weeklies, it becomes apparent that battle scenes were not the most commonly viewed image in the North. Not unlike the newspaper business, where the facts of battle crowded out information on the experience of combat, the portrait trade so deluged markets as to drastically lower the visibility of battle scenes in the public consciousness.[33]

PHOTOGRAPHS

The Civil War occurred at a time when photography offered northerners a new tool to record the battlefield scene, yet technological limitations restricted the distribution of this image to a relatively small part of the public. Photography had existed for about two decades when the war began and had reached a level of sophistication with the development of the wet-plate process in the 1850s. Wet-plate photography superseded previous processes as an efficient method of recording outdoor scenes, and war inevitably became its subject. The Mexican War, the Crimean War, and the Second Opium War in China were recorded by artists using the processes available to them at the time, but their images had a very limited circulation in the United States. These wars were remote to the majority of Americans, and the portrait market dominated the photography business anyway. The carte de visite, a cardboard reproduction small enough to serve as a calling card, became a successful market product in the 1850s. A public taste for landscapes began in the same decade with the successful marketing of the stereo view, with two copies of

---

[33] Jackson, *Time Exposure,* 70–71, 75.

the same image placed in a specially made holder to create a three-dimensional perspective.[34]

Both the carte de visite and the stereo widened the demand for photographs. With the war, photographers rushed to capitalize on public interest. Dozens of portrait artists set up temporary studios near the armies to photograph soldiers, who sent their images home to loved ones. From 1863 to 1865, three hundred civilians applied for passes to set up studios near the armies in Virginia. Over 90 percent of them were portrait artists not interested in outdoor scenes or in battlefield images. Although the number of men primarily interested in photographing the war rather than the soldiers was small, they were among the most talented artists of their day, and they also sought to capitalize on the demand for landscape scenes. A Timothy O'Sullivan view of Grant's army crossing the Rapidan River on May 4, 1864, was issued in stereo to the public within one and a half months. In some cases, then, the buyer had access to realistic images of the war shortly after the events occurred.[35]

The images that drew the greatest interest were the scenes of the slain. Until the Battle of Antietam there had been no circulation of battlefield death scenes in America. Fought in Maryland and thus more readily accessible to northerners, Antietam became a subject for the enterprising Alexander Gardner, who then worked for Matthew Brady. Gardner arrived on the field before all the dead were buried and became the first artist in America to photograph victims of the killing zone in their original condition. Gardner was not yet aware of the market potential of these death scenes; two-thirds of his Antietam images were landscapes and group portraits of participants. When the death images were displayed and sold, he realized he had hit upon a valuable subject, as they created a fever of interest among the public.[36]

Trying to duplicate his Antietam success at Gettysburg, after he had broken from Brady to set up his own business, Gardner exposed sixty negatives of the Pennsylvania battlefield, three-fourths of them

---

[34] William A. Frassanito, *Antietam: The Photographic Legacy of America's Bloodiest Day* (New York: Scribner's, 1978), 24–25.

[35] J. F. Coonley, "Photographic Reminiscences of the Late War," *Anthony's Photographic Bulletin* 13 (September 1882): 311; William A. Frassanito, *Grant and Lee: The Virginia Campaigns, 1864–1865* (New York: Scribner's, 1983), 28, 40.

[36] Frassanito, *Antietam,* 17.

images of the yet unburied dead. Eighty percent of his Gettysburg images were issued to the public in stereo, testifying to the public interest in that photographic format. Other photographers tried to copy Gardner's success when possible, but the exigencies of battle and army movements restricted their work. Actually the dead of only six battles were photographed during the war: Antietam, Corinth, Marye's Heights during the Chancellorsville campaign, Gettysburg, Alsop's Farm during the Spotsylvania campaign, and the capture of Fort Mahone on the Petersburg lines in April 1865. The total number of negatives depicting death scenes probably did not exceed one hundred.[37]

Gardner's technique, which other photographers duplicated, was to expose several negatives of a single body or a cluster of dead from different angles. This was dictated by photographic technology. The wet-plate process required the mixture of chemicals and the coating of the glass plate on the spot. Immediately after exposure the photographer had to develop the plate in a carriage specially designed as a darkroom. It was delicate work that required a minimum of wasted time, and it was much easier to set up the equipment only once for a series of views than to expose only one negative per setting. To maximize the benefit, the camera angle was changed so that the viewer could not readily recognize the bodies in the different views as the same subjects.[38]

The resulting images were stark representations of battle's aftermath. In them bodies lay about, arms and legs akimbo, much as soldiers described them in personal letters. Bloating had done its work, expanding bodies and stretching clothes to the tearing point. Mutilated bodies appeared with abdomens torn open, limbs severed, and faces discolored by decay. Many of the images depicted bodies laid in orderly rows as burial parties gathered them and stopped for a picture at the photographer's request; others showed the killed in their unordered positions. Very few Union dead appeared; in fact, Gettysburg seems to have been the only battle where Union soldiers can be seen lying on the field, and this is only one cluster of dead. This probably was due to the fact that Federal dead were normally

---

[37] Ibid., 285–86; William A. Frassanito, *Gettysburg: A Journey in Time* (New York: Scribner's, 1975), 27, 29; William C. Davis, ed., *The Image of War, 1861–1865,* vol. 1, *Shadows of the Storm* (Garden City, N.Y.: Doubleday, 1981), 325–26.

[38] Frassanito, *Gettysburg,* 228.

buried first when the Union army held the field after a battle. The fact that Gardner mislabeled a view of dead Confederates at Gettysburg as Federals indicated that he sought only battlefield death regardless of side, not that he wished to avoid offending his northern customers with images of rotting countrymen.[39]

In addition to technological limitations, the demands of the market also affected the photographer's work. There was no manipulation of the bodies or the artifacts around them apparent in Gardner's Antietam photographs because they were taken before he realized the market potential of these views. Manipulation occurred often, however, in subsequent photographs by Gardner and those who sought to duplicate his success.

The manipulation took place in an effort to appeal to a sentimental, even romantic, sense in public attitude. At Gettysburg Gardner and his assistants photographed the body of a Confederate infantryman and then carried the body forty yards to a distinctive rock barricade that had been constructed by Confederate sharpshooters during the battle. There they photographed it again and labeled the view as depicting the death of a sharpshooter, although the body had been that of a line infantryman. The second image was much more poignant than the first, which exposed an indistinct body lying in an open field. In the photograph taken near the barricade, the same body was transformed by better photographic composition. Its face was turned to the viewer, and a rifle was carefully placed on the body. The scene was much more evocative of romantic conceptions of battle than the first image.[40]

Props were a regular addition to death scenes. A view of a dead Rebel at Alsop's Farm showed that the photographer, Timothy O'Sullivan, experimented with the position of a bayoneted rifle, placing it at different angles on the gaunt body to achieve the maximum in romantic effect. Some of the most stark, vivid images of battle death, those taken at Fort Mahone, regularly appeared with manipulated props such as a broken artillery sponge carefully placed next to a dead Confederate artilleryman, rifle muskets that appeared in one view of the dead but not in a differently angled view of the same subject, and a bayonet stuck in the mud beside mutilated bodies. No

---

[39] Ibid., 215, 227–29.
[40] Ibid., 187–92.

matter how horrible the scene of death, there was some evidence of the use of props in most photographs of the fallen.[41]

Manipulation went so far that some unscrupulous men foisted spurious death scenes on the public. A photograph apparently depicting dead on the field of First Bull Run was accepted as authentic for a very long time after the war, as were two images of bodies at Gettysburg. Only in the past two decades, thanks to extraordinary detective work on their part, have photographic historians such as William Frassanito judged these pictures to be spurious constructions. The bodies were not bloated, and in the Gettysburg images they were rearranged in the two different scenes. The photographer arranged the "bodies" among the rocks in Devil's Den with the normal draping of carefully placed rifle muskets. In reality he enlisted the aid of live soldiers who obligingly lay down under his direction. These images were accepted as real by a public desiring more and more scenes of carnage. The Gettysburg photographs, as well as the authentic Fort Mahone images, were issued in stereo to increase the vividness of death's appearance.[42]

The use of props and the manipulation of the dead were attempts to conform the authentic image of battle death to romanticized notions about war. When photographers realized the potential these views held for sale to the public, they began to retreat from their role as documenters of the war experience and began to think in terms of packaging their product for the marketplace. The extent to which they manipulated the death scene was the extent to which they tried to alter the understanding of battle and perpetuated imaginative conceptions of war, with the sentimentalism and romanticism attached to those conceptions. Northerners did not see unadorned reality in those images, but reality mediated by culture.

The effect was startling. Gardner exposed a view of an eviscerated Confederate at Gettysburg. His stomach was gone and the ragged hole was clearly visible to the viewer. The soldier's left arm was also gone; a detached hand lay beside him. Even in black and white, his face was so badly discolored as to lose its resemblance to a human being. Yet Gardner placed an unexploded artillery projectile near the body, labeled the picture "War, effect of a shell on a Confederate

---

[41] Frassanito, *Grant and Lee,* 109–12, 345–48, 355–58, 360–63.
[42] Frassanito, *Antietam,* 30; Frassanito, *Gettysburg,* 184.

soldier," and carefully placed a bayoneted rifle musket across his leg. Few soldiers fought with bayonets attached to their rifle muskets; they were seldom used in battle because they got in the way when loading the muzzle of the weapon. Certainly the rifle musket would not have fallen so neatly across the soldier's leg as a shell nearly split his body apart, and another, unexploded shell probably would not have so conveniently fallen within range of Gardner's equipment. These attempts to mediate the scene of carnage for the purpose of success in the marketplace were pitiful, even sordid, compared to one of the most heart-rending demonstrations of how combat could destroy human existence.[43]

The manipulation evident in battlefield death scenes could not completely sanitize them, yet few northerners saw these photographs. No estimates of their circulation exist, but the foremost historian of Civil War photography discovered stereo copies of the Antietam scenes that were sold as late as 1866. Articles describing them appeared in the *New York Times* of October 20, 1862, and the *Atlantic Monthly* of July 1863. As noted earlier, *Harper's Weekly* published some of them as woodcut illustrations on October 18, 1862, and reproduced the Alsop's Farm images on July 9, 1864. Death scenes were distributed by a small number of companies, apparently to local, urban markets. Although larger cities knew of these images, consumers in small town and rural America were probably unaware of their existence.[44]

Gardner's Antietam views were displayed in Brady's New York gallery. An anonymous newspaper reporter who covered the exhibit wrote about the potential these images held for helping the viewer to understand war: "As it is, the dead of the battle-field come up to us very rarely, even in dreams. We see the list in the morning paper at breakfast, but dismiss its recollection with the coffee." Civilians knew battle was a reality, "but it stands as a remote one. It is like a funeral next door. . . . It attracts your attention, but does not enlist your sympathy." Giving the credit to Gardner's boss, this correspondent believed the pictures eliminated that problem. "Mr. Brady has done something to bring home to us the terrible reality and earnestness of war. If he has not brought bodies and laid them in our door-yards and along the streets, he has done something very like it."[45]

[43] Frassanito, *Gettysburg,* 217.
[44] Frassanito, *Antietam,* 286.
[45] *New York Times,* October 20, 1862.

Ironically, this reporter spoke of the photographs in terms that avoided an understanding of the battle experience, rather than enhancing it: "Of all objects of horror one would think the battle-field should stand preeminent, that it should bear away the palm of repulsiveness. But, on the contrary, there is a terrible fascination about it that draws one near these pictures, and makes him loath to leave them. You will see hushed, reverend groups standing around these weird copies of carnage, bending down to look in the pale faces of the dead, chained by the strange spell that dwells in dead men's eyes."[46]

The reporter wrote of these images in much the same way that Holmes wrote of newspaper coverage, as if they induced a fever or spell that hooked the public's attention. These photographs were products of the popular culture industry, made to sell as newspapers were printed to make a profit. Placing a conveyor of battle information on the market inevitably altered it. This happened in newspaper coverage, the illustrations in *Harper's,* and the photographs of such noted imagists as Gardner and O'Sullivan.[47]

Not only was the quality of reporting altered when a conveyor of information was placed on the market, but reaction to it was altered as well. Those civilians who obsessively pored over newspaper reports did so, according to the evidence cited by Holmes, only partly because they wanted news of the war. The rest of their obsession was credited to the manipulation of the medium, the rapid and sensationalized printing of news, which spurred greater and stronger desires for acquiring information. This type of manipulation in today's electronic media is all too palpable to dismiss, and there is no reason to believe it was not a real problem in the 1860s as well.

What could be more sensational than to market photographs of carnage? As the reporter pointed out, "there is a terrible fascination

---

[46] Ibid.

[47] For a discussion of this theme as it relates to twentieth-century warfare, see Mark Crispin Miller, "How TV Covers War," *The New Republic* 187 (November 29, 1982): 26–33; Michael Mandelbaum, "Vietnam: The Television War," *Daedalus* 111 (fall 1982): 157–69; Michael J. Arlen, *Living-Room War* (New York: Viking, 1969). Arlen particularly demonstrates how placing combat reporting in a medium dominated by fast-food commercials, soap operas, and mindless sit-coms can rob it of a profound impact. For an example of a Civil War soldier softening his descriptions of the battlefield dead for publication in newspapers, see Cecil D. Eby, Jr., ed., *A Virginia Yankee in the Civil War: The Diaries of David Hunter Strother* (Chapel Hill: University of North Carolina Press, 1961), xvii.

about it that draws one near these pictures." Patrons could not pull themselves away, "chained by the strange spell that dwells in dead men's eyes." Civilians reacted to these profound artifacts of battle much as they would react to a lurid novel or a fantastic report of a steamboat accident. Despite the reporter's contention that Gardner had brought the war home to New York City, his words indicated that the war was still no closer than before. These terribly vivid conveyors of the experience of battle were incorporated into the popular culture industry, and there they lost much of their impact.

Oliver Wendell Holmes, Sr., also had something to say about these photographs. An avid photography buff, he viewed Gardner's Antietam images but had a very different reaction. Unlike the reporter, who gave no indication of ever having been near Antietam or any other battlefield, Holmes had seen the destructive results of war. He journeyed to the area to find his son after receiving a message that he had been wounded at Antietam. Holmes arrived about four days after the battle, after the dead had been buried, but in plenty of time to see thousands of wounded huddling in makeshift field hospitals and to view the debris left on the killing ground. He found his son, the future Supreme Court Justice, after days of searching.[48]

Holmes agreed with the reporter that these views conveyed reality to the home front, but he felt no fascination. He did not gaze on the dead or eagerly scan each scene for yet another vision of gore: "It was so nearly like visiting the battlefield to look over these views, that all the emotions excited by the actual sight of the stained and sordid scene, strewed with rags and wrecks, came back to us, and we buried them in the recesses of our cabinet as we would have buried the mutilated remains of the dead they too vividly represented."[49]

As Holmes suggested, only those individuals who had first-hand experience with battle or its aftermath could disassociate these conveyors of information from the clutter of other products that appeared on the popular culture market. Only those individuals who

---

[48] Oliver Wendell Holmes, Sr., "My Hunt after 'The Captain,'" *Atlantic Monthly* 10 (December 1862): 749.

[49] Oliver Wendell Holmes, Sr., "Doings of the Sunbeam," *Atlantic Monthly* 12 (July 1863): 11–12. Holmes reinforced the connection between his visit to Antietam and the photographs by using similar language to discuss them. He wrote of "the trodden and stained relics of the stale battle-field" in "My Hunt after 'The Captain,'" 749.

had some personal experience with battle could be touched by them in a profound way. This is what the reporter implied when he commented that, while he and others continued to enjoy viewing the death scenes, he would not want to be present if a woman in the audience should recognize one of the dead as a loved one. For her, the "terrible distinctness" of the photographs would deal a heartfelt blow because it would touch on a personal connection between the woman and the war. Lacking that personal connection, the reporter could remain a viewer and not become a participant in the experience.[50]

What Holmes and the reporter had in common, despite their different reactions to the images, was a positive conclusion regarding the war. Both men ended their discussions with a reaffirmation of the war's worth. Describing it as "poetry," the reporter noted that "Here lie men who have not hesitated to seal and stamp their convictions with their blood—men who have flung themselves into the great gulf of the unknown to teach the world that there are truths dearer than life, wrongs and shames more to be dreaded than death."[51]

In the wake of his painful reaction to the images, Holmes struggled with the question of cost and benefit: "The end to be attained justifies the means, we are willing to believe; but the sight of these pictures is a commentary on civilization such as a savage might well triumph to show its missionaries. Yet through such martyrdom must come our redemption."[52]

Holmes and the reporter came to the same end by way of different routes. The correspondent appears to have been little changed by his exposure to the photographs; his affirmation has the ring of published commentary on the subject of motives and cost, strong and self-assuredly positive. Holmes arrived at affirmation only after a considerable struggle that was sparked by his previous experience with the battlefield. His affirmation was therefore stronger, in one way, for it was tested by doubt and survived. Faced with a serious threat to his conception of what the war effort was worth, Holmes struggled but managed to reassert his faith in the war.[53]

---

[50] *New York Times,* October 20, 1862.

[51] Ibid.

[52] Holmes, "Doings of the Sunbeam," 12.

[53] Alan Trachtenberg discusses the process of mediation that occurs when contemporaries make photographs of historical events and when modern-day scholars exam-

Thus Civil War media—newspapers, illustrated weeklies, photographs—failed to play a decisive role in telling the northern public what the experience of battle was like. Technological limitations, editorial concerns, the demands of the marketplace, even the lack of professional guidelines for those engaged in reporting the war, all combined to restrict the media of the 1860s as a significant conveyor of information about the nature of combat. Northerners had no widely accessible and consistently accurate channel of information about this subject. Perhaps, for the larger issues involved in this and in any major war effort, it was necessary that the public not know what combat was like. Too much information might have threatened their commitment and led more of them to want the war to end without victory. Yet as Oliver Wendell Holmes, Sr., indicated when discussing the Antietam photographs, even those civilians who had insight into the nature of combat were not necessarily dissuaded. In the contest between motives and cost, the former can override the latter if belief and rationalization are strong enough. A clear understanding of the issues at stake could, and in hundreds of thousands of cases actually did, buttress support, no matter how horribly the senses and emotions might have been affected by knowledge of battle. The media could not educate those with only a specious interest in the war, nor could it dissuade those with a personal stake in it.

---

ine them. He points out that photographs are inevitably tied to the cultural background of the society and ought to be considered in the context of political ideologies; Trachtenberg, "Albums of War: On Reading Civil War Photographs," *Representations* 9 (winter 1985): 10, 12, 29.

2

A Thrilling Northern War: Gender, Race, and Sensational Popular War Literature

Alice Fahs

"How I wish I could go and fight for my country!" exclaimed the heroine of *Miriam Rivers, the Lady Soldier; or, General Grant's Spy*, one of a number of northern sensational novels featuring female soldiers published during the war.[1] Louisa May Alcott had expressed much the same desire in April 1861: "I've often longed to see a war," she confided to her journal, "and now I have my wish." Alcott, however, had reluctantly resigned herself to the fact that she could not fight: "I long to be a man," she said, "but as I can't fight, I will content myself with working for those who can."[2] In contrast, in the pages of an extensive sensational war literature, women characters acted on such longings, not only refusing to content themselves with "working for those who can" fight, but often fighting alongside men or even disguising themselves as soldiers.

Beginning in late 1861 and then in a continuing stream throughout the war, "cheap" book publishers, story papers, and illustrated weeklies produced sensational stories of the war that exaggerated the masculinity of white soldiers, scouts, or spies, while simultaneously allowing white women, especially in the border states of Kentucky, Missouri, and Tennessee, dramatic and transgressive roles in the war.[3] Such sensational stories were part of a larger outpouring of

---

[1] *Miriam Rivers, the Lady Soldier; or, General Grant's Spy* (Philadelphia: Barclay & Co., 1865), 42.

[2] Louisa May Alcott, *Journals of Louisa May Alcott*, ed. Joel Myerson and Daniel Shealy (Boston: Little Brown, 1989), 105.

[3] See an 1862 ad by a consortium of cheap publishers referring to their "Cheap Novels" in Walter Sutton, *The Western Book Trade: Cincinnati as a Nineteenth-*

popular war-related literature published during the conflict, including war poetry, sentimental war stories, sensational war novels, war humor, war juveniles, war songs, collections of war-related anecdotes, and war histories. Appearing in newspapers, illustrated weeklies, monthly periodicals, cheap weekly "story" papers, pamphlets, broadsides, song sheets and books, this extensive popular war literature was often widely distributed, sometimes to hundreds of thousands of readers.[4]

Sensational stories occupied a special place within the wider world of northern popular war literature. They emphasized the personal daring, defiance, and risk occasioned by war for both men and women, imagining the war as a series of "exciting," "thrilling," and "stirring" adventures. They not only inflated the masculinity of white soldiers, scouts, or spies, but also allowed white women a heightened sexuality. In doing so, they offered a striking contrast to hundreds of war romances published in mainstream publications such as *Harper's New Monthly Magazine* that concentrated on women's passive suffering on the home front. Sensational stories instead took women out of the home, creating roles for them as cross-dressing soldiers, spies, or scouts to match the roles of men at the battle front. While one scholar has commented that "dime novels were a male-dominated genre" in terms of "publishers, writers, and fictional formulas," a study of Civil War cheap literature reveals instead that sensational war stories often offered equal opportunities for adventure in wartime.[5] It also reveals that within northern popular literary culture, there was room for a wider array of representations of the war than is usually thought to be the case.[6]

Century Publishing and Book-Trade Center (Columbus: Ohio State University Press, 1961), 245.

[4] On the popular literature of the war, see Alice Fahs, "The Feminized War: Gender, Northern Popular Literature, and the Memory of the War, 1861–1900," *Journal of American History* 85 (March 1999): 1461–94; and Fahs, "The Market Value of Memory: Popular War Histories and the Northern Literary Marketplace, 1861–1868," *Book History* 1 (1998): 107–39. See also Kathleen Diffley, *Where My Heart Is Turning Ever: Civil War Stories and Constitutional Reform, 1861–1876* (Athens: University of Georgia Press, 1992).

[5] Christine Bold, "Popular Forms I," in *The Columbia History of the American Novel*, ed. Emory Elliott (New York: Columbia University Press, 1991), 297.

[6] Most literary studies of the Civil War have concentrated on elite literature by canonical writers. See, for example, Daniel Aaron, *The Unwritten War: American Writers and the Civil War* (New York: Knopf, 1973); and George M. Fredrickson,

In sensational war stories women often expressed a desire for danger and excitement: "she did *so* long to be mounted on her gallant Spitfire," commented the narrator of the 1865 *Kate Sharp; or, The Two Conscripts*, "galloping when and where she chose, with enough danger to heighten [sic] the excitement."[7] Acting on this longing, the heroine, Kate Sharp, engaged in a military expedition, leading fifty men "who greeted our heroine with a hearty cheer," against guerrillas and bushwhackers in Tennessee. "I wouldn't miss such an adventure for a great deal," she commented.[8] She even rebutted criticisms of her transgressive role. A dandyish "bandbox hero" told Kate that her "present occupation" was "extremely unladylike, and not such as I should recommend to a sister or friend of mine." Instead, he advised her to "go home, and settle down as the wife of some good, honest fellow, and leave this work of war to bearded men."[9] Kate's scathing put-down of this "pusillanimous puppy," a "martial Adonis" with a "silky mustache," was followed by a meeting with General Sherman in which he absentmindedly handed her a cigar, to her amusement, before authorizing her expedition and telling her that he would promote her if she succeeded.

If sensational war stories approvingly allowed women to transgress norms of gender that prevented them from fighting in the war, they also celebrated the physicality and fighting spirit of men in muscular, swaggering language. In the 1861 *Scotto, the Scout*, for instance, the main character, Scotto, was "tall and athletic," with a "strongly-defined and sun-browned face." "I want to fight!" he announced. "If I don't eat my bigness into rebellion, if I don't cut and hack, hash, slash, and gash, right and left, it'll be because my hand forgets its cunnin', and my arm loses its patriotism, and my brain its sense!"[10] His "Union Rangers" "rallied around Scotto" as their leader because

The Inner Civil War: Northern Intellectuals and the Crisis of the Union (New York: Harper & Row, 1965).

[7] Edward Willett, *Kate Sharp; or, The Two Conscripts* (New York: Frank Starr & Co., 1877), 23, first published in the "American Tales" series in February 1865. For publishing dates, see Albert Johannsen, *The House of Beadle and Adams and Its Dime and Nickel Novels: The Story of a Vanished Literature*, 2 vols. (Norman: University of Oklahoma Press, 1950), 1:xxx.

[8] Willett, *Kate Sharp*, 29–30.

[9] Ibid., 29.

[10] Dr. J. H. Robinson, *Scotto, the Scout; or, the Union Rangers. A Tale of the Great Rebellion* (New York: Frederic A. Brady, 1861), 4.

they knew "he would not flinch, and was the man to lead them to victory, if it were within human attainment. His hardy frame, well-seasoned muscles, and universally accredited courage, gave promise of great effectiveness."[11] An exaggerated physicality and braggadocio marked the portrayal of Scotto throughout the novel, as it marked the portrayal of numerous sensational heroes during the war.

Sensational literature was not new to the conflict. Several publishers drew on their antebellum experiences of producing sensational novels in their response to the Civil War. The sensational publisher Erastus Barclay of Philadelphia, for instance, began his career in the 1840s with "true" crime accounts and sensational novels, including the story of Amanda Bannorris, a female land pirate, and the 1843 *The Female Warrior*, an account of Leonora Siddons, "who, led on by patriotism, joined the Texas army under General Houston" and "fought in the ever memorable battle of San Antonio."[12] With the start of the Civil War Barclay began to publish a new series of sensational fictions, many of them war-related. A number of other publishers also produced what they called "cheap novels" in wartime, including Beadle & Co., Dick & Fitzgerald, Robert M. DeWitt, T. R. Dawley, Frederic A. Brady, and George Munro & Co., all of New York; T. B. Peterson & Co., Barclay & Co., and C. W. Alexander, all of Philadelphia; and U. P. James of Cincinnati.[13]

Antebellum sensationalist novels had frequently featured female heroines, including female warriors and female "land pirates." Portraying girls who ran away from home, disguised themselves as men, and even served as soldiers, sensational novels were often energized by plots of transgression against prevailing norms of behavior for women.[14] At the start of the war, such novels provided a means of imagining women's active participation in the conflict. Indeed, one

---

[11] Ibid., 6.

[12] On Barclay's career, see McDade, "Lurid Literature of the Last Century: The Publications of E. E. Barclay," *American Book Collector* 8 (September 1957): 15–25.

[13] Several of these publishers banded together during the war in an attempt to regulate prices; see Sutton, *The Western Book Trade*, 245.

[14] See David Grimsted, *Melodrama Unveiled: American Theater and Culture, 1800–1850* (Chicago: University of Chicago Press, 1968); David S. Reynolds, *Beneath the American Renaissance: The Subversive Imagination in the Age of Emerson and Melville* (New York: Alfred A. Knopf, 1988); Mary Noel, *Villains Galore* (New York: Macmillan, 1954); Michael Denning, *Mechanic Accents: Dime Novels and Working-Class Culture in America* (London: Verso, 1987); Bold, "Popular Forms I"; and McDade, "Lurid Literature of the Last Century."

author admitted that she had been inspired to disguise herself during the war as a man by an antebellum sensational novel titled *Fanny Campbell, the Female Pirate Captain, A Tale of the Revolution.* Drawing on this and other sensational literature, Sarah Emma Edmonds published a highly embroidered account of her wartime adventures in 1864 titled *Unsexed: or the Female Soldier. The Thrilling Adventures, Experiences and Escapes of a Woman, as Nurse, Spy and Scout, in Hospitals, Camps and Battle-Fields.*[15]

Edmonds actually served as a soldier for part of the war, reminding us that to some extent martial portrayals of women during the war arose out of social realities. By some historians' count, over four hundred women disguised themselves as soldiers during the war, and there were numerous mentions of such female soldiers in popular literature throughout the war.[16] But even "factual" portrayals of female soldiers were usually rooted in the breathless conventions of sensational literature, as the subtitle to Edmonds's book reveals. Likewise, in 1863 the *New York Illustrated News* published an anecdote of one Annie Lillybridge, whose lover was a lieutenant in the 21st Michigan Infantry. Because "the thought of parting from the gay lieutenant nearly drove her mad," Annie "resolved to share his dangers and be near him." After "purchasing male attire," she "behaved with marked gallantry" in the Battle of Pea Ridge, and "by her own hand shot a Rebel captain who was in the act of firing upon Lieutenant W____." Throughout "she managed to keep her secret from all— not even the object of her attachment, who met her every day, was aware of her presence so near him." Both the details of this plot summary and its language were familiar from the pages of sensational fiction. Indeed, the *News* itself acknowledged the blurred line between fact and fiction during the war by publishing this war anecdote under the heading "The Romance of a Poor Young Girl" and commending this "history" to "Miss Braddon [a popular romantic novelist] for elaboration in her next new novel."[17] As Charles Royster has

---

[15] See Frank Schneider, *Post and Tribune,* Detroit, October 1883, in Clarke Historical Library, Central Michigan University, as quoted in Julie Wheelwright, *Amazons and Military Maids: Women Who Dressed as Men in the Pursuit of Life, Liberty and Happiness* (London: Pandora, 1989), 22.

[16] On female soldiers see especially Elizabeth Leonard, *All the Daring of a Soldier: Women of the Civil War Armies* (New York: W. W. Norton, 1999).

[17] "The Romance of a Poor Young Girl," *New York Illustrated News,* June 14, 1863, 99.

noted, the "conventions of popular literature shaped many Americans' expectations when war began."[18] Those conventions also shaped how northerners portrayed the experience of war.

Sensational novels emphasized bold action, striking effects on the emotions, sharply drawn heroes and villains, and highly conventionalized, florid, even lurid language. Advertising for such novels promised to deliver the "romance" and "excitement" of war. A full-page 1863 *New York Times* advertisement for a new war story by the prolific author John Hovey Robinson, for instance, announced "Startling News from Tennessee! Love, War, Adventure! Desperation, Devotion, Heroism!" Extolling *The Round Pack* as a "series of wonderful adventures in the very heart of the guerrilla region of Tennessee," it invited "the million to a peep" into this "grand story" soon to run in the *New-York Mercury,* which offered "such delectable 'notions' as hair-breadth escapes, heroic exploits, thrilling situations, plots and counterplots, and delightful little episodes of a tender nature." "Romance and reality" were most "wonderfully interwoven" in a story that would "stir the Northern heart."[19]

Likewise, the American News Co., the most important distributor of "cheap" literature late in the war, advertised "a series of original and choice ROMANCES OF THE WAR" in 1864, promising a "stirring story of the war" in *The Border Spy;* an "exciting tale" of "the terrors of life on the border" in *The Guerrillas of the Osage;* "one of the most exciting and exhilarating romances of the war yet produced" in *Old Bill Woodworth;* "an exciting tale of scouting life in the West" in *Bob Brant, Patriot and Spy;* and a story "full of all that is novel in war, exciting in adventure and stirring in love," in *The Prisoner of the Mill,* among other war novels.[20] As such advertising revealed, it was widely assumed that war would produce "romance" and "adventure" in addition to deaths on the battlefield.

Sensational war novels and stories were themselves only a small part of a larger sensational literature that included such topics as

---

[18] Charles Royster, *The Destructive War: William Tecumseh Sherman, Stonewall Jackson, and the Americans* (New York: Alfred A. Knopf, 1991), 252.

[19] *New York Times,* May 25, 1863, 5.

[20] Advertisement on back cover of Edward Willett, *The Vicksburg Spy; or, Found and Lost. A Story of the Siege and Fall of the Great Rebel Stronghold* (New York: American News Co., 1864), Dime Novel Collection, American Antiquarian Society, Worcester, Mass.

"the old conventional Indian," with his "wampums, and third-person talking," as well as "trappers & scouts, and masculine young ladies, & pirates and baronets," as one contemporary commentator sarcastically characterized them.[21] Strongly linked to melodrama in language, plot, and characterization, sensational literature emphasized a world of moral certainty composed of dastardly villains and spotless heroes, and of pure good and evil. Herman Melville had commented about melodrama audiences in *The Confidence Man* that they rejected the merely ordinary, looking "not only for more entertainment, but, at bottom, for even more reality than real life itself can show."[22] Sensationalist literature, drawing on the melodrama, approached war in a similar way: rejecting a "commonplace" war, it created a heightened war that stressed the "thrilling," the "exciting"—words used over and over in the titles of sensational works.

The physical appearance of many sensational novels provided a visual cue to their contents. Sensational novels were distinguished from other popular literature by a set of conventions including price, physical appearance, advertising, distribution, and subject matter. Priced at a nickel, a dime, fifteen cents, or a quarter, sensational novels were published in pamphlets running from forty-eight to a little more than a hundred pages. Often published as a series, such as T. R. Dawley's "Dawley's Camp and Fireside Library," their garish, crudely drawn color covers—often but not always yellow—acted as a visual signal to their contents.

Some publishers of "cheap" literature, mindful of what many considered the morally dubious aspect of sensational novels, avoided such garish covers and denied that what they produced was "sensational." "Beadle's Dime Novels are not 'sensational,'" the publisher Beadle & Co. advertised in the *New York Tribune* in 1863. Instead, they were "good, pure, and reliable," "exhilarating without being feverishly or morbidly exciting," and "adapted to all classes, readable at all times, fit for all places."[23] Yet despite this disavowal of sensationalism, the firm's novels, including Civil War novels as well as stories

---

[21] William Everett, "Beadle's Dime Books," manuscript, Charles Eliot Norton Papers, Houghton Library, Harvard University.

[22] Herman Melville, *The Confidence Man* (New York: Holt, Rinehart and Winston, 1964), as quoted in Grimsted, *Melodrama Unveiled*, 234.

[23] *New York Tribune*, November 12, 1863, as quoted in Johannsen, *The House of Beadle and Adams*, 1:45.

of "Border Life and Character, Indian Warfare and Frontier Experience, Early Settlement Romance and Fact, Revolutionary Events and Incidents, Sea and Ship Life," were seen by many to fall within the larger category of sensationalism. As William Everett caustically remarked in an 1864 article about Beadle & Co.'s dime novels, "Not 'sensational.' O dear no: the publishers were determined to see if it would not be popular to offer everything of the best, and the experiment has succeeded! The best!" Everett had "faithfully read through" ten of these novels, he said, and "more uphill work we never had."[24] To an observer like Everett the category of sensational fiction included "dime" and other "cheap" novels of adventure. Indeed, the boundaries among these types of literature often seem arbitrary, and in this article "sensational literature" often includes what publishers described as "cheap" or "dime" literature.

Distributed widely to a home-front audience, sensational novels were particularly noticeable at news dealers' stalls, railway stations, and even saloons. In an article about Beadle's dime novels, William Everett noted in 1864 that the fact that these books "circulate to the extent of many hundred thousands need hardly be stated to any one who is in the way of casting his eye at the counter of any railway bookstall or newsdealer's shop."[25] In addition, he commented, "our readers have probably seen" volumes of Beadle's "Tales" of Daniel Boone and Bob Brant, a sensational war novel, "bound up in bulky volumes alternately with illustrated advertisements, and lying on the tables in refreshment saloons in Boston."[26]

By 1864 and 1865 cheap publishers were producing sensational war literature at a rapidly increasing rate, with both their publication and distribution aided by the merger of several wholesale news agencies into the American News Co. in February 1864. This new company, which sold "about 225,000 'dime' and other ten-cent publications" monthly during 1865,[27] had "facilities for the dissemination of current literature throughout the distant and remote portions of our vast country," the *Round Table* commented in 1866. "Along the line of every car, stage, or steamboat route, and in every

---

[24] Everett, "Beadle's Dime Books."

[25] Ibid.

[26] Ibid.

[27] "Sketches of the Publishers: The American News Company," *Round Table*, April 21, 1866, 250.

large city and town, it has its agents and correspondents, from whom every paper, book, or pamphlet can be obtained as soon as published."[28]

As many publishers of cheap novels recognized during the war, soldiers were an important audience and market for "light literature." Sinclair Tousey, one of the founders of the American News Co., advertised "A New Idea. Army and Navy Literature" composed of "first-class novelettes" in September 1863. "In view of the great demand for light literature among our brave boys in camp and on the ocean," Tousey wrote, who "while not fighting the battles of their country, have nothing to do but to read and write to the dear ones at home," he had "determined to get up, in cheap form," stories that included "romances of the battlefield" among other types of romance.[29] One of the resulting series was the "American Tales," the "romances of the war" listed above.

Other publishers, too, produced series aimed at least in part at soldiers: T. R. Dawley's "Dawley's Camp and Fireside Library" included such 1864 titles as *Justina, the Avenger* and *The Mad Bard*, while "Dawley's War Novels" included a number of sensational war novels by "Dion Haco."[30] So popular was such cheap literature during the war that Boston abolitionist James Redpath was inspired to form his own short-lived publishing company in 1863, with titles intended to be a cut above those of his competitors. His "Books for the Camp Fires," a series of "ten cent" books, were advertised as "of a much higher class than the dime publications now in the market."[31]

That soldiers read "cheap literature" in quantities we know from abundant anecdotal evidence. Looking back over his wartime reading habits, John Billings remembered that "there was no novel so dull, trashy, or sensational as not to find some one so bored with nothing to do that he would wade through it. I, certainly, never read so many such before or since."[32] "I received the Dime Novel," another soldier

---

[28] "Sketches of the Publishers: The American News Company," *Round Table*, April 7, 1866, 218.

[29] Advertisement in *The Phunny Phellow* 4 (September 1863): 16.

[30] Not all such novels were about the war.

[31] Advertisement for "Books for Camp and Home," *Frank Leslie's Illustrated Newspaper*, February 27, 1864, 366. For more on Redpath, see Madeleine B. Stern, *Imprints on History: Book Publishers and American Frontiers* (Bloomington: Indiana University Press, 1956).

[32] John Davis Billings, *Hardtack and Coffee: The Unwritten Story of Army Life*, ed. Richard Harwell (1888; Chicago: R. R. Donnelly & Sons, 1960), 57–58.

wrote home, "and will commence to read it as soon as I am done with this letter."[33] A soldier who fought in Tennessee recalled that "miserable," "worthless" novels "were sold by the thousand." He added, "the minds of the men were so poisoned that they almost scorned the idea of reading a book or journal which contained matter that would benefit their minds. I can remember when the Atlantic and Continental Monthlies were considered dull reading, while the more enticing literary productions, such as Beadle's novels, novelettes and other detestable works were received with popular favor."[34] The artist Edwin Blashfield recalled that during the war he "gloated over" war stories in papers such as the *True Flag* and the *American Union.* A story that "lingers in my memory," he said, was that of a vivandiere named Miss Minnie Ball present at Bull Run.[35] (The minie ball was the bullet used in Civil War rifles.) Confirming soldiers' interest in cheap story papers as well as novels, the New York *Sunday Mercury* ran a regular feature of correspondence from soldiers; the *Mercury* had "been the entire round of the camp," one soldier in New York's 47th Regiment reported from South Carolina.[36]

But it was not only soldiers who read sensational war literature. Children on the home front, too, were eager readers of "cheap" novels. Grenville Norcross, an eleven-year-old Massachusetts boy in 1865, recorded his interest in dime novels in a remarkable wartime journal providing a rare glimpse of a child's war-related reading. Norcross was an avid reader of a wide range of children's books and cheap literature during the war, including a number of war-related dime novels late in the war. On March 2, 1865, for instance, Norcross recorded beginning and finishing the war novel *Kate Sharp* before lending it to a friend a few days later.[37] Since *Kate Sharp* had been published for less than two weeks when Norcross read it, his reading

[33] Bell Irvin Wiley, *The Life of Billy Yank: The Common Soldier of the Union* (Baton Rouge: Louisiana State University Press, 1952; reprint ed., 1978), 154.

[34] Ibid., 155.

[35] Edwin Howland Blashfield, undated memoir, Blashfield Papers, New-York Historical Society. I am indebted to Marc Aronson for this reference.

[36] *Sunday Mercury,* March 2, 1862.

[37] Journal of Grenville Holland Norcross, March 2, 1865, American Antiquarian Society. For his lending of the book, see his March 8, 1865 entry. For his reading of other cheap war novels, see entries for June 5, 1864, November 13, 1864, January 11, 1865, and February 23, 1865. On Norcross, see also James Marten, *The Children's Civil War* (Chapel Hill: University of North Carolina Press, 1998), 31–32.

was a sign of both his avidity for such fiction and the extensive northern distribution system for cheap literature late in the war.[38] During
1864 and 1865 Norcross also read the cheap war novels *Old Bill
Woodworth, Vicksburg Spy, Crazy Dan,* and *Old Hal Williams,* all
part of Beadle's series of "American Tales," in addition to numerous
other dime novels.[39]

Cheap literature of all kinds, including war novels, was popular
with children, as William Everett attested in 1864 in the *North American Review.* "A young friend of ours," he said, was "recently suffering from that most harassing of complaints, *convalescence,* of which
the remedy consists in copious drafts of amusement prescribed by
the patient. Literature was imperatively called for, and administered
in the shape of Sir Walter Scott's novels. These did very well for
one day—when the convalescence running into satiety of the most
malignant type, a new remedy was demanded, and the 'clamor de
profundis arose.' 'I wish I had *a dime novel.*' The coveted medicine
was obtained," Everett reported, "and at once took vigorous hold
of the system."[40] Such cheap literature was an important but often
overlooked part of northern wartime culture.

Sensational war stories often drew upon the actual events of war,
especially in the border states of Tennessee, Missouri, and Kentucky,
where internecine warfare and guerrilla fighting characterized the
conflict in late 1861 and early 1862.[41] Such war stories did not just

---

[38] On the publication date, see Johannsen, *The House of Beadle and Adams,* 1:128.

[39] Albert Johannsen surmises that these were published for Beadle and Co., although they bear the imprint of the American News Co. See Johannsen, *The House
of Beadle and Adams,* I:127–28. See also Edward Willett, *Old Bill Woodworth, the
Scout of the Cumberland* (New York: American News Co., 1864); Willett, *The Vicksburg Spy;* Willett, *Crazy Dan; or, Fight Fire with Fire. A Tale of East Tennessee*
(New York: American News Co., 1864); and J. Thomas Warren, *Old Hal Williams,
the Spy of Atlanta. A Tale of Sherman's Georgia Campaign* (New York: American
News Co., 1865).

[40] Everett, "Beadle's Dime Books." Such a comment supports the contention of
scholars of reading that nineteenth-century readers read a wide variety of material,
with different works filling different needs at different times—whether in a sickbed,
in the parlor, in the railroad car, or in camp. On such diverse reading, see especially
Barbara Sicherman, "Sense and Sensibility: A Case Study of Women's Reading in
Late Victorian America," in *Reading in America: Literature and Social History,* ed.
Cathy Davidson (Baltimore: Johns Hopkins University Press, 1989), 201–25.

[41] On warfare in the border states, see James M. McPherson, *Battle Cry of Freedom: The Civil War Era* (New York: Oxford University Press, 1988). On the violence
of warfare in Missouri in particular, see Michael Fellman, *Inside War: The Guerrilla*

reflect the already-dramatic events of war in these states, however; they superimposed a particular fictional order on the chaos of conflict. Story after story created a narrative arc of disruption and eventual restoration, settling key issues of the war in a tidy narrative form that rarely corresponded to the actual events of war. From early 1862 through the summer of that year *Harper's Weekly*, for instance, published a series of stories exploring the highly charged question of whether Unionism would obtain in those states or be defeated by pro-Confederate forces. These stories often centered around families split in their loyalties by the war, energized by plots in which pro-Confederate bands of men marauded indiscriminately, and with denouements featuring the conversion of erstwhile Confederate sympathizers to staunch Unionists.[42] They also often featured heroines with an intensified sexuality, as well as male characters who embodied a rough but compelling masculinity.

Harper's Weekly's February 1862 "On the Kentucky Border," for instance, featured a Confederate sympathizer converted to staunch Unionism by the end of the story. Described as "about six foot three," Dan spoke in dialect and was a "rough-looking fellow," who made a "homely-attired but manly figure." A "crack shot at turkeys, deer, or 'possum," he counted it "a disgrace not to bring down a squirrel as dead as a hammer with the wind of my bullet." In contrast, his half-brother, Maurice, who had lived in the North, was pro-Union and eventually became a captain in the army, spoke apparently unblemished English, with his politics signaling greater education and refinement. The lesson was clear in this as well as in other border stories: those who were pro-Union were superior in culture and education to those who supported the Confederacy.[43]

Still, it was Dan's rough, manly courage that became the centerpiece of the story. After his disillusionment with "seceshers" and his conversion to Unionism, Dan attempted to fight off a band of Con-

---

Conflict in Missouri during the American Civil War (New York: Oxford University Press, 1989).

[42] The March 1862 "In Western Missouri," for instance, featured the conversion of Squire Jennifer, whose initial diatribe against the "white-livered, blue-bellied Abolitionists" changed dramatically once he learned the "bitter lesson involved in finding himself flying, a fugitive and homeless wanderer, from those whose treason he had virtually abetted"; "In Western Missouri," *Harper's Weekly*, March 1, 1862, 138–39.

[43] On the Kentucky Border," *Harper's Weekly* (February 1, 1862), 70.

federate sympathizers attacking his home. Described "with the light of battle illuminating his rough features," Dan vowed defiance against these attackers, suddenly speaking in the accentless English that signaled Unionism: "Come on, all of you, cowards that you are, and see if I can't use this bowie to some effect!" Outnumbered by his attackers, and beaten to his knees, Dan "still defended himself desperately, having already slain one and wounded two men."[44]

This defiant courage also characterized the heroine of the story, Harry, whose name, "notwithstanding its masculinity, designated a girl of eighteen," in "accordance with a practice" of naming "not yet extinct among the rougher denizens of Kentucky and Tennessee." As her masculine name suggested, Harry possessed great physical courage, refusing to leave her father when their house was threatened with attack. Instead, she "folded her arms with a look of resolution," telling her father that she could "load your rifle for you, if I can do nothing else." "You're true grit, gal," her father replied.[45]

Harry embodied a glowing physicality and sexuality rarely to be seen in domestic fiction. She was "a brilliant brunette, with magnificent black hair and eyes, ripe scarlet lips, and a face whose bold, symmetrical beauty of feature and ruddy health seemed in part to justify her masculine appellation." She was also "tall in stature like her race," "not too neatly dressed," and with "bare, brown, handsome arms" and feet—a detail the author returned to twice in the story. Indeed, the beauty of her bare feet and ankles "made their nudity a matter of congratulations to the masculine spectator," the narrator commented, inviting a form of Victorian voyeurism typical of sensationalist stories.

As such a description suggested, women in the border states were often imagined to embody a heightened sexuality, one whose racialized basis was suggested by recurrent references to these heroines' "brown" skin and black hair. One such heroine was even named "brown Meg."[46] This focus on sexuality was also played out in the plots of several sensational novels, in which the disruptions of war were mirrored by disruptions in the sexual order, as women came under direct sexual threat for their adherence to the Union.

---

[44] Ibid.

[45] Ibid.

[46] See J. H. Robinson, *The Round Pack; a Tale of the Forked Deer* (New York: Frederic A. Brady, 1862), 4.

Several sensational novels took their inspiration for plots that combined physical daring and sexual threat from the highly publicized, though quite possibly apocryphal, actions of Susan Brownlow, the daughter of the famous Parson Brownlow. The "fighting parson" William G. Brownlow of Tennessee toured the North to often tumultuous acclaim during the spring and summer of 1862 before publishing one of the few bestsellers of the war, his 1862 *Sketches of the Rise, Progress, and Decline of Secession; with a Narrative of Personal Adventure among the Rebels.*[47] The Unionist editor of the *Knoxville Whig,* Brownlow had spent months holding forth against the Confederacy from the pages of his newspaper in highly vituperative language before being escorted across Union lines by exasperated Confederate officials in March 1862. What became known simply as *Parson Brownlow's Book* presented dramatic evidence of Unionist sentiment in Tennessee—a subject of intense concern to northerners. But the success of *Parson Brownlow's Book,* which sold over seventy-five thousand copies in thirty days that summer, and eventually more than 200,000 copies, revealed far more, as well: the appeal for northerners of a war framed as sensationalized melodrama.[48] As one Chicago dignitary commented during Brownlow's triumphant lecture tour of the Midwest and East, "our children need no romance to stir their young hearts." Instead, "the truthful picture of your sufferings and heroism will fill the place of high-wrought fiction."[49]

This comment revealed a central source of Brownlow's appeal for northerners. His story was popular not because it was so different from "high-wrought" fiction, but precisely because it was so similar— because he told the tale of his devotion to the Union in the "thrilling" language of popular sensationalism. Indeed, northern audiences met him more than halfway in imagining and celebrating a sensationalist war, especially in response to his daughter Susan. Early in the war Brownlow had defiantly flown the American flag over his house, and an early *Rebellion Record* also reprinted a report that Brownlow's

---

[47] On Brownlow, see particularly E. Merton Coulter, *William G. Brownlow: Fighting Parson of the Southern Highlands* (Chapel Hill: University of North Carolina Press, 1937). For a contemporary description of Brownlow as the "fighting parson," see *Frank Leslie's Illustrated Newspaper,* June 14, 1862, 176.

[48] *New York Tribune,* July 12 and 21,1862. On Brownlow's royalties, see *American Publishers' Circular and Literary Gazette,* October 1, 1862, 97.

[49] Coulter, *William G. Brownlow,* 214, 217.

daughter Susan had used a revolver to defend the flag against two marauders—a story that was "later embellished by saying that two men came back with ninety reinforcements."[50] Whatever the truth of Susan Brownlow's actions may have been (and she may well have defended the flag), she was celebrated throughout the North in the guise of a sensationalist heroine. Accompanying her father on part of his lecture tour, in Hartford she was ceremonially presented with a Colt's revolver; in Philadelphia she was presented with a silk flag.[51] Her picture appeared on "card photographs" available for twenty-five cents.[52] When she appeared with her father in New York, the *New York Times* wrote that "no one can forget her heroic conduct, when, revolver in hand, she kept at bay a crowd of 'chivalry' who threatened and attempted to pull down the Stars and Stripes from her father's house, and no one will forget to yield her all the praise and honor which such patriotism and unflinching bravery deserve."[53]

For Brownlow's northern audiences, his daughter Susan already existed in an imaginary relation to social reality—a relation mediated by the conventions of sensationalist fiction, with its emphasis on differing norms of womanhood from the often passive suffering to be found in the pages of domestic stories. Not surprisingly, her story also inspired sensational novels that emphasized both her daring and sexual threat. The 1864 *Miss Martha Brownlow, or the Heroine of Tennessee* drew directly upon the story of Parson Brownlow and his daughter (whose name unaccountably is changed here) in order to produce "A Truthful and Graphic Account of the Many Perils and Privations Endured by Miss Martha Brownlow, the Lovely and Accomplished Daughter of the Celebrated Parson Brownlow, During Her Residence with Her Father in Knoxville." Close in style to a stage melodrama, it began with "Scene First—Game of the Traitors," in which a Confederate lieutenant and captain wagered "which of us shall lower the 'stars and stripes' at Parson Brownlow's, and kiss his handsome daughter."[54] After suggesting the sexual threat that Martha

---

[50] Frank Moore, ed., *The Rebellion Record: A Diary of American Events, with Documents, Narratives, Illustrative Incidents, Poetry, etc.*, 11 vols. (New York: G. P. Putnam, 1861–63; D. Van Nostrand, 1864–68), 1:109; Coulter, *William G. Brownlow*, 159.

[51] Coulter, *William G. Brownlow*, 231.

[52] Advertisement under "New Publications," *New York Tribune*, July 4, 1862.

[53] *New York Times*, May 14, 1862.

[54] Major W. D. Reynolds, *Miss Martha Brownlow, or the Heroine of Tennessee* (Philadelphia: Barclay, 1864), 21.

faced ("D__n me, I'll have her yet," announced one of the traitors), the novel immediately made clear that Martha would be more than a match for her would-be attackers: she was "a handsome bouncing lass," "a noble girl," who could, "after attending to her domestic duties, cross a sword, handle a musket," and "follow in the chase with success, equal to any man of equal years in Tennessee." Indeed, one character said, "I would forewarn the man who is so fortunate to win the honor of kissing even the hand of that brave girl, to beware; she will not be trifled with."[55]

One of the central ironies that the story exposed was the fact that in wartime the nation could no longer protect its individual members, including women; instead, individuals were often needed to protect the nation. When her father had to leave on a "short journey," Martha told him that she would "feel perfectly safe, even in your absence, father. For *our flag is still there.*' Surely, I am safe beneath its protecting folds." But of course she was not safe—indeed, far from the flag being able to protect her, she must protect the flag, a task she was willing to take on as an heir to Revolutionary womanhood: "Women there were in the American Revolution, who, with their husbands, fathers, brothers, sisters, lovers, braved every danger, faced the foe, and defended that flag against the assaults of our country's invaders. I emulate their daring example, and I'll protect it now." Thus, when the two traitors arrived to demand that she take the flag down just after she had sung the "Star-Spangled Banner" to herself, her response was to level "a musket at her foes": "Back, you cowardly dogs! Leave me, ere I make you bite the dust! Touch not the sacred folds of that good old flag!"[56] Here, once again threats to the Union were linked to a specific sexual threat against a white woman, a threat that due to the disruptions of war took on political overtones.

Such sexual threats also energized the 1862 novel *Six Months among the Secessionists: A Reliable and Thrilling Narrative of the Sufferings and Trials of Miss Sarah L. Palmer, a Native of Pennsylvania who, at the opening of the Great Southern Rebellion, was teaching School in Knoxville, the home of Parson Brownlow.* The heroine of this novel was even reported to have a brief conversation with Parson Brownlow, who told her that the outbreak of war was "bad,

---

[55] Ibid., 22.
[56] Ibid., 24, 25.

bad news for the whole country; but still worse for the South itself. It is suicide!"[57]

In this novel the linkage between political loyalties and sexual danger became immediately clear after the outbreak of war. Sarah Palmer, the heroine, had previously rejected the advances of the villain, the southern planter's son Alfred Poindexter. Now mockingly calling her "my Yankee maid of love and valor," Poindexter locked her in a room and told her that "I have taken care that we shall be undisturbed, and it is my full intention to revenge myself upon you for all the injury your stubbornness has caused me." Although Sarah managed to flee from this threat of rape, she later was caught by a mob, "stripped of my apparel from the waist upward," tied to the tail of a cart and dragged twice around a field. This scene made clear the voyeuristic tendencies of much sensationalist fiction.

If sexual threats to women structured the narratives of several sensational novels, these often alternated with celebrations of the possibilities opened by the war for women. Metta V. Victor's June 1862 *The Unionist's Daughter. A Tale of the Rebellion in Tennessee,* for instance, was an account of the wartime travails of Eleanor Beaufort, another Susan Brownlow–inspired heroine, whose Unionist father was jailed in Nashville for his beliefs and then—unlike the real Parson Brownlow—died.[58] The usefulness of his death as a plot device was clear: as in many sensational novels, such wartime disruption of a family paved the way for adventures outside the home without entirely overturning prevailing ideals of domesticity. After Beaufort's death, Eleanor told her would-be lover, a young Unionist hero named Beverly Bell, that her heart was now "as cold as ice" and that "I am devoted now to my country—it is all that gives me any interest in life." Asking him to "give me work to do," she wanted to know "What are your secret commissions? Can not you trust some of them to a woman's wit?" In return, Bell asked her, "Do you think you could be my courier, Eleanor?—that you could ride on horseback, unmo-

---

[57] Sarah L. Palmer, *Six Months among the Secessionists: A Reliable and Thrilling Narrative of the Sufferings and Trials of Miss Sarah L. Palmer, a Native of Pennsylvania who, at the opening the Great Southern Rebellion, was teaching School in Knoxville, the home of Parson Brownlow* (Philadelphia: Barclay & Co., 1862), 17.

[58] Metta V. Victor, *The Unionist's Daughter. A Tale of the Rebellion in Tennessee* (New York: Beadle & Co., 1862). On Metta Victor's career, see Johannsen, *The House of Beadle and Adams,* 2:278–85.

lested, through an army-cursed, secessionist country for sixty miles?—that you could even play the part of a saucy secessionist lady, if such a ruse should become necessary?"[59] Such questions, with their titillating language ("unmolested") and suggestions of melodrama ("the part of a saucy secessionist lady") could have acted as thumbnail sketches of the plots of a number of sensationalist novels. Eleanor's answer was simple: "Try me," was all she said, but "her eyes lighted with more fire than he had seen in them, of late days."[60]

Throughout, the novel played with ideas of what constituted female courage. One character, for instance, commented that "Women have a heroism of their own." "Theirs is as much in endurance as ours in action. I think they shame us men—even girls." At another point a former suitor of Eleanor's told her that "You have too much courage, Eleanor; you are not womanly enough." She simply replied that "our standards of womanly excellence differ." After Eleanor and Beverly Bell's wedding at the end of the novel, Bell asked her, "How can I take care of such a frail, fair flower?" She responded by asking, "Have I not proven, in the last few months, that I could take care of myself, and others, too, Beverly?"[61]

In focusing on women's courageous deeds during the war, Victor, an established author of Beadle's dime novels as well as other cheap fictions, claimed that she was basing her story on "bare facts." Indeed, at the back of her volume she reproduced a number of "original statements and documents" to buttress the authenticity of her narrative, much as Harriet Beecher Stowe had done in her *Key to Uncle Tom's Cabin.*[62] One of the documents Victor cited, for instance, was "a letter written from the camp of the 1st Tenn. regiment, in the fall of 1861." "One of the features of the 1st Tenn. regiment," this letter reported, "is the person of a brave and accomplished young lady of but eighteen summers, and prepossessing appearance, named Sarah Taylor, of East Tenn.," who had "formed the determination to share with her late companions the dangers and fatigues of a military campaign." Wearing a "neat blue *chapeau,* beneath which her long hair is fantastically arranged," and with "a highly-finished regulation

---

[59] Victor, *The Unionist's Daughter*, 173.

[60] Ibid.

[61] Ibid., 103, 186, 212.

[62] Victor, *The Unionist's Daughter*, "Preliminary Note by the Author," and "Addenda," 217.

sword, and silver-mounted pistols in her belt," she was "quite the idol of the Tennessee boys." Not only did they "look upon her as a second Joan of Arc," but they believed that "victory and glory will perch upon the standard borne in the ranks favored by her loved presence."[63] Significantly, "Miss Captain Taylor" was "all courage and skill." "Having become an adept in the sword exercise, and a sure shot with the pistol, she is determined to lead in the van of the march, bearing her exiled and oppressed countrymen back to their homes, or, if failing, to offer up her own life's blood in the sacrifice."[64] The language in which Sarah Taylor was described bore the marks not of the "bare facts" Victor aspired to but of sensational fiction and pointed to a circular dynamic within the commercial literary culture of war. Sensational fiction often provided a language for representations of the war's events—and the resulting representations were often then used as the "factual" basis for sensational fiction.

Like *The Unionist's Daughter,* several sensational wartime novels imagined disruptions in women's home life that allowed—or even forced—them to step out of their domestic roles and become spies or even soldiers. E. E. Barclay's 1862 *The Lady Lieutenant,* for instance, a slim, forty-page pamphlet, was described as "A wonderful, startling and thrilling narrative of the adventures of Miss Madeline Moore, who, in order to be near her lover, joined the Army, was elected lieutenant, and fought in western Virginia under the renowned General McClellan and afterwards at the great Battle of Bull's Run."[65] *The Lady Lieutenant* promised that "Her Own and Her Lover's Perilous Adventures and Hair-Breadth Escapes" would be "Graphically Delineated."[66]

Like many heroines of sensationalist fiction, Madeline Moore was an orphan—a status that helped to justify her departure from home. Although she lived with an aunt, this relative was "cross, crabbed and tyrannical," and "toward me she behaved with a vindictive boldness," all of which Madeline mentioned "to show how unpleasant was my *home,* and what strong inducements I therefore had for leaving it."[67]

---

[63] Ibid., 222.

[64] Ibid.

[65] For the copyright date, see McDade, "List of Imprints of the E. E. Barclay Co."

[66] Major W. D. Reynolds, *The Lady Lieutenant* (Philadelphia: Barclay & Co., 1862), title page.

[67] Ibid., 13, 14.

As in much domestic fiction of the antebellum era, home was not so much celebrated as scrutinized and found wanting here.[68]

Romance was the keynote of Madeline's character; she described herself as "young, ardent, and rather romantic" and promised to give the reader "an account of the wonderful adventures through which it has been my fortune to pass."[69] When her lover, Frank, decided to join a regiment after the fall of Sumter, initially Madeline "felt lonely and almost heart-broken," but soon grew excited when "suddenly a new idea flashed across my mind"—to disguise herself as a soldier in order to join Frank. Now she was no longer heartbroken over Frank's departure, a change he immediately noticed. As he plaintively remarked, "I think I could go better satisfied could I see you weep."

> I tried to weep to pacify him; but, for my life, I could not start a tear, owing to the rapturous delight I felt in anticipating the result of my new scheme. But I covered my eyes, and forced a few sobs, and in broken sentences and faint tones asked him when he was to go.[70]

Here Madeline was disguising her disguise—and in portraying her as doing so the author of *The Lady Lieutenant* drew on literary conventions stretching back to Shakespeare and beyond.

Sensational literature often emphasized the need for concealment of true or genuine identity—an emphasis that had everything to do with the perceived limitations imposed by class, gender, and race in structuring individual identity. Sensationalist literature thus implicitly offered a commentary on society's limitations; far from being a simple celebration of the possibilities for fluid social identities, it instead arose from a recognition that such fluid identities were unusual. The motif of disguise in *The Lady Lieutenant* had everything to do with a recognition of the limitations imposed on female identity and the shock or titillation value that adhered to overturning gendered norms. *The Lady Lieutenant* also played with a central irony: the only way for a woman to be a genuine soldier was to be an imposter. It presented an implicit theory of female identity outside of the home as inherently theatrical, involving simulation.

---

[68] On domesticity as critique rather than celebration, see Nina Baym, *Woman's Fiction: A Guide to Novels by and about Women in America, 1820–1870* (Ithaca, N.Y.: Cornell University Press, 1978); and Lora Romero, "Domesticity and Fiction," in Elliott, ed., *The Columbia History of the American Novel*, 110–29.

[69] Reynolds, *The Lady Lieutenant*, 13.

[70] Ibid., 16.

It also played with the confused erotic charge that resulted from female disguise. Once Madeline had put on "a complete suit of male attire, with a small pair of whiskers," she found herself attractive in new ways. "I looked in the glass," she confessed, "and must say I fell in love with myself—that is, I should have been apt to take a fancy to just such a youth as I appeared to be."[71] This erotic confusion was shared by Frank, once she joined his regiment under the assumed name Albert Harville. After "Albert" mentioned that Madeline was "a relation" of "his," Frank confessed that he saw "a resemblance between you—enough at all events to cause me to feel a deep interest in your welfare."[72] Frank and "Albert" became inseparable companions; and after Madeline's fake mustache had fallen off, Frank marveled that "Oh, more than ever, Albert, do you resemble my dear, dear Madeline!" Madeline's adoption of male disguise allowed for expressions of autoeroticism and homoeroticism not socially acceptable within the confines of heterosexual society.[73]

It also allowed for nonfeminine experiences proving her bravery. In battle Madeline had no fear, even though "while giving orders to my men a ball whizzed close past my face and lodged in the brain of the sergeant, who stood a little behind me."[74] When she found herself "almost ridden over by a rebel trooper," she not only "drew my revolver and shot my assailant dead," but found it "the work of a moment to seize the fiery animal by the bit and vault upon his back."[75] Twice wounded—once in the "right temple" and once, at "Bull's Run," with "a deep gash in the back of my head"—she nevertheless continued without complaint.[76] In the pages of *The Lady Lieutenant,* war provided a glorious opportunity for physical heroism and personal adventure.

Sensationalist literature like *The Lady Lieutenant* deliberately crossed not only boundaries of gender but also those of class: it invented a war in which persons of "low" status could easily meet those of "high" status as equals. A recurrent motif in such literature was the meeting between the protagonist and an important general: in

[71] Ibid., 17.
[72] Ibid., 19.
[73] Ibid., 33.
[74] Ibid., 22.
[75] Ibid., 36.
[76] Ibid., 25, 37.

The Lady Lieutenant, not only did Frank and "Albert" meet General McClellan, but they also carried his "despatches" [sic] to Washington.[77] Thus sensationalist literature "democratized" the war, in fantasy obliterating the distinctions that existed between ranks, classes, and men and women.

The fantasy that female heroines had ready access to high-ranking generals merged with the fantasy that the wartime nation could offer individuals a new version of family in the 1862 *Pauline of the Potomac,* which marked the literary debut of "Wesley Bradshaw," pseudonym for author and publisher Charles Wesley Alexander of Philadelphia. Born in 1837, Alexander was in his mid-twenties when the war began and, as Philadelphia city directories show, had not yet found a permanent occupation. Listed in 1861 as clerk, in 1862 he appeared as advertising agent, in 1863 as reporter, in 1864 as author, and—finally—in 1865 as publisher, a position he settled into.[78]

Alexander seized the sensational publishing opportunities offered by the war. After publishing *Pauline of the Potomac* with Barclay & Co., Alexander began his own imprint under which he printed a sequel, *Maud of the Mississippi.* During the war he wrote or published a list composed entirely of war-related titles, including *The Volunteer's Roll of Honor* (the only other title he published with Barclay & Co.), *The Picket Slayer, Washington's Vision, General Sherman's Indian Spy,* and *Angel of the Battlefield* (published by the American News Company). In addition, as Wesley Bradshaw he published several pieces of wartime ephemera, including two broadsides, "General McClellan's Dream" and "Jeff Davis' Confession! A Singular Document Found on the Dead Body of a Rebel!"[79]

Barclay made the titillating theme of *Pauline of the Potomac* clear with a cover that pictured his heroine, dressed in Union army uniform, leaning negligently on a cannon. As with several other sensational stories featuring female heroines, what initially energized the plot was family disruption, in this case the death of Pauline's father, "a distinguished French exile" devoted to his adopted country. On

---

[77] Ibid., 34.

[78] See *McElroy's Philadelphia City Directory* (Philadelphia: E. C. & J. Biddle & Co.) for 1861–64; and *McElroy's Philadelphia City Directory* (Philadelphia: A. McElroy) for 1865.

[79] These broadsides can be found in the collection of the American Antiquarian Society.

his deathbed M. D'Estraye made the connection between patriotism and patriarchal authority clear when he told Pauline that he wished to "dedicate" her to a "glorious cause" and then draped the American flag over her head and shoulders "like a bridal veil." "On the battle-field heroes will be wounded beneath its folds," he said; "you will be there to smile upon them, and to give drink to their parching lips. They will die; you will be there to pray for them, to weep for their mothers and sisters, who may be far away." "America," he concluded, "I give you my child, the offering of my heart."[80]

With this dedication of Pauline to country, Alexander carefully authorized her adventures as the last and therefore sacred wish of a dying father. He also addressed any potential criticism of Pauline's role as unfeminine by explaining that though "many might consider the course of Miss D'Estraye as rather masculine or at least out of the established line of conduct for a female and a refined lady," his readers should remember "that Miss D'Estraye was French, and that what would seem indecorous to American women, is by no means so regarded by the gentler sex in France."[81] Both sacred and foreign (and not only foreign but *French*), Pauline was doubly "other."

After her father's death, Pauline initially followed his wishes by "attaching herself to a regiment of volunteers in the capacity of nurse." Present at Bull Run, she afterwards commented, "Oh, what a terrible, what a fearful day was yesterday; and yet its horrors were strangely blended with romance," with "touching and thrilling incidents." As this sensationalist language reveals, within wartime popular culture the meaning of Bull Run was malleable; widely interpreted in the northern press as both a disaster and a goad to strengthen northern resolve, within sensationalist literature it was also a source of romance and adventure.[82]

After Bull Run Pauline "thirsted, however, for a more important part in the great drama than she had hitherto occupied" and decided to go to the "newly appointed Commander in Chief of the Union Army, General M'Clellan [sic], and offer him her services as a scout or spy."[83] This theatrical language—the fact that she wanted a more

---

[80] Wesley Bradshaw [Charles Wesley Alexander], *Pauline of the Potomac, or General McClellan's Spy* (Philadelphia: Barclay & Co., 1862), 31, 33.
[81] Ibid., 49.
[82] Ibid., 34.
[83] Ibid., 45.

important "part" in the "great drama" of war—was telling, a reminder that sensationalist literature and the popular drama of the day tended to inform one another.[84] In a scene that, significantly, transferred the authority for Pauline's actions from father to nation, McClellan decided to accept her "patriotic proposition." Although he cautioned her that the "office of a Scout or a Spy is one of the most responsible ones in the army," and that it was "attended by innumerable and oftentimes insurmountable difficulties and dangers," he was won over by her "knowledge of the geography of the Southern states" as well as her "loyalty to the sacred cause in which we are all engaged."[85]

In the adventures that followed, Pauline was often obligated, "in the performance of this duty, to assume different costumes and even names." Initially deeply veiled, she later procured "the uniform and equipment of a zouave," and later still disguised herself as a "Colonel of the Confederate Army." Like Madeline Moore, Pauline easily performed physical feats of derring-do and was consistently as "cool as she was courageous," often outwitting the enemy. After each of her adventures she returned to McClellan to receive his praise as well as further assignments; at one typical meeting "the General's face was covered with glad and gracious smiles as he cordially greeted Pauline."[86]

By the end she had found a new soldier lover, and "our heroine and her betrothed had confided" to McClellan, "as children to a father, their intentions for the future, and obtained from him his ready assent to honor their nuptials, at the conclusion of the war, with his presence."[87] This ending indicated that there were limits to the transgressive or subversive nature of gendered sensationalism. Sensational novels featuring female "scouts" often made a point of reestablishing their heroines' dependence on a husband or father figure by the end of the narrative, thereby lessening the perceived threat to society of an adventurous single female "on the loose." But their narratives also established a new relationship between women and the nation. The explicit substitution of a national family for the private, nuclear family was an aspect of imagining gendered national-

---

[84] On melodrama, see Grimsted, *Melodrama Unveiled*.
[85] Bradshaw, *Pauline of the Potomac*, 47.
[86] Ibid., 63, 68, 69.
[87] Ibid., 100.

ism in wartime. In the pages of *Pauline of the Potomac* not only did the nation provide a reconstituted family for Pauline, but it also provided a theatrical backdrop against which she could embark on exciting adventures.[88]

A different but related narrative strategy characterized wartime sensational novels featuring male scouts as heroes. Many of these novels began by stressing the solitary character of their protagonists, drawing upon a long-standing antebellum tradition of popular frontier stories in the tradition of James Fenimore Cooper, whose Natty Bumpo lived in harmony with nature but apart from society. The comparison with Cooper was often explicit: "there is nothing finer in the whole range of Cooper's stories," the *New-York Mercury* said about the sensational novel *The Round Pack*.[89] Wartime novels of heroic scouts also began by emphasizing scouts' solitary nature, but typically shifted the contours of the frontier story by integrating their protagonists into a new national economy produced by war. If female scouts eventually became part of a new national "family" by becoming dependent on male authority, male scouts became a functional part of the new nation by working and fighting with other men in an egalitarian "brotherhood."

We can see this process at work in John Hovey Robinson's 1863 *Mountain Max; or, Nick Whiffles on the Border. A Tale of the Bushwhackers in Missouri*. The prolific Robinson, who published numerous cheap novels before the war, attempted to graft the frontier novel tradition onto a Civil War story in this novel and in the process created a new hybrid narrative. In 1858 Robinson had introduced a frontier hero in his *Nick Whiffles: A Drama in Three Acts;* now he self-consciously reintroduced Nick Whiffles in a sensationalist Civil War story. Bursting into a scene in which "villainous" Confederates threatened to hang an aged Missouri Unionist, Whiffles was "dressed like a pilgrim from the far trapping-grounds of the West," in "buckskin frock," "moccasined foot," "leggined calf, and cap of skin," and with a "weather-beaten" face and beard that "presented a flourishing

---

[88] For other examples of sensationalist novels featuring cross-dressing women soldiers, see *Dora, the Heroine of the Cumberland or, the American Amazon* (Philadelphia: Barclay & Co., 1865); *The Modern Niobe; or Leoni Loudo* (Philadelphia: Barclay & Co., 1864); and *Miriam Rivers, the Lady Soldier; or, General Grant's Spy* (Philadelphia: Barclay & Co., 1865).

[89] Advertisement in the *New York Times*, May 25, 1863, 5.

growth of several years."[90] He immediately drew two guns on a "rebel outlaw" so that "each of his brown hands now held six shots." But his intended victim protested against this sudden entrance of the frontier literary tradition into a Civil War setting. "I've heard of you," the well-read Confederate villain announced. "Much has been said and written about you; but I don't believe half on't. You've been published in the newspapers, put on the stage, served up in books, translated into French, and hashed up in every style to suit the modern appetite." Despite his admission of Nick Whiffles's literary fame, however, he questioned Nick's ability to handle the new crisis of war: "This is a bad place for you to come to, Nick Whiffles. There's a different pastime going on here from trapping beaver, shooting bears, and picking off a naked Indian, now and then."[91]

Yet Nick Whiffles's frontier skills were just what the war needed, the novel made clear. "Major-General Fremont had sent for him to come down from the mountains, with a few chosen woodsmen and sharpshooters, to take a hand in playing out the game of Rebellion," the narrator commented.[92] In the course of the story, Whiffles gathered a group of mountain men who "proved a scourge and a terror" to the Missouri bushwhackers. "These brave fellows are doing good service for the Union," the story concluded. "Nick has distinguished himself in many battles." He "occasionally turns a longing eye to the mountains; but no wandering thought can attract his honest heart from its devotion to Liberty and the Old Flag. The star that now directs his steps by day and by night, is not the North star of the old trapping grounds, but the pole-star of Freedom."[93]

One lesson of sensational war novels was that the nation gathered even the staunchest individualists to it in wartime. But as the plot of *Mountain Max* also revealed, as it careened from one adventure to another, sensationalist war novels taught a complementary lesson: that adherence to the nation furthered the possibility of exciting individual adventures.

Such individual adventures had a highly racialized cast. A number of sensational novels featured white characters who disguised them-

---

[90] John Hovey Robinson, *Mountain Max; or, Nick Whiffles on the Border. A Tale of the Bushwhackers in Missouri* (New York: F. A. Brady, 1861).

[91] Ibid., 15.

[92] Ibid., 20.

[93] Ibid., 77.

selves as "contrabands" in order to act as spies or escape from tight situations. In *Kate Sharp* both Kate and her admirer Jim Allen disguised themselves as two old "contrabands."[94] In *Six Months among the Secessionists* the heroine, Sarah, escaped from sexual slavery to the villainous Alfred Poindexter only by being disguised as a slave.[95] These disguises were part of the changeability of identity that generally characterized sensational literature, but also had specific pleasurable and transgressive connotations within a white northern culture that celebrated and enjoyed putting on "blackface" in minstrelsy.[96]

A recurrent motif in these stories was the desire on the part of African Americans to aid whites. In *Six Months among the Secessionists*, it was slaves who helped Sarah escape. Thrust into a "miserable hut occupied only by a negro and his wife," Sarah attracted the sympathy of the "poor old creature" Chloe, who told her, "Dar now, Missus, don't cry no more! Sampson nor Chloe won't let nobody hurt ye!" To help her to escape, they "completely metamorphosed" her "into a young negress, the skin of my face, neck, arms, and hands being ingeniously colored, my own hair after being trimmed, concealed by woolly locks, and my own dress being replaced by the regular attire of a slave girl." The fantasy that blacks would devote themselves to the freedom of whites dominated the remainder of the novel, as Sarah made her way northward *"assisted invariably by negroes!"*[97]

To be sure, many sensational stories and novels did acknowledge African Americans' own desires for freedom, as well as their awareness that the war might result in emancipation. In *Harper's Weekly*'s March 1862 "In Western Missouri," for instance, the female slave Dinah "demanded with great earnestness" whether one character was going to fight for the Union: "You gwine to fight for de Stars and Stripes and Massa Lincoln, ben't you, Cap'n Elliot?" When he told her he was, she blessed him: "De good Lord in hebben bress both you and him! dat's all. Nebber doubt you're in de right and dat He

---

[94] See Willett, *Kate Sharp*, 14, 19.

[95] See Palmer, *Six Months among the Secessionists*, 18, 25.

[96] See Eric Lott, *Love and Theft: Blackface Minstrelsy and the American Working Class* (New York: Oxford University Press, 1993); Jean Baker, *Affairs of Party: The Political Culture of Northern Democrats in the Mid–Nineteenth Century* (Ithaca, N.Y.: Cornell University Press, 1983); and David Roediger, *The Wages of Whiteness: Race and the Making of the American Working Class* (New York: Verso, 1991).

[97] Palmer, *Six Months among the Secessionists*, 34, 35, 36, 37.

will bress you."[98] In other sensational stories, too, black characters emerged briefly from their usual location in the background of the story to state their interest in freedom.

Yet by and large sensational stories and novels depicted African Americans as loyal appendages of whites, interested in freedom only if they could stay with their white masters and mistresses. In *Scotto, the Scout*, the slave Dagon, who "spoke often of the North Star," nevertheless "declared a firm determination not to leave his young mistress."[99] When he thought his mistress had been killed, he exclaimed, "who car's for liberty now? I doesn't! I doesn't car' a hill o' corn for't. I's a miser'ble contraban', I is!"[100] Likewise, though the slave Black Jack allowed that "we should all like to hev the freedom" in *The Round Pack*, he also said that "t'won't make so much dif'rence to me as it does to some others," since "I stays kase I likes to."[101] In *Harper's Weekly's* March 1862 "The Tennessee Blacksmith," the white hero asked the "stalwart negro" Joe whether he would like his freedom. "Well, Massa John," Joe replied, "I wouldn't like much to leabe you, but den I'se like to be a free man." Joe's master then explained a theory of freedom based on masculine whiteness: "Joe, the white race have maintained their liberty by their valor. Are you willing to fight for yours? Ay! fight to the death?" Joe's response, while embracing freedom, also revealed to what extent white authors maintained a fantasy of black love of and subservience to whites. "I'se fight for yous any time, Massa John," Joe said.[102]

The idea that black men deserved freedom only through fighting for (and like) white men was a gendered theory of freedom that also had a feminized counterpart: although black female slaves, in contrast to white women, were never represented as fighting, they were sometimes represented as sacrificing themselves for their white mistresses and obtaining freedom as a result. C. W. Alexander's 1865 *Angel of the Battlefield*, for instance, created a southern heroine, Eleanor Poindexter, who emancipated her mulatto slave Rosa as a reward for total devotion. After Rosa had risked her life for the sake of her mistress, saying, "I'd sooner be killed twenty times over than

---

[98] "In Western Missouri," *Harper's Weekly*, March 1, 1862, 138–39.

[99] Robinson, *Scotto the Scout*, 68.

[100] Ibid., 46.

[101] Robinson, *The Round Pack*, 71.

[102] "The Tennessee Blacksmith," *Harper's Weekly*, March 29, 1862, 202.

have any hurt come to you, Miss Eleanor, God bless you!" Eleanor exclaimed, "'Slave, then, you shall be no longer!'" in "accents that showed she had forever swept from her mind prejudices and opinions which had been inculcated there by lifelong education and custom."[103]

Nevertheless, the severe limitations of this emancipation fantasy were immediately clear. Rosa's emancipation involved paid servitude for her former mistress: "Hereafter," Eleanor told her, "I will pay you four dollars a week."[104] What's more, before Rosa had a chance to exercise her new freedom, the plot demanded that she make the ultimate sacrifice for her former mistress: she died protecting Eleanor from a lascivious villain. As a would-be rapist threatened Eleanor, Rosa "sprang upon him with the fury of a tigress, and, clutching him by the throat, almost bore him to the floor." "Alas! however, the next moment a bowie-knife glittered above her, and flashed down into her bosom like the lightning bolt falls from heaven to earth." Even at the moment of death, this sensational novel imagined that Rosa's last thoughts were of her mistress, emphasizing this point by repeating the word "faithful" twice in one sentence: "The faithful mulatto sank back with a wild shriek of despair; but, faithful to the last, stretched out her arms toward Eleanor, as though to reach and enfold her cherished mistress to her stricken heart."[105]

Rosa's convenient death followed in a long line of "tragic mulatto" stories and vividly revealed the limits that northern racism imposed on conceptions of black life after emancipation within sensational literature, as well as within other forms of popular literature. To solve the "problem" posed by freed slaves, emancipation became no more than the end—quite literally—of blacks' lives as slaves.[106]

There were intriguing exceptions to this general rule. The 1862 *The Rebel Pirate's Fatal Prize*, for instance, was the fictionalized "Life History" of the "brave and daring negro," William Tillman, who early in the war had killed the master of a Confederate privateer after its

---

[103] Wesley Bradshaw [Charles Wesley Alexander], *The Angel of the Battlefield. A Tale of the Rebellion* (New York: American News Co., 1865), 12.

[104] Ibid.

[105] Ibid., 90–91.

[106] On the "tragic mulatto" in literature, see especially Eric J. Sundquist, *To Wake the Nations: Race in the Making of American Literature* (Cambridge, Mass: Harvard University Press, 1993).

capture of the schooner on which Tillman served as steward.[107] This rare sensational novel provided a portrait of Tillman's individual heroism and daring, not his subservience to or love for whites. His was "a stirring history," the novel concluded, and "the next we hear of him, faithful still to his love of country, and desire to serve in some capacity in the good work of crushing out this rebellion,—he accompanied an officer of the Seventh New York Cavalry as an assistant." In response to a Confederate threat to arrest him as a slave, Tillman's "blood is up, and in his course of vengeance through their land, we believe he will make not a few dastardly traitors bite the dust at his feet before this war is closed."[108]

Even more striking a depiction of African American heroism, written as a direct response to Emancipation, was John Townsend Trowbridge's 1863 *Cudjo's Cave*. Trowbridge, an ardent abolitionist before the war, "flung" himself into "the writing of as fiery an antislavery fiction as I was capable of compassing" during the summer and autumn of 1863. Trowbridge felt the "old heat" of antislavery beliefs "fevering me," he said, because "too many calling themselves patriots still opposed emancipation and the arming of blacks, and clung tremblingly to the delusion that the Union and slavery might both be preserved. The idol-house of prejudice was shattered, but not demolished. I was impatient to hurl my firebrand into the breach."[109] Convinced of the political efficacy of fiction, in December Trowbridge published *Cudjo's Cave*, which featured two runaway slaves, Pomp and Cudjo, who lived in an imagined cave deep in the Tennessee wilderness. Like many authors during the war, Trowbridge was fascinated by the Unionist struggle in Tennessee and hoped that his romantic invention of a cave would pique northern readers' curiosity. "Wishing to bring into it some incidents of guerrilla warfare and of the persecutions of the Union men in the border slave States, I cast about for some central fact to give unity to the action, and form at the same time a picturesque feature of the narra-

[107] Circular for *The Rebel Pirate's Fatal Prize; the Bloody Tragedy of the Prize Schooner Waring*, McCallister Civil War Scrapbooks, Library Company of Philadelphia.

[108] *The Rebel Pirate's Fatal Prize; or, the Bloody Tragedy of the Prize Schooner Waring* (Philadelphia: Reichner & Co., 1862), 46.

[109] John Townsend Trowbridge, *My Own Story with Recollections of Noted Persons* (Boston: Houghton Mifflin, 1903), 261.

tive. The idea of a cave somehow suggested itself, and I chose for the scene a region where such things exist."[110]

The resulting novel was a sensationalist work that careened from one violent adventure to another. Trowbridge admitted that *Cudjo's Cave* contained sensational elements: it was a "partisan book, frankly designed to fire the Northern heart," and it "contained scenes of violence such as I never, under other circumstances, have selected as subjects for my pen." But Trowbridge defended such sensationalism in wartime: "I adapted, but did not invent them; the most sensational incidents had their counterparts in the reign of wrath and wrong I was endeavoring to hold up to the abhorrence of all lovers of the Union and all haters of slavery and secession."[111]

Despite the book's title, its hero "was not Cudjo," Trowbridge said, "although I no longer shrank from giving a black man that role." Instead, the "real hero, if the story had one, was the proud and powerful, full-blooded African, Pomp, whom I afterwards carried into the third and last of my war stories, The Three Scouts."[112] Pomp was a significant wartime invention, portrayed as both a fighter and a leader. He and a group of white Unionists fought together against the rebels, and "instinctively they accepted his lead." Though his heroism was racialized—he was "swift and stealthy as a panther," for instance, and his "haughty self-assertion which would have been offensive in a white man, was vastly becoming to the haughty and powerful black"—he was nonetheless a clear attempt to imagine a black military hero and a new wartime departure from antebellum norms of black heroism.[113] Significantly, too, he was not killed at the end. "Have you read the newspaper stories of a certain scout," the narrator asked at the conclusion of the novel, "who by his intrepidity, intelligence, and wonderful celerity of movement, has rendered such important services to the Army of the Cumberland? He is the man."[114]

Trowbridge sincerely meant for his book to combat northern racial prejudice: when Penn Hapgood asked Pomp, "why have you never escaped to the North?" Pomp answered, "Would I be any better off

---

[110] Ibid., 260.
[111] Ibid., 262.
[112] Ibid.
[113] Ibid., 444, 445, 228.
[114] Ibid., 501.

there? Does not the color of a negro's skin, even in your free states, render him an object of suspicion and hatred?" Penn "sadly" agreed, while "contemplating the powerful and intelligent black, and thinking with indignation and shame of the prejudice which excludes men of his race from the privileges of free men, even in the free north."[115]

Still, though *Cudjo's Cave* presented Pomp as a hero, it also constructed a deliberately split image of blacks, reinscribing northern racism in the character of Cudjo. Near the beginning of the novel Pomp and Cudjo were the rescuers of a young Quaker schoolmaster, Penn Hapgood, who had "sunk into a swoon" after being beaten, tarred, and feathered for his abolitionist views. In Hapgood's delirium he imagined his rescuers as two halves of a black servant he knew named Toby: Pomp was "Toby the Good" and Cudjo was "Toby the Malevolent." While the good Toby (Pomp) argued that "We can't leave him dying here," the bad Toby (Cudjo) said, "What dat to me, if him die, or whar him die?"[116]

When Hapgood awoke from his delirium, having been carried to Cudjo's cave by these two, he recognized the "twin Tobys of his dreams." "And what a contrast between the two! There was Toby the Good, otherwise called Pomp, dignified, erect, of noble features; while before him cringed and grimaced Toby the Malign, alias Cudjo, ugly, deformed, with immensely long arms, short bow legs resembling a parenthesis, a body like a frog's, and the countenance of an ape."[117]

Thus Trowbridge unwittingly reinforced the very prejudice he so passionately criticized. In creating Cudjo, he not only suggested that many slaves had been so debased by slavery as to be barely human, but employed a minstrelsy-based imagery to do so. Whereas Pomp's features "lighted up with intelligence and sympathy," when Cudjo laughed he showed "two tremendous rows of ivory glittering from ear to ear" and looked more "like a demon of the cave than a human being."[118] When Cudjo died at the end—a dramatic death in which, after being shot himself, he dragged a cruel overseer down an embankment so that they both drowned in the river below—it was a

---

[115] Ibid., 132–33.

[116] John Townsend Trowbridge, *Cudjo's Cave* (Boston: J. E. Tilton and Co., 1863), 113.

[117] Ibid., 118.

[118] Ibid., 120.

solution to a dilemma that Trowbridge had portrayed as insoluble: how uneducated slaves would be integrated into free society. As in *The Angel of the Battlefield,* clear limitations were affixed to the northern commitment to emancipation—but this time by an avowed abolitionist and promoter of racial equality.

Cudjo's Cave met with immense, even startling success in late 1863 and early 1864, in part atttributable to the tactics of its publisher. J. E. Tilton, "a young and enterprising firm," according to Trowbridge, used "considerable ingenuity and no little audacity in advertising it." Publishers' advertisements and descriptions signaled its sensational elements by emphasizing that the book was "full of interest, excitement, and adventure."[119] Not only were "pictures of the cave" on envelopes and posters, but Trowbridge remembered "a bookseller's window" with a "pile of the freshly bound volumes erected in the similitude of a cave."[120] Significantly, advertisements did not mention that the book was the story of an African American scout.

The book appealed to both adults and children: as one reader remembered, his work was "half a 'juvenile' and half for grown ups" and was "prodigiously popular with young and old."[121] Its antislavery politics made a deep impact on another reader: Elizabeth Boynton of Crawfordsville, Indiana, wrote to her soldier lover in February 1864 that "I sometimes shudder when I think what an *horrible* institution 'American Slavery' *is*—how long before we can say *was*—I have just finished that new story 'Cudjo's Cave' and I wonder how men with any minds can think for an instant that slavery is aught but a *curse.*"[122]

The study of sensational war literature forces us to expand our

---

[119] *American Literary Gazette and Publishers' Circular,* March 1, 1864, 307.

[120] Trowbridge, *My Own Story,* 263–64. Trowbridge also commented that "a private letter to the author from Secretary Chase, then at the zenith of his fame as a national financier, was made to do service in ways he could hardly have anticipated any more than I did when the publishers obtained permission of him to use it. It was printed, and extensively copied by the press, and the interior of every street-car in Boston was placarded with a signed extract from it, outstaring the patient public week after week in a manner that would have made the great Secretary wince, could he have seen it, as it did me" (263–64).

[121] Edwin Howland Blashfield, undated memoir, Blashfield Papers, New-York Historical Society.

[122] Elizabeth Boynton to Will Harbert, February 20, 1864, Elizabeth Boynton Harbert Papers, Huntington Library, San Marino, Calif.

ideas of the cultural meanings of the war in the North. Many writers have assumed, for instance, that northern imaginative writers chose to avert their eyes from the subject of race in wartime. African Americans "figured only peripherally in the War literature" of canonical writers such as Hawthorne and Melville, Daniel Aaron has noted.[123] Similarly, most literary critics have assumed that women were only peripheral characters in war literature. Yet as sensational war literature reveals, both women and African Americans were a vital part of a popular literary war, sometimes appearing in heroic, even dashing roles. We are left with a paradox: though there is no question that sensational literature was conventional, formulaic, derivative, and breathless in style, it also was a rare location in northern wartime culture where both women and African Americans were sometimes imagined to break free of the conventions of a larger society. By studying sensational literature and the popular literary culture of which it was a part, we enlarge our ideas of what constituted a home-front war in the North.

---

[123] Aaron, *The Unwritten War,* xviii.

3

From Necessary Evil to National Blessing: The Northern Protestant Clergy Interpret the Civil War

Peter J. Parish

THE CIVIL WAR was the first war in modern history fought by, and within, a society that embraced political democracy, at least for white males. In such a conflict public opinion, popular support, and civilian as well as soldier morale would be crucially important. But not only was the United States the most advanced democratic society of the age, it was also a profoundly Protestant society. In these circumstances churchmen had a key role as leaders and shapers of opinion, boosters of morale and commitment, and interpreters and justifiers of the cause, or causes, for which the war was being fought.

Northern churchmen showed few inhibitions in supporting the call to arms in 1861. The Rev. A. L. Stone, of Park Street Congregational Church in Boston, saw war as a Christian duty, "as sacred as prayer—as solemn as sacraments." The Methodist Bishop Edward R. Ames declared that, if he were called upon to fight the rebels, he would "fire into them most benevolently." Most of the clergy continued to support the war through the next four years, even as the violence escalated and casualties mounted to levels unimagined and unimaginable when the fighting began. In 1864 Joseph Thompson still took the view that the righteousness of a cause could be referred to God by "the arbitrament of war."[1] Such vigorous support for the

---

[1] A. L. Stone, quoted in Chester F. Dunham, *The Attitude of the Northern Clergy toward the South* (Toledo, Ohio: Gray, 1942; reprint ed., Philadelphia: Porcupine Press, 1974), 111, n.4; Ames, quoted in Charles B. Swaney, *Episcopal Methodism and Slavery, with Sidelights on Ecclesiastical Politics* (Boston: R. G. Badger, 1926), 300; Joseph P. Thompson, *Peace through Victory: A Thanksgiving Sermon* (New York: Loyal Publication Society, 1864), 4.

war was rooted first and foremost in defense of the Union and all that it stood for and did not necessarily include a demand for an end to slavery. There were of course abolitionists in the ranks of northern churchmen, just as there were a few apologists for slavery, and a rather larger number who thought that the federal government had no business to interfere with the South's peculiar institution. If there was a broad middle ground on which the majority of northern ministers stood, it was to be found in abhorrence of slavery as an evil system and hope for its eventual demise, but reluctance to resort to drastic measures to eradicate it immediately. In this respect they mirrored the attitude of Lincoln and his administration when the war began in 1861. Of course, as the war progressed, and Lincoln embraced a policy of emancipation, churchmen were obliged to rethink their ideas on the nature and purpose of the struggle. However, the core belief of most churchmen was always located in the Union—its salvation and, indeed, its rebirth.[2]

How and why were northern churchmen so engaged in the war? What explains the bellicosity of so much of their rhetoric? It is clearly linked to the widely held and deeply rooted belief in the God-given mission of the United States—the confident assumption that the United States had been specially favored by God, in its resources, its liberties, and its opportunities, and that, in return, America would be required to play a unique role in the divine plan for the future of the world.[3] This belief was never more boldly, or indeed baldly, stated than in the words of Bishop Matthew Simpson: "If the world is to be raised to its proper place, I would say it with all reverence, God cannot do without America."[4]

This sense of America's special destiny had been reinforced by the tremendous surge of evangelical and revivalist Protestantism during

---

[2] For general background on the churches during the Civil War, see Sydney E. Ahlstrom, *A Religious History of the American People* (New Haven, Conn.: Yale University Press, 1972), 648–97; and Phillip Shaw Paludan, *"A People's Contest": The Union and the Civil War, 1861–1865* (New York: Harper & Row, 1988), 339–74. A specialized study of crucial importance is James H. Moorhead, *American Apocalypse: Yankee Protestants and the Civil War, 1860–1869* (New Haven, Conn.: Yale University Press, 1978).

[3] On the national mission of the United States, see Ernest L. Tuveson, *Redeemer Nation: The Idea of America's Milliennial Role* (Chicago: University of Chicago Press, 1968).

[4] George R. Crooks, *The Life of Bishop Matthew Simpson of the Methodist Episcopal Church* (New York: Harper, 1891), 382.

the first half of the nineteenth century. In the decades before the Civil War, political democracy, social egalitarianism, and evangelical Protestantism marched forward together and reinforced each other. Many churches and many churchmen had been closely engaged in the philanthropic societies and reform groups that made up the "benevolent empire." Some northern churchmen—but by no means all—extended their concern for individual conversion and salvation into commitment to the improvement and purification of society as a whole.

Secular ideas of progress were buttressed by religious notions of perfectionism, which could be applied to society as a whole as well as to individuals. The evangelical religion of the antebellum decades was shot through with millennialist ideas and millennialist rhetoric. This was more often postmillennial than premillennial in character— that is to say, the predominant belief was not in an imminent return of Christ, a day of judgment, and the end of the world, but in a real historical era of one thousand years of peace, prosperity, and Christian morality, preceding the final judgment. This was a vision of an ideal society toward which people could aspire and strive. This sat quite comfortably with contemporary political beliefs in the world role that the United States should play by the sheer force of its example, as the model of freedom and equality, if only it could cleanse itself of the stains on its political and social character.[5]

To those who cherished such religious and political beliefs, the onset of the Civil War was a massive shock. It posed huge problems, even if, in the eyes of some, it also opened up new possibilities. What now of the moral force of the American example? Was it to give way to physical force and the violent clash of arms? What could be the divine purpose in allowing such a conflict to take place? What had gone wrong with the dreams of America's God-given destiny? The

---

[5] On the Protestant churches during the antebellum decades, see Jon Butler, *Awash in a Sea of Faith: Christianizing the American People* (Cambridge, Mass.: Harvard University Press, 1990); Robert T. Handy, *A Christian America: Protestant Hopes and Historical Realities*, rev. ed. (New York: Oxford University Press, 1984); C. C. Goen, *Broken Churches, Broken Nation: Denominational Schisms and the Coming of the American Civil War* (Macon, Ga.: Mercer University Press, 1985); and Timothy L. Smith, *Revivalism and Social Reform: American Protestantism on the Eve of the Civil War*, rev. ed. (Baltimore: Johns Hopkins University Press, 1980). On the churches and politics, see Richard J. Carwardine, *Evangelicals and Politics in Antebellum America* (New Haven, Conn.: Yale University Press, 1993).

great majority of the Protestant clergy of the time believed in an activist, interventionist deity who would play a direct role in the unfolding of human history, and in the shaping of American destiny. How were they to reconcile their faith in such a God with the calamity that had now struck the United States, and with pain, suffering, and death on an unprecedented scale?

It was at this point that the postmillennial beliefs, which were prevalent in the northern Protestant churches, came to the rescue. It was widely held that the thousand-year age of peace and harmony would be preceded by a period of upheaval and misery, and a final terrible battle between the forces of good and evil. It was not too difficult to cast the war to save the Union in that role. But postmillennialism had much more than that to say about the ultimate meaning of the Civil War. It offered a theory of progress—envisaging an onward march of religious revivalism, material prosperity, and the model American republic—but also, on its darker side, it threatened supernatural judgment and the condemnation of the wicked to eternal punishment. In James Moorhead's words, it was "a compromise between a progressive evolutionary view of history and the apocalyptic outlook of the Book of Revelation." The key lay in the emphasis on human cooperation in achieving the kingdom of God. In Moorhead's memorable phrase: "Postmillennialism was the moral government of God stretched out on the frame of time."[6] There was no guarantee of automatic progress toward the final goal, and there was always the possibility of disaster along the way. America and Americans had to prove themselves worthy of the role prescribed for them, and the coming of the war seemed to suggest that they were failing to meet that challenge. If the war led to mass slaughter, it simply demonstrated the depths of sinfulness, individual and national, into which the United States had lapsed. If America was to fulfill its destiny, the outcome of the war would have to be, not merely the salvation of the Union, but its purification and regeneration.

There were close parallels here with political ideas about the national destiny. However, it is also true that, in both religious and secular thought, there was an inclination to look backward as well as

---

[6] This discussion of postmillennialism draws heavily upon James H. Moorhead, "Between Progress and Apocalypse: A Reassessment of Millennialism in American Religious Thought, 1800–1880," *Journal of American History* 71 (December 1984): 524–42. The quotations are from pp. 541 and 528.

forward. One recurring theme in many periods of American history has been the yearning for a past golden age, the desire to recover a lost innocence or a lost state of grace, whether it was to be found in the Garden of Eden or in the virtuous republic of the Founding Fathers.[7] In this context the Civil War was a punishment visited on the United States for the accumulated sins of several decades—not only slavery, but also all the consequences of luxury and materialism, in the shape of greed, selfishness, intemperance, infidelity, and a whole catalog of other failings. The rhetoric of political leaders, from Abraham Lincoln downwards and of religious leaders of all denominations, was full of such interpretations of the meaning of the war. The horrors of the conflict could be used to purge American society of its evil ways and to bring the republic back to its true path. In short, clergy and politicians looked in both directions—backwards to the restoration of America to its pristine purity and virtue, and forward to the fulfilment of the national destiny and the coming of the millennium. Whether it was entirely logical or not, many of them managed to espouse both views at the same time. With all his skill in articulating the widely shared thoughts and feelings of many people, Lincoln distilled the essence of this conception of the war in his call for a national fast day, issued on March 30, 1863:

> And, insomuch as we know that, by His divine law, nations like individuals are subjected to punishments and chastisements in this world, may we not justly fear that the awful calamity of civil war which now desolates our land, may be but a punishment, inflicted upon us, for our presumptuous sins, to the needful end of our national reformation as a whole People? We have been the recipients of the choicest bounties of Heaven. We have been preserved, these many years, in peace and prosperity. We have grown in numbers, wealth and power, as no other nation has ever grown. But we have forgotten God. We have forgotten the gracious hand which preserved us in peace, and multiplied and enriched and strengthened us; and we have vainly imagined, in the deceitfulness of our hearts, that all these blessings were produced by some superior wisdom and virtue of our own. Intoxicated with unbroken success, we have become too self-sufficient to feel the

---

[7] For one classic statement of this theme, see Richard Hofstadter, *The American Political Tradition and the Men Who Made It* (New York: Alfred A. Knopf, 1948), v–vii and passim.

necessity of redeeming and preserving grace, too proud to pray to the God that made us.[8]

Lincoln's words exemplify the way in which politicians frequently resorted to religious rhetoric in pursuit of their political ends, just as the preaching of churchmen about the war was seldom completely devoid of political implications. Political and religious arguments were intertwined and even interchangeable. Apart from an introduction or conclusion invoking the deity and seeking to elucidate His purposes in the war, many editorials appearing in the northern religious press during the war might equally well have appeared in the *New York Times* or the *New York Tribune*.

This essay offers a small sample of the ideas and attitudes of the northern Protestant clergy during the four years of the war. The predominant theme that emerges is the shift from initial justification of the war as a necessary evil, forced upon the North by the southern attempt to dissolve the Union, to its interpretation as a blessing, a providential opportunity for national atonement, purification, and regeneration. This shift of emphasis is an early example of a recurring pattern in the history of modern wars where champions of a cause face the need to justify the resort to arms, not only to themselves but to a wider constituency of party members or church members—and, beyond them, to public opinion at large. At the moment of entry into a war, and for some time afterwards, the highest priority is to justify participation as an inescapable duty—an act of self-defense, dictated by sheer necessity. However, as the war goes on, and both the costs and the stakes mount, a struggle simply to defend one's interests begins to appear inadequate, even unworthy. Justification of the war then seeks out some higher ground, and the war becomes a crusade for a national rebirth, a spiritual revival, a moral crusade, or some other higher purpose. The development of the arguments advanced by churchmen to justify the war for the Union may have helped to set a pattern in which the escalation of a conflict itself changes the grounds upon which its purpose is justified and its meaning defined.

Case studies of a small sample of individual churchmen may help to give some sharpness and clarity to the complex process through which the struggle to explain and justify the war evolved. The figures

---

[8] Roy P. Basler et al., eds., *The Collected Works of Abraham Lincoln,* 9 vols. (New Brunswick, N.J.: Rutgers University Press, 1953), 6:156.

in this small sample include three enthusiasts for the war, Matthew Simpson and Gilbert Haven, who were both Methodists, and George Ide, who was a Baptist; one agonizer in the person of the Old School Presbyterian Charles Hodge; and one dissident, Bishop John H. Hopkins of the Episcopal Church, who vigorously opposed a war against slavery and blamed the abolitionists for precipitating the conflict.[9] The three enthusiasts for the cause did not share identical priorities. Simpson was a great evangelist of American nationalism, speaking up powerfully for the war to save the Union. Haven, who was the most prominent abolitionist in the Methodist ranks, saw the war as an opportunity to hasten the millennium of racial brotherhood and harmony. Ide cherished the causes of union and emancipation in one huge, undiscriminating embrace.

The clergy in this small sample have deliberately been chosen from the mainstream denominations—and from churches that traditionally had significant strength in both North and South. In the antebellum years they had handled the problem of divisions over slavery in different ways. The Methodists had split, North and South, in the 1840s, and despite their more decentralized structure, the Baptists arrived at a de facto separation at much the same time. The split between Old School and New School Presbyterians was not directly related to the slavery issue, but the New School was essentially a northern church, whereas much of the strength of the Old School was in the South. The Episcopal Church was able to avoid a head-on clash over slavery by permitting each diocese to decide on its own position. Some smaller denominations, such as the Lutherans, adopted a similar approach and avoided as far as possible any commitment to a national stance. It was the northern churches most influenced by the evangelical spirit of the Second Great Awakening that were in the forefront of the crusade for the Union.

Matthew Simpson is probably the most straightforward and un-

---

[9] In addition to biographical studies of these individuals, referred to in subsequent notes, there are useful studies of some of the mainstream Protestant denominations during the Civil War period. See, for example, Donald G. Jones, *The Sectional Crisis and Northern Methodism: A Study in Piety, Political Ethics and Civil Religion* (Metuchen, N.J.: Scarecrow Press, 1979); Lewis G. Vander Velde, *The Presbyterian Churches and the Federal Union, 1861–1869* (Cambridge, Mass.: Harvard University Press, 1932); and George Marsden, *The Evangelical Mind and the New School Presbyterian Experience* (New Haven, Conn.: Yale University Press, 1970). See also Moorhead, *American Apocalypse.*

complicated of these individual case studies. A son of the Ohio frontier, a Methodist circuit rider, then president of a frontier college in
Indiana, an increasingly renowned preacher, and from 1852 a bishop,
he became one of the best-known churchmen in America during the
Civil War. He came to know Lincoln well, tried to use his influence
to secure a healthy share of government patronage for Methodists,
and was asked by Lincoln to deputize for him when the President
declined an invitation to speak at a large fund-raising fair in Philadelphia in 1864. It was Simpson, too, who officiated at Lincoln's burial
in 1865. In many of his views on the war, Simpson was very close to
Lincoln, for example, in his subordination of the slavery issue to the
first priority of salvation of the Union, his rejoicing in the growth of
the nation's resources even during the war, and his sense of the war
as a test of the nation's virtue and of the power of its example to the
world.[10]

During the war Simpson's greatest fame derived from his "war
speech," a patriotic address for which he could command a large fee
and that he delivered in most of the major cities of the North. The
speech went through various versions; it often included some actual,
as well as a good deal of metaphorical, flag-waving, and its dominant
themes were trust in Providence, the value of sacrifice, and the confident expectation that God would ensure the salvation of the Union
because He *needed* America to fulfill His plans for the world. Although Simpson claimed to be above party, it was scarcely a coincidence, for example, that he delivered a supercharged version of his
war speech in New York City three days before presidential Election
Day in November 1864.

At the heart of Simpson's standard speech was the claim that the
war must end in one of four ways. First, America might come under
the control of some foreign power; but this would not happen, he
believed, because the nation's great providential destiny could be
fulfilled only if it retained its unity and independence. Second, the
nation might be permanently divided into two or more confederacies;
but there was no natural geographical basis for such divisions, and
Providence had endowed the whole United States with magnificent

---

[10] On Simpson's career and his wartime role, see Crooks, *Matthew Simpson;* Robert D. Clark, *The Life of Matthew Simpson* (New York: Macmillan, 1956); and James
E. Kirby, "Matthew Simpson and the Mission of America," *Church History* 36 (September 1967): 299–307.

natural boundaries. (He did not explain how the forty-ninth parallel fitted into this picture.) Simpson wanted not some kind of temporary peace that would lead to further strife and further fragmentation, but a lasting peace for a united nation. He deprecated the horrors of war, but rather than face a future of constant turmoil and friction, it was "better now [to] fight for twenty years and have peace than stop where we are."

The third possibility was that the Union would be restored, but with southern institutions and ideas in the ascendancy. Simpson dismissed such an outcome as completely unthinkable. The fourth possibility, and the true outcome of the war, would be that, having passed through its fiery ordeal, the nation would emerge purer, stronger, and more glorious than ever, with the help of divine Providence. This theme of purification may have become more prominent as the war went on, but in truth there is no great sign of evolution or development in Simpson's justification of the war for the Union. He started with an intense belief in the war and never wavered for four years.[11]

However, there was one area where a distinct shift of emphasis can be traced in Simpson's support for the war—and this lay in the relationship of slavery to the conduct and purpose of the war. As a young man in the 1830s, Simpson had voiced some sympathy with the antislavery cause. But, as his career advanced, he became more and more equivocal on this subject and sought to play it down and to avoid controversy.

When the war broke out, he certainly did not see it as an antislavery crusade. By 1864, however, he recognized that the war had done fatal damage to slavery, and he exulted in the thought of its final demise. Nevertheless, he insisted that the war must still be fought, *not* for the purpose of destroying slavery, but for the single purpose of restoring the proper authority of the government. But, with more bluntness than tact or elegance, he went on: "If, while we are striking blows at the rebellion, Slavery will come and put its black head between us and the rebels, then let it perish along with them." Thus, in the divine plan, slavery might become an incidental casualty of the war. Simpson was even ready to welcome the recruitment of black troops; with a racial condescension typical of his age, he boasted that

---

[11] This account of Simpson's war speech is based mainly on Crooks, *Matthew Simpson*, 380–85. See also Clark, *Matthew Simpson*, 236–43.

"it has been demonstrated in this war that a blue coat can make a hero even of a sable skin." By the closing stages of the war, Simpson was in little doubt about the message that God was conveying through the conflict: "He has written a great lesson which the ages may read, that great wrongs must terminate in great catastrophes; and the people have resolved that, cost what it may, the system which could not live within the Constitution shall die beyond it."[12]

When compared with Matthew Simpson, his fellow Methodist, Gilbert Haven, offers a higher idealism, but less of a down-to-earth acceptance of the political and social realities. Haven came from a well-established New England family, underwent a Methodist "conversion" while a student, and emerged as a prominent abolitionist in the 1850s. When the war broke out, his immediate reaction was to volunteer as an army chaplain, perhaps on the emotional rebound from the death of his young wife. He was chaplain to one of the first regiments of ninety-day volunteers from Massachusetts but did not choose to extend his service beyond the initial three-months' term. From May 1862 he spent nine months in Europe and, on his return, resumed his ministry in Boston.[13]

For all his deep-dyed abolitionism, Haven was initially prepared to support the war simply as a harsh necessity. He agonized briefly over the use of force against a portion of the people in a democratic society but quickly accepted that this was a struggle for the perpetuation of national sovereignty, a war in "defense of all that is vital and glorious in our heritage."[14] For the abolitionist Haven, however, the slavery issue could not be thrust into the background for very long. Much more rapidly than most of his fellow clergymen, he raised his interpretation of the war from the level of a struggle for survival to the higher plane of national purification and racial brotherhood.

The first major battle of the war at Bull Run, in July 1861, which was a severe setback to the North and especially to northern morale, seems to have been a turning point for Haven. He was by no means alone in believing that this reverse would change the character of the

---

[12] Crooks, *Matthew Simpson*, 384–85, 393.

[13] On Haven's background and his reactions to events in 1861–62, see William Gravely, *Gilbert Haven, Militant Abolitionist: A Study in Race, Religion and Reform, 1850–1880* (Nashville, Tenn.: Abingdon Press, 1973), especially 76–82, 88–90, 94–109.

[14] Ibid., 78–80.

struggle. If the North had won, it might have swept on to a rapid overall victory and a peace that would have restored the Union very much as it was, with slavery still intact. Initial defeat meant a longer war that would surely lead to the elimination of slavery and progress toward the Union as it should be. God's purpose was now made clear. The war was to liberate "these children of His who have cried day and night unto Him for these many generations." It was also to lead "this nation, stuffed with pride and insolence, into the fires that shall humiliate and purify."[15]

The central themes of Haven's interpretation of the war were now emerging into the open: emancipation of the slaves, regeneration of the South, chastisement and purification of a sinful nation, and preparation for the millennium of racial harmony and equality. In his major sermons and addresses during the latter part of the war, Haven sought to place the conflict both in its broad historical perspective and in its proper millennial context. He saw in history a pattern of progress toward the complete triumph of God's grace and the defeat of sin. The Reformation had destroyed the first enemy, in the shape of an idolatry that had shattered man's allegiance to God. The second enemy was the hostility of man to man, and in its destruction America had the vital role to play; American democracy and popular government, and American ideals of equality and fraternity, were divinely inspired instruments to destroy this second enemy. The unification of mankind required the elimination of various obstacles, notably artificial social barriers of blood, language, color, and caste. For all his idealism, Haven was obliged to recognize that American commitment to the elimination of these barriers was less than complete, but the American people would have to accept these difficult truths, just as sick people had to take very disagreeable draughts in order that they might get well.[16]

In this great unifying process, the Civil War assumed a special historic role—or, at least, God was using the struggle to provide

---

[15] Gilbert Haven, "Letters from Camp," in *National Sermons: Sermons, Speeches and Letters on Slavery and Its War* (Boston: Lee & Shephard, 1869), 266–68. For other examples, religious and secular, of the belief that the initial Bull Run defeat was a blessing in disguise, see George M. Fredrickson, *The Inner Civil War: Northern Intellectuals and the Crisis of the Union* (New York: Harper & Row, 1965), 73–76.

[16] Haven, "The War and the Millennium," in *National Sermons*, 373–92, especially 382–83. Page references in the next five notes are to *National Sermons*.

America with a unique opportunity. The war to defend the Union had fused the passion for Union and the passion for liberty. The shock of war had united both "the centrifugal lovers of liberty and the centripetal lovers of Union." Conservatives and abolitionists now found that they had a common cause. Haven's optimism encouraged him to believe that victory in the war would, or at least could, usher in an age of racial equality and brotherhood. Racial harmony would be the special American contribution to the coming of the millennium, but the repercussions of its achievement would be worldwide. He foresaw a kind of domino effect running on through Europe, Asia, and Africa: "Christendom [once] unified, heathendom and Islamdom will soon be regenerated. Social vices will abate their violence. . . . Intemperance, Sabbath-breaking, infidelity, all the fruits of crowned and Catholic Europe, will be replaced with the graces of Christianity. The Lord Jesus will be the real and recognized, if not visible, sovereign of the world." To those who dismissed such a prospect as a mere dream, Haven pointed, not unjustifiably, to the dramatic change in American attitudes to slavery during three years of war. In 1860 not even the most hopeful souls in America could see any immediate prospect of the demise of slavery, but now its days were numbered. Haven found encouragement in the fact that "the favorite nickname of the negro and the nation, 'Sambo' and 'Samuel' is of the same origin. Is not this prophetic of their future identity?" He added that "Desdemona loved Othello because he had saved her country from destruction; so must we his American kindred."[17]

Crucially, however, Haven did not believe that the achievement of this millennium of racial harmony would automatically follow from the Civil War. God had His own purposes to achieve on earth: "He is pushing us forward to His, not our, millennium. He is using and blessing us *if* we choose to work with Him." In effect, God was offering America a choice, and everything would depend upon the manner of America's response to His call. Either Americans could cooperate in the fulfilment of the divine plan, and gain glory for themselves in the process, or they would be cast aside and become victims of the destruction and chaos that would pave the way for a new order created by direct supernatural intervention. He went on:

---

[17] Haven, "The War and the Millennium," 383, 387; "The Crisis Hour," 436.

For, my friends, be assured that God cares very little for you unless you will aid Him in carrying out His designs on the earth. To that design, if America is willing to contribute, well for her; if not, she is broken in pieces as a potter's wheel. . . . If we cooperate with Him, He will make us His vanguard. If we refuse, He will do with us as He did with His more chosen and more beloved people—cast us off, and raise up another people who shall follow His guidance.[18]

At this point, Haven's millennial vision merges into another common theme in the religious interpretation of the Civil War: the notion that the conflict was a punishment for national sins and a purification of the national soul. The national sins included not only slavery but also all the other vices bred by generations of prosperity. This chastisement theme assumed increasing importance as an explanation of the mounting casualties and costs of the war. One of the remarkable features of both the sermons and the religious press of the war years is that the ardor of clerical support for the cause scarcely wavered or flagged at all, even when the scale of the fighting and the bloodshed reached levels inconceivable at the outset. The notion of divinely ordained national punishment offered a powerful instrument for the explanation, justification, even rationalization, of the escalation of the conflict. The greater the sins, the greater the punishment. For Gilbert Haven, repeated defeats and prolonged conflict were a means of pressing the North toward emancipation, and on toward racial equality. He saw the Union defeats in 1862 as punishments for northern opposition to emancipation and Lincoln's reluctance to act. He then interpreted continuing heavy losses among white troops as a divine message in favor of the recruitment of blacks:

Now comes another word of God. Arm him as a soldier? We refuse; we scream in fear and hatred at that word. . . . Such opposition only new punishment could cure. So God sent our enemies again upon us. They ate up our boys as the ox eateth up grass. He develops demand for work at home to subdue the recruiting fever. He makes the draft unpopular and difficult. He wastes our armies and shows that they cannot be replenished from their previous sources. At length, crushed with calamity and nigh the gates of the grave, we whiningly and meanly, yet honestly, say, 'Come, you nigger, and fight for us.' He comes. . . . We are being led gradually to higher hights [sic]. Providence is using this degradation for the furtherance of His ends.

---

[18] Haven, "The War and the Millennium," 384; "Why Grant Will Succeed," 405.

In 1864 Haven argued that "if Grant is delayed before Richmond, it is not for our destruction but our purification."[19] (Haven does not indicate whether Grant shared this perception of the larger purpose served by his frustration.)

There is ample evidence here of Haven's firm belief in an activist deity who would intervene specifically and selectively in the war. In a breathtaking attempt to have it both ways, he claimed that "our victories are encouraging; so are our defeats." Generals like George B. McClellan and Nathaniel P. Banks had failed precisely because they had not accepted the divine plan for a racially equal and fraternal America. Grant had succeeded because he had seen and accepted the will of God. His armies in both West and East included black regiments fighting alongside whites. In his more reflective moments, however, Haven did probe a little more deeply into the relationship between the divine will and the need for competent human leadership, including generalship on the field of battle. Having said, "we trace our defeats and victories to no incompetent or competent generalship," he goes on: "Not that we despise generalship. Not that we believe victory usually follows virtuous imbecility, and defeat vicious ability. Success requires sagacity, even in the way of righteousness. Folly is not God's favorite."[20]

In his belief in an interventionist God, in a special place for America in the divine plan, in the war as an instrument of chastisement and purification, Haven was typical of many of the northern clergy. What singled him out was his vision of an American future of racial harmony and brotherhood—and his deep conviction that America and Americans were being presented with a choice by God. Postbellum America was to prove a particularly bitter disappointment to him.[21]

---

[19] See Haven, "Why Grant Will Succeed," 390, for a clear exposition of the view of the war as a cleansing of a variety of national and individual sins. On the effect of defeats and the escalation of the war in pushing the North toward emancipation, see ibid., 398–405. The quotations are from "The War and the Millennium," 385–86, and "The Crisis Hour," 436.

[20] Haven, "The Crisis Hour," 436; "Why Grant Will Succeed," 396–405. The quotation is on p. 397.

[21] See Haven, "The Crisis Hour," 421–24, for one of his most sustained examinations of God's purposes in allowing the war and its escalation. See also Gravely, Gilbert Haven, 110–19, for a thoughtful analysis of Haven's understanding of God's purposes in the war and his commitment to the ideal of racial brotherhood. On Haven's postwar career, his appointment as bishop of Atlanta, and his troubled years as a campaigner for racial equality, see Gravely, Gilbert Haven, 139–257.

Some of the main themes developed by the nationalist Simpson and the abolitionist Haven were merged—and perhaps vulgarized—in the preaching of another enthusiastic supporter of the war, the Baptist George B. Ide. In his sermons these ideas were articulated in a more popular and more emotional style, full of extravagant imagery and elaborate (and often far-fetched) figures of speech. Ide was for many years a Baptist minister in Springfield, Massachusetts, and author of a number of works of spiritual uplift. He had also written an antislavery pamphlet before the war, and he was an ardent champion of the Union cause during the war itself. In 1866 he published under the title of *Battle Echoes, or Lessons from the War* a collection of his wartime sermons.[22]

In his 1861 address to a regiment of volunteers about to depart for the front, Ide stressed that this was a war for self-defense, "a grapple for existence." However, from the first he saw larger issues at stake in the conflict, both for America and for the world. As with Simpson and, particularly, Haven, his treatment of these issues—the abolition of slavery and the regeneration of the nation—developed rapidly as the war went on. What had begun as a "grapple for existence" was quickly converted by divine intervention into part of a much grander design and a nobler vision.[23]

Ide underlined arguments deployed by Haven, but with his simpler faith he presented them in a less sophisticated and less complicated style. He showed an unwavering belief, not merely in divine intervention in the war, but in God's total control and manipulation of events. Unlike Haven, he never debated the relationship between human actions and God's overall control. The first paragraph of the preface of *Battle Echoes* declares that there was no stronger or more universal conviction than belief in God's interference in human affairs. During the war, "so clear were the revealings of His hand that even the undevout were compelled to bow before them with awe and

---

[22] George B. Ide, *Battle Echoes, or Lessons from the War* (Boston: Gould & Lincoln, 1866). Ide was a less prominent public figure than Simpson, Haven, or Hodge. However, in May 1864 he was one of a delegation of three from the Baptist Home Missionary Society who presented to Abraham Lincoln resolutions supporting the war and endorsing Lincoln's policies. See Basler et al., eds., *Collected Works of Abraham Lincoln*, 7:365, 368. See also Moorhead, *American Apocalypse*, 51–52, 147.

[23] Ide, "The War for the Union as a Righteous War," in *Battle Echoes*, 21. Page references in the next six notes are to *Battle Echoes*.

reverence." In a later sermon, titled "The Moving Pillar," he argued that, in place of the moving pillar of cloud by day and fire by night that had guided the children of Israel, the American people must be guided by the pillar of God's providence, as revealed in the unfolding of events. Chance had no place in a universe presided over by divine wisdom, and human intellect and passion were but instruments in God's hands. In place of the choice that Haven's God offered His people, Ide's God offered a directing hand that must be followed.[24]

As with Haven, Ide identified very specific examples of divine intervention in the course of the war, for example, in protracting and intensifying the conflict in order to push the North toward emancipation, and to create a new and better Union, rather than preserve the Union as it was. Looking back in 1865, he saw that the great achievement of the destruction of slavery in a few short years had been made possible only by God's direct intervention. "Heaven-led, we chose war—war in its direst form, civil and internecine—war protracted, sanguinary, all-wasting," and yet such a war was preferable to a peace that perpetuated the nation's sinfulness in slavery, as in other matters.[25]

God's interventions covered not only military and political but also economic affairs. Marveling at the North's prosperity even during the war, Ide noted that, just when the government needed extra revenue and the normal sources of funds from abroad had dried up, "the almighty Disposer of events ordained short crops and scarcity for Europe, and ample harvests and overflowing plenty for ourselves; thus creating a demand for bread there, and a supply here, which have caused the tide of wealth to set strongly upon our shores." God, the agricultural economist, was clearly a formidable ally to have on one's side.[26]

As Ide saw it, the divine direction of the war effort aimed at two goals above all. The first was the eradication of slavery from American society—the removal of the greatest of all national sins. In permitting slavery to drive the South to a mad rush into "treason and rebellion," God had created the opportunity to overthrow it. The whole of the United States was now suffering from the war—but all shared in the

---

[24] Ide, Preface, 5; "The Moving Pillar," 137–42.
[25] Ide, "Memories and Lessons," 231–32.
[26] Ide, "Reasons for Grateful Confidence," 41–42, and more generally 40–45.

guilt of slavery. Defeats and suffering had pressed Lincoln into issuing the Emancipation Proclamations, which "allied us with Heaven" and sounded the death knell of slavery. Looking back in 1865, in a sermon entitled "Memories and Lessons," Ide argued that slavery had proved invulnerable to political argument or the criticism of conscience: "We meant to kill it by argument. God meant to kill it with the sword. We purposed to melt it away by the soft breath of Christian influence. God purposed to blow it out of the universe with Parrott guns."[27]

The second and wider purpose behind God's direction of the war was the purification of America through its ordeal by fire. Occasionally Ide spoke in millennial terms not unlike Haven's, but more often he articulated that other great theme of American rhetoric in this era—the need to purge American society of its corruptions and vices, its materialistic excesses and selfish preoccupations, and to return to the purity and integrity of its first principles, whether the ideals of the Founding Fathers or the virtues of the Pilgrim Fathers (or, indeed, some vaguely defined compound of the two).

Ide was at least as sure as Matthew Simpson that the United States "has a grand work to do for humanity and for God." But the relentless pursuit of wealth had distracted the nation from its true purposes. "Materialism, like some monstrous fungus," he claimed, "was rapidly spreading its abnormal growth over the whole body of the nation, poisoning its heart, eating out its vitality, and presaging its sure decay." But help was at hand: "From this peril of self-destruction, the same over-ruling Power, that has been our Guide and Protector in all the eventful epochs of our former history, has mercifully interposed to save us. . . . And the discipline which He has seen fit to employ for this purpose, though severe, is eminently suited to the case, and indispensable."[28]

For Ide the war, with all its horrors, was the divine prescription, not only to overcome materialism but also to destroy slavery. He reserved one of his most extravagant flights of rhetorical fancy to show how an interventionist deity would use the war to achieve emancipation:

---

[27] Ide, "Great Eras Marked by Great Judgments," 92–97; "The Freedmen of the War," 155; "Memories and Lessons," 239–40; and more generally 237–43.
[28] Ide, "Reasons for Grateful Confidence," 46–47.

In the pride of our vain wisdom, we marked out for ourselves the way to political greatness. Across the shaking morasses of Expediency, over the bottomless bog of Compromise, we formed the track, and laid the rails, and put on the train, and got up the steam, and with rush and roar were sweeping onward in our self-confidence, heedless of the abyss which Slavery had dug in our path, and whose yawning depths lay just before us. But God put His hand to the brakes, and switched us off on a new track, which He laid, and not man. There was surprise, terror, outcry at first. There are doubts, apprehensions, tremblings still. But the road is firm and straight, the engine sound, the cars stanch, the Conductor all-wise and all-powerful, and the end of our journey—a vindicated Government, a restored Union, a Free Nation—already in sight.[29]

Ide's bombastic style and overblown imagery may now invite ridicule, but he may well have been more in tune with his popular audience than Haven would have been, and he did not match Matthew Simpson for sheer jingoism. However, for all their differences in style, emphasis, and message, Simpson, Haven, and Ide were all within the mainstream of the contemporary religious interpretation of the war for the Union, and its meaning for America—and indeed the wider world. In their diverse styles, all three reflect the basic theme of a transition from a necessary, defensive war for national survival to a divine instrument of national punishment, purification, and regeneration.

There were some dissident voices, but explicitly pacifist denunciations of the war by any churchman are conspicuous by their absence. Some northern clergy opposed the war as unnecessary and undesirable, and even as contrary to the divine purpose. Often their criticism of the war seemed to be on political as much as a religious grounds. At times they were close to the views of those northern Democrats who thought that the war could have been avoided, who blamed abolitionist agitation for bringing on the secession crisis, who supported the war to save the Union reluctantly, if at all, and who opposed any attempt to convert it into a crusade for emancipation. One such critic was Henry J. Van Dyke, minister of the First Presbyterian Church in Brooklyn, who, in defiance of the patriotic oratory of so many of his fellow ministers, argued that the will of God could not be deduced

---

[29] Ide, "The Freedmen of the War," 153–54.

from the course of American history and ridiculed the idea that Lincoln's Emancipation Proclamations were expressions of the divine will. He was particularly scornful of Bishop Simpson's claim that God needed America.[30]

Another very colorful figure who took a not dissimilar view was Bishop John Henry Hopkins of Vermont, one of the maverick churchmen of his day, and a rare specimen of that increasingly endangered species, a politically naive bishop. A Pennsylvanian by birth and education, Hopkins had become bishop of one of the smallest dioceses of the Episcopal Church in Vermont. By 1860 he was one of the senior bishops of the church, and, by an ironic twist, and through the seniority rule of the church, this eccentric figure became the presiding bishop of the church in 1865.[31]

As with Van Dyke, much of Hopkins's criticism of the war stemmed from his distaste for abolitionism. He was a well-known protagonist of the view that the Bible did not condemn slavery, and in 1860 he had published a pamphlet elaborating the case that slaveholding was not in itself a sin and was not in conflict with the American Constitution. Rejecting any thought of immediate abolition, he professed to believe in gradual emancipation, undertaken by the southern states themselves on grounds of expediency, and not because slavery was morally wrong. Although he believed that a defensive war to save the state might be justified by absolute necessity, he did not regard coercive preservation of the Union as justifiable. The Union as he knew it could not, he thought, be preserved by war. At the 1862 convention of the Episcopal Church, he protested bitterly against a pastoral letter that went too far for his taste in public support of the government and its prosecution of the war. Its authors (some of his fellow bishops) were, he suggested, "more solicitous to please the powers at Washington than the powers of Heaven." Hopkins absented himself from the closing service of the convention until the offending letter had been read.[32]

---

[30] On Van Dyke's attitude to the war, see Moorhead, *American Apocalypse*, 127–28. For a sample of his argument that abolitionists were responsible for the secession crisis, see Van Dyke, *The Character and Influence of Abolitionism: A Sermon Preached in the First Presbyterian Church Brooklyn, on Sabbath Evening, Dec. 9th 1860* (New York: George F. Nesbitt, 1860).

[31] *The Life of the Late Right Reverend John Henry Hopkins, First Bishop of Vermont and Seventh Presiding Bishop, by One of His Sons* (New York: Huntington, 1873).

[32] Ibid., 325–29.

Then, in 1863, he agreed to a request from his old home state of Pennsylvania for the republication of his 1860 pamphlet *A Bible View of Slavery*. The reissued pamphlet was then taken up by the Society for the Diffusion of Political Knowledge, the leading propaganda agency of the Democratic party. It flooded Pennsylvania with copies of the pamphlet in support of the campaign for the state governorship of George L. Woodward, a notorious Copperhead. This aroused the indignation of the Bishop of Pennsylvania, Alonzo Potter, who persuaded 160 of his clergy to join him in signing a protest against this apology for slavery, which, they said, amounted to "an effort to sustain states in rebellion against the government." Hopkins denied this charge but displayed his political naiveté by pleading that, when he consented to republication of the pamphlet, he had not supposed that it would be put to the service of any political party. However, he believed that he had no right to complain if it were so used, because, once published, it became public property.[33] Despite the efforts of family and friends to restrain him, Hopkins refused to let the matter drop, and, working at a furious pace, he produced in 1864 a four-hundred page volume, *A Scriptural, Ecclesiastical and Historical View of Slavery from the Days of the Patriarch Abraham to the Nineteenth Century.*[34]

Hopkins was more notable for the stir that he caused than for any particular arguments that he advanced. His book was about slavery rather than the war, but it repeated his allegation that the abolitionists had caused the war, and his belief that the unity of both church and country could be restored only by a return to the true scriptural doctrine that slavery in itself involved no sin. The one conviction that he shared with his fellow clergy who supported the war and denounced slavery was his belief that the war was God's punishment for national sins. But his catalog of sinners to be punished was directly contrary to theirs: it included those who demanded an antislavery God and an antislavery Bible, and those who were determined

---

[33] Ibid., 330–36.

[34] John Henry Hopkins, *A Scriptural, Ecclesiastical and Historical View of Slavery from the Days of the Patriarch Abraham to the Nineteenth Century. Addressed to the Right Reverend Alonzo Potter D.D.* (New York: Pooley, 1864). The book includes the text of Hopkins's 1860 pamphlet *A Bible View of Slavery* (5–41), the protest by the bishop and clergy of Pennsylvania (42–44), and Hopkins's reply to the protest (44–49). On the circumstances of the book's publication, see *Life of Hopkins*, 336–38.

that the Union should be restored only when all protection for slavery had been abolished. Hopkins's conclusions were pessimistic. The predicted reign of the great Antichrist might well be impending, but, if so, Hopkins wished to be in the tradition of the old martyrs of the primitive church.[35]

Men such as Hopkins and Van Dyke are interesting mainly because they were exceptions to the general rule. Much more important, surely, were those who, unlike Simpson and Ide on the one side or Hopkins on the other, could find no clear or unequivocal answers from God to the questions posed by the war. They were firmly loyal to the Union, but for one reason or another—doubts about the slavery issue, or concern for the unity of their church, or belief that the church should remain detached from political or social controversy—they felt inhibitions about jumping on the national bandwagon. From the ranks of these agonizers, impaled for four years on the horns of one dilemma after another, one name stands out. A man of formidable intellect and energy, Charles Hodge was the most influential voice of conservative Old School Presbyterianism. A professor at Princeton for over a half century, he founded and edited for forty years, *The Biblical Repertory and Princeton Review* (later simply *The Princeton Review*); it has been estimated that his own contributions to that journal would fill some ten volumes, at five or six hundred pages per volume. Throughout the Civil War he analyzed the issues with a subtle, complex, and often tortuous logic, which resisted the easy answers of some of his fellow clerics.[36]

Hodge's reactions to the secession crisis and the coming of the war were instinctively cautious and conservative. He was desperately anxious to save, if he could, the unity of the Old School Presbyterian Church that, unlike some other denominations, had a substantial membership in both North and South. He also believed that the church should steer clear of secular problems wherever possible, and that the church had no right to dictate to its members on political questions, including questions of political allegiance. However, in

---

[35] Hopkins, *Scriptural View*, 16–18, 61–62.

[36] Vander Velde, *Presbyterian Churches and the Federal Union*, 135–40. For biographical information on Hodge, see Archibald A. Hodge, *The Life of Charles Hodge by his Son A. A. Hodge* (New York: Scribner, 1880). There is an excellent brief biographical sketch in Allen Johnson and Dumas Malone, eds., *Dictionary of American Biography*, 20 vols. (New York: Scribner, 1928–36), 9:98–99.

January 1861 he published an article in which, while he denounced
abolitionism, he contended that the United States was one nation,
that the South had no justification for rebellion, and that the right of
secession did not exist. Although he recognized the right of revolution—as any good American would—he regarded rebellion without
adequate cause as a great crime. His article attracted enormous attention, and vigorous criticism from both southern secessionists and
northern abolitionists.[37]

Once war had broken out in April 1861, Hodge and his church
found themselves entangled in further debate. As luck would have it,
the General Assembly of the church was due to meet only a month
later, and it could scarcely ignore the issues raised by civil strife.
Despite a much-reduced southern representation, there was still a
long and heated debate before the adoption of a resolution urging
the church to "strengthen, uphold and encourage the Federal Government." Writing in the *Biblical Repertory* in July, Hodge continued
the protest against the resolution that he had launched at the assembly itself. As an individual, and a loyal citizen, he entirely agreed with
its sentiments, but he denied the right of the General Assembly to
impose its view on church members. All citizens, he argued, owed
loyalty to the government under which they lived—but what if there
was a difference of conviction as to the government to which allegiance was due? Such differences commonly arose between two
countries in Europe, for example, where there were competing
claims to sovereignty over a particular territory. In the American context, the argument was between the claims of the federal and the
state governments. The correct judgment between the two was a
matter of moral indifference to the church. There was a duty of loyalty to the government, but the individual conscience of each citizen
must decide where that duty lay. Hodge reaffirmed his own national
loyalty and belief that secession was unjustifiable. Supporters of secession were guilty of a great crime, but they were not amenable to
church discipline. The General Assembly had, in effect, made allegiance to the Constitution and the government a term of communion,
and they had no right to do so. Loyalty to the federal government

---

[37] Vander Velde, *Presbyterian Churches and the Federal Union*, 29–41.

was not a condition of salvation: "We agree with this decision of the Assembly; we only deny their right to make it."[38]

One year later Hodge underlined yet again his personal support for the war to save the Union. However, while still insisting that the church should not interfere with the state, and vice versa, he now put much greater emphasis on the duty of the church to bear testimony against all error and sin, whether in the magistrate or in the people. He attacked the view that the church was so exclusively spiritual in its preoccupations that it could not pronounce on any political matter, whatever its moral dimensions.[39] The most important of Hodge's wartime articles appeared in January 1863, in the wake of Lincoln's Emancipation Proclamation. Now he took the view that the war touched the conscience at too many points to make silence possible. Moral law took precedence over expediency for both nations and individuals. Unlike many of his fellow churchmen, he also tackled the moral questions arising from methods of waging war as well as the ends for which it was waged. The Union could not be saved by sinful means; proper conduct of the war must include humane treatment of prisoners, respect for the lives of noncombatants, and protection of private property.[40]

Hodge's readiness to court unpopularity showed itself in the scorn that he poured on the widely shared notion that the war was a punishment for national sins. On the contrary, he argued that good and evil were not distributed in this world on the principles of justice, but according to the wise and benevolent sovereignty of God. Some suffering—for example, the sickness of drunkards—was clearly punitive, but it was not always so. God used suffering for many purposes—as punishment, as test, as example, to strengthen and develop character, to make manifest His works. History was not a judicial process, nor were the strong always right. The trials of the American Revolution were not a judgment on the sins of the people, and the same might well be true of the Civil War. Perhaps God was preparing and educat-

---

[38] Charles Hodge, "The General Assembly: The State of the Country," *Biblical Repertory and Princeton Review* 33 (July 1861): 556–66 (hereafter *Bib. Rep.*). There is a detailed account of the General Assembly of 1861 and its consequences in Vander Velde, *Presbyterian Churches and the Federal Union*, 42–107.

[39] Hodge, "The General Assembly," *Bib. Rep.* 34 (July 1862): 518–20.

[40] Hodge, "The War," *Bib. Rep.* 35 (January 1863): 141, 155–57.

ing the nation for higher things. God's providence and His wisdom were a mystery, and His purposes were higher than mere reward and punishment.[41]

By 1863 the relationship of slavery to the war had become the central issue for Hodge and the main challenge to his rigorous, but not inflexible, logic. Like many other conservatives, Hodge placed much of the blame for the war on the agitation of the abolitionists. He did not share their belief that immediate emancipation was a moral duty, but he professed his own strong dislike of southern slavery. Once again, a fine distinction was crucial to his argument; it was not slavery per se that was sinful, but certain features of the southern slave system—for example, denial to the slave of educational opportunity, religious freedom, and a proper married and family life. When the war began, the phrase "the war to save the Union" served Hodge and many others as a kind of code word for disapproval of the notion of a war to free the slaves. The war was justified as a defense of national unity and of a legitimate government, and not as an antislavery crusade. Although Hodge adhered to this basic position throughout the war, the pressure of events and the wonderful workings of Providence brought about a gradual, and often painful, shift in his conception of the relationship of slavery to the conflict.[42]

By July 1862 Hodge conceded that, while he had always hoped for a gradual and peaceful process of emancipation, southern obstinacy and wickedness might bring slavery to a more sudden and violent end. The southern rebellion might well force the northern people to put preservation of the Union ahead of preservation of slavery.[43] In his January 1863 article, he endorsed Lincoln's own justification of emancipation as a means of waging the war for the Union, and not as an end in itself. To make abolition the object of the war would, Hodge still insisted, be morally wrong. Slavery was a great evil, but there were many other evils in the world, such as despotism and false religion—and the mere existence of an evil did not justify war against it. "Nothing can be a legitimate object of a war," he wrote, "but something which a nation has not only a right to attain, but which also it is bound to secure." Legitimate objectives in war would include

---

[41] Ibid., 142–47.

[42] Hodge, "The General Assembly," *Bib. Rep.* 36 (July 1864): 542–51.

[43] Hodge, "The General Assembly," *Bib. Rep.* 34 (July 1862): 519–21.

the security of a nation's territory, the safety of its citizens, and the preservation of national existence. Such was the evil of war that it was justified only by absolute necessity. Under the Constitution the federal government had neither the right nor the obligation to abolish slavery in the states; therefore, to make abolition the object of war would violate the oath of allegiance to the Constitution, as well as the law of God. There was, Hodge claimed, all the difference in the world between abolition as a means of waging war for the Union and abolition as a war aim: "The difference . . . is as great as the difference between blowing up a man's house as a means of arresting a conflagration, and getting up a conflagration for the sake of blowing up his house."[44]

By the last year of the war, it was clear that northern victory would mean the death of slavery. Meeting more than a year after the Emancipation Proclamation, the 1864 General Assembly of the Old School Presbyterian Church resolved that the time had come to end slavery once and for all. Even such retrospective ecclesiastical approval of the policy of emancipation was too much for one ultra-conservative spokesman at the Assembly, who asked, "Could the Church go further in its adulterous intercourse with the State? What are conservative men to do now?"[45]

Hodge's instincts were conservative, but he knew when to accept the logic of events and to perceive in it the will of God. The rebellious southern slaveholders had brought retribution upon themselves. The time had come to get rid of slavery, not because slavery was sinful per se, but because the continuance of the southern slave system in the United States was incompatible with the preservation of the liberty and independence of the nation. The providence of God had, through the course of the war, removed huge obstacles in the way of emancipation. The point had been reached where "either our national life or slavery must be extinguished"—and the nation had made the only possible choice.[46]

In a long retrospective article in 1865, Hodge sought to prove the essential consistency of his journal and of his own position during the war.[47] It was an uphill task. The war always remained, for him, a

[44] Hodge, "The War," *Bib. Rep.* 35 (January 1863): 150–53.

[45] Vander Velde, *Presbyterian Churches and the Federal Union,* 129–30.

[46] Hodge, "The General Assembly," *Bib. Rep.* 36 (July 1864): 550–51.

[47] Hodge, "The Princeton Review on the State of the Country and of the Church," *Bib. Rep.* 37 (October 1865): 627–57.

struggle for national survival, but his interpretation of it changed gradually and, in the end, dramatically. A struggle to defend the Union against the excesses of southern rebels and northern abolitionists alike became a conflict in which emancipation might first be a legitimate means to a legitimate end, and then an achievement of the war that demonstrated the power of God's providence to overcome hitherto insurmountable obstacles.

Hodge, so skilled in drawing fine distinctions, illustrates even more clearly than less subtle and less inhibited observers such as Simpson, Haven, and Ide the progression from justification of a defensive war for national survival to an interpretation of the conflict as serving a higher purpose, as part of God's plan for America. Each of these men differed from the others in his own particular emphasis. Haven's God offered Americans a choice, whereas Ide's brooked no obstacles to the fulfillment of His plan. Hodge derided the notion of the war as punishment for national sins—an idea central to the thinking of Ide and Haven. Again, Haven and Ide were quick to applaud the Almighty for using the war as an instrument for the liberation of the slaves; Hodge and Simpson accepted, more or less graciously, the operation of the divine will in this matter. The central belief that these churchmen held in common lay in their acceptance of an essentially providential interpretation of the war. Simpson, Haven, and Ide clearly believed in a God who would intervene directly and explicitly in order to achieve His ends. They were confident, to a greater or lesser degree, that they knew the will and purpose of God in this terrible conflict. Although he was not always the most modest of men, Hodge was more cautious in his claims to understand the divine will. For him, God's providence was a mystery, and he dismissed simplistic interpretations of historical events as evidence of divinely ordained rewards and punishments.

There is no need to doubt the sincerity of the widely shared belief in the providential interpretation of the meaning of the war. Equally, there is no point in denying that it often proved to be a very convenient belief, capable of reconciling many different points of view, resolving numerous dilemmas, and providing an answer, if not for everything, then at least for many of the awkward questions posed by the war. Each individual citizen—conservative or radical, ardent patriot or dedicated abolitionist—could take what suited him or her from the operation of the divine will through the great American conflict. It might be simply the salvation of the Union or, more ambitiously, the creation of a stronger, more integrated nation. It might be the punishment of national sins, the removal of the stain of slavery, and the purging of the nation's guilt. Or it might be a decisive step on the road to racial harmony and brotherhood, not only in America but also throughout the world.

There was one other key role played by the churchmen who articulated such views in promoting and supporting the Union cause. One of the questions about the Civil War that is most difficult to answer is how and why the northern public—or at least a sufficient proportion of it—went on supporting for four years a war that, in its casualties, its horrors, and its frequent setbacks, exceeded by far all expectations in 1861 of its likely scale and cost. Of course, there is a built-in momentum behind this process. The escalation and intensification of the conflict encourage a raising of the stakes and stimulate bolder and more ambitious statements of the war's meaning and purpose. These in turn give grounds for further enlargement of the scale of the fighting and justify yet more pain and suffering.[48] In this process the explanation and justification of the war as the working of Providence or as part of the divine plan for America offered a powerful reinforcement to support for the war among the people of the North. As leaders and molders of public opinion, the evangelical Protestant churches exerted considerable influence—and not only within the ranks of their own members.[49] Postmillennialist ideas, in particular, offered a framework for understanding the national ordeal within a broader historical framework that combined a call for action, a hope for the future, and a faith in America's mission and destiny.

---

[48] For a fuller examination of this mutually reinforcing escalation of means and ends, see Peter J. Parish, "The War for the Union as a Just War," in *Aspects of War in American History*, eds. David K. Adams and Cornelis A. van Minnen (Keele: Keele University Press, 1997), 81–103.

[49] It is impossible to arrive at any precise estimate of the audience or the readership for prominent clergymen at this time. On the one hand, only a minority of Americans were regular church attenders, and some of the clerics seem to have been mainly concerned with scoring points off each other. On the other hand, the religious press in the 1860s was large and varied, many sermons were published as pamphlets, and churchmen were active contributors to public debate on many issues. Their influence, both direct and indirect, was surely considerable, as their arguments filtered through, or down, to a wider public. In any event, whatever the actual size of their audience, the arguments that the clergy chose to deploy in their attempts to sway public opinion or to support particular causes have a historical significance in their own right.

What made the religious justification of the war even more influential was the way in which it resonated with secular, and specifically political, arguments employed for the same purpose. Even the gradations of opinion within the ranks of the churches correlate quite closely with the shades of opinion within and even beyond the Republican ranks. Matthew Simpson's position was very close to the strong Unionism of Lincoln and many moderate Republicans, who justified emancipation as a means of waging war and then as an inevitable consequence of the kind of struggle that the Civil War became, rather than as a primary war aim. Gilbert Haven, and perhaps George Ide too, used arguments close to those of abolitionists and some radical Republicans, who saw in the war, for all its miseries, a unique opportunity to rid the United States of the incubus of slavery, and to usher in a new era of freedom and racial harmony. Charles Hodge shared many of the doubts and anxieties of conservative Republicans and some War Democrats, who endorsed a defensive war to save the Union, but not a crusade against slavery, and were brought to a reluctant acceptance of emancipation as a result of the war only when it was virtually a fait accompli. Some of the arguments advanced by Bishop Hopkins provided ammunition for the propaganda of those northern Democrats who had grave doubts about the war and were fiercely opposed to a war against slavery. There was no impassable barrier between religious and secular considerations in the minds of either politicians or clerics, and some churchmen had their own political agenda and their own party affiliation. Gilbert Haven's abolitionism and his zeal for racial brotherhood would have made him an uncomfortable partner for all but the most radical of Republicans, but Matthew Simpson was very much a political animal, close to the centers of political power and influence. Charles Hodge wrestled constantly with the relationship between the individual as loyal church member and as politically aware and responsible citizen.

The churchmen who spoke up strongly in support of the war provided the cause with a cloak of respectability—perhaps even an odor of sanctity. They helped the wider public to manage the transition from a limited war to save the Union into a monumental struggle for loftier and more far-reaching purposes. They were part of the support system that enabled the northern home front to cope with a war that cost the lives of over 350,000 Union soldiers and that far surpassed anything that had occurred to them in their worst nightmares.

It would be an exaggeration to describe the evangelical Protestant churches as the Republican party at prayer, but the rhetoric and the propaganda of the two had much in common. The churches were a vital part of the propaganda campaign in support of the war for the Union.

4

Let the Nation Be Your Bank: The Civil War Bond Drives and the Construction of National Patriotism

Melinda Lawson

IN JULY 1894 Jay Cooke, prominent Philadelphia banker and Civil War financier, reflected on his services to the Union: "Like Moses and Washington and Lincoln and Grant," he wrote, "I have been—I firmly believe—God's chosen instrument, especially in the financial work of saving the Union during the greatest war that has ever been fought in the history of Man." Cooke detailed the bond drives he had engineered during the course of the war, then concluded: "I absolutely by my own faith and energy and means saved the nation financially and did not realize any profit therefrom. . . . [T]he public should know even at this late period the unselfishness and sacrifices made by myself and [my] firm."[1]

Written nearly thirty years after the close of the war, Cooke's reminiscences described the bond drives as expressions of a national patriotism defined by civic duty and sacrifice. Contemplating his own role as well as that of the masses of wartime bondholders, Cooke explained how his efforts had rallied Americans behind the war, and how that patriotic uprising had saved the nation. He spoke of volunteerism and obligation, of unheralded national service without expectation of reward. But time had colored Cooke's memories of the war. The bond drives themselves tell a different story.[2]

---

[1] Jay Cooke's Memoir, 2, 82, in Jay Cooke and Company Collection, Baker Library, Harvard Business School, Boston.

[2] Such references are scattered throughout Cooke's Memoir; see, for example, pages 43, 75, 127.

Jay Cooke was indeed the preeminent financier of the Civil War. His services to the North were invaluable: granted nearly exclusive rights to market the nation's first genuinely popular war loans, he raised over $1 billion for the Union cause. Beginning in the fall of 1862, Cooke developed a far-reaching network through which he advertised and distributed the national loans. He sold bonds through his own banking house and contracted with numerous banks around the country. He hired traveling agents to take the offer of the loan into "every nook and corner" of the North and, as Union troops advanced, into the South as well. In less than three years he rose from relative obscurity to become a national legend. Marveling at his accomplishments, contemporaries labeled him "the Napoleon of Finance," "Our Modern Midas," and, after the great financier of the American Revolution, the "Robert Morris of the Civil War."[3]

As Cooke's agents carried war bonds into the farthest reaches of the Union, they brought more with them than the national debt. They also carried distinct notions of the meaning of patriotism and the American nation. But contrary to his own recollections, Cooke taught Americans that patriotism was less about civic duty than it was about opportunity, less a mandate for self-sacrifice than a matter of self-interest. He described a nation whose unique and perhaps most valuable quality was its ability to offer its citizens prosperity; he presented the nation as a source of economic well-being. Thus Cooke crafted a classical liberal understanding of national patriotism, one in which the self-serving actions of individuals would combine to produce the greatest public good. Cooke's own role in the drives suggests that he exemplified the very notions of patriotism he promulgated.[4]

Cooke's campaign was but one of many wartime activities that worked to redefine both the American polity and loyalty to that polity.

---

[3] Harriet Larson, *Jay Cooke: Private Banker* (Cambridge, Mass.: Harvard University Press, 1936), 148; Ellis Paxson Oberholtzer, *Jay Cooke: Financier of the Civil War*, 2 vols. (Philadelphia: A. M. Kelly, 1907), 1:577; Matthew Josephson, *The Robber Barons: The Great American Capitalists 1861–1901* (New York: Harcourt, Brace, 1934), 57; and *Constitutional Union*, no date, cited in Oberholtzer, *Jay Cooke*, 483.

[4] For a discussion of the role of self-interest and nationalism, see David M. Potter, "The Historian's Use of Nationalism and Vice-Versa," *The South and the Sectional Conflict* (Baton Rouge: Louisiana State University Press, 1968), 34–83. For the nation as a source of economic well being, see Hans Kohn, *The Idea of Nationalism: A Study of Its Origins and Background* (New York: Macmillan, 1944).

Throughout the war, political parties, soldiers' aid societies, religious organizations, and even social clubs held meetings, staged assemblies, and waged campaigns that supported and gave meaning to the war effort. Together, these activities propelled the cultural and ideological construction of the American nation-state.

On the eve of the Civil War, the American polity was characterized for the most part by decentralization. The federal government exercised little control over the states, failing even to employ all those powers granted it under the Constitution. With the exception of national elections and trips to the post office, American citizens had almost no contact or interaction with the federal government. Americans' attitudes both shaped and reflected that reality. Suspicions of concentrated power contributed to the formation of a weak national government, and ambivalence about the national state became a mainstay of antebellum political culture. Intense state and local loyalties overshadowed national sentiment. It was, after all, because he was forced to "side . . . with or against my section or my country" that Robert E. Lee chose to fight for the Confederacy.[5]

---

[5] For antebellum national identity, see Merle Curti, *The Roots of American Loyalty* (New York: Columbia University Press, 1946); George Fredrickson, *The Inner Civil War: Northern Intellectuals and the Crisis of the Union* (New York: Harper and Row, 1965); Hans Kohn, *American Nationalism: An Interpretive Essay* (New York: Macmillan, 1957); Paul C. Nagel, *One Nation Indivisible: The Union in American Thought* (New York: Oxford University Press, 1964); Alexis de Toqueville, *Democracy in America*, ed. Phillips Bradley (New York: Vintage, 1945), 1:250–53; Robert Wiebe, *The Opening of American Society: From the Adoption of the Constitution to the Eve of Disunion* (New York: Alfred A. Knopf, 1984); Gordon Wood, *The Radicalism of the American Revolution* (New York: Alfred A. Knopf, 1992); and Wilbur Zelinsky, *Nation into State: The Shifting Symbolic Foundations of American Nationalism* (Chapel Hill: University of North Carolina Press, 1988). For ambivalence about the national state among Democrats, see Marvin Meyers, *The Jacksonian Persuasion: Politics and Belief* (Stanford: Stanford University Press, 1957); Jean H. Baker, *Affairs of Party: The Political Culture of Northern Democrats in the Mid-Nineteenth Century* (Ithaca, N.Y.: Cornell University Press, 1983), esp. 143–46; and Joel Silbey, *A Respectable Minority: The Democratic Party in the Civil War Era, 1860–1868* (New York: W. W. Norton, 1977). For Whigs, see Daniel Walker Howe, *The Political Culture of the American Whigs* (Chicago: University of Chicago Press, 1979); and Merrill D. Peterson, *The Great Triumvirate: Webster, Clay, and Calhoun* (New York: Oxford University Press, 1987), 68–84. For Republicans and support of the national state for the market revolution, see Eric Foner, *Free Soil, Free Labor, Free Men: The Ideology of the Republican Party before the Civil War* (New York: Oxford University Press, 1970), 186–225; and Curti, *Roots of American Loyalty*, 159. Lee is quoted in Alan Nevins, *The War for the Union*, vol. 1, *The Improvised War 1861–1862* (New York: Charles Scribner's Sons, 1959), 107.

It is not that Americans did not entertain a genuine, even ardent, affection for the Union. In speeches and newspapers, sermons and diaries, they described an attachment to Union that historians have labeled mystical or spiritual. They spoke of mission and fraternity, of manifest destiny and "young America." But as historian Robert Wiebe suggests, the "soft glow of the Union" could not compete with "hard local attachments" to villages, towns, cities, and states. In the federative scheme of things, most Americans remained concerned to protect the rights of the states against those of the Union and located their primary identities in Massachusetts or Virginia, not in "these United States." Moreover, Americans did not yet subscribe to a basic nationalist principle: that, particularly in wartime, the duty of national members to their national polity overrode all other civic, and at times, even personal obligations. To the extent that they felt themselves a nation, it was the people, not the national state, that were considered to embody the virtues, ideology, and destiny of America.[6]

This limited nationalism did not immediately present a problem for the Union. It carried America through the War of 1812—before universal white male suffrage placed more importance on citizens' attitudes toward the state—and through the Mexican War—a small-scale war that neither threatened the existence of the Union nor demanded much from the average citizen. Contemporary concerns notwithstanding, it appeared for a while that it might be sufficient to rally the North behind the war for the Union. Northerners responded to the attack on Fort Sumter with an eruption of enthusiastic patriotism.[7]

But popular enthusiasm soon subsided, and as the war progressed American national identity encountered a major challenge. Mobilization for warfare is a remarkable state-building activity. In the North

---

[6] Nagel, *One Nation Indivisible*, 69–103; Wiebe, *Opening of American Society*, 354–55; Eric Hobsbawm, *Nations and Nationalism since 1780: Programme, Myth, Reality* (Cambridge: Cambridge University Press, 1990); and Zelinsky, *Nation into State*, 218–19.

[7] For the effect of the War of 1812 and the Mexican War on American nationalism, see Curti, *Roots of American Loyalty*, 16–29, 152–56; and David M. Potter, *The Impending Crisis: 1848–1861* (New York: Harper and Row, 1976), 12–14. For the North's reaction to the bombing of Fort Sumter, see James M. McPherson, *Battle Cry of Freedom: The Civil War Era* (New York: Oxford University Press, 1988), 274–75. Hobsbawm, *Nations and Nationalism*, 83, discusses the effect of universal suffrage on nation-building.

a rapidly expanding national state taxed and drafted its people, suspended the writ of habeas corpus, and moved to abolish slavery. As
the state expanded, so too did the need to increase the loyalty and
commitment of the people. For the first time the federal government
confronted the need for widespread, protracted support and sacrifice
from a voting citizenry that historically was suspicious of centralized
power. With no official public relations committee equivalent, for
example, to the First World War's Committee on Public Information
to rally the people behind the war, the job of defining the war in
acceptable terms and of redefining the relationship between individual northerners and the national state fell largely to private individuals or associations, each with their own motives and methods. One of
those who stepped into this breach was Jay Cooke.[8]

At a special session of Congress convening on July 4, 1861, President Abraham Lincoln estimated that the government would require
$400 million for the fiscal year beginning July 1 to conduct a "short
and decisive" war. Salmon P. Chase, Ohio lawyer and former governor and the newly appointed Secretary of the Treasury, asked Congress for only $320 million.[9]

The projections of the President and the Secretary did not seem
unreasonable. Fewer than twenty years earlier, the Mexican War had
cost the federal government just over $63 million. But the United
States had never fought a war on the scale to which the Civil War
eventually progressed. By the time the South surrendered, the war
had cost the United States federal government 3.2 billion 1865 dollars.[10]

Had the daunting task of financing this war been at all evident,
Salmon Chase would not have appeared the man for the job. The
Secretary himself acknowledged how "imperfectly" he was qualified

---

[8] On war as a state-building activity, see Charles Tilly, ed., *The Formation of
National States in Western Europe* (Princeton: Princeton University Press, 1975),
74–75.

[9] Bray Hammond, *Sovereignty and an Empty Purse: Banks and Politics in the
Civil War Era* (Princeton: Princeton University Press, 1970), 37–38; and "Report of
the Secretary of the Treasury," *Congressional Globe*, 37th Congress, 1st Session,
July 4, 1861, Appendix.

[10] Paul Studenski and Herman E. Kroos, *Financial History of the United States:
Fiscal, Monetary, Banking and Tariff, Including Financial Administration and State
and Local Finance* (New York: McGraw-Hill, 1952), 123, 159; and Allan Nevins, *The
War for the Union*, vol. 4, *The Organized War to Victory, 1864–1865* (New York:
Charles Scribner's Sons, 1971), 382.

"by experience, by talents, or by special acquirements for such a charge." Indeed, Chase had little knowledge and almost no experience in economics, which, as did many others of his time, he understood primarily in moral and constitutional terms. A strict hard-money man, Chase rejected most of the advice offered him by the banking community.[11]

Chase instead chose to follow an outdated precedent established fifty years earlier by Albert Gallatin, Thomas Jefferson's Secretary of the Treasury. He would rely on revenue to continue the federal government's normal operations, turning to loans to finance the actual war effort. In July and August 1861 Congress authorized $250 million in loans to meet the North's military expenses. Chase proposed that $100 million of the loan be made a popular loan, thus relieving the bankers of a portion of their burden. The nation's pre-eminent bankers would purchase the bonds from the government, but only temporarily; they would in turn market the loan to the people of the North.[12]

The bankers who agreed to undertake this loan assumed many risks, the greatest of which concerned the fact that in the mid-nineteenth century ordinary Americans did not invest in securities. Indeed, this was a people so suspicious of the financial community that the dominant party of the last generation had demanded that its government keep its money in non-interest-producing treasuries and conduct its business in gold. Most Americans knew almost nothing about securities. In a country where only 20 percent of the popula-

---

[11] "Report of the Secretary of the Treasury," *Congressional Globe,* 37th Congress, 1st session, July 4, 1861, Appendix; Frederick J. Blue, *Salmon P. Chase: A Life in Politics* (Kent, Ohio: Kent State University Press, 1987), 129–33; John Niven et al., eds., *The Salmon P. Chase Papers,* 5 vols. (Kent, Ohio: Kent State University Press, 1993), 1: xxxv–xxxvi; and Hammond, *Sovereignty and an Empty Purse,* 73–105.

[12] Hammond, *Sovereignty and an Empty Purse,* 40–41; and "Report of the Secretary of the Treasury," *Congressional Globe,* 37th Congress, 1st Session, July 4, 1861, Appendix; Hammond, *Sovereignty and an Empty Purse,* 43. In his report to Congress, Chase argued that the war was a "contest for national existence and the sovereignty of the people," and it was therefore fitting that an appeal be made first to "the people themselves." By offering the loan in denominations as low as $50, to be paid for in as many as ten installments, at a liberal rate of interest, Chase hoped that it would be possible to "transmute the burden into a benefit," inspiring "satisfaction and hopes of profit rather than annoyance and fears of loss." This was not the federal government's first attempt at a popular loan. In 1813 the Treasury Department had offered a $16 million loan to the public in denominations as low as $100. The loan did not sell (Larson, *Jay Cooke,* 24).

tion lived in urban areas, and 55 percent of the inhabitants still lived off the land, money was saved at home or in local banks or was reinvested in the family farm. Even those Americans who did think in terms of outside investment were unfamiliar with the notion of investing in the federal government. As the Boston *Daily Adviser* explained, "a United States Loan has never hitherto been heard of far outside of the larger cities." Not surprisingly, Chase's loan failed to raise the needed funds.[13]

With declining revenues from tariffs and land sales its only other sources of income, the government had by the end of 1861 reached a crisis point. Its loan was failing, its troops were going unpaid, its wartime suppliers were nearly insolvent. On December 30, 1861, the North's banks, their resources strained to the breaking point, stopped specie payments. The Union's finances looked grim.[14]

In February 1862 Congress passed and the President signed the Legal Tender Act. The bill authorized the issue of $150 million in United States notes and made these notes lawful money. The second section of this bill authorized the sale of $500 million of government bonds bearing 6 percent interest. The bonds, which matured in twenty years but were payable in five, came to be known as "five-twenties."[15]

But the five-twenty bonds were virtually refused in the market. Finally, in October 1862, with the expenses of the war burgeoning and his own loan campaign on the verge of collapse, Chase turned in desperation to Jay Cooke. In an unprecedented move, he offered the private banker sole agency of the government loan.[16]

In his first nineteen months as Secretary of the Treasury, Salmon Chase had worked with numerous private bankers, but it is doubtful that any of them had courted him quite so assiduously as had Jay

---

[13] Hammond, *Sovereignty and an Empty Purse*, 26, 76–77; Robert T. Patterson, "Government Finance on the Eve of the Civil War," *Journal of Economic History* 12 (Winter 1952): 35–44; Oberholtzer, *Jay Cooke*, 162; McPherson, *Battle Cry of Freedom*, 9; Larson, *Jay Cooke*, 119; and *Boston Daily Adviser*, September 11, 1861, cited in Hammond, *Sovereignty and an Empty Purse*, 109.

[14] Hammond, *Sovereignty and an Empty Purse*, 150–59.

[15] Blue, *Salmon P. Chase*, 150–57; and Hammond, *Sovereignty and an Empty Purse*, 159–235. The Revenue Act and the Bank Bill were passed in July 1862 and February 1863, respectively. Chase in Larson, *Jay Cooke*, 117.

[16] Salmon P. Chase to Jay Cooke, October 23, 1862, in *Salmon P. Chase Papers: Microfilm Edition*, ed. John Niven (Bethesda, Md.: University Publications, 1987) (hereinafter cited as *Chase Papers Microfilm*).

Cooke. On March 1, 1861, three days before Abraham Lincoln's inauguration and six weeks before the attack at Fort Sumter, Cooke had written to his brother Henry David Cooke, a personal friend of the Secretary of the Treasury and editor of the *Ohio State Journal,* a Republican organ that had supported Chase in his campaign for reelection as Governor of Ohio. "I see Chase is in the Treasury," Cooke observed; "now what is to be done?—can't you inaugurate something whereby we can all *safely* make some *cash?*" Three weeks later Cooke's father, Eleutheros, wrote his son Jay along similar lines: "H.D.'s plan of getting Chase into the Cabinet and Sherman into the Senate is accomplished, . . . and now is the time for making money by honest contracts out of the government. . . . [T]he door is open to make up all your losses."[17]

Cooke began his campaign to acquire the business of the government. From the beginning, Jay Cooke and Company, a relatively small firm established in January 1861, was active in war finance. Cooke was one of numerous bankers to handle government loans in April and again in September. Although the latter, Chase's National Loan, fared quite poorly, Cooke's agency proved a success. Employing methods similar to those he would use in his own drive a year later, Cooke sold over $5 million of the National Loan.[18]

But Cooke aspired to more. With each task he undertook, he laid the groundwork for the assumption of greater responsibility. To his brother Henry, his Washington representative, he wrote, "We must all study by our watchful care of the interests confided to us to justify this confidence and to show [Chase] that the treasury is a gainer by our confidential connection with it. . . . I want the Governor to trust to our good management, integrity and skill." Cooke continually urged Chase to consider a more active role for his firm in the government's finances, promising strict confidentiality and caution, and assured him that "our movements will be . . . for the best interest of

---

[17] Jay Cooke to Henry David Cooke, March 1, 1861; and Eleutheros Cooke to Jay Cooke, March 25, 1861, Jay Cooke Manuscript Papers, Historical Society of Pennsylvania (HSP). Cooke lost many of his assets in the Panic of 1857; see Larson, *Jay Cooke,* 77–85.

[18] Oberholtzer, *Jay Cooke,* 134; and Salmon P. Chase to Jay Cooke, September 4, 1861, *Chase Papers Microfilm.* For Cooke's methods and reports of progress see Jay Cooke to Salmon P. Chase, September 6, 7, 10, 11, 1862, October 19, 1862; Salmon P. Chase to Jay Cooke, March 7, 1862, *Chase Papers Microfilm;* and Jay Cooke to Henry D. Cooke, March 4, 1862, Jay Cooke Manuscript Papers, HSP.

the government." The Secretary, whose inexperience and stubbornness had alienated many of the nation's largest bankers, appeared to
welcome the association, and in time Cooke came to act as Chase's
financial advisor, making recommendations concerning government
loans, taxation, specie, banking, and legal tender.[19]

In his suggestions to Chase, Cooke prefigured the views of government and private enterprise that would later inform the bond drives.
Impatient with the way the government conducted its affairs, he envisioned a variety of roles for private bankers—preferably his own
firm—in the government economy. In July 1861 Cooke offered to
move to Washington, where, in partnership with another prominent
firm, he would open a "first class banking establishment" and "give
personal attention" to the business of the government, including
management of the nation's wartime loans. Cooke qualified his offer:
"we could not be expected to leave our comfortable homes and positions here without some great inducement and we state frankly that
we would . . . expect a fair commission from the treasury." Although
this particular offer was not accepted, in February 1862 Cooke did
establish a Washington branch of Cooke and Co.[20]

In January 1862 Cooke made a striking suggestion, one that spoke
to his apparently strong belief in the privatization of government finance. He proposed the issue of "circulation" based on a United
States loan and "15 or 20 percent of private capital." In his view,
"private parties (banks and associations) and not the government—
should manage the details of circulation—and that their fifteen or
twenty percent of actual capital should be guaranteed against an irre-
deemable currency. I wished also that some great inducement could
be offered to meet the present emergency. . . . [M]y plan would give
individual enterprise the care of distributing this uniform currency
and with the aid of government keep it always on a sound basis."
Later that month Cooke suggested that Chase allow him to serve as

---

[19] Jay Cooke to Henry D. Cooke, March 4, 1862, Jay Cooke Manuscript Papers,
HSP; and Jay Cooke to Salmon P. Chase, March 6, 1862, *Chase Papers Microfilm.*
For early examples of this advice, see Cooke to Chase, December 27, 1861, January
18, 1862, March 6, 1862, March 22, 1862, April 11, 1862, June 28, 1862, July 2,
1862, August 7, 1862, and October 14, 1862, *Chase Papers Microfilm.*

[20] Jay Cooke to Salmon P. Chase, March 22, 1862, July 12, 1861, *Chase Papers
Microfilm.* For the establishment of Cooke's Washington firm, see Larson, *Jay
Cooke,* 113.

a mediator between the Treasury and the banks of Philadelphia, New York, and Boston.[21]

Cooke also cultivated a personal relationship with Chase. The two men's families frequently visited, and Cooke eventually persuaded Chase to accept personal loans. "I am gratified that you thus allow me to oblige you," Cooke enthused as he sent Chase a check for $2,000. "As I can do so without the slightest inconvenience, command me at all times in any matter for your own or the public good." Cooke also served as Chase's personal investment broker and regularly sent him checks for the proceeds of private stock transactions.[22]

By June 1862 Henry Cooke was able to tell his brother of the Secretary's plans to allow their firm a significant role in the handling of the five-twenty loan. "He has had enough of outside parties," he wrote. Jay Cooke had at last succeeded. His firm was not an outside party; he was, in effect, the government's banker.[23]

On October 23, 1862, the Secretary of the Treasury officially granted Cooke exclusive private agency for the federal government's $500 million "five-twenty" loan. (This was the first of two popular war loans that Cooke was to handle; in January 1865 he contracted with William Fessenden, Chase's successor, for the sale and distribution of the "seven-thirty" war loan.) The five-twenty bonds were to be available in denominations as low as $50, so that "every Capitalist, be he large or small, or Merchant, Mechanic, Farmer, . . . should invest at once his spare funds." Maturing in twenty years but redeemable in five, they would earn 6 percent interest and could be purchased with the newly issued, controversial legal tender.[24]

---

[21] Jay Cooke to Salmon P. Chase, January 18, 31, 1862, *Chase Papers Microfilm.*

[22] For examples of Cooke's and Chase's early social relationship, see Cooke to Chase, October 24, 1861, January 31, 1862, April 26, 1862, June 28, 1862, September 22, 1862, and Chase to Cooke, November 21, 1861, December 16, 24, 1861, October 24, 1862, December 20, 1862, *Chase Papers Microfilm.* For early financial transactions between the two men, see Cooke to Chase, February 8, 1862, March 10, 1862, April 15, 26, 1862, July 5, 1862, August 7, 1862, October 14, 1862, and Chase to Cooke, February 7, 1862, March 7, 1862, April 16, 1862, May 3, 31, 1862, June 17, 1862, August 8, 1862, June 2, 1863, *Chase Papers Microfilm.* For the quotation, see Jay Cooke to Salmon P. Chase, February 8, 1862, *Chase Papers Microfilm.*

[23] Henry D. Cooke to Jay Cooke, June 12, 1862, Jay Cooke Manuscript Papers, HSP.

[24] Salmon P. Chase to Jay Cooke, October 23, 1862; and Cooke's Circular to his agents and subagents, November 7, 1862, *Chase Papers Microfilm.* The U.S. Treasury and designated depositories would also handle the loan. The $830 million seven-thirty loan consisted of short-term bonds redeemable before three years, in

To market the loan, Cooke was allowed one-half of 1 percent of the proceeds for the first $10 million, and three-eighths percent thereafter. With this commission, he was to pay all expenses, including advertising, transportation, distribution, and commission for his agents and subagents. The banker enthusiastically accepted the appointment, promising to "work night and day at it."[25]

Drawing on his experience in the marketing of the National Loan, Cooke developed an impressive and far-reaching network for the advertisement and distribution of the five-twenties and their successors, the seven-thirties. Indeed, through the construction of this network, Cooke laid the foundation for a national popular understanding of securities. He sold bonds through his own banking house and contracted with the nation's most prominent bankers and stockbrokers. In the East, Cooke appointed six leading financial men to organize marketing and sales by region; they in turn arranged with local bankers to act as subagents. In the West, where banking was less well organized, Cooke hired hundreds of traveling agents to recruit and train bankers, first in the larger cities and then, as the campaign progressed, in smaller towns and villages. If no bank was available, Cooke instructed his agents to secure the services of one "competent" person who could give the matter "complete attention": real estate officers, insurance men, or community leaders. In time over twenty-five hundred local and traveling agents and subagents for the five-twenty loan canvassed the nation; for the seven-thirty loan that number increased to between four and five thousand. These agents visited every northern and western state and territory and, as the Union troops moved into Confederate regions, southern states as well: bonds were sold in West Virginia, Virginia, Louisiana, Tennessee, Kentucky, and Missouri. As the northern press noted, "The old saying was that 'wherever the Union Army went, the printing press accompanied it.' The new saying will be, 'Wherever Rebel territory is conquered, JAY COOKE's agents will appear.'"[26]

---

denominations not less than $10, earning 7.3 percent interest (Larson, *Jay Cooke,* 116, 165). The seven-thirty campaign was for the most part merely an elaboration of the five-twenty campaign; for that reason they will be discussed together, though significant differences will be noted.

[25] Salmon P. Chase to Jay Cooke, October 23, 25, 1862, *Chase Papers Microfilm.*

[26] *Bunett, Drake and Co's Reporter and Register of Counterfeit Bank Notes* (Boston: n.p., 1864) in Scrapbook, Jay Cooke Manuscript Papers, HSP. The Jay Cooke Manuscript Papers at the HSP in Philadelphia contain a collection of scrapbooks

Within this broad network of banks and agents, the men who contracted to sell the loan constructed their own intricate networks. To reach their potential customers, Cooke's agents visited local newspaper offices, banks, hotels, post offices, court houses, reading rooms, factories, and railroad stations, courting the cashiers, clerks, and officials they encountered. They left behind circulars, pamphlets, and handbills and posted signs on walls, trees, and telegraph poles. They urged postmasters to mail handbills to town residents; they urged clergymen to recruit their parishioners. During the seven-thirty campaign, agents set up night offices, replete with coffee and doughnuts, so that working women and men could invest their savings. In larger cities such offices were established in the factory districts or along the waterfront; in smaller towns they required only "the counter in a corner drug or grocery store." Near military training grounds agents were instructed to sell bonds to soldiers on payday; once the war was over, they met the soldiers as they were discharged. In rural areas agents traveled into the backwoods and sold the bonds door-to-door. Inspired in part by the promise of a generous commission, they carved out their territories and asked that Cooke keep other agents out, lest "we hit up against each other, and others get the benefit of my circulars."[27]

Cooke managed this sprawling network of agents and capital from his office in Philadelphia. As Henrietta M. Larson notes in her biography of Cooke, at a time when no coordinating agency such as the Federal Reserve System existed, this was a monumental undertaking. In it Cooke was the beneficiary of developments in transportation

---

featuring numerous contemporary newspaper clippings, pamphlets, handbills, and other items. Larson, *Jay Cooke*, 123–26; Oberholtzer, *Jay Cooke*, 222; and Undated Circular to 7-30 Agents; *Lane Express*, March 18, 1863; *New York Tribune*, March 21, 1865; and *Philadelphia Inquirer*, March 24, 1865, all in Scrapbook, Jay Cooke Manuscript Papers, HSP. For Cooke's role in the evolution of the stock market, see Federal Reserve Bank of Boston, *A History of Investment Banking in New England* (Boston: Federal Reserve Bank of Boston, 1965), 14–15.

[27] Jay Cooke to Salmon P. Chase, November 12, December 8, September 18, 1863, *Chase Papers Microfilm;* Albert Van Couss to Jay Cooke, February 11, 1865; Isaac H. Steeves to Jay Cooke, February 11, 1865; Julian Brewer to Jay Cooke, February 12, 1865; Henry D. Cooke to Jay Cooke, September 14, 1863; Jay Cooke, Undated Circular Letter to Agents; Postmaster General Alex W. Randall to Jay Cooke, undated, all in Jay Cooke Manuscript Papers, HSP; and extracts from agents' letters in Jay Cooke to Salmon P. Chase, November 12, 1862, *Chase Papers Microfilm;* Larson, *Jay Cooke*, 123–26, 166–68; Oberholtzer, *Jay Cooke*, 582.

and communication. He used the nation's railroads to carry agents and bonds across the nation, into the farthest reaches of the country. Through aggressive use of the telegraph, Cooke was able to keep in touch with his agents and stay abreast of the progress of the loan, receiving daily or even hourly updates.[28]

Developments in print technology and in mechanisms for the collection and distribution of news also eased Cooke's task. As the process of printing became less expensive, more periodicals appeared, as did advertising agencies. Such phenomena made advertising on a national level possible for the first time, and Cooke made the most of it. Indeed, his exhaustive use of the press to promote the government loan was unprecedented. Whether working through advertising agencies or dealing directly with editors or his own agents, he insisted at all times that the loan be kept before the public with liberal advertising in local papers, including those aimed at immigrant readers.[29]

But Cooke wanted more from the nation's newspapers than room in their advertising columns: he wanted frequent, lengthy, and enthusiastic endorsements as well. His agents paid generously for the advertisements that pervaded the northern press, including foreign-language and religious journals; in return, they extracted promises of "favorable . . . notice" from grateful editors. "My advertising shall not discriminate," Cooke assured Chase, "but give to all parties who will speak a good word for the government and finances—the same patronage."[30]

Cooperative papers featured articles describing the government loans and extolling their virtues. Although the editors themselves were occasionally the authors, more often the articles were copies of editorials penned by Cooke, his brother, his agents, or "able and expert journalist[s]," appearing initially in the nation's more prominent journals and then syndicated to "lesser" papers.[31]

---

[28] Larson, *Jay Cooke*, 125–26; Thomas C. Cochran, *Frontiers of Change: Early Industrialism in America* (New York: Oxford University Press, 1981), 105; and John F. Stover, "Railroads," in *The Reader's Companion to American History*, ed. Eric Foner and John A. Garraty (Boston: Houghton Mifflin, 1991), 907.

[29] Larson, *Jay Cooke*, 127; Jay Cooke, Circular Letter to Agents, July 1, 1863; and Jay Cooke, Undated Circular Letter to 7-30 Agents, Jay Cooke Manuscript Papers, HSP.

[30] Isaac H Stevens to Jay Cooke, February 11, 1865, Jay Cooke Manuscript Papers, HSP; and Jay Cooke to Salmon P. Chase, October 25, 1862, *Chase Papers Microfilm.*

[31] Henry D. Cooke to Jay Cooke, September 11, October 29, 1863, Jay Cooke Manuscript Papers, HSP.

Where advertising patronage was not sufficient, Cooke or his agents tried other tacks. Two prominent New York bankers who served as agents for the five-twenty loan wrote of efforts to coax endorsements—for the bond drive as well as for the fiscal policies of the Treasury—from reluctant editors. They found one local editor "rather opinionated on the subject of bullion and paper," but assured Cooke that "if rightly approached, [Mr. Tinney] can be induced to . . . write for the next number a very different article." During the campaign for the seven-thirty loan, Cooke offered those newspaper men who presented the loan or the nation's financial policies in a positive light options on $50,000 worth of U.S. bonds for a specified period of time. The holder received the profit on the transaction minus 6 percent interest. In a testament to the success of this method, editors clipped their columns and sent them to Philadelphia to persuade Cooke of their loyalty.[32]

Cooke also asked that the papers print daily updates of the progress of the loan in the area. Some printed the names of subscribers in the previous twenty-four hours; others listed local or regional sales figures, hoping to prompt competition between towns, counties, or even states.[33]

Not all press for the loans was favorable. Agents sent into border states or recently reclaimed southern states often encountered skepticism from the Copperhead press. But, as five-twenty agents Paul Jagode and F. L. Loes discovered when the loan received unfavorable notice in an extreme Copperhead newspaper in Milwaukee, any press was good press, and the overall effect of this approach remained the same: Americans across the country, opening newspapers in cities or towns, at home or in reading rooms, in county stores or in courthouses, could not escape notice of the five-twenty, and later the seven-thirty, loan. These ads and editorials, which so pervaded the northern press, most clearly reveal the ideas about the nation and

---

[32] Fisk and Hatch to Jay Cooke, August 18, 1863, Jay Cooke Manuscript Papers, HSP; Oberholtzer, *Jay Cooke*, 581–82. See also Salmon P. Chase to Jay Cooke, September 4, 1863; Jay Cooke to Salmon P. Chase, September 7, 1863, *Chase Papers Microfilm;* and Fitch and Hatch to Jay Cooke, August 15, 1863, Jay Cooke Manuscript Papers, HSP.

[33] Various clippings, Scrapbook, Jay Cooke Manuscript Papers, HSP. The Jay Cooke Scrapbook contains numerous clippings listing the day's subscribers or the daily totals by region.

patriotism that Cooke and his bond campaign set before the American people.[34]

As a seasoned businessman, Jay Cooke was somewhat cynical
about questions of human motivation. His letters to his brother
Henry and to Salmon Chase emphasized the importance of "inducements" in financial operations, both for himself—"we . . . must be
careful not to work for honor alone"—and for others—"no one here
heartily loved their country better than their pockets."[35]

In his loan campaigns Cooke wasted little time appealing to the
"honor" of his prospective buyers. Rarely did he speak of love of
liberty, devotion to country, or the moral obligations of the home
front. Nor did he appeal to Civil War Americans' republican heritage.
Cooke's patriotism was defined in terms of neither civic duty nor civic
virtue. Particularly in the first campaign, when the war was young, its
aim contested, its future unclear, Cooke's main appeal to his customers was as rational, self-interested individuals. He developed a market-model patriotism, wherein the Union faithful came together not
as a moral or social whole, but as appetitive individuals acting in their
own interest, painlessly yet inexorably furthering the public good in
the process.[36]

Cooke's belief in the primacy of self-interest and its role in the
public good had roots in a debate of two centuries' standing. Joyce
Appleby has traced the outlines of this debate to seventeenth-century
England, where a group of economists challenged the dominant notion of a managed economy, suggesting instead that the economy
be viewed as "an aggregation of self-interested individual producer-
consumers." By the late eighteenth century, when Adam Smith's *The
Wealth of Nations* was published, the tenets it propounded were familiar discourse to intellectuals, merchants, and manufacturers in
England as well as in the United States. According to Smith, human
society consisted of a series of market relations between self-interested individuals. Each went about the business of pursuing his or

---

[34] Paul Jagode and F. L. Loes to Jay Cooke, October 31, 1863, Jay Cooke Manuscript Papers, HSP.

[35] Jay Cooke to Henry D. Cooke, March 4, 1862, Jay Cooke Manuscript Papers,
HSP; and Jay Cooke to Salmon P. Chase, April 22, 1864, *Chase Papers Microfilm.*

[36] C. B. Macpherson, *The Political Theory of Possessive Individualism: Hobbes to
Locke* (Oxford: Clarendon Press, 1962), 3. In Cooke's second campaign for the U.S.
government, the seven-thirty campaign, he employed patriotism on a more frequent
(though by no means consistent) basis.

her own good, and from the competition inherent in this pursuit emerged the greatest public good. By the Civil War, Smith's beliefs had entered the mainstream of American thought.[37]

Such liberal tenets did not, however, easily lend themselves to the language of patriotism, particularly a wartime patriotism. Notions of Christian sacrifice, of moral obligation, obedience, and republican civic duty seemed far better suited to the demands on a wartime citizenry than did the idea of self-interest. Cooke's accomplishment was the creation of an alternative definition of loyalty: an accessible and profitable version of national patriotism, rooted in a liberal understanding of citizenship as the pursuit of self-interest, even in times of war.

Cooke laid the groundwork for this appeal by suggesting that the government had chosen to offer the loan to common Americans not as a response to wartime exigencies, but as a democratization of the privilege of investment. Although the decision to appeal to the masses was in fact rooted in the belief that, by themselves, the nation's bankers and capitalists could not or would not finance the war, the bond literature stood this convention on its head. As an article heralding the democratic nature of the five-twenty loan asserted, "The Government with impartial wisdom has not left this loan to rich speculators alone, who would gladly buy up the bonds in vast amounts, but, by taking subscriptions in small sums, has put the permanent advantage of the Loan within the reach of the people." Ads and editorials emphasized that while the loan offered "great advantages" to "large capitalists," it held out "special inducements" to "those who wish to make a safe and profitable investment of small savings."[38]

An obstacle to the success of such an appeal lay in the average American's ignorance of small-scale securities. Agents would have to educate their customers. Fortunately Cooke had developed a model for such an education while marketing the National Loan. Selling

---

[37] Joyce Appleby, *Liberalism and Republicanism in the Historical Imagination* (Cambridge, Mass: Harvard University Press, 1992), 42; and Eric Foner, *Tom Paine and Revolutionary America* (New York: Oxford University Press, 1976), 153.

[38] Unlabeled clipping, May 7, 1863; and *Christian Secretary*, Hartford, November 7, 1862, Scrapbook, Jay Cooke Manuscript Papers, HSP. See also 7-30 Circular, "Interesting Questions and Answers Relative to the 7-30 U.S. Loan," Jay Cooke Manuscript Papers, HSP.

bonds in the front office of his banking house, he had spent hours explaining the "whys and wherefores" of investment. But clearly neither Cooke nor his agents could personally educate the hundreds of thousands of investors he hoped would fund the nation's war debt. Adapting his model to a larger scale, Cooke devised a series of flyers with a question and answer format. In one such circular, a fictional farmer wrote Cooke, asking a number of questions concerning methods of payment, taxes, interest, and maturation. "I have no doubt that a good many of my neighbors would like to take these bonds," the farmer said, "and if you will answer my questions I will show the letter to them." The circular containing these questions along with Cooke's replies became one of the most widely circulated loan publications.[39]

In almost all the bond literature, Cooke emphasized the safety of the government loan. One of his greatest challenges was to convince Americans that the nation and its economy were, in spite of the crisis of war, sound investments offering ready return. Thus, many of the circulars and editorials that described the government loans also detailed the "enormous strength and wealth of the loyal states." They compared the nation's current debt to that of various European countries and found it modest by comparison. They placed that modest debt in the context of the country's glorious future: its ever-increasing population, its flourishing home industries, its unappreciated resources: "We have vast territories untouched by the plow, mines of all precious metals of which we have hardly opened the doors, a population full of life, energy, enterprise and industry, and the accumulated wealth of money and labor of the old countries pouring into the lap of our giant and ever-to-be-united republic." Although such prosperity and prestige might inspire pride, more importantly, they underwrote the nation's popular loan, which could rightly be considered but a "FIRST MORTGAGE upon all Railroads, Canals, Bank Stocks, and Securities, and the immense products of all manufacturers, &c., &c., in the country."[40]

---

[39] Jay Cooke to Salmon P. Chase, September 7, 10, 1861, *Chase Papers Microfilm;* and Circular, "The Best Way to Put Money Out at Interest," Jay Cooke Manuscript Papers, HSP. In another ad Cooke described the advantages of compounded interest over the hoarding of gold; *Danville Democrat,* April 24, 1863, Scrapbook, Jay Cooke Manuscript Papers, HSP.

[40] *Fitzgerald City Stern,* April 18, 1863; *Burlington Sentinel,* April 29, 1865 (this appeared widely); "Supplement to Imlay and Bucknell's Bank Note Reporter," De-

But the strength of the government bonds did not arise solely from their basis in a sound nation and flourishing economy. The bonds were also widely acclaimed for their profitability. As a typical editorial proclaimed, "these Government securities are regarded by Capitalists as the very best in the market." Cooke's ads pointed to security, high rates of interest, legal tender convertibility, and, one of the most frequently heralded features of the loan, exemption from state and municipal taxes. An ad for the seven-thirties urged readers to invest their earnings "where they will be forever safe . . . where Cities, Counties, and States Can't Tax them—and where they will draw the BIGGEST INTEREST!"[41]

This resort to the prospective customer's business sense was particularly well illustrated by the ads that labeled the loan—in fact, the federal government itself—a savings bank. Appealing in particular to the unseasoned investor, ads for the seven-thirties described the advantages of the government loan, then proclaimed it "a National Savings Bank." Another urged readers to "Fetch your little sums of $50 and $100. MAKE THE U.S. GOVERNMENT YOUR SAVINGS BANK."[42]

Only rarely did the ads for government bonds mention the importance of patriotism, citizenship, the war, or even the Union. Although such themes appeared more frequently in the seven-thirty campaign—when the mood of the country as a whole had shifted in support of the Republican war aims—Cooke's main appeal to his customers in *both* bond campaigns was to their self-interest. Thus in making the case for the war loans, a widely syndicated seven-thirty editorial asserted that "The chief arguments for inducing an investment in this loan are . . . 1. The high rate of interest allowed. 2. The convertibility of the notes, in 1867, into a gold interest and principal paying bond. 3. The release of the amount thus invested from state, county, or city tax." The fact that the bonds in question were war bonds was not even mentioned.[43]

---

cember 5, 1862; and *Middletown [Pa.] Weekly Tribune,* April 8, 1863, Scrapbook, all in Jay Cooke Manuscript Collection, HSP.

[41] *Delaware Gazette,* April 17, 1863; and *Delaware County America and Media Advertiser,* Media, Pa., February 22, 1865, Scrapbook, Jay Cooke Manuscript Collection, HSP. For the seven-thirty poster advertising night agencies, see Oberholtzer, *Jay Cooke,* 585.

[42] *Christian Secretary,* Hartford, February 15, 1864, Scrapbook, Jay Cooke Manuscript Papers, HSP; and 7-30 poster in Oberholtzer, *Jay Cooke,* 585.

[43] *Union County Herald,* March 4, 1865, Scrapbook, Jay Cooke Manuscript Papers, HSP.

In fact, when patriotism was invoked, it was often in direct con-
junction with the idea of self-interest. Cooke's ads and editorials regularly linked the two notions. "Self-interest as well as patriotism make
them popular," proclaimed a typical ad, and a second pointed out
that while bondholders would "subserve their own interest, they will
at the same time be patriotically placing at the disposal of the . . .
government, money to carry on the war." A third ad explained, "Patriotism alone, would not have made the Five-Twenty loan so popular. It is popular because people know it is the best, the safest
investment they can find. A man not only lends the Government a
thousand dollars from patriotism, but because he knows that it will
pay him sure profit. . . . Let every one aid [the government], for in
doing so, he helps to shorten the war, and build his own fortune." A
popular circular entitled "The Best Way to Put Out Money at Interest" described just such a man: a "hale old farmer from Berks
county" who invested $5,000, "as he has concluded to put his money
where he is not only sure of interest, but he is aiding the Government."[44]

One ad acknowledged that in theory patriotism might require sacrifice, but offered the ordinary American, who might find it difficult
to subordinate self to country, a more palatable version of civic duty.
Boasting the headline "PATRIOTISM AND PROFIT," a column in the
Boston Traveler read, "Everyone should do all in his power to support the government in the present emergency, however his personal
interests may be affected thereby. The truly patriotic will do so at
the sacrifice of his own individual interests. But it is certainly more
agreeable to aid the government and at the same time promote one's
own advantage."[45]

In March 1863, when it became clear that the bond drives were to
be a smashing success, the bond literature began to employ patriotism in another guise. Still unwilling to rely on love of country to
persuade Americans to buy the loan, the vast majority of bond adver-

---

[44] *City Item,* February 11, 1865; *Phoenix,* February 18, 1865; *Fitzgerald City
Stern,* April 18, 1863, Scrapbook, Jay Cooke Manuscript Papers, HSP; and Circular,
"The Best Way to Put Out Money at Interest," HSP, cited in Oberholtzer, *Jay
Cooke,* 245. See also *Hollidaysburg Register,* March 25, 1863, cited in Oberholtzer,
Jay Cooke, 247.

[45] *Boston Traveler,* February 7, 1865, Scrapbook, Jay Cooke Manuscript Papers,
HSP.

tisements continued to appeal almost solely to Americans' self-interest, but the editorials syndicated by Cooke and his agents began to attribute the popularity of the loan to the patriotism of the people. "Nothing could more forcibly illustrate the determined and unflinching spirit of the Loyal States than the noble subscription to the national "five-twenty" loan," proclaimed one editorial. Another found that increasing sales evidenced "immovable confidence in the government, and . . . overwhelming proof of . . . the immortal patriotism . . . of the American people."[46]

As Americans from all walks of life invested in government bonds, their collective action was proclaimed a patriotic uprising. Inspired perhaps by the hope that social pressure might serve as an effective rallying force, the literature described a community united in action. "The spectacle is really sublime," one article reflected. "Men of all classes, all politics, all professions unite in the determination to make the Government strong with the wealth of a nation. The earnest, hard working Cabinet officer, the earnest, hard working mechanic, stand side-by-side in their devotion to the country. The millionaire invests his hundreds of thousands, the laboring man his fifty or hundred dollars." Such ads and editorials celebrated not just this perceived uprising, but its popular, democratic nature. In images evocative of Walt Whitman's America, they described the masses of diverse customers who daily thronged the agencies: "Americans, Germans, Englishmen, Frenchmen, Spaniards, Irish, Dutch, . . . Soldiers and civilians, the merchant with his thousands, and the mechanic with only his few hundreds, . . . the lady with an annual income of ten thousand and the washer woman with only a few hundred, the farmer who had just sold his fat cattle, and his hired man who had just received his yearly wages . . . a little old Irish woman whose wrinkled face and whitened locks indicated some seventy winters" all stood side by side in the office where war bonds were sold.[47]

The women and men whose purchase of five-twenty and seven-thirty bonds had made this coup possible were publicly acknowledged for their patriotic deeds. *The Philadelphia Inquirer,* for example, listed the names of the day's subscribers in a testament to their

---

[46] *Eastern Express,* May 13, 1863; and *Allentown Democrat,* April 24, 1863, Scrapbook, Jay Cooke Manuscript Papers, HSP.

[47] Unlabeled clipping, May 7, 1863; and *Republican,* March 14, 1865, Scrapbook, Jay Cooke Manuscript Papers, HSP.

devotion to country. Across the nation other papers followed suit, paying tribute to the loyal by name, or, if space did not allow, by state, town, or neighborhood. "Well Done Ohio!" proclaimed a Pennsylvania editorial:

> The same electric impulse that swayed the popular heart as regiment after regiment filed past our doors, amid cheers and music, and the waving of banners, seems to have taken for itself a new direction, and is now manifesting itself by the lavish outpouring of money in exchange for bonds, with which to carry on the war against the Rebellion. A most healthy index of this loyal and generous confidence in the Government is afforded by the State of Ohio. . . . Her sons have fought on every battlefield under the inspiration of cheering assurances from their homes. And now Ohio seals her good works, and glorifies herself by the avidity with which her people subscribe to the Government Loan.[48]

Cooke's message seemed to find a receptive audience. The bond drives were remarkably successful. Sales of the five-twenties soon exceeded even Cooke's expectations. On a single day in April 1863 the campaign brought in over $10 million; one day in October sales reached $15 million. Although military triumphs no doubt encouraged prospective investors, battlefield defeats did not appear to deter them. Sales continued, for instance, at the average of $2 million per day even through the gloom of Fredericksburg. Printers could not keep up with the orders, and bond certificates were soon in short supply. In July 1863 the convertability feature expired, but the loan continued through Cooke's agency. When the five-twenty campaign ended in January 1864, the limit of $500 million had been exceeded: subscriptions totaled $510,776,450. Through his agency Cooke had sold almost $364 million of that amount. The seven-thirty loan was even more successful. Cooke sold $700 million of an $800 million loan.[49]

Although the bulk of these bonds were purchased in the North-

---

[48] Oberholtzer, *Jay Cooke*, 253; for Ohio quotation see *Philadelphia Inquirer*, April 8, 1863, Scrapbook, Jay Cooke Manuscript Papers, HSP.

[49] Jay Cooke to Salmon P. Chase, December 8, 1862, *Chase Papers Microfilm*; Oberholtzer, *Jay Cooke*, 253; Larson, *Jay Cooke*, 145–48; and Undated 5-20 Circular, Jay Cooke Manuscript Papers, HSP. For supply problems, see Jay Cooke to Salmon P. Chase, April 23, 1863; Jay Cooke to Henry D. Cooke, May 28, 1863; Henry D. Cooke to Jay Cooke, April 14, 1863; Jay Cooke Manuscript Papers, HSP; and Oberholtzer, *Jay Cooke*, 577.

east, the loan was distributed in the border states and in the West as well. Contemporaries marveled at the demand for bonds in Maryland, West Virginia, Kentucky, Missouri, Indiana, and Illinois, both because some of this demand arose in sections where there had previously been "no call for this class of investment," and because many subscriptions came from areas that were openly secessionist. William T. Page, a bank agent from Evansville, Indiana, sold over $10,000 worth of five-twenties, reporting the entire amount from a "Copperhead neighborhood. . . . I doubt if a single person who subscribes for the bonds ever had a real Union pulsation of the heart since the rebellion broke out."[50]

It is difficult to determine how many bonds were purchased by small subscribers as opposed to large investors. The bond literature itself points to the purchase of the loan by a wide spectrum of Americans. Its authors may have exaggerated the popular appeal of the drives, yet other evidence suggests that although the greater dollar amount belonged in the hands of large investors, a remarkable number of bonds were held by individuals of lesser means. Over 500,000 different parties subscribed to the loan. The proliferation of night offices during the seven-thirty campaign— Cooke instructed his brother to open thirty to forty in Washington and Georgetown, and the New York Tribune listed twelve in New York City—suggests that many of these subscribers were working- or middle-class men and women. Indeed, when the Tribune attempted to classify the roughly one hundred bond buyers who visited a night office on Bleeker Street one evening, it estimated that sixty were "mechanics or laborers," twenty were "saloon keepers, small dealers, and soldiers," and the remainder were working women, women in mourning, and "vendors, clerks, and even boys." In an article entitled "Who Are the Bondholders?" The Nation called the five-twenties and seven-thirties "a favorite investment of all the thriftiest . . . portion of the working classes." The loan was also taken in rural regions. An agent from

---

[50] Philadelphia Press, April 28, 1863; New York Tribune, March 21, 1865, Scrapbook; Undated Circular, all in Jay Cooke Manuscript Papers, HSP; and W. T. Page to Jay Cooke, April 28, 1863, cited in Oberholtzer, Jay Cooke, 250. An unlabeled clipping in the Cooke Scrapbook broke down the sales for May 15, 1863 as follows: New York and New Jersey: 959,000 / Boston: 440,000 / Rhode Island: 100,000 / Pennsylvania: 61,000 / Washington, D.C.: 33,000 / Baltimore: 23,000 / Kentucky: 27,000 / Missouri: 9,000 / Indiana and Illinois: 17,000.

Vermont wrote, "Farmers who live in little cabins, wear homespun clothes and ride to church and town in two-horse wagons without springs, have in many instances several thousand dollars loaned to the government."[51]

Equally important for our purposes, for every American who purchased a bond, hundreds who did not heard about them. Cooke's agents traveled into every "nook and corner" of the Union; they carried with them not just bonds, but a vision of the government and of the nation. Across the country, in banks, libraries, hotels, reading rooms, and on their doorsteps, millions of Americans—most of whom had heretofore had little contact with the federal government—opened their doors or their papers and encountered Cooke's agents or advertisements.

Emphasizing the financial aspects of the bonds, Cooke told his customers that the federal government could be a source of profit for them. He pointed to the exemptions from state and local taxes that the national loan provided, defining the federal government as protector—as a source of refuge from the financial incursions of states and municipalities. In Cooke's campaigns the federal government overtly offered to serve its citizens as a savings bank. Cooke told them that the nation—in explicit contrast to the states and localities—could be a source of economic well-being.[52]

In defining the nation in these terms, Cooke was extending to middle- and working-class Americans the image of the nation that Alexander Hamilton had offered the financial and commercial classes seventy years earlier: that of directly serving their material interests. Although both Daniel Webster and Henry Carey had previously attempted to give a democratic base to Hamilton's economic nationalism, arguing in effect that the Whigs' protectionist and internal

---

[51] Jay Cooke to Salmon P. Chase, November 17, 1863, *Chase Papers Microfilm;* Larson, *Jay Cooke,* 167; *New York Tribune,* no date, in Oberholtzer, *Jay Cooke,* 585–87; "Who Are the Bondholders?" *The Nation,* February 6, 1868; and undated manuscript containing excerpts from letters, cited in Larson, *Jay Cooke,* 174.

[52] The idea of the nation as a perceived source of economic well-being is discussed in Kohn, *Idea of Nationalism,* 17. The role of self-interest in the creation of a patriotic nationalism is discussed in Potter, *The South and the Sectional Conflict,* 54–56; and in Curti, *Roots of American Loyalty,* 92–121. Both Peter Parish, *The American Civil War* (New York: Holmes and Meier, 1975), 359–60, and Phillip Shaw Paludan, *"A People's Contest": The Union and Civil War 1861–1865* (New York: Harper and Row, 1988), 115–17, mention the role of the bond drives in cultivating loyalty to the nation.

improvement policies would indirectly benefit the masses, never before had America's farmers and artisans, its mechanics and laborers, been offered so direct an economic stake in the welfare of the nation.[53]

The idea that the national loan might cultivate loyalty based on material interest did not go unrecognized. "Every dollar taken of this loan," wrote five-twenty agent S. Davis to Cooke, "is not only a blow against the rebellion, but is cementing the people by the tie of interest to the General Government." During the seven-thirty campaign, an editorial in the *Lane Express* noted that the taking of the loan by the masses "strengthens the Nation. . . . These small subscribers . . . will pinch and save and work to buy more, and thus weave themselves into the very life and interests of the Government. . . . [T]he distribution of SEVEN-THIRTIES among the people is a guarantee of permanent Union between the East and West, and the Centre and the Extremes." And at least one bondholder indicated that he now understood his connection to the Union in different terms: according to the *Philadelphia Press*, a soldier in the Army of the Potomac wrote Cooke that, having invested his surplus earnings in five-twenties, he felt newly inspired to win the war, for "If I fight hard enough, my bonds will be good."[54]

The idea of the nation as a source of economic well-being was furthered by the particular notion of loyalty that Cooke set forward. The United States was a newly centralizing nation; the obligations of its citizens were ill defined. Citizenship might be about asserting a principle, or participation in a polity, or even sacrifice. Appealing to Americans to fund the war debt, the bond literature acknowledged these more conventional forms of patriotism as legitimate. But they were not, Cooke suggested, for all, or even most, Americans. He proposed an alternative form of service to country, in which the demands of citizenship could be met through the act of entering the market to purchase an interest-bearing, profit-producing bond. Linking patriotism and profit, he offered a notion of citizenship that did not require the subordination of private interest to the public good.

---

[53] For the economic nationalism of Carey and Webster, see Curti, *Roots of American Loyalty*, 109–12.

[54] S. Davis to Jay Cooke, June 3, 1863; and *Lane Express*, March 18, 1865, and *Philadelphia Press*, April 31, 1863, Scrapbook, Jay Cooke Manuscript Papers, HSP. See also Paludan, *A People's Contest*, 117.

Rather, he suggested, from the pursuit of private interest, public good would ensue.

In time self-interest came not just to serve, but to be equated with, patriotism in the bond literature. Purchasing the loan with its promise of profit, bondholders were then rewarded with stories of their patriotism, and their names were printed in lists of the loyal. Their acts of pragmatism were redefined: self-interest now equaled patriotism.

There were, of course, limits to the compatibility of self-interest and public good—limits that Cooke himself pushed up against regularly. Forced to choose between furthering the good of his country and that of his estate, Cooke repeatedly denied that such a choice existed, even as he plunged ahead with the pursuit of his own fortune.

Not surprisingly, the tremendous success of the bond drives meant success for Cooke as well. By most accounts, contemporary and historical, he was made rich by the war. Cooke netted at least $220,000 in the fifteen-month five-twenty campaign alone. Given the labor Cooke invested, the risks he undertook, and the amount of money he raised for the Union, many have viewed this sum as fair recompense. But it is not the amount Cooke earned that is disturbing. Rather, it is the fact that though he was clearly making a fortune from the drives, Cooke fought to do better, even when the good of the government and the nation were put at risk thereby.[55]

When Cooke agreed to undertake the agency for the government war loans, he foresaw many benefits. He was aware that a successful bond drive would bring him a substantial commission; he knew he stood to establish a national reputation as well. But the loans also offered another advantage: by keeping the millions collected for bonds on deposit in his own account or in the banks of his more trusted agents for only a short while, Cooke and his banking firm could make untold amounts in interest. This practice no doubt bolstered Cooke's profits significantly, if surreptitiously; more importantly for our purposes, it was a source of constant tension between Cooke, Chase, and their critics. The correspondence that reveals this tension also reveals a somewhat incorrigible Cooke, driven to maximize his personal profit, seemingly incapable of restraint.[56]

---

[55] Larson, *Jay Cooke*, 151, 161; Blue, *Salmon P. Chase*, 155; McPherson, *Battle Cry of Freedom*, 443; and *Congressional Globe*, March 11, 1864, 1046–47.

[56] Cooke established that he saw the potential profits inherent in this practice early on; see Jay Cooke to Salmon P. Chase, September 7, 1861; and Cooke to Chase, March 6, 1862, *Chase Papers Microfilm*.

Salmon Chase was not unaware of these tendencies in Cooke, having confronted them in his dealings with the banker during his agency for the National Loan in 1861. Shortly after his appointment as agent to that loan, Cooke asked to be allowed to keep a "good running balance," increasing his earnings by "letting the balance lay on deposit." Chase does not appear to have assented, for within days Cooke was being chastised for failing to deposit loan proceeds with the government. He may have complied for a short while, but a remarkable incident the following spring illustrates his capacity for flouting the Secretary's authority. On March 22, 1862, Chase authorized Cooke, as one of numerous national agents, to dispose of 750,000 seven-thirty bonds, in order to "make immediate provisions for payment of troops going into the fields." Chase asked that the money for the soldiers' paychecks be submitted to the government as soon as possible. Over a month later, though the Assistant Treasury in New York had sold and relinquished its $3 million in bonds within days of its authorization, Cooke had not yet transferred a significant portion of the loan proceeds in his account to the Treasury, having otherwise invested the funds. Although the government appears to have profited in the transaction, so does Cooke. In an uncharacteristically sharp reprimand, Chase reminded Cooke that the money had been intended to pay soldiers and asked that in the future he be advised if Cooke found "this employment of your means unremunerative."[57]

If Chase thought that Cooke had learned his lesson, he was mistaken. Throughout the five-twenty campaign, Chase continually urged Cooke to deposit into the federal Treasury the large sums collected in the bond drives. He was joined in this quest by Cooke's brother and Washington liaison, Henry David Cooke, who had cautioned Jay before the five-twenty contract "not to show anxiety to keep the deposit." But less than three weeks following his appointment to the five-twenty loan, to the consternation of his brother and Chase, Cooke was holding $1.5 million of the government's money

---

[57] Jay Cooke to Salmon P. Chase, September 7, 1861; and Salmon P. Chase to Jay Cooke, September 10, 1861, March 22, 1862, April 26, 1862 (two letters, both written that day), *Chase Papers Microfilm*. Cooke used the money from the three-year bonds to redeem certificates, which he apparently could not profitably redeem on the terms proposed by Chase. Chase suggested that if he was informed of such situations in the future, he would send Cooke separate sums to carry on this redemption.

in his account. Henry Cooke pleaded with him to deposit the money: "It would look badly if it should get out. . . . Governor C. has boundless confidence in you, . . . hence there seems to be a peculiar obligation, on our part, not to strain it too far." In December Henry David wrote Jay that Chase was again inquiring about Cooke's balance. Although he covered for his brother, suggesting that perhaps sales were slow, Henry urged Jay to "reduce the balance to the *lowest possible point*. . . . [I]t would hardly do for [Chase] to know that you have so large a balance in your hands."[58]

Forced continually to admonish the Philadelphia banker for failing to deliver government funds, both Chase and Henry David grew apologetic. At one point Chase asked that Jay Cooke not think him "parsimonious because I keep an eye on you"; in another letter he acknowledged that Cooke might think him "technical." Henry Cooke tread even more carefully: "We make these suggestions with diffidence, and hope you will not think the pupils are lecturing the teacher, to whom they look up with the sincerest reverence and respect."[59]

But if his close associates were loath to condemn Cooke, the politicians and bankers who questioned the banker's exclusive agency were not. Immediately following the appointment of Cooke to the five-twenty loan, jealous banking interests joined Chase's political enemies in questioning the exclusivity of the arrangement. Amid mounting charges of favoritism, suggestions of corruption emerged. On December 22, 1862, Massachusetts Representative Charles A. Train proposed a congressional investigation of the Treasury to "inquire whether any officer or employee . . . is a partner, or interested di-

---

[58] Henry D. Cooke to Jay Cooke, May 13, 1862, November 12, 1862, December 22, 1862, Jay Cooke Manuscript Papers, HSP. Unmoved, the Philadelphia banker continued to allow the proceeds of the bond drives to sit in his own account as well as those of his agents. The latter practice was particularly galling to Henry, who feared that the agents would lend on stock margins and generate a loss. "I would rather forego the profits arising from the interest in the balances in hands of agents, than to run the risk you are running," he wrote (Henry D. Cooke to Jay Cooke, May 26, 1863, Jay Cooke Manuscript Collection, HSP). Chase chastised Cooke for many other reasons, including sloppy accounting and failing to accept financial responsibility for the acts of his agents. See Salmon P. Chase to Jay Cooke, April 23, 1862, and July 29, 1863, *Chase Papers Microfilm.*

[59] Salmon P. Chase to Jay Cooke, November 13, 1862, April 26, 1862, *Chase Papers Microfilm;* and Henry D. Cooke to Jay Cooke, November 12, 1862, Jay Cooke Manuscript Papers, HSP.

rectly or indirectly in any banking house . . . having contracts with the Government." Although this investigation did not materialize, the acrimony persisted. Cooke's reluctance to forward the proceeds of his sales came to the attention of Chase's correspondents, one remarking to the Secretary that "somebody must be losing a pile of interest by these delays." Speculating on Cooke's profits, the *New York World* announced that the American people were being "humbugged" and "cheated"; in a later congressional debate a Congressman Hendricks charged that Cooke "has been made rich by the drippings of the Treasury."[60]

Such accusations haunted Chase, who pressed Cooke harder, if ineffectively, for compliance. Fearing for his reputation, in June 1863 Chase announced his intention to reduce Cooke's commission. Cooke protested vehemently and threatened to quit. Chase grew impatient. "I have," he pointed out, "a duty to the country to perform which forbids me to pay rates which will not be approved by all right-minded men; and I cannot think that now, when your past services have been fully compensated, and when the necessity for extensive advertising must be greatly reduced and the amount of subscriptions so largely increased that a very low rate will afford you a larger remuneration than a very high rate formerly, the original compensation should be continued." In the end it was left to Henry Cooke to remind his brother that there were more than profits at stake: "We must all make some sacrifices for our country."[61]

Cooke accepted the reduced commission reluctantly, and sales continued unabated. But the struggle had taken its toll on Chase. He continued to use the services of Cooke's firm once the five-twenty loan had closed, but did not suggest another exclusive agency. Neither, until the end of his brief tenure in office, did his successor, William P. Fessenden. Fearing a reprisal of the charges and innuendos faced by Chase, when the need for a second national loan became clear, Fessenden turned to the national banks to sell the second set

---

[60] *Congressional Globe,* December 22, 1862, 167; Henry Cooke to Jay Cooke, June 1, 1863, Jay Cooke Manuscript Papers, HSP; *New York World,* May 20, 1863, in Oberholtzer, *Jay Cooke,* 260; and *Congressional Globe,* March 11, 1864, 1046.

[61] Henry D. Cooke to Jay Cooke, May 14, 1863, Jay Cooke Manuscript Papers, HSP; Salmon P. Chase to Jay Cooke, December 23, 1862, June 1, 1863, *Chase Papers Microfilm;* and Henry D. Cooke to Jay Cooke, June 24, 29, 1863, Jay Cooke Manuscript Papers, HSP.

of bonds, the seven-thirties. By January 1865, however, the national banks had failed to sell a significant portion of the loan. Fessenden offered Cooke the agency, then left office. To Fessenden's successor, Hugh McCullough, was left the trial of coping with Cooke, his intransigence, and yet another round of charges and countercharges.[62]

Jay Cooke's wartime rise to fame and fortune became legendary: "As rich as Jay Cooke" was for many years a popular expression. But if the image was enduring, the money was not. Cooke undertook the financing of the Northern Pacific Railroad and overextended his firm. In 1873 the United States District Court for eastern Pennsylvania declared Cooke and Co. bankrupt. Although later in his life Cooke regained much of his personal fortune through private investments, by the estimation of one biographer, his banking career had ended in failure.[63]

Cooke spent the final years of his life living with his daughter. With her help he began writing his memoirs. Thirty years after the fact, he recounted the sense of duty to country that led him to undertake the government loan "without any hope or expectation of commissions of any kind." But, as the story of the bond drives suggests, Cooke did not accurately depict the nature of his service to the Union.[64]

In fact, far from its alleged roots in civic duty and Christian sacrifice, Cooke's patriotism was grounded instead in classical liberalism. To the project of funding the war debt, he brought both a profound faith in the overriding human drive for economic self-improvement and the assumption that that drive would operate in service of the public good. Cooke's patriot was an economic—not a civic—man, even in the public realm. This belief informed his campaign to acquire the business of the government as well as the conceptualization and execution of the bond drives themselves. Thus Cooke's was a market-model patriotism. In the context of a fluid mid-nineteenth-century political culture—one informed by shifting notions of the relationship between the individual and society—it showed how patriotism in a society based not on republican civic duty, but on the pursuit of individual interest, could work.

Cooke's vision of the nation was perfectly suited to his self-inter-

---

[62] Larson, *Jay Cooke*, 161–65; and Oberholtzer, *Jay Cooke*, 560–62.

[63] Josephson, *Robber Barons*, 57; Larson, *Jay Cooke*, 399–415.

[64] Cooke's Memoir, 75, Jay Cooke and Company Collection.

ested citizen, for it offered the nation, first and foremost, as a source of economic well-being. Cooke detailed the strength and wealth of the Union. He presented the federal government that presided over that Union as one big savings bank, waiting to return high rates of interest, eager to protect its citizens' earnings from the taxes of states and municipalities. He argued that the popular nature of the loan was but an attempt to make the benefits of this nation and this government available to everyday Americans.

The idea that the nation might directly serve its citizens' material interests was not new; it had been the foundation of the Hamiltonian plan to bind the moneyed classes to the federal government. What *was* new was Cooke's democratization of this notion. Setting out to sell bonds to Americans "of all classes, all politics, all professions," through an extensive network of agents and subagents, newspapers and flyers, Cooke brought this vision to America's cities and towns and even into its hinterlands.[65]

---

[65] Unlabeled clipping, May 7, 1863, Scrapbook, Jay Cooke Manuscript Papers, HSP.

5

Freedom, Union, and Power: The Ideology of the Republican Party during the Civil War

Michael S. Green

PERHAPS NO ASPECT of the Civil War, except for the military, has received as much attention from historians as the political developments that caused the war, affected its fighting, and shaped its after-effects. Within the decade before the war and the decade after it, the second party system collapsed and the third party system began and evolved. For the first time, a sectional, minority party captured the presidency and then struggled to become a national, majority party. One region elected that president, and differences in outlook and ambition between northern and southern leaders inspired the other region to refuse to accept the result. The president whom southern-ers denied proved so unpopular with his party as to threaten the survival of his administration and his nomination for a second term, even during wartime; continued exposure to him softened some of his most severe critics, and his assassination made him a martyr.

These plot threads have prompted many efforts to weave a coher-ent whole, and to explore the individual threads. Biographies have illuminated the lives of the individual actors and their times. Studies

This essay is based on my Columbia University dissertation, "Freedom, Union, and Power: The Ideological Transformation of the Republican Party during the Civil War." This article obviously is truncated and does not address the same number of issues in the same depth. I am indebted to my adviser, Eric Foner, for his criticisms of previous chapters addressing these issues, and to Eric McKitrick for similar aid on an earlier study. I also wish to acknowledge my intellectual and personal debt to Professor Xi Wang of Indiana University of Pennsylvania, Professor Michael Voren-berg of Brown University, Professor A. James Fuller of the University of Indianapo-lis, and three colleagues at the Community College of Southern Nevada: Professor DeAnna Beachley, Professor John Hollitz, and the late Professor Gary E. Elliott.

of issues, branches of government, and party factions have described and analyzed crucial aspects of the war, those who affected it, and those who were affected by it. And, despite the increasing and welcome emphasis within the historical profession on history "from the bottom up," those who study the Civil War appear to have heeded Eric Hobsbawm's entreaty to examine not just social history, but the "history of society."[1]

However, no study yet published has sought to explain and analyze how the workings of the Republican party's mind shaped the war as it was fought, and thus the nation as it proved to be. Ideology has been defined as "the system of beliefs, values, fears, prejudices, reflexes, and commitments—in sum, the social consciousness" of a group such as the Republican party during the Civil War. Although this definition is about three decades old, it remains both suitable and appropriate for what Richard Hofstadter described in *The American Political Tradition* as a "central faith" that unites a particular group. The works of Eric Foner, a Hofstadter student, have done much to reveal the Republican mindset and influenced others to produce similarly grounded studies. At the end of *Free Soil, Free Labor, Free Men,* describing the party's rise to power, Foner wrote that "its identification with the aspirations of the farmers, small entrepreneurs, and craftsmen of northern society . . . gave the Republican ideology much of its dynamic, progressive, and optimistic quality. Yet paradox-

---

[1] Quoted in Eric Foner, *Politics and Ideology in the Age of the Civil War* (New York: Oxford University Press, 1980), 6. The books I have in mind include Phillip Shaw Paludan, *"A People's Contest": The Union and the Civil War, 1861–1865* (New York: Harper and Row, 1988); Paludan, *The Presidency of Abraham Lincoln* (Lawrence: University Press of Kansas, 1994); David Herbert Donald, *Lincoln* (New York: Random House, 1995); James A. Rawley, *Abraham Lincoln and a Nation Worth Fighting For* (Chicago: Harlan Davidson, 1996); John Niven, *Salmon P. Chase: A Biography* (New York: Oxford University Press, 1995); Hans L. Trefousse, *Thaddeus Stevens* (Chapel Hill: University of North Carolina Press, 1996); Heather Cox Richardson, *The Greatest Nation of the Earth: Republican Economic Policies during the Civil War* (Cambridge, Mass.: Harvard University Press, 1997); Garry Wills, *Lincoln at Gettysburg: The Words That Remade America* (New York: Simon and Schuster, 1992); Mark E. Neely, Jr., *The Fate of Liberty: Abraham Lincoln and Civil Liberties* (New York: Oxford University Press, 1991); Earl Hess, *Liberty, Virtue, and Progress: Northerners and Their War for the Union,* 2d ed. (New York: Fordham University Press, 1997); James M. McPherson, *What They Fought For: 1861–1865* (Baton Rouge: Louisiana State University Press, 1994); Xi Wang, *The Trial of Democracy: Black Suffrage and Northern Republicans, 1860–1910* (Athens: University of Georgia Press, 1997). These are only a few examples of works that have informed my ideas for this essay.

ically, at the time of its greatest success, the seeds of the later failure
of that ideology were already present." Foner's *Reconstruction:
American's Unfinished Revolution* began with an examination of the
process that led to the Emancipation Proclamation, and how it reflected both the necessity of dealing with slaves coming into Union
lines and the Republican party's genuine hatred for slavery. Near the
end of this work, Foner noted "how closely the Civil War era had tied
the new industrial bourgeoisie to the Republican party and national
state," and that Reconstruction's immediate failure could be linked
to "the weakening of Northern resolve, itself a consequence of social
and political changes that undermined the free labor and egalitarian
precepts at the heart of Reconstruction policy."[2]

Those seeds were indeed sown by the Republican party's history.
A crucial part of that history is what Republicans thought, and a crucial part of both is the years of civil war. Historical knowledge of
this ideology seems akin to Lincoln's description of General William
Tecumseh Sherman's march to the sea. Responding to a serenade
during the period in which Sherman was cut off from his communications, Lincoln told the crowd, "We all know where he went in at, but
I can't tell where he will come out at." We know how Republicans
went into the war. Hindsight tells us where they came out. How they
got there is a story in itself.[3]

The Republicans who won the presidency in 1860 and control of
the federal apparatus for the next four years seemed far more radical
than they actually were. Their presidential candidate had been Lincoln, a moderate who condemned not only slavery, but also radical
abolitionism. Some of the goals they articulated in their party platform read like typical political rhetoric—to rid politics and the government of corruption, for example. Others reflected their
Democratic and Whig antecedents: to promote internal improve-
ments and pass a Homestead Act, which would people the West with
Jeffersonian farmers, and a transcontinental railroad, which would

---

[2] Richard Hofstadter, *The American Political Tradition and the Men Who Made It*
(New York: Alfred A. Knopf, 1948), ix, viii; Eric Foner, *Free Soil, Free Labor, Free
Men: The Ideology of the Republican Party before the Civil War* (New York: Oxford
University Press, 1995 ed.), 4, 316; and Foner, *Reconstruction: America's Unfinished
Revolution, 1863–1877* (New York: Harper and Row, 1988), 584, 603.

[3] "Response to a Serenade," from *New York Tribune*, December 8, 1864, in Roy
P. Basler et al., eds., *The Collected Works of Abraham Lincoln*, 9 vols. (New Brunswick, N.J.: Rutgers University Press, 1953–55), 8:154.

unite the regions and aid business and industry. They also proposed
to ban slavery in the territories. For all of their claims that they would
leave the institution untouched in the states where it existed, Republicans clearly sought to restrict slavery to the status quo, at best, and
to secure the Founding Fathers' dream, as they understood it, to
ensure the slow death of slavery. Southerners who wanted to spread
it, and their northern sympathizers who wanted the whole subject to
go away, charged that Republicans wanted to kill slavery outright and
decried those who hatched the plot as wild-eyed fanatics. Almost
inevitably, secession and war followed.[4]

By the time of Lincoln's death on April 15, 1865, the party had
been more successful than even its most ambitious members could
or should have hoped. Slavery was not just contained, but dying of a
constitutional amendment that would ban it forever. The Homestead
Act promised to open the West to the small-scale, entrepreneurial
farmers whom Republicans expected to form the core of their party.
Construction of the transcontinental railroad was well underway.
Thanks to the war, but also to a protective tariff, the North's industrial economy had achieved supremacy over southern agrarianism,
reaching new heights of profit and productivity. The Democratic
party appeared, if not fatally injured, severely wounded.[5]

These events obviously reflected a triumph of policy and patience,
but Republicans had come into the war committed to a set of principles that had guided them and, they contended, should guide everyone else. At the heart of their ideology was a belief in free labor. To
Republicans, free labor was not only part of a pithy slogan, but also
an accurate depiction of what they wanted for the nation and what
the nation should want for itself. Republicans had long made clear
that they viewed free labor as economically and morally superior to
slave labor. Most importantly, free labor offered the equality of opportunity that Republicans believed to be guaranteed by the Declaration of Independence and the Constitution. "The first great duty of
philanthropists and reformers is to impress upon rising generations

---

[4] For general background relating to the Republican party's beliefs and rise before
the Civil War, see Foner, *Free Soil*, passim; and William E. Gienapp, *The Origins of
the Republican Party, 1852–1856* (New York: Oxford University Press, 1987).

[5] Virtually any text on the Civil War addresses these issues. See generally James
M. McPherson, *Battle Cry of Freedom: The Civil War Era* (New York: Oxford University Press, 1988), passim.

. . . the divine law that by the sweat of a man's brow shall he earn his bread," declared New York party boss Thurlow Weed, who was not given to sentiment or philosophizing. "In our country thousands of poor boys, by industry, honesty, and ambition, have not only acquired wealth, but become useful and honored citizens." For proof of Weed's argument, Republicans needed to point no further than to the leaders of their presidential administration: Lincoln, Secretary of State William Henry Seward, and Secretary of the Treasury Salmon P. Chase, all of whom had risen from humble origins.[6]

In the South, Republicans argued, that kind of social mobility was nonexistent. For the North and its free labor society to triumph at war, Republicans believed, merely confirmed what they had been saying for years about the inferiority and backwardness created by the South's reliance upon slave labor. In his Second Inaugural Address, on March 4, 1865, Lincoln urged his listeners to be neither judgmental nor malicious, but he also observed, "It may seem strange that any men should dare to ask a just God's assistance in wringing their bread from the sweat of other men's faces." Such attitudes demanded reform, and southern secession and its effects availed Republicans of the opportunity to prove their point. As far as Republicans were concerned, if any doubt remained about the superiority of northern society and free labor, the Civil War destroyed it. Thus, victory and social change would go hand in hand. As Charles Leland, a protégé of economic theorist Henry Carey, wrote, "Free labor men of the North wish to see as much made of every man as he is capable of becoming," but slaveowners "do not wish to have the whole continent one busy hum of industry with millions of happy, hardworking mechanics and independent small farmers." Many Republicans of Whig ancestry already were protectionists when it came to the tariff, but party members of every antecedent agreed on the wisdom of enhancing industry and exports—and that the best place to export the free labor ideal was to the South.[7]

---

[6] Thurlow Weed Barnes, *Life of Thurlow Weed, Including His Autobiography and a Memoir* (Boston: Houghton Mifflin, 1884), 7. On the lives of these party leaders, in addition to the aforementioned studies of Lincoln and Chase, see Glyndon G. Van Deusen, *William Henry Seward* (New York: Oxford University Press, 1967).

[7] "Second Inaugural Address," March 4, 1865, in Basler et al., eds., *Lincoln's Works*, 8:332–33; *Philadelphia Bulletin*, May 19, 1863, quoted in George W. Smith, *Henry C. Carey and American Sectional Conflict* (Albuquerque: University of New Mexico Press, 1951). On Republican views of economics as related to the South, see Foner, *Free Soil*, 40–72; and Richardson, *The Greatest Nation of the Earth*, passim.

To Republicans the freedom to labor, to enjoy an equal opportunity to rise in society, was central to a productive society and a victory in the war—indeed, central to the nation's existence. Before the war Republicans had expressed this idea in a variety of ways, from Lincoln 's "House Divided" speech to Seward's warnings of an "irrepressible conflict." During the war they remained as devoted as ever to their belief that slavery, inevitably, must end. "The sacred animosity between Freedom and Slavery can end only with the triumph of Freedom," warned Charles Sumner, the radical senator from Massachusetts. Abolitionists such as Theodore Tilton, pragmatic antislavery advocates such as the editors of the *Chicago Tribune,* and evolving Republicans such as Henry Winter Davis, the one-time Know-Nothing congressman from Maryland, all agreed that it was a war for liberty or freedom, terms that they tended to use interchangeably, long before Republicans realized or acknowledged that slavery had become not just treasonous, but suicidal.[8]

Indeed, as much as they welcomed the opportunity to strike a blow for liberty, most Republicans agreed from the outset that they had gone to war primarily to save the Union. For a few of the more radical Republicans, this required them to admit that a Union with slavery would be worth saving. For most of the rest of the party, the choice was simpler. To allow a Confederate republic to survive might somehow cleanse the Union of what Republicans considered its greatest sin, but it would allow that sin, slavery, to perpetuate itself, and would mean that Republicans, as the "true heirs" to the founding generation, had failed in their responsibility to extend and strengthen the republican experiment. That contradicted the ideology of the Republican party, and that ideology was rooted in the Declaration of Independence and the Constitution—to all but the most radical Republicans, sacred and connected compacts into which all of the American people had entered. Horace Greeley, the influential and quixotic editor of the *New York Tribune,* called the Union "a reality

---

[8] Charles Sumner to Anonymous, November 12, 1860, reel 74, series 2, Papers of Charles Sumner (microfilm), Houghton Library, Harvard University; *The Independent,* June 25, 1863, quoted in Victor B. Howard, *Religion and the Radical Republican Movement, 1860–1870* (Lexington: University Press of Kentucky, 1982), 52; *Chicago Tribune,* July 13, 1864, quoted in Phillip Kinsley, *The Chicago Tribune: The First Hundred Years,* 3 vols. (Chicago: Chicago Tribune, 1960), 1:330; Gerald S. Henig, *Henry Winter Davis: Antebellum and Civil War Congressman from Maryland* (New York: Twayne, 1973), 184 and passim.

. . . a vital force, and not a mere aggregation, like a Fourth of July gathering or a sleighing and supper party."[9]

With far more grace and iron, Lincoln expressed the Republican ideology of unionism. His First Inaugural Address appealed to the "mystic chords of memory" that would "yet swell the chorus of the Union." In December 1862 his second annual message to Congress warned, "The fiery trial through which we pass, will light us down, in honor or dishonor, to the latest generation. We say we are for the Union. . . . We shall nobly save, or meanly lose, the last best, hope of earth." At Gettysburg the entire address concerned the nation's survival and what that meant. In 1864, in his letter to Albert G. Hodges, which is famous for his claim that "events have controlled me," Lincoln made clear that he had acted only with the Union's preservation in mind when he had moved against slavery or left it alone—but at no time had he allowed it to grow. And in his Second Inaugural Address, Lincoln pointed out that one region "would make war rather than let the nation survive; and the other would accept war rather than let it perish."[10]

For Lincoln and the vast majority of his fellow Republicans, the Union and freedom were inextricably linked. When Lincoln became the first president to suggest any form of emancipation while he was in office, in his annual message of December 1862, he reasoned, "We know how to save the Union. The world knows we do know how to save it. . . . In giving freedom to the slave, we assure freedom to the free—honorable alike in what we give, and what we preserve." The story is well known: earlier in the war, some Republicans pushed Lincoln to order emancipation at once; others strenuously opposed even the hint of a suggestion; and Lincoln gradually agreed that saving the Union demanded a blow against slavery. Many Republicans, including the President, already had long suspected, if not hoped, that freedom and union were inseparable. Events proved that to be

---

[9] Glyndon G. Van Deusen, *Horace Greeley: Nineteenth-Century Crusader* (Philadelphia: University of Pennsylvania Press, 1953), 262–63; *The Independent*, April 18, 1861, and May 16, 1861.

[10] "First Inaugural Address—Final Text," March 4, 1861, in Basler et al., eds., *Lincoln's Works*, 4:262–71; "Annual Message to Congress," December 1, 1862, in ibid., 5:518–37; Abraham Lincoln to Albert G. Hodges, April 4, 1864, Robert Todd Lincoln Papers, Manuscript Division, Library of Congress, in ibid., 7:281–83; "Second Inaugural Address," March 4, 1865, in ibid., 8:332–33; Wills, *Lincoln at Gettysburg*, passim.

the case, but Republicans had to believe it in the first place or be willing to accept the idea for it to become reality. As George Boutwell, a Massachusetts radical, later recalled, Republicans "became the party of the Union" and Lincoln "struggled first for the Union, and then for the overthrow of slavery as the only formidable enemy of the Union."[11]

Whether and how Lincoln differed from other Republicans as to means mattered—then and now—less than one crucial point: they agreed on the end. They believed that slavery was wrong, and the South was wrong to secede. If they varied at times over whether the Union would be better off with the South gone, they never wavered in their belief in the value of the Union and the spread of freedom. As president, and thus as constitutional commander-in-chief and presumed leader of his party, Lincoln became the focal point for understanding what Republicans thought about the war.

In a useful and provocative essay, James McPherson likened Lincoln to the hedgehog, which the Greek poet Archilochus and the philosopher Isaiah Berlin called an animal with a "central vision," unlike the fox, which was far nimbler but more discursive and easily distracted. "The Union—with or without slavery—had become . . . the 'single central vision' of Lincoln the hedgehog," McPherson wrote. But when he asked, "What accounted for this apparent reversal of priorities from liberty first to Union first?—from Union as a means to promote liberty to Union as an end in itself?" it was, in some ways, the wrong question, conveying an impression that Lincoln may have put liberty above the Union, rather than side by side. Other Republicans might have ordered them differently, yet they retained shared priorities rooted in a shared ideology.[12]

Yet, to this question McPherson offered an answer that supplies a critical component of Republican ideology during the war. "Unprece-

---

[11] "Annual Message to Congress," December 1, 1862, in Basler et al., eds., *Lincoln's Works,* 5:518–37; Allen Thorndike Rice, ed., *Reminiscences of Abraham Lincoln by Distinguished Men of His Time* (New York: North American Publishing Company, 1886), 134–36; J. David Greenstone, *The Lincoln Persuasion* (Princeton: Princeton University Press, 1992), 18–19, 239–40, and passim; Hans L. Trefousse, *The Radical Republicans: Lincoln's Vanguard for Racial Justice* (New York: Alfred A. Knopf, 1969), passim.

[12] See especially James M. McPherson, "Liberty and Power in the Second American Revolution," in *Abraham Lincoln and the Second American Revolution* (New York: Oxford University Press, 1991), 113–30, 136.

dented power had become necessary to defend liberty against un-precedented peril," he wrote, arguing that Lincoln's presumed shift was due to "the responsibility of power, and Lincoln's conception of constitutional limitations on that power. From the moment he was elected, Lincoln understood his responsibilities. The night of his election, he told reporters, "Well, boys, your troubles are over now, mine have just begun," and immediately began trying to craft a Cabi-net and respond to Republican concerns about the potential and then the reality of secession. Less than two years into his presidency, Lin-coln succinctly summarized the situation to Congress: "We . . . hold the power and bear the responsibility."[13]

Above all else, Republicans agreed, they must use that power and responsibility wisely. When Lincoln took office in March 1861, the Whig party had been dead for less than a decade, the Democratic party was so bitterly divided that it seemed to be teetering near death, and the Know-Nothing and Constitutional Union parties had bloomed and withered within a matter of months. Republicans cer-tainly hoped that their party would prove permanent, but they could hardly be certain. Thus, in the days after Lincoln's election in No-vember 1860, from radical to conservative, they agreed that how they wielded power would play an important role in their success or the lack of it. Senator Lyman Trumbull, a cold-eyed and perspicacious Illinois moderate, told his radical colleague, the blustery Benjamin Wade of Ohio, "With power comes responsibility, and we must now prepare to take it."[14]

Republicans took it, and well, but not always happily. As adroit a political and diplomatic operator as any before or since, and accord-ingly criticized from all sides, Seward often expressed a desire to "leave public life . . . to rest during what remains of life free from the

---

[13] Ibid.; Stephen B. Oates, *With Malice toward None: The Life of Abraham Lin-coln* (New York: Harper and Row, 1978), 195; "Annual Message to Congress," De-cember 1, 1862, in Basler et al., eds., *Lincoln's Works*, 5:518–37.

[14] Lyman Trumbull to Benjamin F. Wade, November 9, 1860, reel 2, Benjamin F. Wade Papers (microfilm), Manuscript Division, Library of Congress. See also James R. Doolittle to Lyman Trumbull, November 10, 1860, reel 6, Lyman Trumbull Pa-pers (microfilm), Manuscript Division, Library of Congress; Burton J. Hendrick, *Lincoln's War Cabinet* (Boston: Little, Brown, 1946), 10–11. On Trumbull and Wade, see Ralph J. Roske, *His Own Counsel: The Life and Times of Lyman Trumbull* (Reno: University of Nevada Press, 1979); Hans L. Trefousse, *Benjamin Franklin Wade: Radical Republican from Ohio* (New York: Twayne, 1963).

suspicions and jealousies of enemies and the reproofs of friends." His increasingly avowed ideological and political enemy, Charles Sumner, tried to disagree with Seward as much as possible, but on this issue they found common ground. Newly ensconced in 1861 as chairman of the Senate Foreign Relations Committee, Sumner complained, as many party leaders of the time did, about the seemingly endless flow of jobseekers. "For myself, I had much rather be in opposition. . . . I am now to see the experiences of power, and I do not like them." But he changed his mind. The prerogatives of power and leadership altered how Republicans saw their new role in the government. Asked what became of a bill he opposed, Sumner replied, "It still sleeps . . . in my committee room," and could take pleasure in knowing that he controlled its fate. Other Republicans agreed that adjusting to power and responsibility was hard. After so many years of dishing out and taking attacks, some of their number proved unable to change what one senator called "the habit of mind which may grow upon a man by constantly fighting in a minority and . . . complaining of the Administration in power."[15]

Now that they were in power, Republicans also had to resolve who among themselves would be in control. The problem was stickier than it might have seemed. Lincoln took office with no executive experience, surrounded by a Cabinet whose members included former governors, senators, government administrators, political bosses, and distinguished attorneys—and most of them were certain of their superiority to the President. When the South seceded, Republicans took over all of the congressional leadership positions. As a result, the party's leaders had to gain control of the gears of government, which took time, just as most of those who had run the government were running the Confederacy and attacking the Union. This pres-

---

[15] Hans L. Trefousse, "The Republican Party, 1854–1864," in *History of U.S. Political Parties*, 4 vols., ed. Arthur M. Schlesinger, Jr. (New York: Chelsea House, 1973), 1161; Norman B. Ferris, *The Trent Affair: A Diplomatic Crisis* (Knoxville: University of Tennessee Press, 1977), 196–201; Charles Sumner to Henry Wadsworth Longfellow, March 16, 1861, and April 7, 1861, in reel 74, series 2, Papers of Charles Sumner, Houghton Library, Harvard University; Sumner to Hamilton Fish, March 16, 1861, ibid.; Sumner to Samuel Gridley Howe, April 7, 1861, reel 64, series 1, ibid.; Sumner to Francis Lieber, April 13, 1864, ibid.; Allen G. Bogue, *The Earnest Men: Republicans of the Civil War Senate* (Ithaca, N.Y.: Cornell University Press, 1961), 61; David Donald, *Charles Sumner and the Rights of Man* (New York: Alfred A. Knopf, 1970), 12; Richard H. Sewell, *John P. Hale and the Politics of Abolition* (Cambridge, Mass.: Harvard University Press, 1965), 197–99.

sure created squabbling, but so did differing conceptions of power. In Congress westerners often complained that most of the committee chairmen were New Englanders; although that was the consequence of the seniority system, the reasoning did little to mitigate the feeling among westerners that easterners viewed them as stepchildren to be bossed around. In turn, most congressmen and Cabinet members expected Lincoln to adhere to the Whig theory of the executive, which was rooted in presidential deference to legislative and ministerial expertise. As commander-in-chief, though, Lincoln had to act as needed to win the war, requiring him to intervene in nonmilitary areas—at times irritating Congress and his Cabinet.[16]

As Republicans adjusted to responsibility for the government, they also articulated what they proposed to do with their new power. The answer lay in perpetuating their ideology of freedom and union. Governor Austin Blair of Michigan announced, "It has been demonstrated beyond cavil, that freedom is the best basis for power," and Winter Davis described the crux of Republican thought and action as "liberty guarded by power." Many Republicans had spent a great deal of their career in the political wilderness, serving in the minority or as a voice for freedom.

For the most part they established reputations rather than records: Lincoln made a bigger name for himself in losing to Senator Stephen Douglas in 1858 than he ever did through his elections to the Illinois legislature or his term in Congress; Chase was far better known as the "attorney general" for fugitive slaves and his stand against the Kansas-Nebraska Act than for any notable achievements as governor of Ohio and one of its United States senators. The most successful Republican politician probably had been Seward, who won his victories in gubernatorial and Senate elections as a Whig. He played a significant role in the debates during the secession winter primarily

---

[16] The main explication of the Whig theory is David Donald, "Abraham Lincoln: Whig in the White House," in Donald, *Lincoln Reconsidered: Essays on the Civil War Era*, 2d ed. (New York: Vintage Books, 1961), 187–208. See also Stephen B. Oates, "Abraham Lincoln: Republican in the White House," in *Abraham Lincoln and the American Political Tradition*, ed. John L. Thomas (Amherst: University of Massachusetts Press, 1986). With all due respect to Professor Donald, I find the Oates argument more compelling, for two reasons: first, Lincoln did intervene in matters that he deemed important; and, second, judging Lincoln's approach to the presidency as Whig or Republican is difficult simply on the grounds that he faced a unique situation. I address this subject further in my dissertation.

because he was the most prominent member of the party not yet in power, but about to be. Indeed, the criticism to which he was subjected for his talk of compromise before the war and his machinations once the war began certainly could be attributed to his reputation as a slippery political boss. But it also reflected a fundamental problem that Republicans had to resolve: never having held power, they were leery of trusting those who seemed to enjoy and take advance of it too much. Republicans tended to view power in terms of principle rather than its pragmatic uses and demands. Power was to be used for freedom and union, not for its own sake.[17]

This commitment to freedom, union, and power united Republicans, but, clearly, it also had the potential to divide them. The issue often was one of degree. Historians have long tried to explain the differences between radical, moderate, and conservative Republicans and generally end up agreeing only that they cannot agree. Both Sumner and Thaddeus Stevens were radicals on racial issues, but one was a New England free trader, the other a Pennsylvania protectionist. They shared the desire of Senator Orville Browning of Illinois and Henry Raymond, founder and editor of the *New York Times,* to restore the Union, but Sumner and Stevens hoped to end slavery and remake southern society in the process; to Browning and Raymond, reconstructing the Union and keeping Republicans in power would be enough of an attack against slavery and the South. They could and did differ over certain issues, yet these too contributed to the formation of a coherent ideology.[18]

Republicans on all sides of the ideological spectrum agreed that their party's beliefs would contribute to a more ordered, peaceful society. Although they debated how much they wanted the government and the nation to change, they generally concurred with *North American Review* editor Andrew Peabody's description of the war as one for a Constitution that "claims our allegiance because it is law and order—the only government possible for us, the only bond of peace and beneficent relations by which our nation can be held to-

---

[17] George N. Fuller, ed., *Messages of the Governors of Michigan,* 2 vols. (Lansing: Michigan Historical Commission, 1926), 2:495–96; Henig, *Henry Winter Davis,* 246.

[18] Besides the previously noted biographical studies, see Maurice G. Baxter, *Orville H. Browning: Lincoln's Friend and Critic* (Bloomington: Indiana University Press, 1957); and Francis Brown, *Raymond of* The Times (New York: W. W. Norton, 1951).

gether" against "disintegration and anarchy." When 100,000 New Yorkers massed for a Union meeting little more than a week after the firing on Fort Sumter, it was no coincidence that the call referred to the importance of "liberty with order, over usurpation and anarchy." From the Republican perspective, when the South refused to accept Lincoln's election, it upset that order and tried to usurp power; when it claimed states rights and the right to spread slavery, it overturned both the Constitution and the progress of civilization itself. For a party dedicated to expanding freedom and continuing the Union, that was too much to bear.[19]

Almost equally unbearable was the Supreme Court. Republicans wanted it to be a bastion for defending the Constitution. Instead, they complained, the Court had become a tool of "the Slave Power," dedicated to defending an institution that the framers of the Constitution had barely protected and disdained so much that they refused to refer to it by name. Making matters worse, as abolitionist John Jay lamented, was "the profound respect and all but implicit obedience that our people are accustomed to render to all the decisions of our courts of law." However, as a Washington observer trenchantly if cynically noted in 1863, "It is easy for the Administration (or for any Administration) to arrange the Supreme Court." Republicans from Lincoln on down paid careful attention to the Court and how to change it from the body that had issued the Dred Scott decision. They succeeded in their efforts. By the end of Lincoln's first term, he had appointed five justices, including a chief justice, Chase. Lincoln's appointees often disagreed with one another after the war, but during the war they upheld the measures that Republicans considered necessary to maintaining the Union and enhancing freedom.[20]

In that regard Republicans sincerely believed that they were merely enacting the intent of the framers of the Declaration and

---

[19] Phillip Shaw Paludan, *A Covenant with Death: The Constitution, Law, and Equality in the Civil War Era* (Urbana: University of Illinois Press, 1975), 28; Margaret A. Clapp, *Forgotten First Citizen: John Bigelow* (Boston: Little, Brown, 1947), 145.

[20] John Jay to John P. Hale, December 13, 1861, box 13, John P. Hale Papers, New Hampshire Historical Society; T. J. Barnett to S. L. M. Barlow, August 17, 1863, box 45, S. L. M. Barlow Papers, Huntington Library, San Marino, Calif.; Phillip Shaw Paludan, "The American Civil War Considered as a Crisis in Law and Order," *American Historical Review* 77 (October 1972): 1013–34; David M. Silver, *Lincoln's Supreme Court* (Urbana: University of Illinois Press, 1956).

Constitution. Their ideology pulled Republicans in both directions: back to Thomas Jefferson's ideal of small farms and equal opportunity, but ahead to a land truly free, with a successful industrial economy of the kind that Alexander Hamilton envisioned. Just as Jefferson and Hamilton, and their disciples, had been at loggerheads, Republicans fought an internal psychological war over them and their reputations during the Civil War. They felt an inherent sense of duty to the Founders to ensure the survival and success of their republican experiment. Thus did Republicans pay homage to their predecessors and seek to push slavery on the road to ultimate extinction that they believed the Founders to have paved.[21]

Another component of Republican ideology also reflected the views of the framers. Shortly after the war began, the party that won the election of 1860 ceased to exist. It became the Union party, although the only readily discernible difference between this new organization and the one it replaced was its name. To be sure, Republicans understood that their appeal had been limited in nature: sectional because they opposed the extension of slavery, largely working class and liberal (in the modern sense of the word) because they seemed dedicated to social change. Accordingly, if they were to save the Union, extend freedom, and gain the power to do both, they needed a broader base of support. The Union party retained the principles and many of the details of the Republican platform of 1860, but it also provided a tent under which Democratic supporters of the war and political independents might safely congregate. After all, the party's name made clear that its goal was the Union's perpetuity. But, just as freedom and union were intertwined, so were the Republican and Union parties.

The 1864 Union party platform called for a constitutional amendment to end slavery, furnishing additional proof of the interlocking nature of freedom and union: the party devoted to preserving the

---

[21] The outstanding study of how Republicans viewed the Framers is George B. Forgie, *Patricide in the House Divided: A Psychological Interpretation of Lincoln and His Age* (New York: W. W. Norton, 1979). While I admire and have profited immensely from Professor Forgie's research, I do not share his conclusion. See also Wills, *Lincoln at Gettysburg,* passim; David Lee Child to Charles Sumner, June 21, 1861, reel 21, Papers of Charles Sumner (microfilm), Houghton Library, Harvard University; "A Song on Our Country and Her Flag. By Francis Lieber. Written in 1861, after the Raising of the Flag on Columbia College, New York. Printed by the Students," in Lieber to Sumner, circa 1861, reel 75, series 2, ibid.

country demanded the ultimate form of freedom, with support from
old Democrats who once had fought against the slightest movement
in that direction. On that platform Lincoln was resoundingly reelected and went on to push the Thirteenth Amendment through the
House of Representatives.[22]

At that point Republicans appeared to have executed the political
equivalent of a military envelopment: they had absorbed some of the
most respected members of the northern Democratic party. This,
too, put them squarely in the tradition of the Founders, although
they were unaware of it. Republicans believed that the war afforded
them the chance not only to consolidate their power and put their
own ideas into practice, but to remove the opposition party as a force.
As Richard Hofstadter explained in *The Idea of a Party System*, the
framers, branding their critics as traitorous, refused to accept the
concept of "legitimate opposition": one of the few points on which
Jeffersonians and Hamiltonians could agree was that their opponents
must be eliminated as a political faction. Not until the rise of Henry
Clay, Daniel Webster, and John Calhoun—and Martin Van Buren,
the guiding force behind the Jacksonians—did parties achieve anything remotely resembling permanence, or their leaders accept the
notion that such organizations might serve a positive purpose. Yet
during the war Republicans seriously, usually sincerely, questioned
Democratic legitimacy. To attack the Republicans, who anointed
themselves as the Union party and attracted several Democratic unionists into their ranks, seemed tantamount to opposing the Union
itself. As David Potter and Eric McKitrick showed, the party system
helped the North by channeling opposition to government policy so
that it could be controlled and might do some good, but Republicans
doubted the wisdom of dissent in all its political and constitutional
colors. It was a far cry from their days in the opposition, and easily

---

[22] On the Union party's evolution and the 1864 election, see William Zornow,
Lincoln and the Party Divided (Norman: University of Oklahoma Press, 1954);
David E. Long, *The Jewel of Liberty: Abraham Lincoln's Reelection and the End of
Slavery* (Mechanicsburg, Pa.: Stackpole Books, 1994); John C. Waugh, *Reelecting
Lincoln: The Battle for the 1864 Presidency* (New York: Crown Publishers, 1997);
LaWanda Cox and John H. Cox, *Politics, Principle, and Prejudice, 1865–1866: Di-
lemma of Reconstruction America* (New York: Macmillan, 1963). A work that has
greatly informed my thinking on this subject is Michael A. Vorenberg, "Final Freedom: The Civil War, the End of Slavery, and the Thirteenth Amendment" (Ph.D.
diss., Harvard University, 1995).

explained: their wartime ideology of freedom and union, and sense of power and responsibility for perpetuating them, made criticism seem not constructive, but destructive, even treasonous.[23]

If Republicans were, indeed, to perpetuate their beliefs, the western territories provided an almost ideal laboratory. Thus, the West itself played a large role in the party ethos. Most of the land west of the Mississippi was sparsely populated and without organized government. To fill it with Republicans, settlers of like mind, would extend the party's base of support, and with it those who shared its ideology. The Republican platform of 1860, and the policies that Lincoln and Congress pursued once in power, reflected this belief. The Homestead Act of 1862 was designed to turn the Jeffersonian vision of the nation into a reality by making cheap land available to small farmers. The Morrill Land Grant College Act of 1862 would spread agricultural and industrial education throughout the country, expanding the economy and tying two seemingly disparate parts of it together. The Pacific Railroad Act of 1862 would build the transcontinental line that had been at the heart of political controversy in the 1850s, link the east and west coasts, and connect farms and factories. Although these measures worked out differently than anticipated, helping instead to make the big business of railroads even bigger, the West proved to be mostly Republican for decades to come—and if it was a different brand of Republicanism than that practiced during the Civil War, the party never claimed total clairvoyance among its talents. More important, these policies helped keep the region loyal during wartime and make it supportive of the Republican party and what it believed.[24]

---

[23] Richard Hofstadter, *The Idea of a Party System: The Rise of Legitimate Opposition in the United States, 1780–1840* (Berkeley: University of California Press, 1969), passim; David M. Potter, "Jefferson Davis and the Political Factors in Confederate Defeat," in David Donald, ed., *Why the North Won the Civil War* (Baton Rouge: Louisiana State University Press, 1960), 91–112; Eric L. McKitrick, "Party Politics and the Union and Confederate War Efforts," in *The American Party Systems: Stages of Political Development* ed. William N. Chambers and Walter Dean Burnham (New York: Oxford University Press, 1967), 117–51.

[24] Richardson, *The Greatest Nation of the Earth,* addresses the background behind many of these issues. There is no need or desire here for immersion in western history. Two recent syntheses that deal, at least to some extent, with the impact of these measures on the trans-Mississippi West are Patricia Nelson Limerick, *The Legacy of Conquest: The Unbroken Past of the American West* (New York: W. W. Norton, 1987); and Richard White, *"It's Your Misfortune and None of My Own": A New History of the American West* (Norman: University of Oklahoma Press, 1991).

Nor was the growth of big business antithetical to what Republicans believed. Before the war, and at times during it, some party members had disdained businessmen. Greeley warned Congress to pay attention not to "cotton loving merchants" who always "eat a little dirt for the sake of slavery," but to "men who fill the workshops and till the farms. . . . In this large class there is no timidity and hesitation." As Massachusetts radical Samuel Gridley Howe told Sumner, "The tendency of capital is to subvert legislation to its own interest;—to hedge itself . . . with privileges and exceptions; to strengthen and perpetuate itself in the establishment of castes. . . . [S]ociety never will, and never ought to rest upon solid and peaceful foundations so long as the labour and drudgery of the world is thrown entirely upon one class, while another class is entirely exempt from it." However, Republicans sought and expected the triumph of free labor and its concomitant, the elimination of slave labor, which would benefit everyone, free and slave. "The interests of the capitalist and the laborer are in perfect harmony with each other," the intellectual leader of the party's protectionists, Henry Carey, claimed, because each benefited the other. Power also played a part in the equation: achieving these goals required control of the government and victory in the war, which required money—the kind of funding available only from large banks and businesses. Republicans had to convince their owners and managers that their party was dedicated to the sort of fiscal responsibility that could win wars and preserve both governments and credit ratings. As long as this cultivation was part of a larger cause and ideology, Republicans could easily rationalize it— and did. Only after the war, as a new generation of leaders who came of age with the party in power supplanted the old, would the party lose its ideological moorings.[25]

Not that the early Republicans never fought over just this kind of issue. No two Republicans seemed more alike or differed more ex-

---

[25] Bruce Levine, *Half Slave and Half Free: The Roots of the Civil War* (New York: Hill and Wang, 1991), 230; Samuel Gridley Howe to Charles Sumner, February 14, 1865, reel 79, series 2, Papers of Charles Sumner, Houghton Library, Harvard University; Smith, *Henry C. Carey,* , 101. See also Paludan, *"A People's Contest,"* passim; Francis W. Bird to Charles Francis Adams, East Walpole, December 24, 1860, IV, "Letters Received and Other Loose Papers," August-December 1860, reel 550, the Adams Family Papers (microfilm), Massachusetts Historical Society; Philip S. Foner, *Business and Slavery: The New York Merchants and the Irrepressible Conflict* (Chapel Hill: University of North Carolina Press, 1941).

plicitly than Charles Sumner and William Pitt Fessenden. Both were senators from New England, the cradle of abolitionism—Sumner from Massachusetts, Fessenden from Maine—and opposed slavery. Both understood the loneliness and powerlessness of serving in the minority; before the Civil War, for most of their tenure in the Senate, southerners and their sympathizers had controlled the key committees, the Supreme Court, and the presidency. Both could be hard to get along with: Sumner was vain, pompous, egotistical, elegant, and eloquent, and increasingly difficult and hateful toward the South after suffering a caning at the hands of a South Carolinian in 1856; Fessenden was waspish, dyspeptic, and often impatient. Yet, with southern secession and the coming of the Civil War, both became powers in the Senate—Fessenden as chairman of the Finance Committee and majority leader in all but title, Sumner as chairman of the Foreign Relations Committee, a close adviser to Lincoln on diplomatic issues, a connection to the European powers and thinkers whose influence could affect the outcome of the war, and the leading political voice of abolition and emancipation. They also could be pithy in explaining their guiding political principles. Fessenden declared, "I have been taught since I have been in public life to consider it a matter of proper statesmanship, when we aim at an object which we think is valuable and important, if that object . . . is unattainable, to get as much of it and come as near it as we may be able to go." Sumner said, "A moral principle cannot be compromised."[26]

In these two men, and those two quotations, lies the basis for much of the history of the Republican party and its ideology during the Civil War. One was a voice of politics tinged with commitment, the other of idealism unwilling to bend. Yet Fessenden fought the Legal Tender Act, which did much to enable Lincoln's government to finance the war, until he finally agreed to support it. Privately, and at times publicly, he blistered Lincoln and his ministers, but he eventually joined the Cabinet and ended up attesting to the President's political genius. Sumner, the emancipationist, avoided any public break with Lincoln, despite what he considered the President's snail-

---

[26] Michael Les Benedict, *A Compromise of Principle: Congressional Republicans and Reconstruction, 1863–1869* (New York: W. W. Norton, 1974), frontispiece. On these two men, see Charles Jellison, *Fessenden of Maine: Civil War Senator* (Syracuse, N.Y.: Syracuse University Press, 1962); and Donald, *Sumner and the Rights of Man.*

like pace in moving against slavery. And during the murky negotia-
tions involving the party ticket in 1864, the evidence strongly suggests
that Sumner maneuvered against the renomination of Vice President
Hannibal Hamlin, whom he hoped to support for election to the
Senate from Maine in 1865, when Fessenden's term would be up.
Thus, Fessenden could be the ideologue, Sumner the wire-pulling
politician.[27]

These differences were largely personal, and they do much to explain Republican thought during the war. To overstate the obvious,
Republican leaders were politicians. Although they might criticize
those of their number who revealed too much in the political game,
all of them had scratched and clawed their way from the local level
to the national level. Some of them had previously done so as Democrats, some as Whigs, some from factions and splinter groups, some
from the center of party organizations and some from the periphery.
Their backgrounds and personalities also affected how they functioned in office. Lincoln long had run a disorganized law office, and
his administrative habits changed little when he reached the White
House. Seward got along well with others and could be, at turns, a
jocular, profane, tippling, shifty raconteur whom Lincoln greatly enjoyed and who maneuvered his ministers and foreign powers like a
grand master in chess. Chase was serious and devout, finding Lincoln
and Seward too light-hearted and given to political gamesmanship;
the Treasury Secretary was too honestly ambitious to be shrewd
enough to win the presidential nomination, but so honestly well-
meaning as to finance the war and remain largely untainted by scan-
dal in the process.

The Cabinet that Lincoln appointed as he took office provides a
portrait of the Republican party and the role of the personality in
shaping its actions: divided in and by background and region, united
by a common desire to preserve the Union and work against slavery,
and riven by personal dislikes having little to do with ideology. Three
ministers had been Democrats: Chase, Secretary of the Navy Gideon
Welles, and Postmaster General Montgomery Blair. Three of them
had been Whigs: Seward, Attorney General Edward Bates, and Secretary of the Interior Caleb Smith. One, Secretary of War Simon
Cameron, had belonged to both parties and proved corrupt in each

---

[27] Donald, *Lincoln*, addresses relations between Lincoln, Sumner, and Fessenden.

of them; his successor, Edwin Stanton, was a former Democrat who worked closely with Seward during the secession winter and insinuated himself into radical good graces upon taking office. Only Chase began the war as a true radical and remained one. Seward's radical reputation suffered as he moved increasingly into the conservative Republican wing. Bates and Smith were conservatives who never really left the Whig party. As a border state spokesman, Blair felt squeamish about moving too rapidly against slavery and continued to believe that the Democratic party could be redeemed.[28]

More important for the Cabinet's operations were the many personal dislikes and ambitions among the ministers. Seward considered himself the premier, superior at first to Lincoln and always to his colleagues, and interfered in the administering of other departments. Chase distrusted Seward, grew to hate Blair and his family, and desperately wanted to be president; accordingly, he cultivated good relations with anyone who might help and was so lacking in subtlety that he harmed his chances more than he helped them. Blair and Welles were closely allied and equally disdainful of whiggery and radicalism, so that they detested even Seward, who shared much of their conservatism. Cameron and Stanton oscillated between their colleagues, each abandoning Seward for Chase and Stanton largely ignoring the wishes of everyone but Lincoln, whom he also viewed as overly political. Yet Lincoln controlled them, mainly by keeping them separate and rarely meeting with them, annoying Chase and congressional Republicans who believed that he was too close to Seward and too willing to follow him.

All of these factors and factions bubbled to the surface in December 1862 and proved to be a defining moment in the party's wartime evolution, ideologically and politically. The war effort had stalled: Lincoln had removed George McClellan from command of the Army

---

[28] In addition to more general studies such as Paludan, *Presidency of Abraham Lincoln,* Hendrick, *Lincoln's War Cabinet,* and the aforementioned biographical studies, see also Erwin S. Bradley, *Simon Cameron, Lincoln's Secretary of War: A Political Biography* (Philadelphia: University of Pennsylvania Press, 1966); Marvin R. Cain, *Lincoln's Attorney General: Edward Bates of Missouri* (Columbia: University of Missouri Press, 1965); John Niven, *Gideon Welles: Lincoln's Secretary of the Navy* (New York: Oxford University Press, 1973); William E. Smith, *The Francis Preston Blair Family in Politics,* 2 vols. (New York: Macmillan, 1933); Benjamin P. Thomas and Harold M. Hyman, *Stanton: The Life and Times of Lincoln's Secretary of War* (New York: Alfred A. Knopf, 1962).

of the Potomac, and his replacement, Ambrose Burnside, led his men to disaster at Fredericksburg. The Preliminary Emancipation Proclamation seemed a failure: many moderate and conservative Republicans blamed it for the party's poor showing during the recent election. A Senate caucus decided that the problem lay with Lincoln's failure to consult his Cabinet often enough and with Seward's control over him. Bolstered by Chase's complaints about the absence of genuine Cabinet meetings, the senators decided that "public confidence in the present administration would be increased by a reconstruction of the Cabinet," and Sumner suggested sending a committee to Lincoln to recommend changes. Upon learning of the meeting and vote, Seward offered Lincoln his resignation. On the night of December 18 the committee met with Lincoln. Hearing how the senators quietly presented their views, Bates wrote, "To use the President's quaint language . . . they seemed to think that when he had in him any good purposes, Mr. Seward contrived to suck them out of him unperceived."[29] Assuring Lincoln that he had the Senate's confidence, Fessenden claimed that the Constitution gave his colleagues power to advise and consent, and they advised a change, wholly in the spirit of helpfulness. Lincoln felt differently, and invited them back the next night. They encountered a disagreeable surprise: all of the Cabinet but Seward. For several hours the ministers, including Chase, defended themselves and professed to work well together. While claiming that he consulted his ministers as much as necessary,

---

[29] A good summary is found in Donald, *Lincoln*, 398–406. See Lafayette Foster to Hamilton Fish, December 16, 1862, vol. 49, Hamilton Fish Papers, Manuscript Division, Library of Congress; Leonard P. Curry, *Blueprint for Modern America: Nonmilitary Legislation of the First Civil War Congress* (Nashville: Vanderbilt University Press, 1968), 217–20; Hendrick, *Lincoln's War Cabinet*, 390–93; Theodore C. Pease and James G. Randall, eds., *The Diary of Orville Hickman Browning*, 2 vols. (Springfield: Illinois State Historical Library, 1925–33), entry for December 16–17, 1862, 2:597–99; William Henry Seward to Abraham Lincoln, December 16, 1862, reel 74, William Henry Seward Papers (microfilm), University of Rochester; Frederick W. Seward to Lincoln, ibid.; Howard K. Beale, ed., *Diary of Edward Bates, 1859–1866* (Washington, D.C.: Government Printing Office [volume 4 of the Annual Report of the American Historical Association for the Year 1930]), 1933), entry for December 19, 1862, 268–69; Francis Fessenden, *Life and Public Services of William Pitt Fessenden*, 2 vols. (Boston: Houghton Mifflin, 1907), 1:231–38, 251–52; John Jay to Charles Sumner, December 18, 1862, reel 27, Papers of Charles Sumner (microfilm), Houghton Library, Harvard University; Samuel Wilkeson to Sydney Howard Gay, December 19, 1862, reel 6, Sydney Howard Gay Papers (microfilm), Department of Rare Books and Manuscripts, Butler Library, Columbia University.

Lincoln confessed to making key decisions, mostly affecting McClellan, on his own. But he made clear that he expected "a general smash-up" if Seward walked the plank and asked his ministers for their opinions. Chase "seemed offended, and said he wouldn't have come if he had expected to be arraigned." Browning later asked how Chase could say such things. Senator Jacob Collamer of Vermont replied, "He lied." Embarrassed, Chase offered his resignation, which Lincoln accepted, replying, "I have a pumpkin in each end of my bag." Lincoln told Seward and Chase that he needed them both, and they stayed in the Cabinet.[30]

In returning to the Cabinet, Seward's position was clearer than Chase's. Many radicals abhorred Seward, believing that he had become irretrievably and impossibly conservative. What they thought, however, mattered less than what Lincoln wished to do. Aware that he lacked party support, Seward fully devoted himself to serving Lincoln and to his diplomatic duties. A radical who claimed to be glad that Seward stayed called it "almost pusillanimous" to drive him out for his loyalty to Lincoln. That was Chase, who added, "And, besides, Seward is the only distinctive and original anti-slavery man besides myself in the Cabinet."[31]

Ironically, Chase's actions, and the Senate's failure to jettison Seward, served precisely the purposes they were intended to thwart. Not only did they enhance Lincoln's powers, but they diminished the

[30] Pease and Randall, eds., *Browning Diary*, entry for December 18–22, 1862, 2:600–603; Beale, ed., *Bates Diary*, entry for December 19, 1862, 269–70; Fessenden, *Life of Fessenden*, 1:238–51; James G. Randall, *Lincoln the President*, 2 vols. (New York: Dodd, Mead, 1945), 2:241–49; Curry, *Blueprint for Modern America*, 223; Salmon P. Chase to Flamen Ball, December 20, 1862, series 1, reel 24, Salmon P. Chase Papers (microfilm), Historical Society of Pennsylvania; Chase to Jay Cooke, December 20, 1862, ibid.; Chase to Lincoln, December 20, 1862, Robert Todd Lincoln Papers, Manuscript Division, Library of Congress.

[31] Joseph Medill to Salmon P. Chase, December 28, 1862, box 7, Salmon P. Chase Papers, Historical Society of Pennsylvania; John C. Hamilton to Chase, December 23, 1862, series 1, reel 24, Salmon P. Chase Papers (microfilm); Chase to Richard C. Parsons, December 24, 1862, ibid.; John G. Nicolay to Therena Bates, December 23, 1862, typescript, box 7, John G. Nicolay Papers, Manuscript Division, Library of Congress; Hendrick, *Lincoln's War Cabinet*, 409; Albert Bushnell Hart, *Salmon Portland Chase* (Boston: Houghton Mifflin, 1899), 302–3; Chase to William Henry Seward, December 1862, reel 74, Seward Papers (microfilm), University of Rochester; Chase to Lincoln, December 22, 1862, Robert Todd Lincoln Papers, Manuscript Division, Library of Congress; Chase to Hiram Barney, December 27, 1862, Hiram Barney Papers, Huntington Library, San Marino, Calif.

influence of the Cabinet and Congress. Governor William Dennison of Ohio asked, "Is it not a dangerous innovation for Senators to interfere with Cabinet matters in caucus form? Will it not be a precedent that may in the future completely subordinate the Executive to the Legislative branch of the Govt and thus virtually destroy the whole theory of our political system?" The answer, many Republicans felt, was yes. The Constitution under which they wielded power for freedom and union said nothing about that kind of power. Lincoln did not just outfox or overwhelm two feuding ministers and a captious Senate; he made a forceful statement in behalf of presidential power and authority over the Cabinet, and he did it for the sake of preserving freedom and the Union.[32]

Yet the actions of Lincoln, his Cabinet, and the Senate had far less to do with ideology than with personalities and politics. "People might take sharply adversarial positions on fairly basic issues and still find their meanings within essentially the same structure of ideas and values, the same body of reference," wrote two historians of an early period of political and Cabinet strife. "Or, to turn the case around, overwhelming numbers of them might support the same cause . . . from a variety of divergent individual motives and interests, yet still be drawing upon the same enveloping tradition of thought for whatever community of purpose and meaning they might reach." Chase and Republican congressional leaders had proved far less influential with Lincoln and his administration than they had hoped or expected. That had nothing to do with radicalism, conservatism, or anything in between. Nor was it due to Seward's influence or Lincoln's presumed pliability. Ideologically the crisis grew out of different perceptions of how much power the Cabinet should have in an administration, and what the Senate's constitutional right to "advise and consent" really meant. Much more important, however, were what Lincoln's biographers might call his mysterious nature and tendency to dissemble, which made it hard to know him and harder to know what he was up to; Seward's greater reputation for political and ethical slipperiness;

---

[32] William Dennison to Francis Preston Blair, Sr., December 22, 1862, box 9, Blair-Lee Family Papers, Princeton University; *Daily Alta California,* December 24, 1862, quoted in Curry, *Blueprint for Modern America,* 227; *Chicago Tribune,* December 25, 1862, quoted in Joseph Logsdon, *Horace White: Nineteenth-Century Liberal* (Westport, Conn.: Greenwood Press, 1971), 93; Cain, *Lincoln's Attorney General,* 206–10.

and Chase's desire for place. What they seemed mattered far more than what they believed, because those beliefs were shared, and Republicans knew what they were.[33]

Nor did Lincoln always get his way. On April 14, 1865, he met with his Cabinet to discuss what to do with the states that comprised the defeated Confederacy. Three days before, the President had gently, almost diffidently, advocated suffrage for some blacks, such as soldiers and the literate—a significant step, too great for some Republicans, that prompted one listener, actor John Wilkes Booth, to tell a friend, "That means nigger citizenship." But on that Good Friday Lincoln wanted to conciliate the seceded states, smoothing their path back into the Union. Most of the Cabinet agreed on the wisdom of reconstructing the Union as painlessly as possible, but preferred to move more slowly than Lincoln. His ministers thought that it was at least as important not to allow those who had been traitors a week before to wield too much power—or even any power—too soon.[34]

Granting that Cabinet meetings had gone on for seventy-five years, this gathering was unusual. The key issue facing Lincoln and his Cabinet was the status of the former slaves. Four years before, Republicans had been trying to reassure the South that its slaves would remain unfree. Now Lincoln and his advisers were arbitrarily—within limits set by Congress—deciding how and whether the South could return to the Union, and what rights the freed people would enjoy. It proved the accuracy of a prediction made on April 13, 1861, the day after the South fired the first shot. "Whatever you may think of the signs of the time, the Government will arise from this strife greater, stronger, and more prosperous than ever. It will display energy and military power," Senator John Sherman, who helped guide

---

[33] The quotation is from Stanley M. Elkins and Eric L. McKitrick, *The Age of Federalism: Birth of the Republic, 1788–1800* (New York: Oxford University Press, 1993), 13–14. On Lincoln's leadership style, see LaWanda Cox, *Lincoln and Black Freedom: A Study in Presidential Leadership* (Urbana: University of Illinois Press, 1985).

[34] Basler et al., eds., *Lincoln's Works,* 8:399–405; Donald, *Lincoln,* 588–92; Foner, *Reconstruction,* 74–75; William Hanchett, *The Lincoln Murder Conspiracies* (Urbana: University of Illinois Press, 1987), 37; Cox, *Lincoln and Black Freedom,* 144–46; Thomas and Hyman, *Stanton,* 357–58; Howard K. Beale, ed., *Diary of Gideon Welles,* 3 vols. (New York: W. W. Norton, 1960), 2:281; Fawn M. Brodie, *Thaddeus Stevens: Scourge of the South* (New York: W. W. Norton, 1959), 213–14. On the issues and problems with black suffrage, as far as Republicans were concerned, see Wang, *Trial of Democracy,* passim.

the government through the thicket of greenbacks and taxes as a member of the Finance Committee, told his brother, the general whose march to the sea devastated a once-proud region.[35]

Four years of civil war caused great change throughout the nation. Not the least among those changes, the war stepped up the Republican party's efforts to make itself, and its beliefs, truly national. To do so demanded a refinement of the party's principles. In opposition it could call for freedom, and in power it could continue to do so. With power, however, came responsibility—for the government, the Union, and the winning of a war to preserve them all. However, on the night the Cabinet dissuaded Lincoln from undue, perhaps unbecoming, mercy and forgiveness, Booth killed the President. His bullet also shattered the Civil War party. At heart a states-rights, racist Jacksonian Democrat, Andrew Johnson reacted accordingly to the nationalistic Republicans who sought to protect the freedmen's rights. Circumstances changed for the Republicans when they won the presidency in 1860, and again when the war began. The end of the war presented a new set of problems for them to try to solve and required further refinements in their belief system. But for the war itself, the Republican ideology of freedom, union, and power sustained the party, and sustained a nation.

---

[35] Winfield Scott Kerr, *John Sherman: His Life and Public Service*, 2 vols. (Boston: Sherman, French, 1906), 1:128.

6

Beyond Politics: Patriotism and Partisanship on the Northern Home Front

Adam I. P. Smith

THE SETTLED JUDGMENT of a generation of historians has been that the two-party competition between Republicans and Democrats behind the lines during the Civil War was a source of strength to the Union. In a brilliant essay, published in 1967, Eric McKitrick pointed out that in comparison to the partyless (and faction-riven) Confederacy, electoral competition provided a means by which opposition to the war could be channeled into the familiar, orchestrated conflict of party politics.[1] The system harmonized state–federal relations even while providing a salutary check on disloyal opposition. Yet, this was not the perception of most of those who experienced the war, any more than it was the perception of people living in the 1790s that conflicts between Jeffersonians and Federalists were conducive to the health of the republic.

Political parties shaped popular engagement in public life in mid-nineteenth-century America in at least two ways: as organizations they were powerful mechanisms for mobilizing voters and distributing information; as symbols that embodied distinct sets of identities they provided a language that enabled citizens to engage more fully and systematically in the public sphere. Both the organizational and the symbolic functions of parties were challenged by the outbreak of civil war. Lincoln's call for troops was accompanied by pleas for a cessation of party conflict. How could party opposition to the admin-

---

[1] Eric McKitrick "Party Politics and the Union and Confederate War Efforts," in *The American Party Systems: Stages of Political Development*, ed. William N. Chambers and Walter Dean Burnham (New York: Oxford University Press, 1967), 117–51.

istration be reconciled with the need to "rally round the flag"? It was a question that remained a deeply troubling undercurrent throughout the rest of the war, sometimes surging to the surface when war weariness was at its height. The relationship between partisanship and patriotism created such anxiety because calls for unity were met by an ever-greater intensification of deep political divisions. The well-established rituals of election time—nominating conventions, overblown rhetoric, parades, canvasses, and polling-day treating— continued as before. The political process was bound up in constructive as well as damaging ways with the task of mobilizing the northern people behind the war effort.

Because politics was so central to the lives of antebellum northerners, it provides a natural explanation for the way in which northern commitment to the war effort was generated. Parties were the connecting tissue between local and national spheres, a means of enabling people to interpret the meaning of the war, and through which information could be disseminated. Only churches performed a similar role, and, during the war the functions of political and religious meetings were never closer. The purpose of this essay, then, is to consider how the meaning of partisanship was tested by the pressures of war and how, in that context, the political process aided the Union war effort.

The political world of James Batterson, chairman of the Connecticut Union party committee during the war, provides a window on the impact of the war on parties and the political process.[2] A businesslike, affable man, he was representative of the class of political organizers that had been spawned by the growth of mass-based political parties since the Jacksonian era.[3] In the campaign to reelect Lincoln

---

[2] I am grateful for the kindness of Sharon Steinberg at the Connecticut Historical Society, who, on my behalf, went to great lengths uncovering biographical material on James Batterson.

[3] On the development of political parties in the antebellum period see Richard Hofstadter, *The Idea of a Party System: The Rise of Legitimate Opposition in the United States, 1780–1840* (Berkeley: University of California Press, 1969); Michael Wallace, "Changing Concepts of Party in the United States: New York, 1815–1828," *American Historical Review* 74 (April 1968): 453–91; William N. Chambers and Phillip C. Davis, "Party Competition, and Mass Participation: The Case of the Democratizing Party System, 1824–1852," in *The History of American Electoral Behavior*, ed. Joel H. Silbey, Allan G. Bogue, and William H. Flanigan (Princeton: Princeton University Press, 1978), 174–97; William G. Shade, "Political Pluralism and Party Development: The Creation of a Modern Party System, 1815–1852," in

in 1864, Batterson and his committee were involved in the production and distribution of broadsides and the organization of public meetings. He corresponded with the Union Party National Committee in New York and the Congressional Committee in Washington, both of which were sources of centrally raised funds and printed campaign documents. It was Batterson who organized the printing of distinctively designed yellow paper ballots and sent them out to every ward and township in the state.[4] Beneath the familiarity of electoral battle, though, it is clear that for this particular party man the 1864 campaign was more than just another election. "Three Hundred and Fifty Years before the Christian era the liberty of Greece was sacrificed upon the altar of Party differences and internal strife," he reminded a political meeting. "Jealous of each other the Grecian states ruined their united strength by failing to agree upon the administration of a central government. Party strife then as now was the hot bed of treason—and the enemies of Greece could never have power . . . had not party traitors barely betrayed and sold their country and with it their own liberty."[5] Although this kind of rhetoric was part of the tradition of electoral hyperbole familiar to the Civil War generation, this time everyone knew that the threats were real.

To dramatize the issues at stake, Batterson arranged for soldiers who had been furloughed home to parade and symbolically deposit ballots at pro-Lincoln rallies. Whereas in 1860 the Republicans had

---

The Evolution of American Electoral Systems, ed. Paul Kleppner (Westport, Conn.: Greenwood Press, 1981), 77–112; Ronald P. Formisano, The Transformation of Political Culture: Massachusetts Parties, 1790s–1840s (New York: Oxford University Press, 1983); Formisano, "Boston, 1800–1840: From Deferential-Participant to Party Politics," in Boston, 1700–1980: The Evolution of Urban Politics, ed. Ronald P. Formisano and Constance K. Burns (Westport, Conn.: Greenwood Press, 1984), 29–57; Richard P. McCormick, The Second American Party System: Party Formation in the Jacksonian Era (Chapel Hill: University of North Carolina Press, 1966); Lee Benson, The Concept of Jacksonian Democracy: New York as a Test Case (Princeton: Princeton University Press, 1967); and Michael F. Holt, "The Election of 1840, Voter Mobilisation, and the Emergence of the Second American Party System: A Reappraisal of Jacksonian Voting Behavior," in his Political Parties and American Political Development from the Age of Jackson to the Age of Lincoln (Baton Rouge: Louisiana State University Press, 1991), 151–91.

[4] The James G. Batterson Papers in the Connecticut Historical Society contain his correspondence on all these matters. See, for example, Henry J. Raymond to James G. Batterson, undated [Oct. 1864]; H. H. Starkweather to Batterson, October 27, 1864; J. M. Sperry to Batterson, October 20, 1864; William Buckingham to Batterson, October 10; D. N. Cooley to Batterson, October 10, 1864.

[5] Fragment of a speech, undated, Batterson Papers.

carried the election with the aid of "Wide Awake" marching clubs, they now did so with the aid of real soldiers fighting a real, and very bloody, war. Here was a deeply committed party organizer railing against the destructive, treacherous, partisanship of his opponents. Just as he and his fellow Republicans advocated fighting the rebels until a "just peace" was achieved, he also believed in crushing the political opposition at home, so that partisanship would not bedevil the Union war effort. As Batterson's remarks indicate, Republicans' anxiety about the ability of their opponents to use the political process to wreck the war effort created the most polarized and unstable political strife since the 1790s. It was in this overwrought context, with sincerely meant accusations of treason and tyranny a staple of political battle and with huge questions about the future character of their republic at stake, that northerners encountered the arguments and engaged in public debate about the war.

The wartime experience of northerners illuminates the limits of partisanship as a means of generating popular political participation; a deepened popular engagement in politics was accompanied, as Batterson's attitude indicates, by an upsurge of antiparty sentiment. As McKitrick recognized, the theater of elections and the functioning of political parties are integral to an understanding of how popular support for the war effort was generated and maintained. But the relationship between party politics and the heightened civic engagement generated by the crisis was more contested and ambiguous than McKitrick allowed.

When mid-nineteenth-century Americans referred to "politics," they almost always narrowly used the term to describe the system by which parties won control of government through elections. Although the boundaries were not always clear, most people recognized that there were public institutions and activities outside the realm of partisanship. There were high-minded collective efforts for the public good, often of a charitable kind, led by middle-class civic leaders, which consciously tried to make themselves distinct from the "grubbiness" of party politics. Town meetings, which were infrequent but important features of local government in New England, were theoretically nonpartisan as well. So too were community celebrations such as the Fourth of July, where readings of George Washington's "Farewell Address," in which he warned of the curse of faction, often took center stage.

At the start of the war this pattern of locally based, nonpartisan civic activism briefly appeared to be the most appropriate model for popular participation, revealing the underlying tension between a partisan political culture and the continuing power of republicanism. Lincoln's call for volunteers was met with an overwhelming and spontaneous public response that was channeled by civic leaders and local businessmen who formed regiments and equipped the men, initially at their own expense. It was common for town meetings to be held in 1861 in order to coordinate a community's response to a crisis, and every effort was made to distance these gatherings from any "taint of partisanship."[6] However, the war gradually prompted a drive for greater centralization of everything from the recruitment of soldiers to the diffusion of political propaganda. The result was a complex, two-way relationship between local communities and national organizational efforts. In his survey of the northern home front, Matthew Gallman has described what he calls a "national war fought by local communities."[7] The massive expansion of governmental authority in a culture that was not prepared, at least initially, for big bureaucratic organization compounded this lack of clarity about pri-

---

[6] See, for example, Concord (N.H.) *Monitor,* May 23, 1861. On public meetings, see Glenn Altschuler and Stuart Blumin, *Rude Republic: Americans and Their Politics in the Nineteenth Century* (Princeton: Princeton University Press, 2000), 172.

[7] J. Matthew Gallman, *The North Fights the Civil War: The Home Front* (Chicago: Ivan R. Dee, 1994), 188. There are a number of excellent community studies that cover the war years. See Michael Frisch, *Town into City: Springfield, Massachusetts, and the Meaning of Community, 1840–1880* (Cambridge, Mass.: Harvard University Press, 1972); Stuart Blumin, *The Urban Threshold: Growth and Change in a Nineteenth-Century American Community* (Chicago: University of Chicago Press, 1976); Don Harrison Doyle, *The Social Order of a Frontier Community: Jacksonville, Illinois, 1825–1870* (Urbana: University of Illinois Press, 1978); John Mack Faragher, *Sugar Creek: Life on the Illinois Prairie* (New Haven, Conn.: Yale University Press, 1986); Grace Palladino, *Another Civil War: Labor, Capital, and the State in the Anthracite Regions of Pennsylvania, 1840–68* (Urbana: University of Illinois Press, 1990); Thomas R. Kemp, "Community and War: The Civil War Experience of Two New Hampshire Towns," in *Toward a Social History of the American Civil War: Exploratory Essays,* ed. Maris A. Vinovskis (Cambridge: Cambridge University Press, 1990), 31–77. A number of studies have recently explored the role of the big northern cities in the conflict. See Thomas H. O'Connor, *Civil War Boston: Home Front and Battlefield* (Boston: Northeastern University Press, 1997); J. Matthew Gallman, *Mastering Wartime: A Social History of Philadelphia during the Civil War* (Cambridge: Cambridge University Press, 1990); Ernest A. McKay, *The Civil War and New York City* (Syracuse, N.Y.: Syracuse University Press, 1990); and Iver Bernstein, *The New York City Draft Riots: Their Significance for American Society and Politics in the Age of the Civil War* (New York: Oxford University Press, 1990).

vate and public functions, as individual citizens and private organizations set about fulfilling public roles such as recruiting for the army and organizing aid to soldiers. This confusion of public and private had immediate implications for politics because of the concurrent lack of certainty about what was political and what was nonpolitical.

In this context participation in church work, attending lyceums, and even teaching in schools assumed an increased political significance. In their study of political engagement in nineteenth-century America, Glenn C. Altschuler and Stuart M. Blumin quote a wartime resolution of the Iowa teachers association proclaiming that certification should be revoked from "all persons who show, by act, or word, sympathy with the designs of rebels and traitors." Such commitments could have political consequences, including a backlash from "Copperheads": the same authors report an incident where a Democratic schoolmaster suspended "several little girls" who had left school to help their mothers at an Iowa Sanitary Commission fair.[8] Celebrations of the Fourth of July were politicized as well. Many communities reported that separate partisan celebrations had been held for the first time that anyone could remember, even during the most turbulent days of the Jackson administration.[9]

Politics became intertwined with war work. The United States Sanitary Commission (USSC) was an organization set up by a group of elite Republican men in New York to coordinate the voluntary war work of northern women. Seeking to capitalize on what, in the dominant gender ideology of the time, was understood to be the moral authority and disinterested patriotism of women, the USSC was a determinedly nonpartisan body, despite the political roles of its directors. In her study of women's war work, Jeanie Attie has argued that "while offering a way of expressing commitment to the Union cause, it [the USSC] also allowed national issues to intervene in community life with a new forcefulness."[10] Women were regarded by their friends and neighbors as making political statements when they decided to work—or not—for a Soldiers' Aid association.

---

[8] Altschuler and Blumin, *Rude Republic*, 167.

[9] See, for instance, the contrasting reports on Fourth of July celebrations in the *Daily Illinois State Register* and the *Illinois State Journal* (both of Springfield, Illinois), July 5, 1864.

[10] Jeanie Attie, *Patriotic Toil: Northern Women in the American Civil War* (Ithaca, N.Y.: Cornell University Press, 1998), 139.

The most obvious wartime institution that broadened the bounds of political life for ordinary northerners was the mass citizen army. Being part of the army meant being surrounded by politics; it created a forum for political action that had not previously existed. One Illinois regiment exercised its collective political muscle by passing a resolution that "all C[ommanding] officers who do not endorse the president's proclamation, and who will not to the utmost of their ability endorse and sustain the administration in its efforts to crush the rebellion, be politely requested to go home and let better men fill their place."[11] In another regiment a Democratic soldier reported that his company had been compelled to vote for Lincoln. When the men were in rank, he reported, there was an order that all who wished to vote for McClellan should take a step back and "all those who favor the re-election of Lincoln will stand fast."[12] The allegorical quality of this anecdote does not detract from its significance: enlisted men were deemed to be taking part in a political as well as a patriotic undertaking. Indeed, the distinction between those two concepts was barely recognized.

The government was also able to use its command of the army to political effect even well behind the lines. Assistant Secretary of War Charles Dana later recalled that "all the power and influence of the War Department, then something enormous from the vast expenditure and extensive relations of the war, was employed to secure the re-election of Mr. Lincoln."[13] The Republican party's control of the apparatus of state governments over most of the North pushed up their majorities among Union troops in many ways. In Connecticut, for example, a state that had passed a constitutional amendment to allow soldier voting, local Union party officials were quite open about the fact that they exercised partisan discretion when drawing up lists of registered soldiers.[14] During 1864 Union party leaders made clear

---

[11] Charles Pearce to Father, March 15, 1863 (GLC 00066.115), Gilder Lehrman Collection, on deposit at the Pierpont Morgan Library, New York, N.Y.

[12] "Letter from a soldier," printed in the *Daily Illinois State Register*, September 30, 1864.

[13] Charles A. Dana, *Recollections of the Civil War: With Leaders in Washington and in the Field in the Sixties* (New York: D. Appleton and Company, 1898), 261.

[14] Rufus Griswold to James G. Batterson, October 27, 1864, Batterson Papers. For a thorough discussion of the problem of soldier voting, see Samuel T. McSeveney, "Re-electing Lincoln: The Union Party Campaign and the Military Vote in Connecticut," *Civil War History* 32 (June 1986): 139–58; and Adam I. P. Smith, "The Elec-

to immigrants that if they sought to become naturalized they would be drafted.[15] For the first time ever federal soldiers were highly visible on the streets of New York on Election Day 1864. Troops were also deployed in Baltimore during the presidential campaign, and local Democrats bitterly blamed the visible military presence on the five-to-one margin in Lincoln's favor. The reach of the government had been very limited in the antebellum period. Now war expanded the power of the federal government and so increased the ways in which the authorities could be a factor in the electoral process.

As in any war, the churches also played a crucial political role. Touching almost every community in the North, the northern Protestant churches rallied in support of the government in 1861, and, like the rest of the country, their patriotic role became increasingly politicized as the parties polarized over the meaning and future direction of the war. Protestant churches had the manpower, the money, and the buildings to host political meetings and to publish and distribute campaign literature. The leadership of ministers in the "crusade" to reelect Lincoln gave a powerful moral momentum to the Union party campaign. Throughout the war churchmen were in the vanguard of the movement to identify opposition to the administration with treason.[16] At the outset of the 1864 campaign, the most widely read Christian weekly newspaper, Henry Ward Beecher's *Independent,* urged ministers to "take fit and early opportunity to make known the Christian duties of a citizen in a crisis such as this."[17] The Christian duty was to vote for Lincoln, and to use the influence of the churches to further that Godly and patriotic end. Many ministers—especially Presbyterians and Congregationalists—took heed of the *Independent*'s exhortation and became heavily involved in the campaign. Po-

---

tion of 1864: Party Politics and Political Mobilisation during the American Civil War" (Ph.D. diss., Cambridge University, 1999), 227–45.

[15] H. H. Starkweather to Batterson, October 27, 1864, Batterson Papers; *New York Tribune,* July 28, 1864; Ella Lonn, *Foreigners in the Union Army and Navy* (Baton Rouge: Louisiana State University Press, 1951), 331–32.

[16] James H. Moorhead, *American Apocalypse: Yankee Protestants and the American Civil War* (New Haven, Conn.: Yale University Press), 152; *Appleton's Annual Cyclopaedia and Register of Important Events . . . for 1864* (New York: D. Appleton and Company, 1865), 680–84.

[17] *Independent,* editorial reprinted in a broadside published by the New England Loyal Publication Society, Houghton Library, Harvard University.

litical sermons were frequently printed and circulated, just as Sunday services became a distribution outlet for pro-Lincoln broadsides.[18]

The role played by the churches is the most striking example of the blurring of the boundaries between politics and other spheres of civic activity. It is evident that the partisan support for Lincoln from the churches was driven not by political partisanship as that term was traditionally understood.[19] "It is not the triumph of Abraham Lincoln we celebrate," one minister told his congregation after the election, "nor the victory of any political party; it is the predominance of patriotism, and the conquest of the grandest ideas which ever inspired a nation."[20]

"Politics never much interested me before . . . but they seem to matter now," wrote Mattie Blanchard of Foster, Connecticut, in 1863, echoing the sentiments of many other letter writers and diarists.[21] Although their voices were seldom heard in public, women had been highly visible in antebellum politics at parades and meetings, and the absence of husbands and sons increased opportunities for women to engage in political life. Blanchard wrote to her husband about her participation in town meetings and concluded, "they ought to let the soldiers wives vote while they are gone."[22] Many women wrote extensively about politics to their men in the army.[23] Typical of many similar comments was the woman who defended her right to disagree with her cousin in the army: "Henry don't be offended by

---

[18] An example of a sermon that was reproduced by the Union League is the Rev. Samuel T. Spear, *Our Country and Its Cause. A Discourse Preached October 2nd, 1864, in the South Presbyterian Church, of Brooklyn* (New York: Union Steam Presses, 1864). Sermons published by and distributed by other loyal organizations included Rev. R. D. Hitchcock, *Thanksgiving for Victories. Discourse by Rev. R. D. Hitchcock* (New York: W. E. Whiting, 1864).

[19] Gilbert Haven, *National Sermons* (Boston: Lee and Shepard, 1869), 481–82; Moorhead, *American Apocalypse,* 157.

[20] Rev. William S. Apsey, *Causes for National Thanksgiving: A Discourse Delivered in the First Baptist Church, Bennington, November 24th, 1864, by the Rev. Wm. S. Apsey, Pastor of the Church* (n.p., [1864]).

[21] Mattie Blanchard to Caleb Blanchard, March 26, 1863, in Nina Silber and Mary Beth Sievens, eds., *Yankee Correspondence: Civil War Letters between New England Soldiers and the Home Front* (Charlottesville: University Press of Virginia, 1996), 115.

[22] Ibid.

[23] See, for example, James R. Kelly correspondence (GLC 4197) in the Gilder Lehrman Collection.

what I have written. I have a right to my own opinion the same as you."[24] For most women political awareness was derived from their own experience of war work and of the drastic changes in their lives when their men were away in the army. Suddenly political decisions intruded into domestic concerns.

A heightened political consciousness did not necessarily reinforce traditional patterns of political engagement. Indeed, there is no evidence that the war increased participation at purely partisan events such as nominating conventions. The rituals of election time attracted the same mixture of humbug, theater, passion, and display that they always had. More money was spent producing more campaign literature than in any previous election, and, at least according to politicians and the political press, popular enthusiasm was immense.[25] "Night and Day, without cessation," recalled Abram J. Dittenhoefer, a pro-Lincoln campaigner, "young men like myself, in halls, upon

---

[24] Quoted in Altschuler and Blumin, *Rude Republic,* 162.

[25] As early as mid-September Elihu B. Washburne, chairman of the Union Congressional Committee, was "sending out from fifty to a hundred thousand documents a day"; Washburne to E. B. Warner, September 15, 1864, in Warner Papers, Illinois Historical Survey, Urbana, Illinois, quoted in James G. Randall and Richard N. Current, *Lincoln the President: The Last Full Measure,* reprint ed. (Urbana: University of Illinois Press, 1991), 239. The Secretary of the Union League of Philadelphia rhapsodized that "there is scarcely a homestead so retired into which one or more of our documents have not found a way of entrance, to the enlightenment of its secluded inmates"; Union League of Philadelphia, *Second Annual Report of the Board of Directors* (Philadelphia: The League, 1864), 6. Senator James Harlan, the chairman of the Union Congressional Committee, thought that his committee alone had "circulated among the reading masses over six millions of documents"; James Harlan to Elihu B. Washburne, November 19, 1864, Elihu B. Washburne Papers, Library of Congress, Washington, D.C. This seems highly plausible given the scale of the congressional committee's activities. The Union League of Philadelphia, with fewer resources and a policy of concentrating its efforts only in Pennsylvania, still managed to produce 1,044,904 copies of various pamphlets, in both English and German, according to its annual report; Union League of Philadelphia, *Second Annual Report of the Board of Directors,* 6. The Loyal Publication Society distributed 470,000 documents in 1864; Loyal Publication Society of New York, *Proceedings at the Second Anniversary Meeting of the Loyal Publication Society, February 11, 1865, with the annual reports, prepared by order of the society, by the secretary* [J. A. Stevens] (New York: Loyal Publication Society, 1865). The National Union Executive Committee in New York published over twenty different pamphlets and several dozen broadsides, the total numbers for which can be estimated to have run to over two million. Figures for the various organizations distributing pamphlets in the West, from Chicago and Cincinnati, are harder to establish, and although much less material would have been produced there, a sizeable additional contribution to the total is likely.

street corners, and from cart-tails, were haranguing, pleading, ser-
monising, orating, arguing, extolling our cause and our candidate,
and denouncing our opponents. A deal of oratory, elocution, rhetoric,
declamation, and eloquence was hurled into the troubled air by
speakers on both sides."[26] It should be noted that nothing in this
passage indicates the response of the public to this barrage of politics,
a point that emphasizes the complexity of understanding how much
nineteenth-century Americans knew or cared about politics—even in
wartime. It is certainly dangerous to accept at face value politicians'
assessments of the enthusiasm and commitment of the electorate.
High turnouts at election time were maintained during the Civil War,
and party newspapers continued to make extravagant claims about
the success of their own parades and public meetings. Partisan newspapers have long been a staple source for political historians, and so
it is unsurprising that so many of them see high turnout rates as
indicative of a deeply partisan public culture in which everyone knew
which "side" they were on and acted accordingly in the public
sphere.[27] Evidence that supports this interpretation of the depth of
popular partisanship is the way in which party leaders always knew,
to a remarkable degree, precisely who was going to vote for whom in
advance of an election. For example, James Batterson wrote to every
town committee in Connecticut in early October asking them to give
him an assessment of the political situation in their area. A typical
reply read: "We have just completed the canvass of our town [New
Fairfield]. The vote will be about as follows: Copperhead, 114; Union
89; Doubtful, *none*. . . . [I]f we can make the figures any more favorable on election day we shall do so, but they will not vary *much* if any
from the above."[28]

It was common for a small number of "doubtful" voters to be recorded, but rarely more than about 5 percent of the total. In any case,
"doubtful" usually seems to have meant uncertain about whether to
vote at all.[29] Overall, the canvass returns Batterson received (about

---

[26] Abram J. Dittenhoeffer, *How We Elected Lincoln* (New York, Harper & Brothers, 1916), 87–88.

[27] See especially Joel Silbey, *The American Political Nation, 1838–1893* (Stanford,
Calif.: Stanford University Press, 1991).

[28] T. D. Rogers (Chairman of the Union Party town committee of Columbia,
Conn.) to James G. Batterson, October 28, 1864, Batterson Papers.

[29] Party organizers sometimes made clear that there were sections of the community that were not expected to vote. For example, John Law of Cheshire County,

ten days before election day) were an accurate prediction of the vote to within 3 percent (although this was less than the margin of Union victory in November, and so the result remained in doubt until all the ballots were counted).[30] This seems to suggest that most voters were open and reliable in their political loyalties. Furthermore, the capacity of the voters for serious and sustained argument can be deduced from the considerable sums of money that political organizers like Batterson spent on publishing long—and often very long-winded—pamphlets and reprinted speeches. There was unquestionably an appetite for political talk from many citizens.[31] Effective speakers could hold an audience for two hours or more—and this in spite of the fact that one town committee in Connecticut defined a "good speaker" as one who "cracked no jokes."[32]

The strenuous nature of electioneering efforts may, however, suggest a rather ambiguous relationship between the strength of party organization and the depth of popular political engagement. Batterson's local party organizers reported openness about political affiliation but not necessarily an informed electorate. During the war party newspapers always made extravagant claims about the spontaneity of their rallies, even while they exhorted party activists to work tirelessly for the cause. The republican ideal of popularly mandated government ensured that this rhetoric was an essential part of any mid-nineteenth-century election. Yet party organizers, even in as apparently as crucial an election as that of 1864, often found that their efforts met with dispiriting indifference. "Our village sadly needs stirring up by an eloquent convincing speaker," wrote one.[33] Another wrote an irritable letter to Batterson remarking, "I have seen today a gentleman who has just been spending a few days in Hartford and the only flags he saw were two for [Lincoln's Democratic opponent]

Connecticut, wrote to Batterson explaining that "most of the doubtful are a bad set and the best we can hope is that they will not vote"; John Law to James G. Batterson, October 28, 1864, Batterson Papers.

[30] Calculations based on a comparison of the canvass returns in the Batterson Papers with the detailed breakdown of the vote given in the *Hartford Times*, November 10, 1864.

[31] See, for instance, the enthusiastic first-hand report about a speaker meeting in Bridgeport, Connecticut, in J. V. Smith to James G. Batterson, October 8, 1864, Batterson Papers.

[32] James M. Henderson to James G. Batterson, October 29, 1864, Batterson Papers.

[33] Frank Blair to James G. Batterson, September 27, 1864, Batterson Papers.

George B. McClellan. I think unless our people *wake up* they will find themselves disappointed next November."[34] During the crucial 1863 gubernatorial election in Ohio, which pitted the arch-Copperhead Clement L. Vallandigham against War Democrat John Brough, the correspondent of the London *Times* attended a Union party mass meeting and discovered that more than just enthusiasm for "the cause" had attracted people:

> To eat, drink and be merry was the great business of the political meeting. Here and there, indeed, in a corner under a canopy of some huge tree, Mr Somebody from Indiana, or Mr Nobody from Illinois, stumped away for very life, with a cluster of listless loafers around his extempore platform, pretending to listen, cheering occasionally, jeering more frequently; all this in a din of discordant music, the racking fire of great and small guns, and the shrill cries of apple women and vendors of fire-water. For the rest there were children squalling, young people flirting, angry men swearing, drunken men reeling—all the varieties of a swarming, bustling crowd.[35]

This was a rather jaded, if not jaundiced, perspective, but it is an important counterbalance to the tales of enthused citizens to be found in party newspapers. As Altschuler and Blumin have recently argued, the geography of small towns and villages that characterized the United States in the 1860s may be the key to the success of party managers in mobilizing voters rather than especially intense political commitment. The party committees in each township with whom James Batterson corresponded were "responsible" for as few as two hundred eligible voters. For example, there were at least nine active Unionists in Prospect, Connecticut, a town with only 124 eligible voters, 68 of whom were considered likely to vote Union, and seven of whom were "doubtful."[36] The ratio of enthusiastic Union party worker to hapless likely Union voter would have been only one to seven. In such circumstances the visibility of each man within his community meant that, as Altschuler and Blumin point out, it might well have been "more bothersome not to vote than to have voted."[37]

---

[34] George Leavens to James G. Batterson, September 30, 1864, Batterson Papers.

[35] *The Times* (London), October 23, 1863, quoted in George Winston Smith and Charles Judah, *Life in the North during the Civil War: A Source History* (Albuquerque: University of New Mexico Press, 1966), 112–13.

[36] C. S. Tyler to James G. Batterson, October 28, 1864, Batterson Papers.

[37] Altschuler and Blumin, *Rude Republic*, 71.

Furthermore, leading figures in each community were clearly important in determining the outcome of an election, a fact recognized
by party organizers. For instance, a young Union party organizer in
Westford, Connecticut, wrote to Batterson blaming the likely "Copperhead" majority on the effect of the unpopular military draft,
which, he said, had "made its ravages among our Republicans, turning 2 or 3 of our leading men—men of considerable influence in
Town."[38]

Political energies were certainly not always orchestrated by parties.
Tensions were brought to the surface by election campaigns that revealed deep divides within communities. Often this resulted in violence, or what newspapers would often refer to as "rowdyism." A
typical incident occurred in the Boston area in October 1864 when a
McClellan "caravan" left Marblehead by train en route for Lynn. The
Boston Post, the leading Democratic journal in the area, reported
that the train had been "stoned" as it left the station. After it had
arrived in Lynn, "all terms of insults to be found in the blackguard's
vocabulary were applied to the Democrats in the procession, followed by stones and other dangerous missiles cast at the men, seriously injuring citizens and destroying the emblem they wore."
According to the *Post,* which insisted that the Republican party was
to blame, hundreds of men were involved in this attack. Even the
pro-Lincoln press in Boston reported that a severe disturbance had
occurred in Lynn that night, although it spared readers the political
details.[39] On another occasion three people were killed in Cincinnati
by "roughs" who attacked a torchlight procession of Lincoln supporters after a mass rally at which Secretary of the Treasury Salmon P.
Chase had spoken.[40] The experience of T. W. Bergley, one of the
several hundred accredited speakers sent out by the Union Party
Congressional Committee during the presidential election of 1864,
reveals the rough partisanship that could be embedded in, and sanctioned by, collective community values. Stump speaking in Demo-
cratic-dominated southern Indiana, Bergley soon felt as if he had
wandered deep into rebel country. His speech in Huntingburg was

---

[38] C. L. Dean to James G. Batterson, September 26, 1864, Batterson Papers.

[39] *Boston Post,* October 11 and October 25, 1864. This incident is described in
O'Connor, *Civil War Boston,* 213–14.

[40] *Chicago Tribune,* September 28, 1864; *Cincinnati Daily Enquirer,* September
28, 1864.

disrupted by what he called "roughs," many of whom, he reported, were "openly shout[ing] for Jeff Davis." Bergley's right leg was, as he put it, "somewhat damaged" in a fight outside the tavern where he was staying. And the following day he was violently attacked "by a fellow called 'Mike Wotcher'" and lost the use of his left eye. When he arrived in Holland, Indiana, "a number of Democrats were assembled to prevent me speaking [and] one of the worst of them 'Byron Spratly' told me 'I will kill you and any man that speaks for Lincoln.'" One-eyed and limping, Bergley valiantly continued into more sympathetic parts of the state, simply remarking of his treatment, "poor deluded fellows!"[41]

These scenes were part of a long tradition of violence surrounding election campaigns. Still, the war seems to have emboldened and even legitimized these acts of naked intimidation. Altschuler and Blumin's analysis of disputed election returns concluded that at no other time was there "such clear evidence of voters speaking out on substantive—if crude and simple—terms about what they and their parties stood for."[42] War clarified issues, identities, and enemies.

The army provided an important means of politicizing the previously unpolitical citizens in various ways: pressure from above, discussion in camps, and, most of all, the fact of their being there—hundreds of thousands of farmers and mechanics and small businessmen in arms to maintain the Union. Joseph Allen Frank has estimated that about 25 percent of northern Civil War soldiers were highly politically aware, judged by their knowledge, scope of interest, and sense of political agency. "These were the true believers," Frank has written, "the most articulate and most important in motivating their fellow citizen-soldiers."[43]

To some extent this mobilization of popular political energies was clearly a reflection of a war-induced patriotism that was separable from politics. Civil War soldiers' letters frequently refer in a generalized way to patriotic feelings but much less often to specific political questions. Voting for Lincoln was a highly important symbol of the close relationship of the political and the military campaigns. Many soldiers concurred with the sentiments of an infantryman from Con-

---

[41] T. W. Bergley to Elihu B. Washburne, October 3, 1864, Washburne Papers.

[42] Altschuler and Blumin, *Rude Republic*, 177.

[43] Joseph Allen Frank, *With Ballot and Bayonet: The Political Socialization of American Civil War Soldiers* (Athens: University of Georgia Press, 1998), 39.

necticut who declared that he felt as if he was using the bayonet against the enemy on the field and the ballot against the traitors in the rear.[44] After casting his ballot for Lincoln, another soldier wrote: "The day of the greatest battle & I believe the greatest victory . . . has been fought and I know won today."[45]

Political participation was an important manifestation of the status of the soldier as citizen, something that was affirmed by the field voting laws passed by several states in time for the 1864 election. Many soldiers regarded elections as solemn political festivals that affirmed republican government, a faith illustrated by the many occasions, recorded in soldiers' letters and diaries (and later in newspaper reports), on which voting took place, even when it was clear that it could have no impact on who was elected. Prisoners of war held in Confederate jails rigged up polling booths on Election Day and solemnly cast their ballots. Soldiers reported how keenly their units had supported the cause by voting for Lincoln with as much zeal as if reporting the outcome of a battle.[46]

Nevertheless, the army was not a mirror of the home-front political experience. Even if they kept up with the issues through newspapers, soldiers were detached from the electoral seasons that punctuated civilian life. In the correspondence between soldiers and their families, it is common to find a great deal more partisan passion from wives than from their more weary and cynical husbands in the field. For example, George W. Tillotson of the 89th New York Volunteers, who had voted for Lincoln in 1860, responded wryly to his wife's remark that he would "grind his teeth" if he heard the "rebel democrats" back home: "I'll bet anything that I can hear full as plain and treasonable talk from the soldiers every day and that not from one or to [sic] only, but from hundreds, and thousands."[47]

These variable levels of engagement in politics and the ways in which the war affected them are illustrated by the experience of Elizabeth A. Livermore. Unmarried and in her forties when war broke

[44] Frey to [illegible], [1864], Augustus Beardsley Frey Letters, Illinois State Historical Society, Springfield.

[45] William H. Pittenger diary, November 8, 1864, Ohio Historical Society, quoted in Frank, *With Ballot and Bayonet*, 91.

[46] John W. Northrop Diary of Prison Life (transcript), [November] 16, 1864, Western Reserve Historical Society, quoted in Frank, *With Ballot and Bayonet*, 93.

[47] George W. Tillotson to Elizabeth Tillotson, February 27, 1863, Tillotson Correspondence, (GLC 4558), Gilder Lehrman Collection.

out, Livermore lived with her elderly mother in Milford, New Hampshire. She had a long-standing interest in politics and had been to Republican party rallies since 1856 when she had keenly supported John C. Frémont's presidential campaign (she later recalled that she had been "certain he would be elected!"). Her wartime diaries record the approach of upcoming elections with some anxiety: "I wish I could know *now* what is to be the result of the election," she wrote of a race for state governor three weeks before it took place. At the start of the war Livermore helped to organize her town's effort to supply New Hampshire troops with clothes and medical supplies. Frequent letters from her nephew in the Army of the Potomac gave a personal edge both to her work for the Sanitary Commission and to her hope that Lincoln would be reelected and that "copperheads would be soundly beaten" everywhere. A week before the 1864 election, she went with "ever so many people" to nearby Amherst, New Hampshire, to hear Vice President Hannibal Hamlin speak. It was a "beautiful day" and was clearly a great public occasion, but Livermore was most impressed by the "solemnity" and "decisiveness" of the crowd. "Everywhere," she wrote, "there is the greatest hope that Lincoln will be elected." She herself was much less confident, though, and as she listened to the speeches she was "thinking much" of her nephew. In her earnest commitment to the Union cause and her clear linkage of Lincoln's reelection with her familial concern for her relatives in the army, Livermore seemed to exemplify the idealized role that women played in the Republican party campaign.

On Election Day itself, however, she was acutely aware of her own impotence: "It seems to me that men must think themselves monarchs of a great power today—almost kings in their powers and prerogatives," she wrote. Meanwhile she was sharply reminded of the nature of her own proscribed role by the arrival of a note from the Sanitary Commission: "The pickles were all right," she was assured. Livermore spent the morning and early part of the afternoon in the town, shopping and talking to her neighbors. Despite her own concern about the significance of the day, the talk of the town was by no means all politics. Family and local gossip clearly concerned most of the people she met. "Old Mr. Clark" told Livermore that "it was his most solemn duty to vote for Abraham Lincoln for President," but she notes that he did not bother to do so. He had "been sick," Livermore conceded, but it wasn't stopping him visiting "Aunt Sarah in

Concord" the following day. Most eligible voters did manage to cast a ballot, of course, but perhaps the gap between Mr. Clark's professed expression of determination and his actual level of commitment was not so unusual. Livermore's aging and infirm mother, meanwhile, was stuck at home, her face pressed to the window, "watching all that was going on with great consternation."[48]

Precisely because this was an exceptional time, there was a great deal of public interest in the issues, but it does not mean that the rough or ritualized aspects of electioneering created a forum for rational-critical discourse. The war may well have seen a politicization of many aspects of everyday life, but the terse diary entry for November 8, 1864, of Nathan Abbott, a New Hampshire farmer, puts politics in its place: "Had 4½ bushels of corn ground at the mill—attended our Ward meeting to vote for President and Vice President—finished spreading the manure."[49]

If the war complicated the relationship between politics and the rest of the public sphere, and if this expansion of politics served to intensify the engagement of both individuals and whole communities in political matters, then where did that leave the role of the institutions that had shaped and defined the American political nation for the past generation? How did the wartime expansion of popular engagement in politics relate to political parties, both as mechanisms for generating political engagement and as objects of loyalty?

The conventional picture of the mid-nineteenth-century political nation explains high levels of participation in politics in terms that sometimes conflate popular partisanship with strong party organization. The Civil War presents a rather more complex story: there was increased engagement and evidence of widespread active discussion about politics; there were also closely fought election campaigns. But by transcending the boundaries of the traditional political sphere, the wartime experience of northerners intensified political engagement in a way that did not automatically reinforce traditional partisanship.

War seemed to demonstrate the failure of party politics. Newspapers on both sides frequently pointed out partisanship had brought

[48] Elizabeth Livermore Diaries, New Hampshire Historical Society, Concord, entries for March 11, 1862, November 1, 1864, November 7, 1864, November 8, 1864, November 9, 1864.

[49] Nathan Kilbourn Abbot diaries, vol. 7, entry for November 8, 1864, New Hampshire Historical Society.

the nation to this state of "Armageddon."[50] A soldier in an Illinois regiment was sure that "this partyism . . . is sapping the north[.] The people are very slow to learn that there are only loyal men and traitors[;] it seems to me it will be time enough to cavil about politics when our government is secure, and not before."[51] Reflecting this feeling, the strategies used by partisans to win over "doubtful" voters suggested the weakness of partisan appeals. Especially in places where there was a strong Democratic organization, Unionist organizers were anxious not to appear too partisan. The Union party town committee of Collinsville, Connecticut, wrote angrily to James Batterson, complaining that a speaker he had sent them had done them "positive harm" by giving a speech consisting of nothing but "abuse of McClellan and the Copperheads and that of the smallest kind."[52]

In "normal" circumstances partisanship reduced the need for a constant engagement with the issues. Parties provided a shorthand means of comprehending political problems. As Altschuler and Blumin have argued, they were "instrumental to most Americans who wanted to perform, but not become absorbed in, their duties as citizens."[53] In wartime citizens were often actively performing public duties (as soldiers and on the home front) and engaging with the government in a way they had not before. Parties therefore lost their function as the crucial mediating channel between the citizen and the government.

Cynicism about "wire-pullers" and the political class in general was hardly new. Antipartyism was a continual counterpoint to the "hoopla" campaigns of the party-dominated nineteenth century. But the war made such rhetoric the dominant note in political discourse. An election appeal in Philadelphia spoke of politics as having become a "synonym for all that is mean and low."[54] In the same spirit the

---

[50] See, for instance, *American destiny, what shall it be, Republican or Cossack? An argument addressed to the people of the late Union, North and South* (New York: Published for the Columbian Association, 1864), 4. See also *Cincinnati Daily Enquirer,* October 11, 1861.

[51] Charles Pearce to Father, March 15, 1863 (GLC 00066.115), Gilder Lehrman Collection.

[52] The Town Committee of Collinsville to James G. Batterson, October 28, 1864, Batterson Papers.

[53] Altschuler and Blumin, *Rude Republic,* 82.

[54] *A Workingman's reasons for the re-election of Abraham Lincoln* (Philadelphia: n.p.,1864), on microfiche in the New York Public Library, New York, N.Y.

New York Herald offered a cynical analysis of the 1864 election season: "This war, which should have sobered the people and merged politics in patriotism, has had precisely the opposite effect upon politicians of all parties. Never were roorbachs so tremendous, frauds so plentiful, fabrications so numerous, delusions so popular, humbugs so transparent, and falsehoods so generally circulated."[55] In this context antipartisanship took the form of an assertion by both parties, but especially by the Republicans, that they were the embodiment of the nation, that they transcended party in their selfless devotion to the Union. The continuation of party conflict conflated the electoral struggle with the military one.

Antipartisanship appealed to republican values, to a fear of faction and a need for virtue to combat corruption: it suited the Romantic ideal of selfless sacrifice for democratic government. In the week of the 1864 presidential election, an editorial in *Harper's Weekly* warned its readers that the contest would decide "the most important question in history," whether the American republic would succumb to the fate of all previous republics and allow "party spirit" to "overpower patriotism."[56]

The Republican party emerged out of an antiparty tradition that provided its speakers with a ready-made language with which to reflect this distrust of parties. The Free Soil and Anti-Nebraska parties had rallied against the "baneful and corrupting spirit of partyism." Before the war Republicans had denounced Democrats for their "slavish devotion to party" and connected the discipline of the Democratic organization with the ability of the "slave Power aristocrats" in the South to control their lackeys in the free states.[57] In wartime Republicans (or Unionists) argued that elections were "not a party contest."[58] They referred to themselves as "stout-hearted inflexible

---

[55] *New York Herald*, October 14, 1864.

[56] *Harper's Weekly*, November 12, 1864.

[57] Michael Holt, *The Political Crisis of the 1850s* (New York: John Wiley & Sons, 1978), 163–69, 175–76. In chapter 11 of *The American Political Nation*, Joel Silbey focuses on those who dissented from the political norms he describes. However, his concern is with those he describes as "outsiders," challengers to two-party hegemony who resorted to third-party "guerrilla" tactics. "Their schismatic behavior," he writes, "roiled the political waters but did not re-channel the mainstream of two-party politics" (197).

[58] *How Shall We End the Rebellion: Shall we coax it or crush it?* (New York: National Union Executive Committee, 1864). See, for instance, a Union party ticket from one of the most Republican states in the Union—Massachusetts—which was

men," who transcended "mere politics."[59] Their candidates, they said, had been chosen on the basis of "personal integrity, without regard to party," or because they were, in a rather graphic phrase, "fresh from the loins of the people."[60] Seeming to vindicate this electoral strategy, a private in a New York regiment told his wife, "I wouldn't vote a *republican* ticket merely because it *was* republican but I should most assuredly vote for the Union, and those that would maintain it, let the principle appear under any name whatsoever."[61]

Of course, Democrats also tried to rally support beyond their traditional supporters. One Democratic newspaper appealed for the support of "honest political opponents, who, relinquishing party ties, will unite with us."[62] For the sake of the country, urged the *Boston Post,* "whether you call yourselves Whigs, Republicans or Democrats, sink party now deeper than plummet can sound, say goodbye to bye gones . . . and elect McClellan! . . . In the name of the country vote for him!"[63] But the Union party represented a style of politics that prized antipartisanship as an end in itself, defining itself as the noble and independent arbiters of the public good, without the taint of corruption that they saw as characteristic of the Democrats. Although the Union party had all the same trappings of partisan politics as their Democratic opponents, its mode of operation was still to claim that its candidates had been chosen on the basis of "personal integrity, without regard to party," because of their "tried and tested devotion to the Union" or because they were simply "men of character."[64] Civil War politics were therefore a clash between two different approaches to the problem of political mobilization as well as over substantive ideological and political questions.

---

emblazoned with the slogan "One flag, one country, one government": Alfred Whital Stern Collection of Lincolniana, Library of Congress. Newspapers carried party tickets above their editorial columns, which provide the easiest means of surveying the slogans used. See, for instance, *Cincinnati Daily Commercial,* September 19 to November 9, 1864.

[59] M. A. Croft to Simon Cameron, August 31, 1864, Cameron Papers, Library of Congress.

[60] *New York Times,* June 18, 1864; *Cincinnati Daily Enquirer,* July 28, 1864; *Chicago Tribune,* September 2, 1864.

[61] George W. Tillotson to Elizabeth Tillotson, November 21, 1863, Tillotson Correspondence.

[62] *Cleveland Plain Dealer,* September 12, 1864.

[63] *Boston Post,* September 9, 1864.

[64] *New York Times,* June 18, 1864; *Cincinnati Daily Enquirer,* July 28, 1864; *Chicago Tribune,* September 2, 1864.

In all elections in the North between 1861 and 1864, the antiparty campaign of the Republicans was aided by a faction of the Democratic party that campaigned for Lincoln. A meeting of the War Democrats at the Cooper Union in New York on November 1, 1864, generated a great deal of press attention; the *New York Herald* described the gathering as a "political movement of greater importance than any of the ordinary *partizan* assemblages of the day."[65] Union party publicists also worked hard to persuade as many former Democratic voters as possible, especially in the swing states, that the Union party represented the best in the Democratic political tradition.[66] One ambitious Union campaign broadside stressed the antislavery achievements of Democrats in the past and argued that their natural home was with the Union party.[67] Rather than merely reinforcing preexisting party loyalties, Union propaganda was designed to persuade habitual non-Republicans with flattery and threats. This poster slogan, for instance, exploiting the Jacksonian politics of Lincoln's running mate, had the punchy sound-bite quality of a modern-day bumper sticker:

> Are you a Democrat?
> So is Andrew Johnson of Tennessee.[68]

---

[65] *New York Herald*, undated, quoted in *The Campaign for the Union*, November 5, 1864. (This was a Union party campaign newspaper published in Boston in October and November 1864. Holdings in the Boston Public Library.) Reports also appeared in, for example, *Pittsburgh Gazette*, June 9, 1864; *New York Times*, June 9, 1864; *Chicago Tribune*, June 10, 1864; *Proceedings of the Grand Meeting of the War Democracy in the Cooper Union* (New York: n.p. 1864); Hiram Walbridge, *Speech of Gen. Hiram Walbridge, delivered before the convention of the War Democracy at Cooper Institute, New York, Tuesday, November 1, 1864* (New York: n.p., 1864), Illinois State Historical Library; *Pittsburgh Gazette*, November 3, 1864.

[66] For instance, the image of Andrew Jackson was exploited by Unionists as well as by Democrats. A very powerful image distributed by administration supporters contrasted the "Democracy of 1832" with that of 1864. In one-half of the picture a fiery President Jackson imposes his physical presence upon a penitent Calhoun and other South Carolina nullifiers. The other half of the image shows Jeff Davis lording it over "Little Mac," who cravenly implores that "we should like to have Union and Peace, dear Mr. Davis, but if such is not your pleasure then please state your terms for a friendly separation"; cartoon in the Stern Collection of Lincolniana, box 4, pt. 2, no. 30, Prints and Broadsides Collection, Library of Congress.

[67] "Who are the Real Democrats?" address of the Democratic [Loyal] League (n.p., n.d.), Collection of Pamphlets, Election of 1864, Houghton Library, Harvard University. See also "The Real Chicago Platform, as expounded by the Democratic Orators at Chicago," Collection of Broadsides, Houghton Library, Harvard University.

[68] *The Campaign for the Union*, November 2, 1864.

Antipartisanship was a political tool, not merely a description of an attitude. The tension between the need to maintain a national patriotic consensus behind the war effort and the continuation of two-party politics created deep suspicions and fears on each side, which reinforced the tendency to deny the legitimacy of the opposition implicit in the Republican name change. In other words, antipartisanship was intensified by fierce partisan conflict. To borrow a suggestive phrase from David Waldstreicher's book on the rites of nationalism in the early republic, the practice of politics during the Civil War can be aptly described as "partisan antipartisanship."[69] The political triumph of the Republican (or Union) party during the war is in part the story of the successful manipulation of this antiparty tradition. Wartime political culture reveals that partisanship and antipartisanship were not—as is often assumed—polar opposites. Instead, they were mutually dependent and reinforcing.

A massive celebration in Cleveland, Ohio, in October 1864 exemplified this mutually reinforcing connection between electoral politics and patriotic celebration. To the accompaniment of several dozen brass bands playing patriotic tunes, the marchers held aloft nonpartisan symbols such as live eagles and images of George Washington. Delegations from all over the state had created "transparencies"—illuminated canvasses—displaying patriotic slogans such as "the three P's we propose: Patriotism, Perseverance and Pluck." Companies of soldiers furloughed home from battle were showered with ribbons and feted by the crowd. A highlight of the procession was a horse-drawn wagon bearing "thirty-five beautiful young ladies, representing the States, with Columbia in the center." At the climax of the evening, rockets flew up from a dozen places at once, missiles exploded, sending up showers of golden and crimson fire, bonfires blazed, and for a time the night sky was "lit up with the most extraordinary pyrotechnic display." The crowd remained long into the early hours "lustily" singing patriotic songs.[70] This was a political meeting, designed to endorse Lincoln's bid for reelection. But no one mentioned a party, or used partisan imagery to rally people to the cause. There is clearly a fine line between the exaggerated language of election

---

[69] David Waldstreicher, *The Making of American Nationalism, 1776–1820* (Chapel Hill: University of North Carolina Press, 1997), 202.

[70] Cleveland *Herald,* October 6; *Chicago Tribune,* October 8, 1864.

campaigns and the denial of the legitimacy of the opposition. The point is that during the war partisanship and party were dirty words: one's own loyalty to a party was patriotism, one's opponents' was "mere" partisanship.

The significance of the antiparty strategy did not lie in the number of Democrats who were persuaded to support the administration (most Democrats, after all, remained loyal to their organization). In 1864 rallying support in the name of the nation and the "loyal, earnest, patriotic" public was the means by which an increasingly divisive war could be presented as a genuinely national cause. Writing about popular fetes and parades in the early republic, Waldstreicher has argued that "such rituals might have aspired to a unity beyond political division, but, because of their origins and the political needs of various groups, they did not and could not merely reflect ideological consensus."[71] Similarly, the patriotic rallies, meetings, concerts, and parades of the Civil War years were inseparable from party strategies and electoral contests.

Drawing parallels with the heroism of the revolutionary generation, the grand Union parades with their bright lights and bonfires also conveyed a sense of national purification, an image often emphasized by ministers speaking from the podiums.[72] The return home of companies of soldiers (often furloughed in order to be able to vote) was frequently the occasion for a pro-Lincoln meeting. Eight thousand of the "loyal citizens" of Douglas County, Illinois, gathered in Tuscola on September 23, 1864, to "show their appreciation of the services rendered by their boys in blue." After prayers and a musical interlude by the Tuscola Glee Club and two brass bands, the local Union party congressional candidate spoke for over an hour, castigating the Democratic party's Chicago platform, and reminding his au-

---

[71] Waldstreicher, *In the Midst of Perpetual Fetes: The Making of American Nationalism, 1776–1802* (Chapel Hill: University of North Carolina Press, 1997), 8.

[72] *Chicago Tribune,* November 4, 1864. For a discussion of the symbolic and psychological significance of party activity within a cultural context see Jean H. Baker, "The Ceremonies of Politics: Nineteenth-Century Rituals of National Affirmation," in *A Master's Due: Essays in Honor of David Donald,* ed. William J. Cooper et al. (Baton Rouge: Louisiana State University Press, 1985), 161–78; Jean H. Baker, *Affairs of Party: The Political Culture of the Northern Democrats in the Mid-Nineteenth Century* (Ithaca, N.Y.: Cornell University Press, 1983); and Daniel Walker Howe, *The Political Culture of the American Whigs* (Chicago: University of Chicago Press, 1979).

dience that "we have duties at home as imperative as those in the field." When he had finished speaking, the soldiers present marched to the front of the gathering and, to the cheers of the crowd, symbolically deposited ballots for Lincoln.[73] Through the expression of these rites of nationhood, citizens participated in partisan politics, just as in antebellum times, in acting as partisans, Democrats and Republicans had "learned to be Americans."[74]

Mattie Blanchard was right: politics did matter more in wartime. The exceptional national crisis naturally turned the minds of northern women and men on the home front to political questions, creating a genuinely engaged citizenry. In fact, the political experience of wartime northerners helps to explain how popular commitment to the war effort was maintained. Parties were important to this process in an organizational sense, being agencies through which information and opinion could be disseminated. And as many historians have observed, the patronage networks that lubricated the process of politics were greatly expanded by the war, providing the administration with a powerful means of compelling loyalty. Local, state, and national parties were linked by mutually beneficial ties of patronage. Parties also provided big public occasions at which commitment to the war effort could be demonstrated and generated. Nevertheless, the language of politics reflected voters' rejection of the concept of partisanship even while they cheered for their party's candidates. This disjunction suggests that it is misleading to describe the conflict within the North over the conduct and meaning of the war as if it were "merely" a continuation of the old party battles of the antebellum era. The institutions and rituals of partisan politics remained in place, but the wartime context altered the meanings ascribed to them by voters and political leaders alike. As the anxiety of partisan organizers like James Batterson suggests, the electoral process became an integral part of the process of putting down the rebellion, but in a conflictual rather than a consensual way. As a Union party election broadside put it, "for four summers the loyal North has been firing *bullets* at the rebellion. The time has now come to fire *ballots*."[75]

---

[73] *Chicago Tribune,* September 26, 1864.

[74] Baker, *Affairs of Party,* 101.

[75] *Worcester Palladium* [date unknown], quoted in a Union party election newspaper, *The Campaign for the Union,* November 3, 1864.

7

A Monstrous Doctrine?
Northern Women on Dependency
during the Civil War

Rachel Filene Seidman

IN APRIL 1861 a young woman in Philadelphia started a journal. Smart, articulate, and engaged in the world around her, Amanda Meshler made an interesting decision about how to organize her diary. At the top of the journal's right-hand page she inscribed the heading "Personal," and at the top of the left-hand page she wrote "War Statistics." Over the next two years Meshler recorded weekly entries on each side of the book. On the "Personal" side, she wrote of family and friends, the weather, her church attendance, and local news. Under "War Statistics," Meshler recorded news of the battles, estimates of the numbers killed and wounded, and reports of military strategy, all of which she gleaned from newspapers and her neighbors.[1]

By dividing her diary into two parts, Meshler constructed it to reflect her belief that the war existed, or at least should have existed, in a realm apart from her own personal life. Over the course of the war, however, the division in Amanda Meshler's life between "war statistics" and "personal" began to blur. Which was it when Amanda's male friends joined the army, or told her stories of the battles they had seen, or died from their wounds? Where should she record her own exposure to the sight of maimed men? Or her decision to get involved in a ladies' aid society, canvasing the neighborhood for

---

[1] Entry for July 23, 1861, Amanda L. Meshen Memorandum Book. Historical Society of Pennsylvania, Philadelphia. While her diary is recorded in the Historical Society of Pennsylvania under the name Amanda Meshen, I believe this is a misreading of the handwriting, and I read her surname as Meshler.

money and goods to send to the soldiers? Entries like these, in fact, showed up on both sides of her journal. And when, having filled up one book, she started a new journal in 1863, Amanda gave up on trying to keep the war and her personal life separate. For the rest of her wartime diary, the two were completely intertwined.

Like Amanda Meshler in 1861, historians have often assumed that narratives of the Civil War and narratives of women's lives should occupy separate pages in the history books. "The Brothers' War" has captivated generations of historians, but until recently few have paid any attention to the soldiers' sisters, mothers, wives, and daughters. Practitioners of women's history, on the other hand, eager to uncover the hidden world of women's experience, have often ignored war as too traditional a topic. The result is, like the first half of Meshler's diary, a falsely divided story.

Historians need to follow the example of the second half of Meshler's journal and integrate the narratives of the Civil War and women's lives during the mid–nineteenth century. The war is clearly one of our nation's most important political dramas, and it continues to reward historians with new insights. If we expand our definition of politics to encompass the various ways that Civil War women tried to exert influence and gain power over their lives, we gain an even more nuanced picture of American political culture.

During the Civil War northern women used their understanding of their rights to shape the debate over their place in American political culture. Women's involvement in the war effort led them to a new sense of entitlement. They sought new ways to describe what they felt the country owed them, and what they owed the country. Although some adopted the nascent language of "woman's rights," many women defined their rights very differently from more famous activists such as Lucretia Mott, Elizabeth Cady Stanton, and Susan B. Anthony.

In this essay I explore the approaches to women's role as citizens formulated by middle-class women reformers, working-class seamstresses, and a broad-based population of northern women who wrote to President Abraham Lincoln and other Union officials for the release of their sons and husbands from the army. Each of these groups grappled with the popular assumption that women were "dependent" on men. At the same time, each group asserted strikingly different interpretations of what that assumption meant for its particular relationship to the nation. Taken together, the similarities and differences between these arguments suggest how the Civil War era reshaped northern women's ideas about their position as citizens in the United States.

Historians have shown that the concept of dependency evolved over time, from a status that most white men and women shared to one that by the nineteenth century was considered proper only for women, children, slaves, and paupers. In preindustrial England, "dependency" usually referred to subordination. Since in the hierarchical social structure of the era most people were subordinate to someone else, dependency was normal. In the late eighteenth and nineteenth centuries, an age of "democratic revolutions," this assumption began to change—at least for men. As Nancy Fraser and Linda Gordon have pointed out, "the developing new concept of citizenship rested on independence; dependency was deemed antithetical to citizenship."[2] Women, the theory went, were *naturally* dependent on men for economic support and protection. This rationale enabled men to disqualify women as voters and full citizens.[3] Whereas dependency for white men became shameful, for women it was considered appropriate and even necessary. As Dru Stanley has argued, the "fundamental premise of the marriage bond" was the relationship between male protection and female dependency.[4]

In 1837 Massachusetts clergymen issued a "Pastoral Letter" denouncing the abolitionist sisters Angelina and Sarah Grimké for lecturing to "mixed audiences" of men and women. In a scathing response, Sarah Grimké outlined one of the first public challenges to the assumption that women's "dependency" constricted their role in American society.[5] The pastoral letter argued that "The appropriate duties and influence of woman are clearly stated in the New Testament. Those duties are unobtrusive and private, but the sources of *mighty power*. When the mild, *dependent*, softening influence of

---

[2] Nancy Fraser and Linda Gordon, "A Genealogy of *Dependency:* Tracing a Keyword of the U.S. Welfare State," *Signs* 19 (winter 1994): 309–36, quotation on 315.

[3] Joan Gundersen, "Independence, Citizenship, and the American Revolution," *Signs* 13 (autumn 1987): 65.

[4] Amy Dru Stanley, "Contract Rights in the Age of Emancipation" (Ph.D. diss., Yale University, 1990), 283.

[5] The Grimké sisters grew up in the South but were forced to leave because their views put their physical safety at risk. The rest of the women in this article are northern by residence.

woman upon the sternness of man's opinions, is fully exercised, society feels the effects of it in a thousand ways." Grimké replied:

> How monstrous is the doctrine that woman is to be dependent on man! Where in all the sacred scriptures is this taught? . . . The poet has sung in sickly strains the loveliness of woman's dependence upon man, and now we find it re-echoed by those who profess to teach the religion of the Bible. . . . This doctrine of dependence upon man is utterly at variance with the doctrine of the Bible. In that book I find nothing like the softness of woman, nor the sternness of man; both are equally commanded to bring forth the fruits of the Spirit—Love, meekness, gentleness.
>
> But we are told "the power of woman is in her dependence, flowing from a consciousness of that weakness which God has given her for her protection." If physical weakness is alluded to, I cheerfully concede the superiority . . . but no where does God say that he made any distinction between us as moral and intelligent beings.[6]

Grimké asserted that, contrary to the clergymen's prescriptions, women had every right, and indeed the duty, to speak publicly on controversial moral and political topics. "Men and women were CREATED EQUAL; they are both moral and accountable beings, and whatever it is right for man to do, is right for woman to do."[7]

Following Grimké, women's rights activists continued to argue that any restriction of women's legal rights based on the cultural assumption of their dependence was oppressive. The Declaration of Sentiments issued by the first national women's rights convention in Seneca Falls, New York, in 1848 outlined the myriad ways that men legally, economically, and intellectually established "an absolute tyranny over" women. Formulated in large part by Elizabeth Cady Stanton and Susan B. Anthony, the Declaration concluded that "[Man] has endeavored, in every way that he could, to destroy [woman's] confidence in her own powers, to lessen her self-respect, and to make her willing to lead a dependent and abject life." In response, it called for women's "immediate admission to all the rights and privileges which belong to them as citizens of the United States."[8]

---

[6] Sarah Grimké, "Province of Women: The Pastoral Letter," *The Liberator*, October 6, 1837, reprinted in Nancy Woloch, ed., *Early American Women: A Documentary History, 1600–1900* (New York: McGraw-Hill, 1997), 262–65.

[7] Ibid., 264.

[8] Declaration of Sentiments, Seneca Falls Convention, 1848, in Elizabeth Cady

Grimké, Stanton, and other antebellum women's rights activists trained in the abolitionist movement argued that coverture laws—laws that subsumed married women under their husband's legal identity, depriving them of the right to own property, to sign contracts, or to keep wages they earned—made married women's legal status little better than that of slaves, and they demanded legal reform to emancipate women from dependency on their husbands.

While women's rights activists decried dependency, other mid-nineteenth-century women reformers rejected this stance. They, too, connected the issue of women's dependency to the nature of women's role as American citizens, but with very different results. One of the best-known reformers in the era, Catharine Beecher, directly countered Sarah Grimké's assertion that women should participate in politics in the same ways as men. Formulated as a response to Grimké, Beecher's *Essay on Slavery and Abolitionism with Reference to the Duty of American Females* insisted that indeed women were dependent on men. But unlike the Massachusetts clergymen who had raised Grimké's ire, Beecher argued that women could still play an essentially political role. She agreed that God had assigned women to a "subordinate station," but that "it is not because it was designed that her duties or her influence should be any the less important, or all-pervading." She believed that as women they could act as mediators in the contentious politics of the democratic nation.[9]

In effect, as Kathryn Kish Sklar has written, Beecher's ideas "politicized the traditional female sphere of the home." Observing the increasingly rancorous political debates around her, Beecher asserted that "unrestrained party-spirit and ungoverned factions" threatened the survival of the nation. In her best-selling *Treatise on Domestic Economy*, Beecher argued that as democracy flourished, the social and political tensions in the country would only increase. By removing themselves from the realm of political and economic competition and accepting their subservience to men in the public sphere, women could help hold the nation together by improving and managing the

---

Stanton, Susan B. Anthony, and Matilda Joslyn Gage, eds., *The History of Woman Suffrage*, 6 vols.(New York: Fowler & Wells, 1881–1922), 1:70–73, reprinted in Woolch, ed., *Early American Women*, 265–69.

[9] Catharine Beecher, "Essay on Slavery and Abolitionism with Reference to the Duties of American Females," 98–101, quoted in Kathryn Kish Sklar, *Catharine Beecher: A Study in American Domesticity* (New York: W. W. Norton, 1976), 135.

private sphere. She insisted that "a system of laws must be established, which sustain certain relations and dependencies in social and civil life." Although not *naturally* subservient, women had to subordinate themselves to men if the country was going to be able to "go forward harmoniously."[10] By accepting dependence on men, Beecher argued, women could help save the nation from its own destructive forces.

Reformer Elizabeth Ware Packard, too, believed that women ought to be dependent on men, and, like Beecher, she put a political spin on this stance. Packard had been institutionalized against her will by her Calvinist minister husband after she insisted on teaching a Bible class addressing the new religious movements of perfectionism and spiritualism. In the 1860s she wrote a series of popular books and pamphlets seeking reform of the laws regarding insane asylums, and she took her concerns directly to several state legislatures. Legal historian Hendrik Hartog has explored how Packard argued for the "right to be a married woman." Packard did not reject the concept of dependency as Elizabeth Cady Stanton had. She saw coverture as essential to her identity and so insisted that her "moral autonomy" depended on protective men and male institutions. Instead of fighting dependency, Packard sought legal confirmation of a specifically female dependent status. But Packard also claimed the "right" to governmental intervention and protection from the men who were defined as her protectors.[11] Hartog argues that for Packard, dependency on men did not necessarily preclude a woman from claiming autonomy as a rights-holder. Packard wanted the state to ensure that men used their authority over women fairly.[12] Whereas Beecher believed that by accepting their dependency women could help protect the state, Packard argued that the state needed to protect women in their dependency.

In the decades leading up to the Civil War, then, middle-class female reformers had been debating why women were dependent on

---

[10] Catharine Beecher, *Treatise on Domestic Economy for the Use of Young Ladies at Home and at School*, 25–26, quoted in Sklar, *Catherine Beecher*, 157–58. Beecher's ideology was full of contradictions, among them her belief that teaching was important for single women partly as a way for them to avoid dependence on others. See Sklar, *Catherine Beecher*, 223.

[11] Hendrik Hartog, "Mrs. Packard on Dependency," *Yale Journal of Law and the Humanities* 1 (December 1988): 93.

[12] Ibid., 102.

men (whether it was ordained by God or imposed by men) and what that meant for women's relationship to the national state (whether "dependency" meant women should stay out of public debates or not, and whether it meant the government owed women special protection). The Civil War highlighted the issue of dependency and prompted a wider population of American women to address this thorny problem. Many of them approached the subject differently than the earlier reformers. One group who did so were working-class seamstresses in Philadelphia and other cities, who focused on the financial aspect of women's dependency. Although working-class women had protested their plight earlier in the century, the Civil War changed the economic and political context and sparked new levels of organization. In their wartime efforts sewing women, allied at times with middle-class reformers and at other times against them, challenged the very notion that women were, in fact, dependent on men at all.

The general assumption of women's dependence had long had particular ramifications in the labor market. The understanding that wives and mothers were not supposed to be a family's main breadwinner had historically justified wretchedly low pay in the few "respectable" jobs open to women. In cities such as Philadelphia the image of the haggard sewing woman had been a familiar one throughout the antebellum period. Wealthy women had focused their benevolent efforts on ameliorating the lives of seamstresses, while at the same time often reinforcing the idea that the only appropriate jobs for women were sewing or domestic work. The Ladies Depository, a benevolent organization that paid poor women for sewing at its rooms on Philadelphia's South Eleventh Street, had been in existence for twenty-eight years when the war began.[13] The Northern Association for the Relief and Employment of Poor Women, founded in 1844 and incorporated in 1856, gave "proper employment," mainly sewing and domestic service work, "and compensation therefor" to both black and white women.[14]

Middle-class observers had been made aware of sewing women's

---

[13] Ladies Depository, *Twenty-eighth Annual Report of the Board of Managers* (Philadelphia: L. R. Bailey, 1861), copy at the Library Company of Philadelphia.

[14] Northern Association of the City and County of Philadelphia for the Relief and Employment of Poor Women, *Eighteenth Annual Report* (Philadelphia: Deacon & Paterson, 1862), copy at the Library Company of Philadelphia.

desperate circumstances by the actions of the working women themselves. In 1835 five hundred women workers from the sewing and other trades had formed the Female Improvement Society for the City and County of Philadelphia. They drew up wage demands, submitted them to employers, and formed a committee to protest their low wages.[15] During this same period women took part in local strikes. In March 1836 women shoe corders and binders in Philadelphia created the Female Boot and Shoe Binders Society. They struck, together with the men's cordwainers' union, for a rate advance and won the men's support. Although the outcome of the strike remains unknown, in June of that year the society remained "large and growing."[16] Fifteen years later seamstresses in Philadelphia again brought their concerns to the public. In 1850 sewing women formed an Industrial Union, a cooperative shop for manufacturing and selling clothing. Lucretia Mott and other middle-class reformers helped organize a second cooperative shop, which continued until the economic crisis of 1857.[17] By the time of the Civil War, then, working women in Philadelphia had a history of organization and experience publicizing their plight. They had raised the awareness of the middle classes and had utilized the petition, the strike, and the cooperative to try to better their own condition.

The Civil War only exacerbated the sewing women's problems. Thousands of women entered the wage-labor force for the first time when their husbands and sons joined the army, and most of them sought work as seamstresses. This highly visible increase in the numbers of working women was accompanied by the harsh effects of a subcontracting system. At the start of the war the federal government paid thousands of women directly to sew army uniforms, which were distributed from so-called "arsenals" like the one in Philadelphia on the Schuylkill River. Soon, however, subcontractors began purchasing enormous lots of the fabric and distributing it to women in the suburbs or to home workers in the city. The subcontractors routinely paid less than half the price that the government had paid women.

---

[15] Philip Foner, *Women and the American Labor Movement: From Colonial Times to the Eve of World War I* (New York: Free Press, 1979), 46.

[16] Ibid., 48.

[17] Ibid., 88–89. Further research might reveal interesting interplay between Mott's support for women's rights and her experience with working women in Philadelphia.

Whereas the Schuylkill Arsenal paid twelve and a half cents per hat, for example, a subcontractor paid only five cents. Women trying to support their families earned as little as $1.50 per week.[18] Meanwhile, inflation in the North, although nowhere near the 9,000 percent experienced by the Confederacy, reached nearly 80 percent. Real wages in general declined by about 20 percent.[19]

In the context of the Civil War, the plight of the sewing women won greater sympathy. Middle-class observers noted that the sewing women were now working to clothe the Union soldiers and, in many cases, were soldiers' wives. Reformers were moved by the thought that the seamstresses' poverty grew out of sacrifice for the country. During the war middle-class reformers began to stress the fact that, through no fault of the women's own, many seamstresses were not receiving any money from male protectors. They pointed out that, because of the war, many women could not be dependent on men for financial support. Mary Livermore, the famous leader of the Sanitary Commission, wrote in 1864 that "Scarcely a day of our life passes that we are not obliged to confront the question, 'How shall women, dependent on their own exertions for a livelihood, find remunerative employment?'" She noted that the question was "daily urged upon us by soldiers' wives, widows, and children." "[B]ut what," Livermore continued, "is there for them to do? . . . There is sewing, which is another name for suicide or starvation."[20] Writing her "business manual for women" published in 1863, Virginia Penny noted, "At no time in our country's history have so many women been thrown upon their own exertions. A million of men are on the battle field, and thousands of women, formerly dependent on them, have lost or may lose their only support."[21] Penny went so far as to support women's right to strike in order to protect their livelihood.[22] The Civil War created not only increased numbers of sewing women and harsher conditions, but also a new political climate that encouraged an intensified and more widely publicized concern about them on the part of middle-

---

[18] Virginia Penny, *The Employments of Women* (Boston: Walker, Wise, 1863), 308.

[19] James M. McPherson, *Ordeal by Fire: The Civil War and Reconstruction* (New York: Alfred A. Knopf, 1982), 205.

[20] *Fincher's Trades Review*, April 23, 1864.

[21] Penny, *Employments of Women*, v.

[22] Virginia Penny, *Think and Act: A Series of Articles Pertaining to Men and Women, Work, and Wages* (Philadelphia: Claxton, Remsen, & Haffelfinger, 1869; reprint ed., New York: Arno Press, 1971), 38.

class reformers.[23] These Civil War–era reformers stressed the discrepancy between the assumption of women's dependence on men and the reality of these working women's lives.[24]

More importantly than prodding the consciences of the middle class, the Civil War prompted a new level of organization on the part of sewing women themselves. In Philadelphia sewing women, working together with both male and female middle-class reformers, launched a highly publicized and at least partially successful petition campaign for higher wages, in which they developed their political voice, drawing on their vocation's history of activism. Dissatisfied with that approach, another group of seamstresses allied themselves with male working-class advocates and explored unionization. In so doing, they forged a new relationship for working women with the male labor movement. Although their tactics differed dramatically, both the seamstresses who chose to petition and those who unionized demanded that the government recognize that not all women were financially dependent on men.

The sewing women's wartime movement in Philadelphia began in the summer of 1863, after two years of falling wages and rising prices. In August Colonel Crossman, the overseer of Philadelphia's Schuylkill Arsenal, issued a directive discharging all women employees who were not near relatives of soldiers. On August 8 two hundred sewing women from the arsenal met at Jefferson Hall and issued a series of resolutions, naming Colonel Crossman's conduct "oppressive and prejudicial to the working women." The sewing women from the

---

[23] Lynn Weiner has argued that it was during the 1860s that "self-supporting women" became "visible as a social group"; Weiner, *From Working Girl to Working Mother: The Female Labor Force in the United States, 1820–1980* (Chapel Hill: University of North Carolina Press, 1985), 14.

[24] Not all middle-class reformers saw the problem of women's wages in the same light, however. Gail Hamilton (the pen name of Mary Abigail Dodge) argued that sewing women whose wages were too low should either simply learn to sew better clothing or go into household service. "We do not see why American women starve on needle wages when they can live comfortably, and save money, as house servants," she wrote. Likewise, Sarah Josepha Hale, the influential editor of Philadelphia-based *Godey's Lady's Book,* argued that it was wrong to "place women in competition with men in their industrial pursuits." Virginia Penny refutes Hamilton's arguments from an article entitled "Woman's Wrongs"; see Penny, *Think and Act,* 27. An article expressing these views, most probably written by Hamilton, is reprinted in *Fincher's Trades Review,* December 5, 1863. See also Sarah Josepha Hale, *Manners: or, Happy Homes and Good Society All the Year Round* (Boston: J. E. Tilton, 1868; reprint ed., New York: Arno Press, 1972), 356.

arsenal strongly objected to the government's drawing a connection between personal relationships to soldiers and the right to employment. The women admitted that although female employees with relatives in the army were "fully entitled" to work, "the claims of other poor sewing women were more urgent, as the former received the pay and bounties of the soldiers, while the latter had to depend on a small pittance, earned from week to week." Even several soldiers' widows spoke out against the colonel's orders. In addition, the women pointed out that many of the men working at the arsenal had no relatives in the army.

Philadelphia working women took issue with the economic and political roles assigned them by Colonel Crossman. They rejected equating a familial relation to a soldier with the right to employment. One woman drew attention to the problematic nature of such an assumption by stating that "although she had no relatives engaged in the present war, her immediate ancestors had fought for this country, and if patriotism of kindred was to be made the test . . . she would not be deprived of her employment while she could raise a hand against such a proceeding." The women called for Crossman's discharge from his post and claimed that he had "always acted adverse to the interests of the laboring classes of Philadelphia." They wanted him replaced with someone who would "fully appreciate the necessities of the poor sewing women." The women then expressed their confidence that the Secretary of War would act justly, and determined to send him a copy of their resolutions.[25]

Philadelphia's sewing women were not alone in their efforts. A sewing women's movement developed across the Northeast that autumn. In October 1863 the umbrella sewers of New York and Brooklyn unionized and struck; shirt makers in New York City struck in November, and lost. Later that month between three and four hundred New York City women gathered to discuss their wages and working conditions. They soon founded the Working Women's Union and formed the Sewing Women's Protective and Benevolent Union. According to newspaper reports, "the object of the working girls was to bring about such a state of affairs that they could ask a fair price, and not be wholly at the mercy of the employer."[26] The organization

---

[25] *Fincher's Trades Review*, August 8, 1863.
[26] Ibid., November 21, 1863.

combined aspects of benevolent organizations with those of trade unions. They instituted an initiation fee and dues and offered support in times of sickness or unemployment.[27] One week later the labor newspaper *Fincher's Trades Review* reported that the journeymen house painters' union of Boston had "tendered the use of their Hall to the Sewing Girls of that city, in consequence of a contemplated movement on the part of the women to secure better wages."[28] Sewing women across the Northeast were beginning to organize and call attention to their efforts.

In the spring of 1864 sewing women in Philadelphia stepped up their activities. Divisions within the movement soon surfaced, however, and the women separated into two camps. One, following the advice of middle-class male reformers who attended their meetings, formed the Working Women's Relief Association, wrote an "appeal to employers," and drew up a petition to the United States Congress. In a move that captured the attention of the national press, four seamstresses personally delivered the petition to President Abraham Lincoln in the winter of 1865. After listening to the women's description of seamstresses' distressed circumstances, the President called in the Quartermaster General and told him, "I shall consider myself personally obliged if you can hereafter manage the supplies of contract work for the Government made up by women so as to give them remunerative wages for their labor."[29] Another group of Philadelphia sewing women rejected this method of protest. They worked closely with William Sylvis, the leader of the Iron Molder's Union, and Jonathan Fincher, editor of *Fincher's Trades Review,* and formed the Sewing Women's Union no. 1, which, according to newspaper announcements, met weekly throughout the war.

Even within the sewing women's movement, then, there was disagreement about women's proper mode of political action. Those who were swayed by middle-class male reformers favored petitioning. Those who sided with the working-class union activists rejected this approach as too dependent on the goodwill of wealthy men. They took the advice of the District Attorney William B. Mann who told the women to "fix your prices, and then strike. Say you won't work.

---

[27] Foner, *Women and the American Labor Movement,* 114.
[28] *Fincher's Trades Review,* November 28, 1863.
[29] Foner, *Women and the American Labor Movement,* 116.

Then put a fair price on the different articles, and the community will sustain you."[30] In a practical sense the unionizing women depended on men to help them start their new organization—they approached the men's Trades' Assembly, which formed a committee to make the "necessary arrangements for the formation of a Protective Union" and sponsored a lecture by the two labor activists Sylvis and Fincher.[31] But in choosing to unionize, this group of sewing women rejected the petition's inherent sense of dependency on authority. As Linda Kerber has argued, "the formulation of a petition begins in the acknowledgement of subordination," and the members of Sewing Women's Union no. 1 dismissed that approach.[32]

Other groups of sewing women pressed the government to recognize their independence even after the war ended. Working women in Boston petitioned the Massachusetts legislature in 1869, arguing that because of the postwar population disparity between the sexes, it was not their fault that they could not find husbands. They demanded that the legislature help them build a community that would support them in their necessarily autonomous state. In what must be read as a satirical play on the traditional forms of women's pleas, they deemed themselves "poor, ignorant women," who would not "presume to dictate any plan for our own relief." They continued, however, with an elegantly specific and detailed plan, perhaps drawing on radical Republican Reconstruction proposals for aid to the freedpeople with land in the South. The women suggested that the legislature buy a large tract of land, divide it into small plots, and provide each with its own house and garden. The houses were to be rented to "poor working women" to whom the State would "furnish rations, tools, seeds and instruction in gardening, until such time as the women would be able to raise their own food, or otherwise be-

---

[30] *Fincher's Trades Review,* May 21, 1864.

[31] Ibid., May 28, 1864. See also Edgar B. Cale, *The Organization of Labor in Philadelphia 1850–1870* (Philadelphia: University of Pennsylvania Press, 1940), 55.

[32] Linda Kerber, *Women of the Republic: Intellect and Ideology in Revolutionary America* (New York: W. W. Norton, 1986), 85. There were other women's trade unions during the war as well. The laundry workers of Troy, New York, founded their union in 1864. New York City sewing women followed a path similar to those in Philadelphia. When the Working Women's Union, formed in November 1863, "abandoned the goal of organizing women for higher wages in favor of 'protective' aims . . . some of their number created yet another organization"; see Alice Kessler-Harris, *Out to Work: A History of Wage-Earning Women in the United States* (New York: W. W. Norton, 1982), 83.

come self-supporting; the payment of rent to commence with the third year only, and the rent to be then so graduated . . . that each woman might, in a reasonable time, pay off, in the form of rent, the entire cost to the State for the lot on which she lives." The houses would be passed on to their female heirs.[33]

Both the Boston and Philadelphia seamstresses' most basic and important argument was that, because of the Civil War, there was no guarantee that all women could be dependent on men. The war and their class status shaped their arguments in ways that differed from earlier middle-class reformers. In a sense they took a more pragmatic approach, pointing out that, financially speaking, they simply *were not* dependent on men. In Philadelphia the two groups of women activists pursued this same message, with different tactics and results. The wartime petition drive gave some working women a chance to speak for themselves and define their own political voice. They found a way to take control of their cause in a manner that drew unprecedented national attention and succeeded in obtaining at least a minimum of relief from the President of the United States. This movement contributed to working women's sense of their own direct relationship to the federal government, and the possibility of shaping that relationship themselves. The women who unionized forced male labor leaders to understand the reality of working women's lives and paved the way for women's unprecedented participation in the national labor movement after the war.[34] Both groups argued that women who supported themselves and their families deserved jobs as much or more than women who received money from male family

---

[33] *The Revolution,* May 13, 1869. In a fascinating look at Reconstruction era approaches to the idea of dependency, Carol Faulkner has found that there was a significant group of women active in the freedmen's aid movement who saw the issue very differently than their male counterparts. Whereas the Freedmen's Bureau and the freedmen's aid movement in general aimed to cut back on "charity" in an effort to increase freedpeople's "independence," these women insisted that the nation in fact owed freedpeople goods and services. See Carol Faulkner, "'How Much Wiser a Charity to Help a Man Become More Manly!' Women in the Freedmen's Aid Movement," paper presented at 1999 annual meeting of the Organization of American Historians, Toronto, Canada, manuscript in author's possession.

[34] William Sylvis would go on to head the National Labor Union, and I believe his willingness to sponsor women's participation grew directly out of his experience with Philadelphia's sewing women during the war. See Rachel Filene Seidman, "Beyond Sacrifice: Women and Politics on the Pennsylvania Homefront during the Civil War" (Ph.D. diss., Yale University, 1995), chapter 3.

members, whether soldiers or not. These working women argued that their own active, productive participation in the war effort, not the sacrifice of male family members to the Union cause, should be the measure of their virtuous citizenship and their right to work.

Antebellum middle-class reformers had argued that women *should not* be dependent on men. Working-class women during the war argued that they *could not* be dependent on men. In thousands of letters to Abraham Lincoln, Secretary of War Edwin Stanton, and other federal officials, another group of women took yet another approach to the issue of dependency and women's relationship to the government. In most of these letters women pleaded for the release of their sons and husbands from the army. In trying to obtain discharges for their relatives, these women embraced the definition of themselves as dependents. Reminiscent of Elizabeth Packard, they did not see dependency as a barrier to their rights, but argued that it in fact *guaranteed* them a claim to certain rights. Indeed, they insisted to the federal government that they had the *right* to be economically dependent on men. These women used the notion of their dependency to construct their identity as citizens.[35]

A few women drew expressly on the language of women's rights, reflecting their exposure to ideas like Grimké's and Stanton's. Mary Herrick's language revealed her adoption of both women's rights and abolitionist rhetoric when she wrote to accuse the Lincoln administration of unfair practices. "I am left all a lone I have a small plase and dont want to be taxed to death," she wrote. She continued: "[B]y good rights you should pass a law to exemt such as I am from heavey taxes. . . . [I]t is unjust and cruel to tax a poor woman to death[;] you have plenty of simpathy for the slaves and I think slaverey is an abomination in the sight of god, that is one reason why I dont want

---

[35] My work intersects here in interesting ways with the recent work of historian Drew Faust, whose superb book *Mothers of Invention: Women of the Slaveholding South in the American Civil War* (Chapel Hill: University of North Carolina Press, 1996) explores the wartime experience of women in the South, where for many the war was more immediate and harsh than in the North. Faust argues that southern women lamented their wartime independence and faced it with great insecurity. On the one hand, they clung to the idea of themselves as dependents, but on the other hand, they began to see both men and God as failing them in their roles as protectors and guides. They started to view dependency not as a natural state, but as part of a contractual bargain, contingent on men's fulfilling of their part by offering protection and support. Faust argues that this new critique of male superiority derives not from a sense of self-esteem, but out of desperation and the fundamental need to survive.

to be a slave to this *war!*"[36] One week later, Mrs. Herrick wrote to the Adjutant General: "I think a *woman* has all the rights of a *free* american sitisen and I want the american as it was without *slavery*. I dont want one star or stripe less in that dear old flag that has floated over me ever since I was born in this land of the *brave* and this *contrey of the free!*[37]"

Unlike Herrick, most northern women who wrote to the administration adopted a stance more similar to Elizabeth Ware Packard's idea that the government should protect women's dependency on men. On the one hand, they went out of their way to explain that they had been doing all that they could on their own, including working outside the home, before turning to the state for help. Marie Kellog told Lincoln, "willingly have I toiled early and late to help . . . in the glorious cause of freedom and to earn my own support. Left a widow, for many long weary years I have struggled for my living and kept myself from the iron fetters of abject poverty."[38] Mrs. J. Johnson wrote, "We are in a sad fix . . . but I hear you ask, why you do not work?" She informed Lincoln, "I do as much as I can but my health being poor I am not able to do more."[39] These women anticipated the expectation that they would at least try to support their families. They knew they could not rely solely on their femininity as an excuse for their need; they claimed to be either too old, or too sick, or too poor to survive on their own.[40]

On the other hand, Civil War wives and mothers insisted that they were indeed dependent on men for support and argued that their position as dependents meant that the government owed them rec-

---

[36] Mary W. Herrick to E. M. Stanton, May 30, 1863, Enlisted Branch Records, 1863, Records of the Adjutant General's Office, Record Group 94, National Archives, Washington, D.C. (hereinafter cited as RG 94).

[37] Mary W. Herrick to Sam Beck, Adjutant General, June 8, 1863, Enlisted Branch, 1863, RG 94.

[38] Marie Kellog to Abraham Lincoln, May 14, 1863, Enlisted Branch, 1863, RG 94.

[39] Mrs. J. Johnson to Abraham Lincoln, May 18, 1863, Enlisted Branch, 1863, RG 94.

[40] Interestingly, Mary Beth Norton has shown that, in their petitions to the Continental Congress after the Revolution, many women described themselves as "helpless." None of the women in this study used that term to describe themselves. See Mary Beth Norton, "Eighteenth-Century American Women in Peace and War: The Case of the Loyalists," in *A Heritage of Her Own: Toward a New Social History of American Women*, eds. Nancy Cott and Elizabeth Pleck (New York: Simon and Schuster, 1979), 136–61.

ompense, whether in the form of favors or the support of their sons and husbands. Their ideas may have been influenced as much by military policy as by Packard, Beecher, or any other reformer. In the summer of 1862 Congress passed legislation granting pensions to widows, children, and other "dependent relatives" of soldiers who had died in the war. Although the military policy regarding dependents applied only to pensions, and not to discharges, many women turned the language of dependence to their own ends. Emeline Herman told Lincoln that she had "been dependant" on her son "before and since he left me."[41] Nancy Harris pleaded with the Secretary of War to "think of my poor boy . . . and a poor old mother['s] dependance."[42] Mary Ann Henry wrote for the discharge of Joseph Irish, "as he has an aged mother and orphan Brothers and sisters dependant solely on his exertions for support."[43] Jane Welcom told Lincoln "my head is blossoming for the grave," and that she wanted her son Mart released from the Colored Troops because he was "all the subport" she had.[44]

The military defined the payment of soldiers' wages as "support," but women sometimes insisted on more. Especially for women who lived on farms, money was not always enough; physical labor was necessary for survival. Of course, the two—labor and money—were inherently linked. Maria Swett informed the Secretary of War that she had recently bought a small farm, a pair of horses, and two cows, assuming that her son would help her with the work and with paying off the debts she assumed. She told the Secretary of War that already one horse, worth fifty dollars, had died of neglect. "I do think I ought to have pay for [my son's] time. . . . [I]f you was to pay me 2 dollars a day for his time, it would not be recompense for the losses . . . but I do hope you will pay me enough so that I can pay the remaining debts." She added, "I require that you send him home if he is willing to come *and* pay me for his time."[45]

---

[41] Emeline Herman to His Excelency [sic], the President of the United States, June 15, 1863, Enlisted Branch, 1863, RG 94.

[42] Nancy Harris to Mr. Stanton, April 20, 1863, Enlisted Branch, 1863, RG 94.

[43] Mary Ann Henry to the Hon. E. M. Stanton, January 27, 1863, Enlisted Branch, 1863, RG 94.

[44] [Jane Welcom] to abraham lincon [sic], November 21, 1864, box 188, Letters Received, Colored Troops Division, RG 94.

[45] Maria Swett to Mr. Stanton Secretary of War, February 17, 1862, box 49, Addison Files, RG 94; emphasis in original.

Fannie Hayndon pointed out she had already lost three brothers on the battlefield, and her father and two more brothers were serving in the army. She requested the discharge of her sixteen-year-old brother: "All of my relatives able to fight are in the United States Service[.] We have no acquaintances South or fighting for the Rebels so of course we have some claim on your generosity."[46] Sarah Langley told Lincoln that her husband was in the army, and her father had fought in the War of 1812. "And as this is the only favor we have asked of Congress," she wrote, "please grant my request."[47] Jane Henry demanded that the military address the terrible conditions soldiers faced in military prisons not just for the men's sake, but for "their friends who were patriotic enough to let them go."[48]

These Civil War women used their dependency to prove their patriotism, demonstrating how, despite their need for the men at home, they had given them up to support the nation's cause. But women also used their dependency as a way to place limits on the scope of their patriotic duty, arguing that, despite their love for the country, their need for the men superseded all. Sophrona Southland wrote: "I love the man who loves his Country but there is another side to the question. A widowed mother without a home weeping and mourning by day and night for her only dependence is gone. . . . [I]f [George] Washington could speak methinks he would say go home to thy mother take care of her in her old age and be the means of drying thy sisters tears."[49]

Many women, especially mothers, defined the limits on their duty in terms of the numbers of men they thought they owed the country. Jane Goones had already lost three sons in the war when she tried to get a discharge for her son Michael. She told the man writing the letter for her that she "thinks she has lost enough for one family."[50] Lydia Hagar wanted a discharge for her youngest son, who had joined the army against her will. "i have to sons out b sides," she explained,

---

[46] Fannie E. Hayndon to the Secretary of War, December 6, 1862, box 50, Addison Files.

[47] Sarah Langley to Mr. Cameron, January 18, 1862, box 50, Addison Files, RG 94.

[48] Jane Henry to Hon. Abraham Lincoln, February 5, 1863, Enlisted Branch, 1863, RG 94.

[49] Sophrona Southland to Hon. Sir, October 12, 1861, box 47, Addison Files, RG 94.

[50] Simon Albright to Lorenzo Thomas, March 10, 1864, Enlisted Branch, 1864, RG 94.

one of whom had been in the army "ever since the War Commenst so i think i have don My duty to the War plese to do all you Can for Mee."[51] Emily Miller wrote, "I think it harde after encountering great hardships in raising my children to be deprived of the aide of *both* my sons, one of them . . . I consider enough to give my country."[52] Adaline Feel was illiterate, but through a justice of the peace she communicated that she was "willing to spare one son for her country but thinks both would be more of a sacrifice than she can bear."[53] Lucinda Applegate wrote, "I think two sons is sufficient for one woman to give her country and I beg of you for one to be left with me."[54] Northern women used the definition of themselves as dependents on men both to construct themselves as patriots and citizens to whom the government owed recompense, and to place limits on how much they felt they owed the government.

Elizabeth Cady Stanton, writing in the 1880s, remarked, "The lessons of the war were not lost on the women of this nation; through varied forms of suffering and humiliation, they learned that they had an equal interest with man in the administration of the Government, enjoying or suffering alike its blessings or its miseries."[55] As Stanton suggests, many northern women did recognize during the Civil War the increasingly important role that government played in their lives. They did not, though, all respond by demanding the vote, as Stanton wanted. Reformers wrote treatises, seamstresses took to the streets, mothers penned letters to political leaders, but their demands were less a political platform than a cultural critique. Taken together, their actions constituted a challenge to the assumption that women's dependency on men limited their ability to play a role in public, political debate. Although not all of these women would have agreed with Sarah Grimké that their dependence on men was a "monstrous doctrine," they each in their own way asserted their status as American citizens and claimed rights to which they felt that status entitled them.

---

[51] Lydia Hagar to "Dear Friend," January 5, 1864 [noted on the letter "should be 1865"] Enlisted Branch, 1865, RG 94.

[52] Emily Miller to Honrlle [sic] S. Cameron, October 29, 1861, box 47, Addison Files, RG 94.

[53] Adaline Feel, affidavit, May 3, 1862, box 49, Addison Files, RG 94.

[54] Lucinda Applegate to Secretary of War, February 4, 1862, box 49, Addison Files, RG 94.

[55] Stanton et al., eds., *History of Woman Suffrage,* 2:88.

8

Joseph Henry's Smithsonian during the Civil War

Michael F. Conlin

JOSEPH HENRY viewed the Civil War as yet another obstacle to his mission as Secretary of the Smithsonian Institution to follow James Smithson's directive to labor for the "increase & diffusion of knowledge among men." Henry, the leading American physicist of his generation, saw this English chemist's bequest as a unique opportunity to support basic scientific research in the United States, but others advocated endowing a museum or a library. Rather than resolving the dispute, Congress had provided for a library, a museum, and a research center in the bill that established the Smithsonian in 1846. From the beginning, Henry tried to upset the congressional compromise in favor of what he called the active operations of scientific research and publication, but various factions on the Board of Regents, charged by Congress to administer the Institution, resisted his efforts. The Board, which consisted of the Vice President, the Chief Justice of the Supreme Court, the Mayor of Washington, three U. S. Representatives, three U. S. Senators, and six private citizens (the last twelve Regents to be selected by Congress), approved expenditures and prepared an annual report. In the 1850s Henry defeated the library supporters on the Board by making a truce with the Regents who advocated a museum. As a result of this alliance, Henry fired the Smithsonian librarian and accepted the collections of the National Museum on the condition that the federal government would pay for their maintenance. The Civil War created additional challenges for Joseph Henry's Smithsonian Institution by exposing it to new political attacks, diverting resources away from basic research and toward applied science, and by disrupting the conditions necessary for science: the free flow of ideas, people, and money.[1]

Trying to keep above politics in a partisan time, Henry did not openly endorse a party or advocate principles. Maintaining good relations with Whigs and Democrats, Henry had placed the Smithsonian Institution on the neutral ground of science in the 1850s. A staunch Unionist, he blamed both fire-eaters and abolitionists for the secession crisis. Henry viewed the rise of the Republican party with trepidation as it upset the sectional balance in Congress and his alliances on the Board of Regents. Staying as Henry's guest during the 1861 inauguration, John Torrey, a botanist, found Henry "bitterly opposed" to President Abraham Lincoln because of the Smithsonian secretary's "strong attachment" to the Constitutional Union party. Despite their political differences, Henry and Lincoln developed a mutual respect after several meetings. Although never adopting Republican principles, Henry was pleased that Lincoln supported the Smithsonian and would leave its administration to him. Impressed by Henry's "comprehensive grasp" of every subject on which he spoke, Lincoln regarded him as a valuable resource after their first meeting. Previously the President had thought that the Smithsonian was "printing a great amount of useless information," but concluded, "it must be a grand school if it produces such thinkers" as Henry.[2]

Henry's enthusiasm for the war was as tepid as his endorsement of

---

[1] "The Will of James Smithson," reprinted in William Jones Rhees, ed., *The Smithsonian Institution: Documents Relative to Its Origin and History* (Washington, D.C.: Government Printing Office, 1901), 1:6. For more on the political battles Henry fought to keep the Smithsonian Institution a center of scientific research, see Wilcomb E. Washburn, "Joseph Henry's Conception of the Purpose of the Smithsonian Institution," in *A Cabinet of Curiosities: Five Episodes in the Evolution of American Museums*, ed. Walter Muir Whitehall (Charlottesville: University Press of Virginia, 1967), 106–66; Joel J. Orosz, "Disloyalty, Dismissal, and a Deal: The Development of the National Museum at the Smithsonian Institution, 1846–1855," *Museum Studies Journal* 2 (spring 1986): 22–33; and Kenneth Hafertepe, *America's Castle: The Evolution of the Smithsonian Building and Its Institution, 1840–1878* (Washington, D.C.: Smithsonian Institution Press, 1984).

[2] Robert V. Bruce, *The Launching of American Science, 1846–1876* (New York: Alfred A. Knopf, 1987), 272–76; Patricia Jahns, *Matthew Fontaine Maury & Joseph Henry: Scientists of the Civil War* (New York: Hastings House, 1961), 154–59; Andrew Denny Rodgers III, *John Torrey: A Story of North American Botany* (Princeton: Princeton University Press, 1942), 272; L. E. Chittenden, *Recollections of President Lincoln and His Administration* (New York: Harper & Bros., 1891), 236, 238; Robert V. Bruce, *Lincoln and the Tools of War* (Indianapolis: Bobbs-Merrill, 1956), 85.

the President. In private he wondered whether there were "any proper grounds for a civil war?" Believing that blacks could live with whites only in a state of servitude, Henry feared that civil war and the abolition of slavery would lead to further discord. Wary of the exigencies of war, he predicted that the Smithsonian Institution would not be able to "conduct its affairs with same persistence and success" as it had before the bombardment of Fort Sumter. As Washingtonians braced for the expected Confederate invasion in the first few days of the war, Secretary of War Simon Cameron issued muskets and ammunition to the Institution for defense. While Spencer F. Baird, assistant secretary of the Smithsonian Institution, packed the National Museum's collection of bird eggs, Henry planned diplomacy in the event of a Confederate occupation of Washington. Seeking to protect the Smithsonian with the cloak of scientific neutrality, he determined that the Institution would not fly the American flag and would rely on the "sense of propriety of the besiegers" to respect the sanctity of Smithson's bequest. The threat passed without incident, but Henry continued this unpopular policy for the duration of the war.[3]

Although Henry quickly began scientific work on behalf of the federal government, his refusal to fly the American flag and his friendship with Jefferson Davis led to rumors of disloyalty. Rather than expressing shock that Davis had accepted the presidency of the Confederate States of America, Henry thought that his friend's "talents and integrity" would acquit the office well. In May 1861 a correspondent to the *National Republican* charged that "several secessionists are in office at the Smithsonian Institution." The Lazzaroni, an influential clique of scientists led by Alexander Dallas Bache, Superintendent of the United States Coast Survey, which wanted to improve American science, feared for Henry's reputation. Reporting the "extraordinary stories in circulation" about Henry's loyalty to Bache, Wolcott Gibbs, professor at the Free Academy of New York, concluded that they were the result of the Smithsonian Secretary's "timidity and want of tact." These rumors dogged Henry throughout the war. As late as August 1864, midnight experiments conducted for

[3] Bruce, *The Launching of American Science*, 275–76, 299–300; Jahns, *Maury & Henry*, 4–5, 255; J. Henry to S. Alexander, April 26, 1861, Joseph Henry Papers, Smithsonian Institution Archives, Washington, D.C.; *Smithsonian Institution Annual Report for 1861*, 13.

the navy to test the transmission of signals by lanterns between the Smithsonian high tower and the tower of the Soldiers' Home prompted rumors of Henry's sending information to the rebels.[4]

Not all of the Smithsonian staff dreaded the war, but its changes on Washington and the Smithsonian Institution were evident. Ferdinand V. Hayden, a visiting researcher in residence at the Institution, confessed that the sights and sounds of the fifty thousand volunteers who marched and paraded around the national metropolis made "anything so peaceful in its character as Geology" distasteful. These soldiers transformed Washington from a sleepy political town into a bustling military center, leaving no part of the city untouched, not even the Smithsonian. Men answered Lincoln's call with such alacrity and in such great numbers that they overwhelmed the facilities established for them. As a result, they were quartered in the Capitol, the Patent Office, the Navy Yard, and the Interior Department. Unable to accommodate troops, the Naval Observatory allowed its grounds to be used by the Quartermaster Corps as a base for wagons and mules. Having exhausted government facilities, Cameron pressed private institutions into service. Georgetown College, Trinity Church, and the American Colonization Society quartered troops, but the Smithsonian did not. Henry, disinclined to allow Mars to distract Athena, agreed to house troops but observed that use of the building as an infirmary would be "more in accordance with the spirit of the Institution." Sensing Henry's reluctance and having no authority over the Smithsonian, Cameron made other arrangements. In the first weeks of the war, Henry opened the castle doors only to the soldiers who visited the National Museum and who attended a concert held for their entertainment. When these soldiers returned to Washington

---

[4] Constance McLaughlin Green, *Washington: Village and Capital, 1800–1878* (Princeton: Princeton University Press, 1962), 1:245–46; Jörg Nagler, "Loyalty and Dissent: The Home Front in the American Civil War," in *On the Road to Total War: The American Civil War and the German Wars of Unification, 1861–1871*, eds. Stig Förster and Jörg Nagler (Cambridge: Cambridge University Press, 1997), 343–44; Thomas Coulson, *Joseph Henry: His Life and Work* (Princeton: Princeton University Press, 1950), 235–36; J. Henry to F. A. P. Barnard, February 23, 1861, Frederick A. P. Barnard Papers, Rare Book Room and Manuscript Library, Columbia University, New York; *National Republican* May 17, 1861; W. Gibbs to A. D. Bache, February 2, 1862, William Jones Rhees Collection, Huntington Library, San Marino, Calif.; Carl Sandburg, *Abraham Lincoln: The War Years,* 4 vols. (New York: Harcourt, Brace, 1939), 2:320; J. Henry to A. D. Bache, August 21, 1864, Alexander Dallas Bache Papers, Smithsonian Institution Archives.

as casualties, filling many churches, half the government buildings, and some fifteen hospitals, Henry did not open the castle doors to them, but instead supplied the hospitals and medical wards with disinfectant made in the Smithsonian laboratory.[5]

As rumors questioning Henry's loyalty circulated, abolitionists dragged the Smithsonian Institution into their campaign for the emancipation of slaves and a vigorous prosecution of the war against the southern people. Lincoln shied away from pursuing these policies for fear of pushing any wavering Unionists into the Confederacy. Because of the "distraction of the public mind in regard to the war" in 1861, Henry had decided to cancel the course of popular lectures given each winter at the Smithsonian lecture hall. A group of abolitionists offered to sponsor a series of lectures, but Henry, repelled by their doctrines, declined. Styling themselves the Washington Lecture Association, the abolitionists renewed their application. Prominent Republicans, including members of Lincoln's Cabinet and several Smithsonian Regents, pressured Henry into allowing the Association to give a "partial course" of lectures to place Washington on a "higher plane in regard to Literature, Loyalty, and Liberty." Henry felt especially vulnerable because of the absence of many of his allies on the Board of Regents due to death, retirement, and the ascendancy of the Republican party. With the deaths of Senator Stephen A. Douglas and Senator James A. Pearce as well as the removal of Washington Mayor James Berret for refusing to take the federal loyalty oath, Henry lost allies on the Board. Exacerbating these difficulties, Congress loaded the Board with Republicans, including Senator William Fessenden, Senator Lyman Trumbull, and Representative Schuyler Colfax. Henry still counted Bache and Chief Justice Roger B. Taney as supporters, but time was not on his side. Abolitionists wanted to secure the Smithsonian lecture hall to force Henry to support their principles and to command a national forum. John Pierpont, Washington Lecture Association president and a Unitarian clergyman,

---

[5] F. V. Hayden to F. B. Meek, May 24, 1861; F. V. Hayden to F. B. Meek, June 30, 1861, Fielding B. Meek Papers, Smithsonian Institution Archives; Green, *Washington*, 1:244, 247, 261; *National Republican*, April 18, 24, May 2, 3, 6, 7, 9, June 14, 1861; Jan K. Herman, *A Hilltop in Foggy Bottom: Home of the Old Naval Observatory and the Navy Medical Department* (Washington, D.C.: Naval Medical Command, Department of the Navy, 1984), 21–22; *Smithsonian Institution Annual Report for 1861*, 13; *Evening Star*, December 6, 1861; *Smithsonian Institution Annual Report for 1862*, 33.

pledged to invite lecturers "who have earned a reputation for the highest culture and the most earnest patriotism," ranging from college presidents to men of letters.[6]

Fearing that the Washington Lecture Association would entangle the Smithsonian in political disputes, Henry demanded that the Institution be absolved of any connection with its lectures. To keep the Smithsonian out of the partisan storms that had darkened the Washington sky, Henry had limited the use of the lecture hall to benevolent societies and to groups whose objects were "in accordance with the general operations" of the Institution, such as the United States Agricultural Society and the American Colonization Society, but he made an exception for the Association. Pierpont had placated Henry's concerns with a promise to limit the course to twelve lectures and to invite scholars such as Orestes A. Brownson, Ralph Waldo Emerson, Edward Everett, and James Russell Lowell, but he extended the course and loaded the program with abolitionists. The Association stretched the course from twelve lectures to twenty-six, spanning from December 1861 to April 1862. Of those with a literary reputation, only Brownson and Emerson accepted Pierpont's invitation, and they chose to lecture on politics rather than literature. Most of the two dozen orators who spoke in the lecture course were abolitionists who supported a vigorous prosecution of the war. All but three of these lectures treated political subjects that aroused violent opinions in the national metropolis.[7]

The course of the Washington Lecture Association was part of a Republican campaign to pressure Lincoln into prosecuting the Civil War on abolitionist principles. Prominent Republicans, including Senators Trumbull, Charles Sumner, Preston King, Henry Wilson, Samuel Pomeroy, and James Lane as well as Representatives Colfax, Galusha Grow, Owen Lovejoy, John Hutchins, Thaddeus Stevens,

---

[6] Jahns, *Maury & Henry*, 174–76; *Smithsonian Institution Annual Report for 1861*, 47; *Liberator* 32 (January 3, 1862): 4; *National Republican*, December 9 and 17, 1861; Green, *Washington*, 234–35, 248–49, 272; Hans L. Trefousse, *The Radical Republicans: Lincoln's Vanguard for Racial Justice* (New York: Alfred A. Knopf, 1969), 11–15.

[7] *Evening Star*, January 9, 1861, March 21, 1862; *Daily National Intelligencer*, January 16, 1861; Bruce, *Launching of Modern American Science*, 275; William J. Rhees, ed., *The Smithsonian Institution: Journals of the Board of Regents, Reports of Committees, Statistics, Etc.* (Washington, D.C.: Government Printing Office, 1879), 172–73; *National Republican*, December 9, 1861.

and Thomas Edwards, made a point of attending at least one lecture. *The Liberator* noted with satisfaction that battles in the Senate chamber, the concert hall, the streets, the army camps, and the Smithsonian lecture hall were part of a war waged between freedom and slavery in the capital city. At the same time that the Association lecturers supported the suspension of the writ of habeas corpus in Maryland, advocated the confiscation of southern slaves by generals on the battlefield, and chastised the incompetence of Democratic generals, the Republican Congress passed a Confiscation Act that forfeited the claim of ownership to all slaves employed in a manner hostile to the United States, tried to repeal the Fugitive Slave Act, and established the Joint Committee for the Conduct of the War to demonstrate the damage limited war aims did to the army.[8]

Intrigued by the controversy as much as the quality of the speakers, Washingtonians crowded the Smithsonian lecture hall for every lecture. The brightest of the luminaries assembled by the Washington Lecture Association were Horace Greeley, editor of the *New York Tribune;* George B. Cheever, a Congregational minister from New York City; Ralph Waldo Emerson, the leading American philosopher; and Wendell Phillips, a Boston lawyer and abolitionist who was so controversial that he was forced to carry a revolver to his lectures. On January 3, 1862, Greeley lectured on "The Nation," with Lincoln in attendance. Setting the tone that almost all the other lecturers followed, Greeley called for emancipation, the enrollment of former slaves into the army, and vigorous prosecution of the war. After being hectored by abolitionists throughout the lecture, the President did not attend the remainder of the course. Instead, he met the speakers privately. To appreciate the volatility of these lectures, consider Phillips's reception in Cincinnati several days after he spoke at the Smithsonian, where he was pelted with rotten eggs and threatened by a mob.[9]

---

[8] *Evening Star,* December 24, 1861, January 1, 1862; *National Republican,* December 21, 1861; *Liberator* 32 (February 28, 1862): 36; Bruce Tap, *Over Lincoln's Shoulder: The Committee on the Conduct of the War* (Lawrence: University Press of Kansas, 1998), 55–58; Leonard P. Curry, *Blueprint for Modern America: Nonmilitary Legislation of the First Civil War Congress* (Nashville: Vanderbilt University Press, 1968), 37–74, passim.

[9] *National Republican,* January 3, 4, 11, 13, February 1, 15, March 15, 1862; *Evening Star,* January 4, 11, February 1, March 15, 19, 1862; *Independent* 14 (January 9, 1862): 5; Don C. Seitz, *Horace Greeley: Founder of the New York Tribune* (India-

Henry became increasingly dismayed by the Washington Lecture Association's controversial topics and its seemingly endless course. Desperate to show the public what proper Smithsonian lectures were, Henry began his own course of eight speakers. Unlike the Association's narrow course, the official Smithsonian lectures ranged from science to travel and from history to philology. The highlight of Henry's course was four lectures on "Arctic Exploration" by Isaac I. Hayes, who had returned from an Arctic expedition. Reflecting the interest Americans had shown in the Arctic in the 1850s, Washingtonians thronged the hall to hear Hayes. At the beginning of each Smithsonian lecture, Henry disclaimed the responsibility of the Institution for lectures on partisan issues that were beyond its control.[10]

Despite Pierpont's repeated disavowals of any connection between the lecturers and the Smithsonian Institution, Henry chafed at the notoriety the lectures brought. Most galling to Henry was the fact that the only two lecturers who spoke twice—Cheever and Phillips— were the most radical speakers of the course. Henry privately urged that the lectures be toned down, but the Association refused and then leaked the incident to the press to keep him quiescent. Hoping that freedom of speech could be enjoyed in the national metropolis, the *New York Evening Post* regretted Henry's "solemn protest" against the lecturers' patriotic addresses. Rejecting a proposal to invite Frederick Douglass to finish the course, Henry informed the Association that he "would not permit the lecture of a coloured man to be given in the room of the Institution." Henry's resistance to these lectures added new impetus to questions about his loyalty.[11]

Many others shared Henry's frustration with the Washington Lecture Association course. Washingtonians attacked the course in newspaper letters, threatened violence at the lectures, and mutilated the

---

napolis: Bobbs-Merrill, 1926), 238; *New York Tribune,* January 15, 1862; *Boston Traveller,* reprinted in *Liberator* 32 (January 17, 1862); Len Gougeon, *Virtue's Hero: Emerson, Antislavery, and Reform* (Athens: University of Georgia Press, 1990), 281; *New York Tribune,* reprinted in *Liberator* 32 (March 21, 1862): 45–46; James Brewer Stewart, *Wendell Phillips: Liberty's Hero* (Baton Rouge: Louisiana State University Press, 1986), 213–15, 220, 231–37.

[10] *Evening Star,* January 15, 30, February 21, 25, 1862; *Daily National Intelligencer,* October 12, 1861; *New York Commercial Advertiser,* reprinted in *Daily National Intelligencer,* October 25, 1861.

[11] *New York Evening Post,* reprinted in *National Republican,* January 20, 1862; J. Henry to A. D. Bache, April 4, 1862, William Jones Rhees Collection.

posted bills giving notice of them. With less than a third of the course completed, the *Evening Star* hoped that some of the speakers would choose "some topic not political. Cannot the Lecture Association manage it? We have had now eight abolition lectures in succession; a 'popular course' ought to show a little more variety." Although many of the Regents supported the lectures, Senator Garrett Davis, a Democrat from Kentucky, did not. He complained that abolitionists had "desecrated the Smithsonian Institution" in an attempt to "destroy the Union, so as to secure over its broken fragments the emancipation of slaves." The Washington correspondent of the *Boston Herald* reported that the lectures "raised the dormant pro-slavery feeling" in the District "until it vents itself in the churches, on the street, and in private circles. People who are strongly Union are so incensed that they freely admit that they are rebels, if worshipping Wendell Phillips be loyalty."[12]

Of course, abolitionists were pleased by the Washington Lecture Association course. The Washington correspondents of *The Independent* and *The Liberator* marveled that abolitionists could speak in the national metropolis, where Sumner had been assaulted and the Slave Power conspiracy had trampled free speech for thirty years. Aware that some were pleased that abolitionists could speak in Washington, the *New York Evening Post* and the *New York Tribune* took little solace that free speech was tolerated in the capital of the United States, observing that only the presence of a large army and the temporary preponderance of Union sentiment allowed them to lecture without risking their lives.[13]

Henry regretted seeing "party wranglings obtrude themselves on the neutral grounds of science," disrupting the Smithsonian Institution. After the Washington Lecture Association lecture course had finished, he restricted use of the lecture room to the lectures given under Smithsonian auspices because of the "impossibility of preventing the name of the Institution from being associated in the mind of

[12] *Evening Star,* December 5 and 13, 1861, January 25, February 14, 1862; *Boston Courier,* reprinted in *Liberator* 32 (January 31, 1862): 17; Randall C. Jimerson, *The Private Civil War: Popular Thought during the Sectional Conflict* (Baton Rouge: Louisiana State University Press, 1988), 38–40; *Boston Herald,* reprinted in *Liberator* 32 (March 28, 1862): 51.

[13] *Independent* 14 (March 20, 1862): 5; *Liberator* 32 (February 14, 1862): 27; *New York Evening Post,* reprinted in *National Republican,* January 20, 1862; *New York Tribune,* reprinted in *Liberator* 32 (March 21, 1862): 46.

the public with topics foreign to its peaceful character and scientific reputation." In his annual report to Congress, Henry explained that the course was an "exposition of political principles" that exposed the Smithsonian to "acrimonious attacks" by "members of Congress and editors of papers holding different political opinions." If the Smithsonian were to survive the political vagaries of Washington, Henry believed that "men of the most extreme political views" must continue to meet in the castle "as on a common ground of friendly sympathy" with no motivation other than sustaining "the Institution in its mission of advancing and diffusing knowledge."[14]

In June 1862 several Washingtonians, including at least one Congressman, made arrangements for Parson William G. Brownlow, a Unionist newspaper editor from Tennessee, to lecture at the Smithsonian Institution to answer the abolitionists. Assuming that since the castle was "a public building of the United States" it could be used for "public purposes," they did not inform Henry of the lecture until announcements had been made in local newspapers. Although sympathetic, Henry informed Brownlow and his supporters that the Smithsonian was a private body that no longer hosted political lectures. Brownlow was angry that Henry allowed abolitionists to speak at the Institution but refused him the opportunity to rebut. On June 30 Brownlow came to Washington and spoke at Ford's Athenaeum, a smaller venue than the Smithsonian. Brownlow championed vigorous prosecution of the war and attacked the Institution. At the same time the Washington Lecture Association requested the use of the lecture room for another course of lectures. Henry rejected their application and received more abuse. Henry believed that these public attacks had hurt the reputation of the Smithsonian. Indeed they had. As late March 1863, friends of the spurned lecturers circulated rumors that Henry was to be removed from the Institution, presumably because of disloyalty.[15]

These rumors proved to be groundless. From the beginning of the

---

[14] *Smithsonian Institution Annual Report for 1862*, 43–44; *Smithsonian Institution Annual Report for 1864*, 15; *Evening Star*, June 11, 1862.

[15] *Smithsonian Institution Annual Report for 1862*, 44–45; J. Henry to T. D. Woolsey, August 8, 1862, Theodore D. Woolsey Papers, Sterling Library, Yale University; *Daily National Intelligencer*, June 28, 30, 1862; *Evening Star*, July 1, 1862; J. Henry to W. D. Whitney, December 16, 1862, William D. Whitney Papers, Sterling Library, Yale University; J. Henry to J. Hall, March 13, 1863, G. P. Merrill Collection, Smithsonian Institution Archives.

war, Henry, despite concerns that the demands of war would distract the Smithsonian from supporting basic research, had opened the Institution to the "requests made by different departments of the government." Most of the activities of the Smithsonian on behalf of the government during the war were by necessity those of its tireless secretary, who dominated the Institution. Henry evaluated proposals for inventions, reported on government policies, and conducted experiments to address wartime problems. Henry noted that the Smithsonian staff made "several hundred" reports, but the exact number of investigations will never be known because the records were destroyed by fire in 1865. On occasion Henry was pressed into service to do an odd job no one else could do, such as debunking a spiritualist. Henry's seemingly random activities on behalf of the Union war effort reflected the federal government's failure to make long-range plans for scientific research. Because strategists expected the war to end quickly, the federal government did not sponsor a systematic research program to address specific problems. Consequently the process of government agencies requesting technical assistance was informal, ad hoc, and sporadic. Similar difficulties troubled the Confederate States during the Civil War and the United States at the beginning of World War I and World War II.[16]

Henry's first service for the federal government was to evaluate the plans of inventors. The *Scientific American* exhorted "men of genius" to "make an improvement on some well-known machine" or to "strike out into some new field of discovery," and they responded. Henry rejected most of them as impractical or impossible, but he lobbied for those that showed promise. Henry took proposals advanced by scientists more seriously than those made by amateurs, but the military authorities ignored these innovations in the cases of Henry Wurtz, Thaddeus Sobeski Constantine Lowe, and Robert L. Stevens. In December 1861 Henry supported Wurtz's attempts to improve percussion caps, incendiary shells, and canister shot. He arranged for Wurtz, who had been released from his position as an examiner in the Patent Office, to demonstrate his percussion caps

---

[16] *Smithsonian Institution Annual Report for 1862*, 14; *Smithsonian Institution Annual Report for 1864*, 47; A. Hunter Dupree, *Science in the Federal Government: A History of Policies and Activities to 1940* (Cambridge, Mass.: Harvard University Press, 1957), 121; Bruce, *Launching of American Science*, 306–7; Alex Roland, "Science and War," *Osiris*, 2d series, 1 (1985): 255–57.

before then Commander John A. B. Dahlgren, Chief of the Ordnance Bureau of the Navy. After Dahlgren dismissed Wurtz following an unimpressive showing, Henry allowed him to perfect the project in the Smithsonian laboratory. Lincoln ordered another trial, probably because of Henry's intercession, but the gun burst to pieces, thus ending the project.[17]

The most famous proposal Henry supported was a suggestion by Lowe to use a manned balloon outfitted with a telegraph for military reconnaissance. Intrigued by Lowe's plan, Henry arranged for the aeronaut to conduct demonstrations in Washington. During ascents in June 1861, Lowe successfully transmitted telegrams to observers on the ground, to stations as far away as Philadelphia and Baltimore, and to Lincoln as evidence of the "availability of the science of aeronautics in the military service of the country." After a demonstration on the Smithsonian grounds allayed fears that atmospheric disturbances might interfere with the telegraph, Henry endorsed Lowe. Confident that "important information may be obtained in regard to the topography of the country, and to the position and movements of an enemy by means of the balloon," Henry introduced Lowe to Cameron. Despite the promise of Lowe's trials, the War Department showed little enthusiasm. Chafing at its slow response, Henry sent Lowe to Secretary of the Treasury Salmon P. Chase. Chase eventually made Lowe chief balloonist of the Army of the Potomac's Balloon Corps, which was comprised of seven aeronauts who served with distinction at the Peninsular Campaign, Fredericksburg, and Chancellorsville. The difficulties of transporting an inflated balloon proved insuperable, so Lowe constructed gas generators fixed on carriages. He also developed a pulley and tackle system to keep a balloon moored to the ground over the battlefield, allowing many officers to make observations. After overcoming the additional problems of signaling and aerial observation, Lowe could not surmount the half-hearted support of the army. On the march to Gettysburg, General George C. Meade disbanded the Balloon Corps, and Lowe abandoned the project.[18]

---

[17] *Scientific American* 5 (September 21, 1861): 185; Bruce, *Lincoln and the Tools of War,* 268; H. Wurtz to J. Henry, November 9, 1861; J. Henry to H. Wurtz, December 10, 1861, Henry Wurtz Papers, New York Public Library.

[18] J. Henry to T. S. C. Lowe, February 25, 1861, reprinted in *Scientific American* 5 (December 14, 1861): 373; F. Stansbury Hayden, *Aeronautics in the Union and*

At the request of Congress, Navy Secretary Gideon Welles appointed Henry to the commission charged with determining whether the Stevens battery, an immense ironclad ship, should be completed. Word that the Confederates were building ironclads to break the Union blockade spurred the United States Navy to build its own and to consider completing the half-finished Stevens Battery, which had languished in dry dock since 1856. During a revolution in naval ordnance as a result of a European arms race, Stevens and his brothers had begun construction of an impregnable steamer for the federal government in 1842. After spending $700,000 over fourteen years to keep up with these innovations, the navy gave up on the ironclad, preferring to construct wooden vessels instead. The outbreak of the Civil War renewed interest in the Stevens Battery. "No marine structure," the *Scientific American* observed, "has so largely excited the curiosity as the Stevens battery from the mystery that has ever hung over its origin, character, size, appearance, destruction, and perhaps its very existence." Following a brief review, a commission rejected the project largely because the hull could not withstand the weight of the vessel. Henry, the only civilian on the committee, dissented. He asserted that the ship was capable of short voyages. After the battle of Hampton Roads showed the value of ironclads, the navy appointed another commission to evaluate the Stevens Battery, replacing Henry with then Captain Charles H. Davis. After the second commission reported against completing the vessel, Congress abandoned the project.[19]

The navy's need for a review of inventions coincided with the Lazzaroni's desire to found an official agency to provide technical assis-

---

Confederate Armies with a Survey of Military Aeronautics Prior to 1861, 2 vols. (Baltimore: Johns Hopkins University Press, 1941), 1:161–78; J. Henry to S. Cameron, June 21, 1861, Thaddeus Sobeski Constantine Lowe Papers, Library of Congress; *National Republican,* July 15, 1861; Coulson, *Joseph Henry,* 267; *Evening Star,* June 24, 1861; Dupree, *Science in the Federal Government,* 128; *Daily National Intelligence,* June 25, 1862.

[19] John Niven, *Gideon Welles, Lincoln's Secretary of the Navy* (New York: Oxford University Press, 1973), 364–70; James Phinney Baxter, *The Introduction of the Ironclad Warship* (Cambridge, Mass.: Harvard University Press, 1933), 48–52, 211–19; Joseph Henry Locked Book, October 11, 1861, Joseph Henry Papers; *Scientific American* 5 (August 31, 1861): 129–32; *Scientific American* 6 (January 18, 1862): 41–42; J. Henry to H. Henry, December 18, 1861, Joseph Henry Papers; *Daily National Intelligencer,* March 10, 21, April 17, 1862; J. Henry to A. D. Bache, April 22, 1862, William Jones Rhees Collection.

tance to the federal government, resulting in the formation of the National Academy of Sciences and the Permanent Commission of the Navy Department. Although Bache led Henry to believe that the Lazzaroni had dropped the National Academy in favor of the Permanent Commission, a select group of scientists who would screen inventions for the navy, he pursued both courses. In February 1863 Welles established the Permanent Commission "to which all subjects of a scientific character on which the government may require information may be referred." At the same time that Bache and Rear-Admiral Charles H. Davis sat with Henry on the Commission, they worked in secret to establish the National Academy. Although objecting to the surreptitious organization of the National Academy, Henry accepted an invitation to join the group because he wanted to "remedy as far as possible the evils which may have been done." In practice, the National Academy, which met as a body once during the war, referred matters to the Commission. Because of the overlapping memberships of the two bodies, these referrals amounted to only slight changes in the people who examined proposals. Meeting three times a week from February 1863 to September 1865, the Commission rotated through the offices of the members at the Smithsonian Institution, the Coast Survey, and the Bureau of Navigation. The Commission issued over two hundred reports on subjects such as designs for torpedoes, underwater guns, and ironclads, dismissing many as "entirely crude and undigested." The Commission was as close to a central scientific agency as the Union got during the Civil War, but it never enjoyed the resources to address research problems independently. The navy viewed the Commission only as a negative mechanism for rejecting crackpot schemes, not as a positive device for improving the fleet. The Commission was, however, an advance over the corrupt system of development that favored political connections over scientific research and eased Secretary of the Navy Gideon Welles's burden.[20]

---

[20] Nathan Reingold, "Science in the Civil War: The Permanent Commission of the Navy Department," *Isis* 49 (September 1958): 308–17; J. Henry to S. Alexander, March 9, 1863; J. Henry to M. Henry, April 24, 1863, Joseph Henry Papers; Green, *Washington*, 267; Coulson, *Joseph Henry*, 259; Bruce, *Launching of American Science*, 308; Bruce, *Lincoln and the Tools of War*, 224; J. Henry to A. D. Bache, August 21, 1862, Alexander Dallas Bache Papers; Dupree, *Science in the Federal Government*, 121, 137.

In addition to evaluating proposals for the government, Henry also performed experiments to address pressing war problems, such as the possible shortage of potassium nitrate or niter. By fall 1861 Union stores of niter, the main component of gunpowder, fell to low levels because the military had consumed domestic stocks and importation from India was slow. In 1857 the Department of War alerted Henry that the United States relied too heavily on British sources of niter. He had hoped to develop a method of producing niter in the laboratory, but Congress failed to fund the project. Instead, Henry employed B. F. Craig, an assistant in the Army Medical Department, to find alternative sources. Working in the Smithsonian laboratory, Craig determined that sodium nitrate, which was abundant in Chile, might prove useful as an alternative. In response to the 1861 niter crisis, Henry published Craig's "Report on Nitrification" in the Smithsonian annual report and sent Craig back to the Smithsonian laboratory. Joining Craig in the laboratory, Henry conducted experiments on the combustion of gunpowder in various gases. The United States met the crisis with English niter, but still groped for a cheap and reliable supply. To stimulate interest in the subject, Henry reprinted Craig's translation of a German essay on gun cotton (cotton dipped in sulfuric and nitric acids), which began to supplant gunpowder as the propellant in European firearms during the 1860s. To disseminate this information, Henry invited Wurtz to lecture on "Gunpowder" and Eben Horsford, Rumsford Professor on the Application of Science to the Useful Arts at Harvard College, to lecture on the "Munitions of War."[21]

Reflecting his confidence in the Smithsonian Institution, Lincoln referred unusual problems to Henry. To placate opponents of emancipation, Lincoln advocated voluntary repatriation of former slaves in Central America. Ambrose W. Thompson, a Philadelphia merchant who owned large tracts of land on the Isthmus of Panama, convinced Lincoln that substantial coal deposits in Panama made it the best location for such a colony. At the request of Secretary of State William H. Seward, Henry examined the coal deposits in the region.

---

[21] Jahns, *Maury & Henry*, 171–72; Alfred D. Chandler, "Du Pont, Dahlgren, and the Civil War Nitre Shortage," *Military Affairs* 13 (fall 1949): 142–49; *Smithsonian Institution Annual Report for 1861*, 38, 311, 317–318; *Smithsonian Institution Annual Report for 1862*, 45; *Smithsonian Institution Annual Report for 1863*, 234; *Daily National Intelligencer*, January 17, February 18, 1863.

Henry supported voluntary colonization of freed blacks as a solution to the problem of slavery in the South and racial discrimination in the North, but rejected Thompson's scheme as a swindle. Despite Seward's endorsement of the plan and an offer of shares in the colony for a favorable report by the speculators, Henry reported that the coal from the region was as "nearly worthless as any fuel can be." Although ignoring Henry's advice, the President abandoned the plan largely because of the protests raised by Central American diplomats, who resented an American encroachment on their territories.[22]

The President also recruited the Smithsonian Secretary to discredit a spiritualist, who took the name Lord Colchester and was preying on Mary Todd Lincoln's grief over the death of her son, Willie. Uncomfortable with the influence Colchester had over the First Lady, Lincoln wanted to reveal the medium as a charlatan. Unable to debunk Colchester himself, Lincoln called upon Henry, who had long opposed spiritualism, to investigate. After Colchester held a séance in the Smithsonian Institution, Henry concluded that the sounds came from the medium himself and that he made them even when both of his hands were held, but Henry could not prove that these sounds did not come from the spirit world. Several weeks later, Henry accidentally met a man who had sold the medium a telegraphic device that enabled him to make noises by flexing his biceps. Colchester left Washington soon after Henry made his report to Lincoln.[23]

In a review of the February 1862 number of the *American Journal of Science*, the *National Intelligencer* hoped that the "truths of science will not be lost in the pomp and circumstance of war." If not lost, the truths of science pursued by the Smithsonian Institution were at least obscured by the distractions of war. In his reports to Congress Henry put on a brave face, observing that modern warfare

---

[22] Warren A. Beck, "Lincoln and Negro Colonization in Central America," *Abraham Lincoln Quarterly* 6 (September 1950): 167–75, 181–83; *Daily National Intelligencer*, September 1 and 18, 1862; J. Henry to A. Gray, May 22, 1862, Asa Gray Papers, Gray Herbarium Library, Harvard University; J. Henry to J. P. Lesley, May 28, 1862, John Peter Lesley Papers, American Philosophical Society, Philadelphia.

[23] J. Henry to J. D. Dana, May 24, 1855, Dana Family Papers, Sterling Library, Yale University; Jahns, *Maury & Henry*, 212–13; Ruth Painter Randall, *Mary Lincoln: A Biography of a Marriage* (Boston: Little, Brown, 1953), 292–93; R. Laurence Moore, "Spiritualism and Science: Reflections on the First Decade of the Spirit Rappings," *American Quarterly* 24 (October 1972): 474–75, 486–89, 493–95.

encouraged the development of important "scientific truths" because it demanded the "application of scientific principles on a scale of magnitude which would never be attempted in time of peace." In his private correspondence he was not so sanguine. "Of all places in the country," Henry complained, "Washington is . . . the worst in which to pursue scientific investigations. The constant drudgery and anxiety of an office unfit a man for profound and continuous thought; and as he is under the restraint of the sentiment of the dominant party, he finally loses his manly independence and that love of truth which constitutes an honest man." Despite the threat of Confederate invasion, the excitement of partisan politics, and the distraction of war-related research, Henry pursued the active operations of research and publication as best he could. Unable to communicate with the southern contingent of his meteorological network, Henry continued to collect data from observers in the North. Although the federal government sent no more specimens to the Smithsonian museum because of the recall of military explorers to war duty, Baird disseminated specimens from previous expeditions to naturalists for classification. Overcoming the disruption of oceanic traffic by Union blockaders and Confederate privateers, the Smithsonian system of exchanges continued to transmit scientific materials between the United States and the rest of the scientific world.[24]

The greatest obstacle posed by the Civil War to the Smithsonian Institution research program was the economic dislocation that diminished the funds that Henry could devote to research and publication. After the Confederate states repudiated their debts to the North, William Howard Russell, special correspondent of the London *Times*, reported that Arkansas had repudiated the bonds in which the Smithsonian funds had been invested, placing the Institution in financial straits. Fearing that his enemies might charge that he had carelessly invested Smithsonian funds, Henry explained in his annual report that Congress made the federal government the trustee of Smithson's bequest in 1846 so that the Treasury invested those monies and paid the interest to the Institution. Although this policy "saves the Smithsonian" from this repudiation, Henry privately acknowledged that it "really makes our Government, and not the fund

[24] *Smithsonian Institution Annual Report for 1862*, 13–14; *Daily National Intelligencer*, February 8, 1862; J. Henry to H. Wurtz, July 26, 1861, Henry Wurtz Papers.

set apart by Mr. Smithson, the supporter of the Institution." Unfortunately not all of the Smithsonian funds were protected by the federal government. In an effort to increase the principal, Henry had saved some of the interest accrued from Smithson's bequest. After attempts to convince Congress to add this sum to the endowment guaranteed by the federal government failed, the Board of Regents invested in the bonds of Tennessee and Virginia. These states also repudiated their debts, costing the Smithsonian about $4,000 in expected annual income, about 10 percent of its operating budget. To avoid further retraction of Smithsonian income, Henry lobbied Chase to pay the Institution in specie or its equivalent value instead of depreciated Treasury notes, but the Treasury Secretary had no choice but to send notes because of the scarcity of specie.[25]

With the Smithsonian finances exposed to the "disturbing incidents of a theatre of war," Henry decided to "curtail the expenditures of the Institution, as far as practicable," without suspending the active operations. Applying a rigid economy, Henry cut all superfluous expenses and was "exceedingly cautious in attempting any new enterprises." Stopping gas service at the Smithsonian in August 1863, Henry observed to the staff that "sun light is cheaper than gas light and answers all purposes equally well." At that same time Henry halted "all expenditures on new investigations in natural history" and told all of the visiting naturalists except Fielding B. Meek, a paleontologist who had resided at the Smithsonian since 1859, to "find lodgings elsewhere." Because of the depreciation of Treasury notes, Henry was unable to furnish instruments to the Smithsonian meteorological observers in 1863. Hampered by the scarcity of paper, Henry canceled the publication of some memoirs and delayed the publication of others. Lacking specie, he suspended the purchase of books and apparatus from Europe.[26]

---

[25] *Daily National Intelligencer,* August 24, 1861; *Smithsonian Institution Annual Report for 1861,* 14–15; J. Henry to A. Gray, July 12, 1861, Gray Herbarium Library; J. Henry to J. H. Coffin, December 10, 1861, Joseph Henry Papers; Rhees, ed., *Journals of the Board of Regents,* 243.

[26] *Smithsonian Institution Annual Report for 1861,* 15–16; J. Henry to A. Gray, July 12, 1861, Gray Herbarium Library; J. Henry to C. W. Eliot, February 17, 1862, Charles W. Eliot Papers, Houghton Library, Harvard University; J. Henry to Baron R. Ostensacken, December 22, 1864, Louis Agassiz Museum of Comparative Zoology, Houghton Library, Harvard University; J. Henry to S. F. Baird, August 24, 1863, Spencer F. Baird Papers, Smithsonian Institution Archives; J. Henry to S. P. Chase,

A labor shortage exacerbated the strained finances of the Smithsonian Institution. In the heady days of the spring of 1861, Baird regretted the loss of several assistants who left the drudgery of the museum for the glory of the battlefield. After consecutive Union defeats dampened war enthusiasm, enlistments slumped. To raise enough troops to prosecute the war, Congress passed a military draft, conscripting all able-bodied men aged twenty to forty-five. Baird, thirty-nine years old, feared that he would be enrolled. Although Baird was not drafted, Meek, William J. Rhees, chief clerk of the Smithsonian Institution, and Solomon Brown, an assistant in the museum, were. All three received exemptions, but not all scientists were so reluctant to serve their country. On June 20, 1863, Bache and Lieutenant James. M. Gilliss, director of the Naval Observatory, were among the pallbearers for the coffin of Lieutenant Colonel William R. Palmer of the Topographical Engineers, who died on the battlefield.[27]

The receipt of the Smithsonian's income in Treasury notes hurt the Institution's system of international exchanges more than almost any other part of the active operations because of its dependence on specie. Thanks to the presence of the Union navy, transatlantic steamer traffic continued unvexed, but the hand of war weighed on the exchanges. Henry was unable to advance the postage of several American scientific societies to Felix Flügel, the Smithsonian agent in Leipzig. Baird exchanged thousands of packages of scientific books and apparatus with Flügel, Gustave Bossange in Paris, William Wesley in London, and Frederick Müller in Amsterdam over the course of the war, but the suspension of postal service with the South cut off southern scientists and scientific societies from sending or receiving packages. As the southern part of the system was comparatively small,

---

June 22, 1864, General Records of the Treasury, Record Group 56, National Archives and Records Administration, Washington, D.C.; *Smithsonian Institution Annual Report for 1862,* 15.

[27] *Smithsonian Institution Annual Report for 1862,* 36; Green, *Washington,* 257; Mark E. Neely, Jr., *The Fate of Liberty: Abraham Lincoln and Civil Liberties* (New York: Oxford University Press, 1991), 52–53; Eugene Converse Murdock, *Patriotism Limited, 1862–1865: The Civil War Draft and the Bounty System* (Kent, Ohio: Kent State University Press, 1967), 5–11; J. Henry to S. F. Baird, August 16, 1862, Spencer F. Baird Papers; A. C. Heamlin to the Director of the Board of Enrollment of the 7th District, September 29, 1864, Fielding B. Meek Papers; J. Henry to C. Wetherill, October 17, 1864, Joseph Henry Papers; Bruce, *Launching of American Science,* 279; *Daily National Intelligencer,* June 20, 1862.

its absence was not a grievous blow. Despite these difficulties, Baird managed to transmit about the same volume of packages during the war as in "preceding years."[28]

Perhaps Henry's greatest war-related disappointment was the disruption of the network of meteorological observers, which "suffered more than any other part" of the Smithsonian research program. Provided with instruments and registers, these friends of science took a variety of observations and transmitted their records to the Institution. After the suspension of postal service with the rebellious states, Henry received no registers from southern members. Enlistments claimed some northern members of the network. These martial encroachments took a great toll on the Smithsonian observers, cutting their number from a high of over five hundred in the late 1850s to below three hundred during the Civil War. Henry's difficulties in maintaining the meteorological network were pushed to the breaking point when Congress passed a postal act in 1863, which inadvertently prohibited the Smithsonian observers from sending their registers without postage, a privilege they had enjoyed by virtue of the Smithsonian Institution's collaboration with the Patent Office. After taking observations three times a day, most observers were unwilling to pay the postage to send the data. Faced with the prospect of the meteorological network's dissolution, Henry successfully lobbied Congress to amend the law in 1864. Henry feared that there would be no results from 1863, but the Commissioner of Agriculture paid the postage for one hundred observers. Henry had hoped to outfit the observers with barometers calibrated to an international standard agreed to by European meteorologists, but the uncertain state of Smithsonian finances precluded the purchase of new instruments until after the war. Henry also had to discontinue the practice of updating a climatic map of North America with daily telegraphic reports of weather conditions because the telegraph lines to the South were cut and the lines to the West were "so entirely occupied by public business that no use of them could be obtained for scientific business."[29]

[28] S. F. Baird to F. Flügel, March 9, 1861, Spencer F. Baird Papers; J. Henry to H. Stevens, May 12, 1863, Henry Stevens Papers, Charles E. Young Research Library, University of California, Los Angeles; *Smithsonian Institution Annual Report for 1861*, 44–45, 48, 51, 57; *Smithsonian Institution Annual Report for 1862*, 41, 47; *Smithsonian Institution Annual Report for 1863*, 41.

[29] *Smithsonian Institution Annual Report for 1861*, 35–36; *Daily National Intelligencer*, June 27, 1861; James Rodger Fleming, *Meteorology in America, 1800–1870*

Although the scarcity of paper delayed the publication of the observations from the meteorological network, Henry managed to publish the meteorological observations of the Arctic taken by American explorer Elisha K. Kane and British explorer Sir F. L. McClintock on separate expeditions in search of Sir John Franklin, a British Arctic explorer who was lost at sea. "It would be a great interest to science, and particularly to the meteorology of this country," Henry noted, if all subsequent meteorological observations of the Arctic would be made and reduced on a "uniform plan, like that adopted in regard to the observations of Dr. Kane." Showing his interest in meteorology, Henry published these memoirs before others. The difficulties in publication were offset by the decline in scientific memoirs submitted. During the war the number of papers submitted to the Smithsonian each year was fewer than for any previous year. Henry believed that the martial ethos favored the "collection of facts" over the "deduction of general principles" because the disorder of war distracted the mind from "continued application to the development of a single idea."[30]

Despite the uncertainties of war, Henry inaugurated a new journal, the *Smithsonian Miscellaneous Collections,* to introduce newcomers to the natural sciences and to encourage them to "co-operate with all others engaged in the same pursuit." In the first of the two volumes published in 1862, Henry provided directions for the use of meteorological instruments and tables of conversions that were prepared by Arnold H. Guyot, professor of physical geography and geology at Princeton College. Although developed for use by the observers in the Smithsonian meteorological network, the tables were useful to all of the "friends of meteorology" to reduce their observations to a form that would be useful to meteorologists. In the second volume Henry included natural history catalogs of birds, reptiles, and shells, as well as directions for collecting and preserving natural history specimens. With the help of several other naturalists, Baird developed a simple protocol that would allow "any one, with but little practice, to pre-

---

(Baltimore: Johns Hopkins University Press, 1990), 82, 146–47; *Smithsonian Institution Annual Report for 1862,* 28–32; *Smithsonian Institution Annual Report for 1863,* 31–32; *Smithsonian Institution Annual Report for 1865,* 51, 56–57; [H.] Grinnell to J. Henry, August 4, 1863, Joseph Henry Papers.

[30] *Smithsonian Institution Annual Report for 1861,* 16, 18–20, 24; *Smithsonian Institution Annual Report for 1862,* 16, 28–29.

serve, specimens, sufficiently well for the ordinary purposes of science."[31]

Offering a more elementary introduction to natural history than that provided by the *Smithsonian Miscellaneous Collections*, the National Museum of the Smithsonian Institution entertained the tens of thousands soldiers and civilians who swelled the national metropolis during the war. Discounting transient soldiers, the population in Washington doubled from sixty thousand in 1861 to 120,000 in 1863. With some trepidation, Henry noted that this unprecedented exodus of "strangers" to Washington "continually thronged" the museum. From March to May 1863 over twenty-three thousand people—half of whom were soldiers or sailors—visited the museum. Henry encouraged the soldiers to visit "as often as their duties permit," but exhortation was not necessary. Only the discipline imposed by General George B. McClellan stemmed the flood of soldiers who visited, and only temporarily. George Templeton Strong, the Treasurer of the United States Sanitary Commission, found the museum to be "magnificent," but regarded the laboratory and the working rooms as "shabby, dusty, listless, and feeble." Not all visitors were impressed with the museum. Walt Whitman, an occasional correspondent for the *New York Tribune* and hospital attendant, preferred the Smithsonian grounds to the "old-fogy concern" of the museum.[32]

While visitors gawked at the "bird wonders" in the display cases, Baird and his staff processed the tens of thousands of specimens that had accumulated from government exploring expeditions. As the federal government recalled its exploring expeditions, reassigning soldiers and sailors from the frontier to the front, the flood of additions to the museum was reduced to a trickle. This respite allowed Baird to make great progress in describing and labeling specimens. To diffuse

[31] *Smithsonian Institution Annual Report for 1861*, 26–29; *Smithsonian Institution Annual Report for 1862*, 14, 26; Arnold Guyot, "Tables, Meteorological and Physical, Prepared for the Smithsonian Institution," *Smithsonian Miscellaneous Collections* 1 (1862): 3; [Spencer F. Baird], "Directions for Collecting, Preserving, and Transporting Specimens of Natural History, Prepared for the Smithsonian Institution," *Smithsonian Miscellaneous Collections* 2 (1862): 3.

[32] Green, *Washington*, 250; Walter Lowenfels, ed., *Walt Whitman's Civil War, Compiled & Edited from Published & Unpublished Sources* (New York: Da Capo Press, 1960), 65, 144–45; *Smithsonian Institution Annual Report for 1861*, 44; *Daily National Intelligencer*, May 23, 1863; J. Varden to S. F. Baird, August 3, 1861, Spencer F. Baird Papers; Allan Nevins and Milton Halsey Thomas, eds., *The Diary of George Templeton Strong*, 4 vols. (New York: Macmillan, 1952), 3:438.

knowledge, Henry determined that duplicates of described specimens should be distributed to museums, natural history societies,
and colleges. During the war Baird distributed tens of thousands of
duplicates. The devaluation of payments from the federal government to support the museum prompted Henry to renew his efforts
to transfer the museum and the castle to the federal government and
devote the Smithsonian bequest to the "active operations" of scientific research and publication. Observing in his annual report that the
"principal end attained by the public museum of the Institution has
been the gratification and incidental instruction of the visitors to the
city of Washington," Henry asserted that the collection and distribution of specimens that formed the primary scientific advantage of
the Smithsonian collections required "no costly building nor corps of
attendants, and indeed, the charge of them might well be assumed
by other establishments." The addition of Louis Agassiz, the leading
American naturalist, as a Regent in 1864 added a sympathetic and
powerful ally to Henry's effort to sever ties with the museum and the
castle, but the rest of the Board showed little enthusiasm.[33]

The event that proved most disruptive to the operations of the
Smithsonian Institution during the Civil War had nothing to do with
the unusual contingencies of a war, but rather with a universal danger—that of fire. On the afternoon of January 24, 1865, a fire broke
out in the attic of the building. The District fire department arrived
on the scene in a matter of minutes, but an inadequate supply of
water, the consequence of a mud-clogged aqueduct, hampered its
work. The fire destroyed the towers, razed the rooms in the upper
story, and collapsed the roof, but did not damage the first floor or the
wings. While a detachment of soldiers kept looters away, Henry
worked to protect what remained of the Smithsonian castle. At Henry's request, Lincoln ordered the army to construct a temporary roof
to protect the exposed interior of the building from the elements.
Henry assured the Board of Regents that the fire had spared the

---

[33] *Daily National Intelligencer,* October 29, 1862; *Smithsonian Institution Annual
Report for 1861,* 41–43, 58–64; *Smithsonian Institution Annual Report for 1862,*
34–35, 37–39, 55–56; *Smithsonian Institution Annual Report for 1863,* 52–53;
Smithsonian Institution Annual Report for 1864, 31; J. Henry to L. Agassiz, June 10,
1863, and Henry Locked Book, March 15, 1864, Jospeh Henry Papers; Rhees, ed.,
Journals of the Board of Regents, 218–22, 233–34; J. Henry to A. D. Bache, August
15, 1864, Alexander Dallas Bache Papers.

meteorological records and the duplicate specimens ready for distribution and did not "materially affect the essential operations of the
Institution, which would be continued as usual." The Board determined that a stove that had been temporarily placed in the attic by
workmen caused the fire. Henry totaled the damages: approximately
eighty-five thousand pages of official correspondence, twelve volumes of meteorological observations collected in 1860, the records
of war-related research, four manuscripts of scientific monographs
accepted for publication, and James Smithson's personal effects and
apparatus. Refusing to allow the fire to slow the advance of science,
Henry completed the next volume of the *Smithsonian Contributions
to Knowledge* on time.[34]

Joseph Henry greeted the end of the war more with a weary sense
of loss than with satisfaction at a successfully completed task, no
doubt in large part because of the toll the conflict had taken on his
institution. By diverting resources from science, by distracting scientists from research, and by disrupting communication between scientists, the Civil War placed heavy burdens on American science.
Southern scientists suffered the greatest hardships because of the
dislocation and isolation the war brought to their region, but northern
scientists endured the distractions and deprivations of the conflict
as well. As the leading patron of antebellum American science, the
Smithsonian Institution had much to lose and little to gain from the
shock of war. The charged atmosphere of wartime Washington and
Henry's stubborn independence opened the Smithsonian to political
attacks. Rapid inflation, labor shortages, and the high cost of paper
hamstrung the Institution's active operations of research and publication. The demands of war shifted the Smithsonian program from
basic to applied research. Although conducting research on behalf of
the Union war effort, the Smithsonian savants and other American
scientists did not reap the rewards that their counterparts enjoyed
after World War II. Despite its consolidation of power as a result of

---

[34] *Daily National Intelligencer,* January 25, 1865; Hafertepe, *America's Castle,*
132–37; Henry Desk Diary, January 25 and 26, 1865, Joseph Henry Papers; Rhees,
ed., *Journals of the Board of Regents,* 234–39; Fleming, *Meteorology in America,
1800–1870,* 147; *Smithsonian Institution Annual Report for 1864,* 29; *Smithsonian
Institution Annual Report for 1861,* 47; J. Henry to L. Agassiz, January 31, 1865,
William Jones Rhees Collection; Hafertepe, *America's Castle,* 138–40; J. Henry to
[A. Gray], February 13, 1865, Joseph Henry Papers.

the war, the federal government remained an observer rather than a supporter of science. Overcoming all of these difficulties, the Smithsonian Institution pursed the abstruse truths of science in the midst of war. Henry and Spencer F. Baird preserved the meteorological network, maintained the system of international exchanges, continued the transmission of natural history specimens, and ensured that the Smithsonian publications remained on the press. After the Civil War ended, Henry fought a holding action against the encroachment of the museum on research and publication. However, after his death in 1878, Baird became the Smithsonian Secretary, completing the transformation of the Institution from a center of scientific research to a museum.[35]

---

[35] Bruce, *The Launching of American Science*, 272; Howard S. Miller, *Dollars for Research: Science and Its Patrons in Nineteenth-Century America* (Seattle: University of Washington Press, 1970), 185.

9

Civil War Church Trials: Repressing Dissent on the Northern Home Front

Bryon C. Andreasen

AT FIRST BLUSH, the well-worn diaries of itinerant preacher John H. Excell do not seem promising sources for historians of the Civil War home front. Terse, generally undescriptive, void of retrospection, the good minister's entries simply chronicle the daily travels and appointments of a busy, dedicated United Brethren clergyman serving on the circuits of the Western Reserve Conference in Ohio during the war years.[1] There is, however, this interesting entry for May 18, 1864:

> Ate breakfast went to Bro Burnetts found him at home talked with him found out that I must bring him to trial he is in sympathy with Slavery & Vallandigham[.][2]

Brother Burnett was a Democrat, and as such, he had by the spring of 1864 become increasingly suspect in the eyes of most clergymen and lay members of the United Brethren in Christ, a denomination that prided itself on its wartime abolitionist credentials and its support for the state and federal Republican administrations. At the next

---

[1] John J. Excell Papers, 1850–87 (hereinafter cited as Excell Papers), Ohio Historical Society, Columbus, Ohio. Besides keeping a diary, Rev. Excell occasionally sent correspondence to the official organ of the United Brethren in Christ, the *Religious Telescope*. For example, see issues for May 14, 1862, and May 13, 1863.

[2] Diary, 1863–64, folder 5, box 1, Excell Papers. Clement L. Vallandigham, Ohio Congressman and gubernatorial candidate in 1863, was the leader of the Democratic party's "Peace" wing and was declaimed as a leading Copperhead. For a biography of Vallandigham, see Frank L. Klement, *The Limits of Dissent: Clement L. Vallandigham and the Civil War* (Lexington: University Press of Kentucky, 1970; reprint ed., New York: Fordham University Press, 1998).

Quarterly Conference held at the end of June 1864, Excell brought Burnett to trial.[3] On June 30 Excell recorded:

> This is the day appointed to try Bro Burnett so I must go clear up there to attend to it Bro Evan & Merwin came Strong went with The Elder B[urnett] came his son pettifogged his case Evans & Merwin chose Bro Strong for 3d man so the trial went off B[urnett] had quite a lot of democrats there our main witnesses would not come the committee condemned him on 2 specifications I came home Bro Strong rode with me[.][4]

This is the extent of the record of the church trial of Brother Burnett. The Democrat was "condemned" by a committee of three clergymen. The precise charges and specifications on which he was convicted are unrecorded, though it is clear Burnett's political views were at the core of the complaint. Neither is the committee's sentence for the "condemned" recorded, though the usual procedure would have been "suspension" until the next annual meeting, when the full Conference would affirm or overturn the verdict of the Quarterly Conference. Even the defendant's full name and his church status are unclear, though he was probably a traveling minister, since

---

[3] In general, the United Brethren followed the same pattern of ecclesiastical organization as the Methodist Episcopal Church—Civil War America's largest Protestant denomination (see note 11). The Methodists divided their churches into ecclesiastical jurisdictions called "Conferences" for administrative purposes. At the time of the Civil War, there were twelve Conferences in Illinois, Indiana, and Ohio, four in each state (though part of a fifth Ohio Conference overlapped into Pennsylvania). Each Conference was subdivided into districts that would meet in quarterly Conferences. And each district, in turn, was divided into circuits consisting of several appointments (local congregations) that were served by an itinerant minister who traveled around the circuit on a regular schedule to preach and perform ecclesiastical duties (hence the term "circuit preacher"). The traveling minister was sometimes assisted by local ministers or superannuated preachers (retired ministers) who were associated with local congregations. For an informative description of nineteenth-century Methodist Church organization, see chapter 7, "Structures That Formed the Church," in J. Gordon Melton's denominational history, *Log Cabins to Steeples: The Complete Story of the United Methodist Way in Illinois, including All Constituent Elements of the United Methodist Church* (Nashville: Commissions on Archives and History of the Northern, Central, and Southern Illinois Conferences, 1974), 109–19.

[4] Diary, 1863–64, folder 5, box 1, Excell Papers. Rev. Excell's diary provides other glimpses of the prevailing anti-Democratic bias among Protestant clergymen. On June 12, 1864, for example, he recorded that he "staid [sic] at home" and read, rather than attend a Sabbath School conducted by a man who "voted for Vallandigham."

the official church newspaper noted several months later that the expulsions of "J. Burnett" and two other ministers were confirmed during the Annual Conference meeting in mid-October 1864.[5] This personally traumatic episode in the life of one of the Civil War's many faceless Democratic dissidents would be lost to history but for its mention in an obscure preacher's diary and a solitary, unrevealing notation in a forgotten church newspaper.

Exploring "the limits of dissent" is an important topic for scholars studying the home front of any war. For historians of the American Civil War, the traditional concern in this regard has been the civil liberties record of the Lincoln administration—the extent, if any, to which the President and his men manipulated the government's internal security apparatus to suppress political opposition. In his 1992 Pulitzer Prize–winning study *The Fate of Liberty*, for example, Mark E. Neely, Jr., examined wartime federal arrest records of civilians. He concluded that most arrests "had nothing to do with dissent or political opposition in the loyal states above the border states."[6] Excerpts like the one from the Rev. John Excell's diary about the trial and conviction of Democratic church members, however, suggest that historians should look beyond the reach of formal government authority and look also at the power of local social institutions—such as the church—in matters of repressing dissent on the northern home front.

There is no doubt that northern Protestants played an influential role in national affairs during the Civil War. In studies like James Moorhead's *American Apocalypse,* scholars have examined how "Holy War" interpretations of the conflict, articulated and espoused primarily by northeastern clergymen, served to rationalize and support the North's conduct of the war.[7] Others, like Victor Howard in

---

[5] "Western Reserve," *Religious Telescope*, November 9, 1864, 43. Usually only disciplinary actions against traveling ministers, who were higher in the church hierarchy than local ministers, were reported in the denomination's newspaper. The other expelled ministers were "V. B. Jones" and "Jos. Heickle." Also noted with no explanatory comment is a suspension—"S. D. Stone"; two "erasiers" [sic] (withdrawals)—"J. W. Kilbern" and "J. Bradish"; and one dismissal by letter—"O. Card."

[6] Mark E. Neely, Jr., *The Fate of Liberty: Abraham Lincoln and Civil Liberties* (New York: Oxford University Press, 1991), 137–38.

[7] James H. Moorhead, *American Apocalypse: Yankee Protestants and the Civil War, 1860–1869* (New Haven, Conn.: Yale University Press, 1978). This important book is the most ambitious study yet undertaken of northern religious interpreta-

Religion and the Radical Republican Movement, have demonstrated the important influence that Protestant clergymen had in shaping and justifying the political agenda of Republican politicians.[8] Studies such as these tend to emphasize the attitudes and contributions of the Protestant majority who generally supported the war aims and policies of the ruling party.[9]

Clearly the Protestant churches significantly influenced the character and outcome of the Union war effort. But these churches also had an influential role in shaping the character and extent of attempts to repress dissent on the northern home front. Those most directly affected by these efforts were clergymen who were members of the Democratic party. This essay surveys church disciplinary actions against Democrats in some key states of the Civil War West—Illinois, Indiana, and Ohio—and suggests that attempts to pressure dissenting churchmen to conform to the political expectations of the clerical majority created an oppressive wartime atmosphere for many dissenting clergymen and church members.[10]

---

tions of the Civil War. Moorhead focuses on the four major denominations of the North's Protestant establishment: Baptists, Congregationalists, Methodists, and Presbyterians (Old and New Schools); he uses evidence from published sermons, tracts, church Conference resolutions, and popular evangelical weeklies in an effort to "gauge . . . rank and file opinion." Nevertheless, his work tends to reflect more heavily the thinking of the church leadership elite from eastern sections of the North.

[8] Victor B. Howard, *Religion and the Radical Republican Movement, 1860–1870* (Lexington: University Press of Kentucky, 1990), 1–6, 212, and passim, credits "radical Christians" in the northern Protestant churches with making antislavery sentiment more respectable in northern circles and with successfully exerting their moral influence on the Republican politicians who implemented radical war and Reconstruction policies. John R. McKivigan, *The War against Proslavery Religion: Abolitionism and the Northern Churches, 1830–1865* (Ithaca, N.Y.: Cornell University Press, 1984), 188, 191, 200, however, is more critical of the churches, admitting their instrumentality in sustaining the government's war policies, but attributing it chiefly to antisouthern prejudice and passion rather than to moral convictions.

[9] See also Chester Forrester Dunham, *The Attitude of the Northern Clergy toward the South, 1860–1865* (Philadelphia: Porcupine Press, 1974); Lewis Vander Velde, *The Presbyterian Churches and the Federal Union, 1861–1869* (Cambridge, Mass.: Harvard University Press, 1932); William Warren Sweet, *The Methodist Episcopal Church and the Civil War* (Cincinnati: Methodist Book Concern, 1912); Richard Chrisman, "'For God and Country': Illinois Methodist Support for President Lincoln during the Civil War," *Lincoln Herald* 99 (summer 1997): 80–89.

[10] It is simply not possible to determine with precision the denominational affiliation of Democratic voters, given the paucity of firm data from the mid–nineteenth century. On the difficulty of obtaining religious quantitative data for the period, see

The experience of Democrats in the Illinois Annual Conference of the Methodist Episcopal Church (MEC) is illustrative.[11] The Conference boundaries extended across central Illinois from the Mississippi River to the Indiana border and included such important cities as Jacksonville, Springfield, Decatur, and Charleston. The political atmosphere throughout Illinois was tense. Democratic politicians were arrested. Democratic newspapers were suppressed or attacked. Secret societies called "Union Leagues" (which originated in Pekin, Illinois, and quickly spread throughout the state and beyond) functioned as an underground Republican "home guard." Some party leaders disclaimed these Union "vigilance" committees. Nevertheless, it was convenient, as one historian has noted, that suitable

---

Stephen L. Hansen, *The Making of the Third Party System: Voters and Parties in Illinois, 1850–1876* (Ann Arbor: UMI Research Press, 1980), 216. My assumption is based on the sheer magnitude of the evangelical Protestant presence in Civil War America. Evangelical Protestantism reached its zenith of cultural and social influence in America in the mid–nineteenth century. If children, seekers, and casual attenders are added to official church membership numbers, historians estimate that as much as 60 percent of the population came under direct evangelical influence (this inclusive percentage suggests that church influence may have had a broader impact than just the number of official church members may suggest). The leading evangelical Protestant denominations at the time of the Civil War were Methodists, Baptists, Presbyterians, Congregationalists, Disciples of Christ, and evangelical Episcopalians; see Richard J. Carwardine, *Evangelicals and Politics in Antebellum America* (New Haven, Conn.: Yale University Press, 1993), 4–6; Curtis D. Johnson, *Redeeming America: Evangelicals and the Road to Civil War* (Chicago: Ivan R. Dee, 1993), 3–4.

[11] The Illinois Conference was one of four Methodist Conferences in Illinois at the time of the Civil War. The others (descending geographically from north to south) were the Rock River Annual Conference, the Central Illinois Annual Conference, and the Southern Illinois Annual Conference. One nineteenth-century counting of Illinois church membership put the number of Methodists in the state in 1860 at 98,982 persons, served by 715 ministers. The closest Protestant rival, the Baptists, had a reported 36,062 members and 431 preachers; see John Moses, *Illinois Historical and Statistical*, 2d ed. revised, 2 vols. (Chicago: Fergus Printing, 1895), 2:1070–71.

It is difficult to determine with any precision the number of church members in the various Christian denominations in the nineteenth century. Church membership information was not collected until the 1890 census. The 1860 census does provide, however, the seating capacity of American churches on the eve of the Civil War. In the northern non-slave-holding states at that time, Methodists could accommodate the most people in their churches—3,471,461; second were the Baptists—1,630,402; Presbyterians of all types were a close third—1,622,203; Statistics of the United States . . . in 1860, compiled from Bureau of the Census, *Eighth Census of the United States*, vol. 4, *Miscellaneous* (Washington, D.C.: [Government Printing Office], 1866), 352–501.

"champions" could be found "to administer severe thrashings" to antiwar spokesmen, and Republican neighbors sat quietly by as bands of "union regulators" sought to silence Democrats "by threats and intimidation, if not by physical violence." In some areas Democrats responded in kind. Rumors abounded of Copperhead militias drilling in public places, and of secret meetings of antigovernment societies like the infamous Knights of the Golden Circle. Political assemblies of both parties were disrupted. In several instances people died in the violence. Civil discourse in many areas of the Illinois Conference seemed on the verge of breaking down.[12]

In this wartime atmosphere a spirit of super-patriotism pervaded the pulpits of the MEC Illinois Conference. Many clergymen and church members seemed to equate partisan loyalty for President Abraham Lincoln, the Republican party, and its war policies with church loyalty and Christian duty. Church-going Democrats, even many so-called War Democrats who opposed secession and supported the war in principle, came under suspicion and ridicule in church circles if they did not openly endorse the administration and

---

[12] The quotation is from Arthur Charles Cole, *The Era of the Civil War, 1848–1870* (Chicago: A. C. McClurg, 1922), which is still the best general overview of the political turmoil on the Illinois home front. Other works that cover aspects of the volatile Illinois home front include Theodore J. Karamanski, *Rally 'Round the Flag: Chicago and the Civil War* (Chicago: Nelson-Hall Publishers, 1993); Camilla A. Quinn, *Lincoln's Springfield in the Civil War* (Macomb: Western Illinois University, 1991); Neely, *The Fate of Liberty*; Frank J. Klement, *The Copperheads in the Middle West* (Chicago: University of Chicago Press, 1960); Wood Gray, *The Hidden Civil War: The Story of the Copperheads* (New York: Viking Press, 1942); David Costigan, "A City in Wartime: Quincy, Illinois and the Civil War" (D.A. diss., Illinois State University, 1994); Jasper William Cross, Jr., "Divided Loyalties in Southern Illinois during the Civil War" (Ph.D. diss., University of Illinois at Urbana-Champaign, 1942); Robert D. Sampson, " 'Pretty Damned Warm Times': The 1864 Charleston Riot and 'the Inalienable Right of Revolution,' " *Illinois Historical Journal* 89 (summer 1996): 99–116; William M. Anderson, "The Fulton County War at Home and in the Field," *Illinois Historical Journal* 85 (spring 1992): 23–36; Frank L. Klement, "Copperhead Secret Societies in Illinois during the Civil War," *Journal of the Illinois State Historical Society* 48 (summer 1955): 152–80; Charles H. Coleman and Paul H. Spence, "The Charleston Riot, March 28, 1864," *Journal of the Illinois State Historical Society* 33 (March 1940): 7–56; Bluford Wilson, "Southern Illinois in the Civil War," *Transactions of the Illinois State Historical Society 1911* 16 (spring 1913): 93–103; Thomas F. Schwartz, "Lincoln's 'Fire in the Rear': Civil Unrest in Illinois," copy in the possession of the author. On the development of the Union Leagues originating in Pekin, Illinois, see Frank L. Klement, *Dark Lanterns: Secret Political Societies, Conspiracies, and Treason Trials in the Civil War* (Baton Rouge: Louisiana State University Press, 1984), chapter 2.

Republican war aims, which by September 1862 came to include the controversial policy of emancipation. What were church-going Democrats supposed to think, for instance, when circuit ministers admonished congregants from the pulpit with warnings such as "He who does not adopt, maintain and defend a correct theory relative to 'matters of state' . . . will 'certainly lose his soul' "?[13]

To purge the Conference of its most outspoken minority clerics (and to set a warning example for others), some local presiding elders began resorting to church disciplinary measures. These could range from pressuring dissenting ministers into "requesting" to be located (relieved of circuit assignments) or "voluntarily" assuming superannuated status (retirement), to instigating full-fledged trial proceedings at which church membership was at stake.[14]

A well-publicized example occurred in the month preceding the 1863 Annual Conference meeting. Oliver H. McEuen, a local deacon

---

[13] "Preaching Politics," *Pike County [Ill.] Democrat*, January 21, 1864.

[14] *The Doctrines and Discipline of the Methodist Episcopal Church, 1860* (New York: Carlton & Porter, 1860), contained the rules and procedures that governed MEC disciplinary proceedings for most of the Civil War years. A charge or complaint against a minister or church member could be filed at any time with the presiding elder of a district or the traveling minister in charge of a circuit. Complaints could also be withheld until a quarterly (district) Conference meeting or the Annual Conference meeting, and then voiced when the offending minister's name was called for confirmation by the assembly as having sufficiently "good character" to merit continued association with the Conference. When complaints were filed, the presiding official usually appointed an investigating committee. If procedures for ameliorating the difficulty were unavailing, the presiding official would then order a formal trial and arbitrarily appoint other Conference ministers to act as prosecutors, defense counsel, or members of an adjudicating committee (jury). Trials would proceed in similar fashion to civil trials, with direct examination, cross-examination, and redirect examination of witnesses. The defendant was supposed to be present in person. Testimony was supposed to be recorded verbatim and sent to the Annual Conference.

The most serious grounds for misconduct by a churchman were dishonesty, immorality, or disseminating doctrines contrary to the church's articles. Cases deemed slightly less serious included "improper tempers, words, or actions," or conduct rendering a minister "so unacceptable, inefficient, or secular, as to be no longer useful in his work." Conviction at a district trial meant suspension until the next Annual Conference meeting, where the case would be reviewed by a committee, and the entire Conference would vote to confirm or reject the committee's disciplinary recommendation. Disciplinary sanctions could include a formal censure or reprimand, forced "location" (being relieved of circuit assignments), forced superannuated status (retirement), or formal expulsion from the church. Both traveling ministers and local ministers had the right to appeal convictions to the next higher jurisdiction. Appeals could go all the way to the quadrennial national Conference.

living on the New Hartford Circuit in Pike County in west central Illinois, was tried for his membership before a fifteen-member district tribunal. He was charged with sowing dissension for allegedly saying that the Methodist Church was becoming corrupt with "political preaching" and that Democrats should consider organizing a more conservative church. He was denounced for preferring secular Democratic newspapers to the Conference's organ, *Central Christian Advocate*, which McEuen believed was biased in favor of Republicans.

Democratic observers deemed the proceeding a "mock trial":

> [McEuen] was not allowed to read the reply to the charges . . . he was not allowed to finish his arguments to his plea of abatement. The President was generally in a very great hurry when the defendant was speaking or examining witnesses; but generally . . . had time sufficient when the prosecution spoke or examined a witness. . . . The Methodist Discipline and the Bill were laid aside, as to the management of Church offences . . . party spirit was the moving cause of it.[15]

Prosecution witnesses were invariably Republicans; defense witnesses were Democrats. It appeared that the Republicans on the tribunal, who constituted a sizeable majority, had already made up their minds as to a verdict before the trial commenced. Not surprisingly, the tribunal sustained both charges and summarily expelled McEuen from the church. "[H]e was proscribed for his opposition to the pollution of the pulpit and religious press with politics," dissidents protested. They feared that similar intolerance would be manifested toward other Democratic members of the church. It was time, they said, for all honest people to "pause and consider well" if they should remain in such a church any longer.[16]

The McEuen trial was a foreshadowing of what transpired at the Annual Conference meeting held in Springfield the following month,

---

[15] The reporters were several men and women, presumably married couples and class members on the New Hartford Circuit; see "A Mock Trial," *Pike County (Ill.) Democrat*, November 5, 1863. The Pike County article was republished in the *Quincy Herald*, November 14, 1863, and a shorter notice of the article later appeared in the *Chicago Times*, December 1, 1863. The United Brethren's newspaper also reported that Methodist "Rev. O. H. McEwen [sic], a local minister, on New Hartford circuit, Ill. was recently tried and expelled from the church for disloyalty to the government. Served him right"; *Religious Telescope*, November 18, 1863.

[16] "A Mock Trial," *Pike County [Ill.] Democrat*, November 5, 1863.

October 1863. There the politically enthused Conference members, whipped into a patriotic frenzy by a two-hour-long partisan harangue delivered by Republican Governor Richard Yates, brought disciplinary charges against a number of their fellow ministers on account of their Democratic politics.[17]

The first target was one of the pioneer preachers of the Conference, the Rev. William Blundell of Clark County.[18] Blundell was an old Jackson Democrat, but one who had not been in the habit of attending political meetings or of conversing on political subjects. As political excitement mounted during the war years, however, Blundell occasionally expressed his private opinions in day-to-day conversations with neighbors. In the summer of 1862, for example, he voiced disapproval of the Confiscation Act passed by Congress, believing it to be a federal "usurpation of power." In mid-September when President Lincoln issued the preliminary Emancipation Proclamation, Blundell opposed it, thinking it was an "unwise policy." At other times he said he did not think the rebellion could be put down by military force. These sentiments were not unusual among Illinois Democrats going in to the 1862 fall elections. When Blundell attended the 1862 Annual Conference meeting a few weeks before the elections, it was well known that he was a Democrat and that he generally disapproved of the way in which the government was prosecuting the war. So it was not coincidental that during the meeting Blundell was relegated to a superannuated (retired) relation with the Conference.

---

[17] Governor Richard Yates was not a Methodist church member, nor was he known for his religiosity. He was, for example, embarrassingly intoxicated at his own inauguration. Democrats complained bitterly that the governor's speech "turned the conference into a political convention"; see Bryon C. Andreasen, "'As Good a Right to Pray': Copperhead Christians on the Northern Civil War Home Front" (Ph.D. diss., University of Illinois at Urbana-Champaign, 1998), 150–51.

[18] Material quoted or related herein regarding the Blundell episode is from the William C. Blundell File (1864), Illinois Annual Conference Trial Records, Archives of the United Methodist Church Illinois Great Rivers Annual Conference, Bloomington, Ill. Certain aspects of the Blundell case were also reported in the *Illinois Daily State Register*, October 10, 11, 1863; *Peoria (Ill.) Morning Mail*, October 11, 1863; *Belleville (Ill.) Democrat*, October 17, 1863; and Roy W. Ennis, ed., *Journal and Records of the Forty-first Session of the Illinois Annual Conference of the Methodist Episcopal Church Held at Danville, Illinois Commencing September 29th and Ending October 3rd, 1864* (Springfield: Illinois Conference Historical Society, 1906), 4, 7. For a more detailed treatment of the Rev. Blundell and turmoil in the MEC Illinois Conference during the war, see Andreasen, "As Good a Right to Pray," chapter 4.

Despite his superannuated status, Blundell had continued to serve occasionally as a local preacher (as was customary with superannuated Conference members) in and around his Clark County home. So now, a year later, some in the Conference were intent on making a lesson out of him. When Blundell's name was called during the 1863 annual meeting for routine approval as a superannuated Conference member, critics challenged his fitness to serve as a Methodist preacher.[19] A special committee convened, and it formulated charges that included the following:

- Disloyalty to the Government of the United States for failing to identify with any of the movements looking to support the government [in other words he had declined to join the local Union League] . . .
- For failing to pray in public for the President or Armies of the United States . . .
- Gross immorality for failing to observe a day of National Thanksgiving as proclaimed by the President.

Added to these sins of omission was the sin of improper association, that of being seen in the company of persons alleged to be in sympathy with the rebellion. Blundell's accusers, however, had not brought along witnesses or other evidence to substantiate their charges. Most importantly, Blundell was not in attendance to face his accusers, as required by disciplinary procedural rules. The immediate purpose of those charging Blundell was apparently to make a political statement in front of their assembled colleagues, rather than actually to conduct a trial of the accused. By airing the charges in the large public forum of the Conference, the instigators scored their desired political points. Conference members then voted to send Blundell's case to the presiding elder in Clark County for formal adjudication, where he was later convicted.[20]

---

[19] One of the main items of business each year at the annual meeting of a Methodist Conference was approving the ministerial character of each individual Conference member. Usually this was a routine matter, with the presiding elder for each district vouching for the worthiness and integrity of those ministers he had supervised over the preceding year.

[20] At the subsequent quarterly Conference trial, Blundell pleaded not guilty to all charges. The forty-page manuscript trial transcript reveals the inane level on which these trials could proceed. This exchange on cross-examination about the nature of Blundell's prayers is illustrative:

Q. [by prosecution]: Do you remember about the language he used in praying for the President?

Political repercussions from the charges against Blundell reverberated beyond Republican religious circles. Blundell became a momentary cause célèbre among dissenting Democrats. If the accused was forced "to walk the plank," declared one, "then every Democrat belonging to the Conference ought to have self-respect enough to leave a religious body that has resolved itself into a political caucus." Conference officials became so exasperated with Democratic complaints and ridicule that they barred reporters from Springfield's leading Democratic newspaper from entering the building for the remaining days of the Conference. This act precipitated even louder protests from Democrats against ecclesiastical repression.[21]

After dispensing with the Blundell matter and expelling Democratic newspaper reporters, Conference members next passed a strongly worded "Report on the State of the Country" that read in many respects like a Republican campaign document. It concluded by stating that anyone who withheld his "hearty support from the administration of the government may be justly suspected of want of sympathy with, and loyalty to, the government of his country."[22] Sev-

---

Ans.: As near as I can remember, he prayed that the blessing of the Lord might rest upon the President and our Armies; and that God would confound the wrong and bless the right.

Q.: Did he pray that our armies might succeed in crushing the rebellion?

Ans.: I never heard him pray in those words.

Q. [by the Chair]: What did you understand his meaning to be when he asked the Lord to confound the wrong and bless the right?

Ans.: I understood him to mean both sides were wrong.

Q. [by Committee]: When, and how often have you heard Bro. Blundell pray for the President and our armies?

Ans.: When he was on the Livingston Circuit, [I] heard him about 4 or 5 times . . .

Following his conviction, Blundell joined one of the "new church" movements fostered by local Democratic dissidents. For a brief overview of the "new church" movements in Illinois, see Bryon C. Andreasen, "Proscribed Preachers, New Churches: Civil War in the Illinois Protestant Churches during the Civil War," *Civil War History* 44 (spring 1998): 194–211. For more detail, see Andreasen, "As Good a Right to Pray," chapters 12 and 13.

[21] "Degeneracy of the Church," *Belleville [Ill.] Democrat,* October 17, 1863; "No Democrats in the Church," *Peoria [Ill.] Morning Mail,* October 11, 1863; *Chicago Times,* October 13, 1863; see also Andreasen, "As Good a Right to Pray," 154–55.

[22] In addition, the "Report on the State of the Country" identified slavery as "the primary cause of this wicked rebellion"; it proclaimed that God was "compelling the nation to recognize the manhood of the negro"; it declared that the President's Emancipation Proclamation was "justified, not only by military necessity, but by the moral sense of the civilized world"; and it "cordially" approved "the administration in the enforcement of the Conscription Act and the suspension of the writ of *habeas corpus." Minutes of the Fortieth Session of the Illinois Annual Conference of the*

eral prominent Democrats, among them the venerable Rev. Peter Cartwright, a War Democrat, "spoke earnestly in opposition" to some of the Report's resolutions, and the Rev. James L. Crane of Springfield proposed some substitute "minority" resolutions. In the end only seven ministers out of the 127 in attendance dared to vote against the resolutions in their final form. The Conference then promptly proceeded to bring charges against two of the ministers who voted with the minority.[23]

The Rev. William P. Paxson, a young preacher with much promise, was charged with the effrontery of speaking at Democratic rallies in Christian County; the Rev. William C. Howard of the Moawequa Circuit, a ten-year Conference veteran, was charged with failing to pray for Abraham Lincoln and for proclaiming that if he was an Ohio citizen he would vote for the maligned "Copperhead" Clement Vallandigham for governor. "Rumors of disloyalty" regarding the two preachers circulated around the Convention. Suspense mounted as the assembled ministers waited for the names of the suspect preachers to be called during the routine roll call of Conference members.[24]

Paxson's name came first. As soon as it was called, several ministers rose to accuse him of making political speeches. Others took the floor to provide incriminating details. Many of the allegations regarding the unpatriotic nature of Paxson's political discourses were based on hearsay, there being few actual witnesses present to testify. After some heated discussion, the meeting chairman permitted the young reverend to address the entire Conference in response to the accusations. This turned out to be a tactical mistake.

Methodist Episcopal Church, held at Springfield, Illinois, from October 8th to October 13, 1863 (Chicago: Methodist Book Depository 1863), 26–27 (hereinafter *Published Minutes, 1863 Illinois Conference*). Virtually all Methodist Conferences in Illinois, Indiana, and Ohio adopted strongly worded endorsements of the Republican war policies.

[23] Andreasen, "As Good a Right to Pray," 148–51.

[24] "Illinois Conference Minutes in Manuscript Form, 1848–1864" (Bound Volume), 431–44, Archives of the United Methodist Church Illinois Great Rivers Annual Conference, Bloomington (hereinafter "1863 Manuscript Minutes"); *State Register*, October 13 and 14, 1863; "Meeting in Christian County," *Chicago Times*, August 24, 1863. Detailed retellings of the Paxson and Howard controversies are preserved in stenographic-like transcriptions in "Case of Rev. W. P. Paxson," *Pike County [Ill.] Democrat*, October 29, 1863; and "Speech of the Rev. Mr. Howard in the Methodist Conference," *Pike County [Ill.] Democrat*, November 26, 1863. Unless otherwise noted, the accounts and quotations that follow regarding the cases of

Paxson carefully explained each of the offending remarks attributed to him, showing how they had been taken out of context. He was for the Union and the original war aims of the Republican administration, but could not support the new, revolutionary direction the government had taken since the Emancipation Proclamation. As for the charge of making political speeches, "I have done so," he admitted unapologetically, "and I base my justification not so much as a moral but as a political right." He did not think it was proper for preachers to enter the political arena, he continued, "but just as long as the Conference sanctions speeches on the one side, I claim as a good loyal citizen the right to present the other side." He was willing, however, to make a covenant with his fellow ministers: if they would make no political speeches during the new Conference year, neither would he. He concluded with an emotional appeal:

> Mr. President, five years ago, in the first bloom of youth, I offered my services to the Church, and I . . . had hoped to live with you, labor with you, and die in the service of the Church; but, if for opinion's sake, I must be proscribed, and can retain my connection with you only at the sacrifice of my convictions of right, then I gladly leave you, and go out into some other field of action, where I can serve God and yet be free.

Paxson's oratory was effective. The entire Conference acting as jury passed on Paxson's character.[25]

Next called was the Rev. William R. Howard. The effective oratorical defense just delivered by Rev. Paxson apparently caused the Conference managers to adopt a different strategy in Howard's case. They quickly shuffled the matter off to a committee before there could be any general discussion on the Conference floor. The next day the Committee submitted a report that was not sufficiently strict for the majority of patriotic Conference members. Instead, they adopted a substitute measure from the floor:

Paxson and Howard are all based on or quoted from the respective *Pike County Democrat* articles. See also Andreasen, "As Good a Right to Pray," 156–65.

[25] Persistent Conference leaders managed to have the vote on Paxson's character "reconsidered," and his case was sent to a committee for review. The next day the Conference again voted not to censure or discipline Paxson. Nevertheless, it appears that the young reverend never fully recovered from the 1863 Annual Conference attacks. In 1865 Paxson was "located" (relieved of circuit duties); his name never appears in Conference records again.

WHEREAS, Our country is in a terrible conflict with rebels, and whereas, Brother Howard has, by common rumor and by his own statements before Conference confirming that rumor, been imprudent in his position on the great questions involving loyalty to the Government so as to impair his usefulness as a Methodist preacher therefore,

RESOLVED, That he be reprimanded by the Chair, and that his character pass.[26]

Before members voted on the substitute measure, however, the Conference president relented and finally allowed Howard to address the Conference in his own defense. The beleaguered minister declared, "[if] this Conference will not pass my character on account of my political opinions, I want this issue to go before the people, and I intend that it shall." It seemed the Conference intended "to close the mouths of those who differ with them," he exclaimed. He warned, however, "there is no power in heaven or earth, or hell, that can close my mouth or deny me the right to express my opinions as a free man." "I love the Constitution of my country next to my bible," he proclaimed. But the Lincoln administration was wrong. "I do not and cannot endorse its policy," he declared. Nevertheless, he would never propose that anyone "interfere with, or resist the action of the Administration so long as the ballot-box is free and the way thereto untrammelled." He, as did Paxson, concluded emotionally, but perhaps with more defiance:

I am arraigned before this Conference as a criminal, not charged with inefficiency or immorality or unacceptability, but . . . wholly on account of political sentiments, in a word that I am a Democrat. But being firmly and religiously convinced of the correctness of my political opinions, I shall think for myself and vote for whosoever I please, regardless of consequences.

Howard's truculent address did not have the same effect as had Paxson's. The Conference adopted the condemnatory measure, whereupon the visiting bishop "administered a reprimand" to Howard. Humiliated, the aggrieved minister asked to be "located" or relieved of a circuit assignment.[27] At the conclusion of the Howard

---

[26] In addition to the *Pike County [Ill.] Democrat* article, the substitute report is also in the 1863 Manuscript Minutes, 433–34.

[27] In the substitute report, the Conference requested the bishop to furnish a copy of his remarks for the minutes. But they do not appear in either the manuscript or printed version of the minutes, nor in any of the Methodist newspapers. The *Pike*

affair the august Rev. Peter Cartwright was so disturbed by what had transpired that he rose and publicly rebuked the Conference for its conduct toward those Democrats who had dared openly to question the political nature of some of the Conference proceedings.[28]

Next, Conference members voted for the delegates who would represent the Illinois Annual Conference at the quadrennial General Conference meeting to be held the following summer. Everyone knew the 1864 General Conference would be an important one, since its action on the question of slavery would help define and justify the national MEC position on the Union war effort. Three of the Democrats who had spoken out against the politicized "Report on the State of the Country" had served as delegates to the previous General Conference meeting in 1860—Peter Cartwright, James L. Crane, and William S. Prentice. Each was in the running again, but none was reelected. "Rev. Dr. Cartwright was rejected," opined the repressed Springfield Democratic newspaper, because "he was not ultra enough for modern abolitionism."[29]

As the 1863 Annual Illinois Conference meeting drew to a close, Conference members adopted a "Report on the State of the Church" that concluded with an ominous warning. In view of the "great number" of persons who accused the church of preaching "purely political subjects," and in view of the "magnitude of the offenses, partaking as they do of the nature of treason against both the church and the state," the Report resolved that if after "prudent" and "affectionate" public and private "monitions and exhortations" such mistaken brethren failed to acknowledge the error of their ways, they should be tried by the church, and if guilty, expelled from it. Beyond the Report's threatening words, Democrats in the church also had the Conference's demonstrable action in the cases of Blundell, Paxson, and Howard to contemplate as they weighed the likely consequences of quietly conforming or standing on political principles.[30]

County [Ill.] Democrat's article reported that "Democratic Methodists at Pleasant Plains . . . are going to employ Mr. Howard, at a liberal salary, to preach at their church during the coming year." Howard does not appear in Conference records again until 1876, when he was apparently readmitted. During the intervening decade Howard participated in one of the "new church" movements that arose among Democrats in 1863 and 1864; see Andreasen, "As Good a Right to Pray," 523.

[28] Ibid., 165.

[29] State Register, October 10, 11, 1863; Western Christian Advocate, October 21, 1863; 1863 Manuscript Minutes, 428–29; Andreasen, "As Good a Right to Pray," 152.

[30] Published Minutes, 1863 Illinois Conference, 24–25.

The relatively small number of ministers who voted for dissident measures at the Conference may not be a true indication of the scope of dissenting sentiment present. The "witch-hunt" atmosphere made it perilous to betray any sign of sympathy for vocal Democrats or doubts about the efficacy of the Republican war program. Even staunch War Democrats like Peter Cartwright paid a price for their political affiliations. As the traveling ministers took their leave and fanned out across the countryside, the hand of institutional repression reached out against Democrats in the broader church in the days following the controversial 1863 meeting of the MEC Illinois Annual Conference.

The other three Illinois Methodist Conferences also took politically motivated action against individual ministers in their jurisdictions. An example from the Rock River Conference in northern Illinois was the case of the Rev. Nathan Jewett, a twenty-five-year veteran of the circuits, who, in a manner similar to the Rev. Blundell, was relegated to a retired status at the 1862 Annual Conference meeting. According to the official minutes Jewett retired at his own request.[31] Democrats thought differently. The old preacher "was thrown aside because he could not adopt all the policies of Abraham," one newspaper correspondent wrote. "He is turned out in his old age to take care of himself; and for what? He dares to be a democrat . . . this is the only charge."[32] A year later Democrats claimed that Rev. Dewitt C. Howard—"a man of talent and great popularity"—was retired under similar circumstances as Jewett's.[33] Even a presiding elder, the Rev. John W. Agard, had the pulpit "shut against him" on account of his Democratic politics.[34] Official minutes record only that Agard was retired.[35] Democrats believed these preachers were disciplined

---

[31] *Minutes of the Twenty-third Session of the Rock River Annual Conference, of the Methodist Episcopal Church, Held at Joliet, Illinois, September, 1862* (Chicago: Dunlop, Sewell, & Spalding, 1862): 13–14.

[32] *Chicago Times,* October 12, 1863.

[33] Ibid.

[34] Ibid.

[35] *Register of the Twenty-fifth Session of the Rock River Annual Conference of the Methodist Episcopal Church, Held at the City of Chicago, Commencing Thursday, October 6, 1864* (Chicago: Methodist Book Depository, 1864), 12. Interestingly, both Agard and D. C. Howard are noted as "visitors" at the politically charged 1863 Illinois Annual Conference meeting in Springfield—where the Paxson and Howard cases were aired.

because they cannot consistently with their calling as ministers of the gospel, preach politics. There is no other impediment. Has it come to pass that the democracy of the North must be compelled to hear [political] preaching upon the Sabbath and that men who dare preach Christ and Him crucified must be rejected and thrown aside with the taunt "You copperheads"? Shame on those who set such examples to their flocks. What can they expect of us poor sinners, if they take this course to reform men?[36]

Other Methodist Democratic clergymen who felt the heavy hand of attempted ecclesiastical repression included the Reverends Rumsey Smithson, Ira Norris, Francis M. Mills, Butler Presson, William A. Presson, and Joseph Richmond of the Central Illinois Conference, and the Reverends James Rowe, Alexander Caldwell, John W. Westcott, James D. Gray, and Absolum L. Davis of the Southern Illinois Conference.[37]

Attempts to quash Democratic dissent within Methodist ranks were not limited to the four Illinois Conferences. Indeed, the political scenes in Indiana and Ohio were just as turbulent as in Illinois. And in the emotional turmoil, the Republican clerical majorities in those states also tried to rid the churches of war dissent. One of the most completely documented cases comes from Dearborn County, Indiana, located across the Ohio border from Cincinnati. There the Rev. Judge Alfred Cotton, a local minister and minor Republican politico, "cracked a Butternut preacher" as he called it, through a nasty twelve-month campaign that illustrates how a calculating individual could take advantage of the fearful wartime climate by adeptly co-opting the disciplinary apparatus of the church to pursue a personal agenda for self-promotion or revenge.

The Rev. Samuel B. Chamberlain, a Democratic preacher serving on a circuit in the South East Indiana Conference, had delivered two controversial sermons in the spring of 1863, in which he made indiscreet statements such as:

- I love this Union, but I am opposed to this war . . . I am for an honorable peace . . .
- Our Generals are not fighting for the country, but for the money they are making out of it . . .

---

[36] *Chicago Times*, October 12, 1863.
[37] See Andreasen, "As Good a Right to Pray," chapters 8, 12, and 13.

- There is as much deep mourning in the South as there is here in the North . . .
- The South fully believes that she is right as much as we do . . .
- If God does not come to our rescue soon, we are gone as sure as you live . . .
- [If we win this war] should we hang the rebels? No, my friends . . . we should at once drop the subject and receive them all kindly. This is . . . the only way that we can ever be a free and happy people again. We may censure and punish their wicked acts, but we must excuse the actors.

Judge Cotton sat in the audience and secretly copied statements like these on a slate. He persuaded a dozen witnesses to swear to the truth of his transcriptions and then brought charges for disloyalty and immorality against Chamberlain. Shrewdly, Cotton marshaled the social and psychological pressures the church disciplinary system could bring to bear—playing on fears like the loss of livelihood, loss of social standing, loss of God's grace by treason to the church. He ticked off the names of twenty-one Methodist preachers—every minister in the District but two—who were "all true to the President"; could anyone believe, he asked, "that God and right and victory are with these two yellow butternut preachers, and against all this other host of eminent divines?" Chamberlain cracked under the pressure, came out "four square" for the Union, attended Union rallies, and more, but to no avail. He was suspended at the Quarterly Conference and lost his appeal at the Annual Conference, where he was expelled.[38]

Another Indiana case—that of the Rev. Enos W. Errick of the North Indiana Conference—illustrates how even "War Democrats" who unquestionably supported vigorous prosecution of the war sometimes faced harassment through ecclesiastical channels. Errick

---

[38] Case of Samuel B. Chamberlain, South Eastern Indiana Conference Trials, Archives of DePauw University and Indiana United Methodism, Roy O. West Library, DePauw University, Greencastle, Ind.; *Minutes of the South-Eastern Indiana Conference of the Methodist Church Held in Columbus, IA., September 16–21, 1863* (Cincinnati: Methodist Book Concern, 1863), 7, 22; *Minutes of the South-Eastern Indiana Conference of the Methodist Church Held in Shelbyville, Ind., September 21–26, 1864* (Cincinnati: Methodist Book Concern, 1864), 5, 8, 11–2, 16. Chamberlain, like Blundell, eventually joined a "new church" movement. For a more detailed discussion of the Chamberlain case, see Andreasen, "As Good a Right to Pray," chapter 5.

rode the circuit in the Fort Wayne area and was a successful preacher—too successful, perhaps. A jealous rival who took over one of Errick's previous circuits did not fare as well in the assignment as had Errick before him. Probably embarrassed and looking for a way to deflect criticism, he latched onto Errick's political affiliation with the Democrats to strike at him. He filed charges of "Immoral Conduct" against Errick for voting for Democrats and for failing to use his influence with the public to campaign on behalf of a fellow Methodist who was a Republican candidate for the state senate. Testimony in the trial transcript shows that Errick did indeed vote the Democratic ticket except for state senator, where he crossed over and voted for his fellow Methodist. He had refused, however, to campaign for the Republican candidate, he said, because he felt it was unseemly to preach politics from God's pulpit. Errick was convicted by the Quarterly Conference and suspended. Deeply offended that a jealous rival had taken advantage of wartime prejudice against Democrats to discredit and embarrass him, he promptly severed his connections with the Methodists.[39]

The MEC Ohio Conference boasted one of the most celebrated attempts by the church to stifle wartime dissent—the case of the Rev. James F. Given. Given had preached for sixteen years on Ohio Conference circuits. During that time he filled some of the most important and responsible stations in the Conference with "great ability and honor." His politics were wrong, however. On the Sabbath and from the pulpit he was circumspect about not addressing "public issues"; but in private he did not hesitate to express his Democratic views and his support for Vallandigham. In three successive annual circuit assignments beginning in 1861, murmurings about his "loyalty" impaired his ministerial effectiveness. While serving as minister of St. Paul's Church at Ohio Wesleyan University, in

---

[39] Case of Enos W. Errick, North Indiana Conference Trials, Archives of DePauw University and Indiana United Methodism; *Minutes of the Twentieth Session of the North Indiana Conference of the Methodist Episcopal Church, Held in Wabash, IA., April 9, 1863* (Cincinnati: Methodist Book Concern, 1863), 4; *Minutes of the Twenty-first Session of the North Indiana Conference of the Methodist Episcopal Church, Held in Knightstown, Henry County, IA., April 6, 1864* (Cincinnati: Methodist Book Concern, 1864), 5, 18. After leaving the Methodists, Rev. Errick joined the Evangelical Lutheran Church, where he continued a successful preaching career. For a more detailed discussion of the Errick case, see Andreasen, "As Good a Right to Pray," 244–57.

Delaware, Ohio, Given was besieged by an angry mob out to intimidate the only Democratic preacher in town. He was saved by the timely intervention of the president of the college, who was able to forestall the mob until cooler heads prevailed. Nevertheless, threats against Given continued, including a hangman's noose that he discovered one morning ominously extended from the parsonage door. Church officials quietly moved him to a lower-profile post. During the summer of 1863, the bitterly contested Ohio gubernatorial contest between Clement Vallandigham and John Brough heated up. Church members on Given's circuit split into contending factions, with the larger Republican faction refusing to pay their minister, and the Democratic faction conducting special subscriptions to sustain him.[40]

Finally, formal action was taken against Given during the Annual Conference meeting in September 1863, a month before the state election. There Conference leaders entertained charges accusing Given of making several political speeches that allegedly rendered him "unacceptable" to church members throughout the Conference.[41] Given twice tried to gain the convention floor to deliver a defense. Unlike in the Illinois Conference cases of Paxson and Howard, however, Ohio Conference officials, perhaps fearing his eloquence, never gave Given the opportunity to address the full assembly. Rather, the Conference voted without debate to adopt a special committee's recommendation that Given not receive a circuit assignment for the new year, pending a formal investigation to be headed by his former presiding elder. Livid over the shabby treatment he believed he had received at the convention, Given published in Democratic newspapers the "defense" he had not been allowed to deliver. "It is clear," he argued, "that this Conference cannot single me out for censuring from the number who have

---

[40] A. S. Addison, "Death of Rev. James F. Given," *Christian Witness,* September 19, 1867; Kenneth O. Brown, "'Building Father's House Anew': James F. Given and the Founding of the Christian Union," *Methodist History* 20 (July 1982): 209–18; Isaac Crook, *The Great Five: The First Faculty of the Ohio Wesleyan University* (Cincinnati: Jennings & Graham, 1908), 50; "Donation Party to the Rev. Mr. Given," *Crisis,* July 22, 1863.

[41] "Journal Minutes of the Ohio Conference, Volume 3—1840–1867" (manuscript), United Methodist Archives Center, Ohio Wesleyan University, Delaware, Ohio, 431–32. The Given investigation committee report was excluded from the published version of the Conference Minutes.

done likewise [made political speeches] without glaring injustice." Pressured and aggrieved, Given severed his Methodist connections.[42]

Another Ohio example of church action against Democrats was the case of the Rev. Moses T. Bowman. Bowman resided in the boundaries of the Cincinnati Conference during the war years. In September 1861 he was "requested" to "locate" (cease circuit duties), and by 1863 his Democratic politics had triggered a church investigation that eventually resulted in his formal expulsion in 1864.[43]

High-profile Conference ministers such as James F. Given and Moses T. Bowman were not the only targets of attempted repression in Ohio MEC Conferences. The experience of Brother Jeremiah White, a local preacher in the Central Ohio Annual Conference, who lost his preaching privileges in a less formal manner than church rules prescribed, reveals how Democrats on the lower rungs of the clerical ladder could be coerced. Brother White attended his circuit's Quarterly Conference in mid-August 1863 to renew his license as a local preacher. He was able to answer satisfactorily a series of questions: yes, he was a "Union Man"; yes, he was a "War Man"; yes, he favored vigorous prosecution of the war. Then he was asked, "Are you going to vote for Vallandigham?" Yes, he was; he was, after all, a Democrat. This was an inappropriate answer. Did he not think that he would be embarrassed to preach when "nine-tenths of the Methodist ministers [were] opposed to Vallandigham?" "No, sir, I should not," was White's reply. "When I preach I endeavor to preach the Gospel." Lively discussion ensued. Everyone present ad-

---

[42] "Political Proscription in the Methodist Church in Ohio," *Crisis*, October 7, 1863; "Rev. J. F. Given and the Ohio Conference: His Defense and Vindication," *Delaware [Ohio] Democratic Standard*, October 15, 1863. According to the archivist at Ohio Wesleyan University, none of the documents pertaining to the James F. Given case have survived. After leaving the MEC, Given assumed spiritual leadership of a "new church" movement initiated by prominent local Democrats—the Christian Union. For a detailed discussion of the Given case and his role in the creation of the Christian Union, see Andreasen, "As Good a Right to Pray," chapters 9 and 11.

[43] After his expulsion, Bowman associated with the same "new church" movement as did Rev. James F. Given. The Bowman case is yet another instance where apparently no official records of the investigation or disciplinary proceedings have survived; see Andreasen, "As Good a Right to Pray," 417–18, and chapter 11.

mitted that Brother White possessed "all the gifts and graces necessary to qualify him for a local preacher." But the presiding elder
concluded, "I cannot conscientiously vote to license any man who is
a supporter of Vallandigham." Nevertheless, the first vote on White's
character went in his favor by a small majority, with a large number
of ministers abstaining. The presiding elder informed the abstainers
they would have to vote or leave the Conference. This caused some
of the disgruntled ministers to stalk out of the meeting. The revote
was a tie, which the presiding elder broke by deciding against White.
Thereafter, all other ministers who expressed sympathy for the
Democratic gubernatorial candidate were sent home without their
licenses.[44]

During the six-year period 1860 through 1865, formal complaints
were lodged against 121 ministers at Annual Conference meetings
held by the twelve Conferences covering Illinois, Indiana, and Ohio.
This number does not include any actions taken against local ministers that were never appealed to an Annual Conference meeting.
Thirty ministers were formally expelled. During those same years,
101 ministers withdrew or discontinued their affiliation with their
respective Conferences; 244 ministers were "superannuated" (retired); 197 ministers were "located" (relieved of circuit duties). Minute entries show that after the war started in 1861, the number of
challenges to the "character" (ministerial fitness) of Conference ministers increased each year of the war until 1865, when the number
dropped back to a prewar level. Interestingly, the largest numbers of
ministers were expelled in years coinciding with congressional and
presidential elections—1860, 1862, and 1864. The year with perhaps
the highest overall level of clerical unrest—1862—was the year
Democrats scored impressive gains on both the federal and state levels in the off-year congressional elections. The figures intimate a possible political impetus behind the numbers.[45]

---

[44] "Clerical Tyranny—A Vallandigham Democrat Not Allowed to Preach the Gos-
pel—Alarming Demoralization in the Church," quoted from the *Circleville [Ohio]
Democrat,* in the *Cincinnati Enquirer,* September 15, 1863; see Andreasen, "As
Good a Right to Pray," 257–59.

[45] The following figures are derived from the official minutes for the twelve Methodist Conferences covering the states of Illinois, Indiana, and Ohio for the years
1860–65 (Rock River, Illinois, Central Illinois, Southern Illinois, Indiana, North Indiana, Northwest Indiana, Southeast Indiana, Ohio, Central Ohio, Cincinnati, and
North Ohio Conferences):

Still, it is not possible to know for sure in how many of these incidents politics may have been a contributing factor. Official minutes are cryptic on this score at best, as in the cases of Jewett, Howard, and Agard from the Rock River Conference, where there are no indications of political considerations in the record. But the Rock River Conference was not alone in keeping evidence of political intrigue out of its minutes. For example, the Central Ohio Conference minutes for 1863 give no indication that eleven of its preachers withdrew because they had been charged with disloyalty for supporting Vallandigham.[46] In the published minutes of the 1863 Ohio Conference there is nothing to indicate that three preachers listed as "located" or under terms of suspension (including Given) were actually under condemnation for political disloyalty.[47] Other Conferences were just as likely to keep out of their minutes any reference to political disputations that underlay reported actions.[48]

	Charges Brought	Superannuated	Located	Withdrawn/ Discontinued	Expelled
1860	17	30	35	16	5
1861	16	32	44	21	3
1862	20	37	51	21	9
1863	25	56	26	11	4
1864	29	44	15	16	8
1865	14	45	26	16	1
Total	121	244	197	101	30

The published figures are not complete, as some Conferences failed to include in their published minutes every action that was taken during the course of the annual meeting. On the problematic nature of church records, see Andreasen, "As Good a Right to Pray," 259–68.

[46] *Crisis,* September 23, 1863. Reference in the *Crisis* article to "a North-West Conference" most likely refers to the geographical location of a Quarterly Conference within the Central Ohio Annual Conference, probably the one that expelled Jeremiah White and his supporters.

[47] Ibid.; *Minutes of the Ohio Annual Conference of the Methodist Episcopal Church, for the Year 1862–3* (Cincinnati: Methodist Book Concern, 1863), 4.

[48] Not only does the official language used in reporting the verdicts of church disciplinary proceedings sometimes obfuscate the true nature of those proceedings, so too does the language used to describe the charges. As the church trials of Blundell, Chamberlain, and Errick show, for example, it sometimes turned out that what official church minutes brusquely labeled charges of "immoral conduct" were actually based on matters of partisan politics. This was true as well in several other prominent Civil War church trials, such as those for Methodist Reverends Moses T. Bowman of the Cincinnati Conference and Rumsey Smithson of the Central Illinois Conference, as well as that of Rev. John Van Buren Flack of the United Brethren in

Methodists were not alone in using church disciplinary apparatus to encourage conformity in political views. Brother Burnett and his persecutor John Excell, as we recall, were members of the United Brethren. So, too, was proscribed Illinois preacher John Van Buren Flack. The Brethrens' Auglaize Conference in northwest Indiana and northeast Ohio lost seven Democratic ministers in a single incident in 1864.[49] Various Baptist associations suffered from war-engendered difficulties.[50] Presbyterians in Ohio barred pro-Vallandigham ministers from their pulpits, and Old School Presbyterians in particular experienced politically related tensions in their ranks.[51] Even the conservative Protestant Episcopal Church, which took great pains to appear politically neutral and to minimize political controversy within its ranks, suffered its share of turmoil. A letter from the Bishop of the Indiana Diocese, George Upfold, is indicative of the problems that beset even those in the highest ranks of church leadership:

> [T]he people . . . do not appreciate [their Rector] as he deserves. They want him to go to Union meetings and blaat on politics, with Methodist and Presbyterian preachers—They think and talk of nothing else than politics, and that of the intensest [sic] abolition stripe. I have had to defend [the Rector], and to say that he would meet my disapproval, were here [sic] to do, as he is desired and expected to do. This accursed war is doing religion and the Church serious injury. It is my

Christ. In each case the official charges were couched in terms of "immoral conduct" from which those unfamiliar with the particulars of the case could have inferred that it was moral lapses like theft, dishonesty, or sexual impropriety that were at issue, rather than charges of a political nature. What this ultimately means is that one cannot merely assume that the perfunctory descriptions of proceedings in official church records convey an accurate sense of what the disciplinary proceedings were really about. If newspaper accounts or other types of corroborating evidence do not exist for a particular case reported in the official minutes or official church newspapers, one is left to speculate about the degree to which action taken respecting that person was motivated by questions of political worthiness as opposed to moral or spiritual worthiness.

[49] *Crisis*, January 20, 1864; see also Andreasen, "As Good a Right to Pray," chapter 7 (Flack) and chapter 10 (Auglaize Conference).

[50] This is based on review of the American Baptist Churches of the Great Rivers Region Collection, boxes 1, 2, 16, and 18, Illinois State Historical Library, Springfield. It seems, however, that the Baptists, with their looser ecclesiastical structure and greater local church autonomy, were a little more tolerant than Methodists of the Democratic minority in their midst.

[51] Klement, *Limits of Dissent*, 236. In general, see Vander Velde's still valuable study, *The Presbyterian Churches and the Federal Union*.

painful experience in every parish and missionary station I have visited.[52]

Indeed, a systematic examination of each evangelical denomination
would help to verify the extent of wartime repression by Protestant
churches. It would also help to explain the dynamics behind the re-
pressive attitude and conduct of the Republican religious majority.[53]

Nevertheless, in the course of his study of the Lincoln administration's civil liberties record, Neely realized that "even counting every
last relevant scrap of paper remaining in the National Archives would
not tell a historian how many civilians were arrested" during the war.
He concluded, "the time had come to abandon the count" and focus
on the meaning of the evidence at hand.[54] This approach may be
particularly apt where one is attempting to recapture or imagine the
essence, the feeling, and the mood prevalent among church-going
Democrats on the northern home front, matters that are not readily
amenable to quantification.

This essay suggests that immersion in literary sources and other
traditional kinds of impressionistic evidence points to a home front

---

[52] Bishop George Upfold [Bristol, Elkhart County] to "My dear daughter," May
15, 1863, George Upfold Papers, Indiana State Historical Library, Indianapolis.
Bishop Upfold's son-in-law was Joseph J. Bingham, an editor of the *Indianapolis
Daily State Sentinel,* the leading Democratic newspaper in the state. Bishop Whitehouse of the Illinois Diocese even earned the epithet of "Copperhead Bishop" for
praying at the 1864 Democratic National Convention in Chicago and for excommu-
nicating an entire congregation in Galesburg for failing to dismiss a Radical Republican rector; see Bruce T. Brown, "Grace Church, Galesburg, Illinois, 1864–1866:
The Supposed Neutrality of the Episcopal Church during the Years of the Civil
War," *Historical Magazine of the Protestant Episcopal Church* 46 (June 1977): 187–
208; Percy V. Norwood, "Bishop Whitehouse and the Church in Illinois," *Historical
Magazine of the Protestant Episcopal Church* 16 (June 1947): 167–80.

[53] For various reasons—the loss or failure to record disciplinary hearing transcripts, the incomplete and sometimes misleading nature of official minute entries,
and the sheer diffusion of bits of evidence buried in the columns of scores of religious and secular newspapers and among the personal papers of obscure individuals—it may never be possible precisely to determine, even just for the Methodists,
the number, location, timing, and consequences of all wartime church disciplinary
proceedings involving dissenting Democrats, nor identify all of those involved. Such
a time and labor-intensive quantitative study, if someone were to undertake it, would
be interesting and valuable in terms of producing a statistical portrait of where and
when ecclesiastical repression was most prevalent, and who were the persons most
likely to suffer. Also, quantification for periods before and after 1861–65 would help
determine what impact the war had on the churches.

[54] Neely, *Fate of Liberty,* 234.

rife with frustration and anxiety for many church-going Protestant Democrats, at least in midwestern states. Wartime newspapers are replete with accounts of proscribed clergymen and examples of church attempts to discourage dissent.[55] These and personal papers and manuscripts indicate an evolving sense of discouragement and foreboding among church-going Protestant Democrats in the face of escalating hostility from the religious and political majority, particularly during volatile election years.[56] Ecclesiastical trial records, such as the Methodist church trial transcripts examined for this essay,[57]

[55] Religious papers examined for this essay include the Methodist publications *Western Christian Advocate* (Cincinnati), *Northwestern Christian Advocate* (Chicago), and the United Brethren organ, *The Religious Telescope* (Dayton). Democratic newspapers include, by state: (Illinois) *Illinois Daily State Register, Chicago Times, Ottawa Free Trader, Jonesboro Gazette, Belleville Democrat, Peoria Morning Mail, Pike County Democrat, Salem Advocate;* (Indiana) *Indianapolis Sentinel, Columbia City News; Sullivan Democrat;* (Ohio) *The Crisis, Cincinnati Enquirer, Delaware Democratic Standard, Scioto Gazette, Dayton Daily Empire.*

[56] These sources also illustrate that matters of church discipline did not always, perhaps did not even usually, make it into official church records—either because they were never properly recorded, or because they were later lost or discarded.

[57] For this essay I examined all the church trial records for the period 1860–65 located in the Archives of the United Methodist Church Illinois Great Rivers Annual Conference in Bloomington, Illinois (Illinois Conference and Central Illinois Conference), and the DePauw University archives in Greencastle, Indiana (all four war-era Indiana Conferences). Most of the files reveal little more than the information given in the Annual Conference minutes (which are sometimes deceptive regarding the apparent absence of political motives), but many files did indicate important political dimensions to the proceedings.

The Illinois records were apparently consulted by William Warren Sweet and his seminar student, Paul A. Varg, in connection with chapter 13, "Church Trials among the Methodists in the Early West," in *Religion on the American Frontier,* vol. 4, *The Methodists, 1783–1840* (Chicago: University of Chicago Press, 1946), 640–79. This study did not extend to the Civil War years, however. Robert H. Williams in "Methodist Church Trials in Illinois," *Methodist History* 1 (October 1962): 14–32, looked at these records again while comparing changes in Illinois disciplinary proceedings for the period 1824–1931. Regarding the Civil War, he briefly concluded in passing that "the great crime of the war years was disloyalty" and cited the cases of W. P. Paxson, W. R. Howard, and William C. Blundell, though without providing much context or analysis.

It is unfortunate that many, if not most, transcripts of wartime church trial proceedings have not survived (if they were ever recorded). Relatively few full verbatim church trial transcripts like those for the Blundell, Chamberlain, and Errick trials remain from the war years. Transcripts of the trials for some of the most prominent Methodist dissidents, men like Rev. James F. Given of Columbus, Ohio, Rev. Moses T. Bowman of Cincinnati, Ohio, and Reverends Rumsey Smithson and Butler Presson of central Illinois, are now missing; other trial transcripts of lesser figures no doubt suffered similar fates. To the extent such records have been lost, our under-provide an important, intriguing, and heretofore unused window onto certain oppressive aspects of wartime northern society. One candid minister admitted in his church newspaper that "as a general thing . . . church trials . . . are a nuisance, a bore, or anything but profitable affairs, to either the parties concerned, the church, or the world outside . . . it is bad business of which one might be ashamed."[58] Be that as it may, the seemingly banal questions and answers provided in scribbled trial interrogatories provide rich details for historians that reveal narrow partisan mindsets, frequent acts of pettiness, and a general atmosphere that fostered intolerance for dissent.

In their tedious entirety, trial transcripts reveal that the test for what constituted acceptable behavior for church membership had been skewed by the war—political tests became the measure of religious faith. They show it was not enough for dissenting ministers to leave their Democratic politics outside the chapel door each Sunday; passivity or neutrality in the interest of church harmony was not enough. Staying away from antigovernment rallies was not enough; actual attendance at progovernment Union meetings was required. Praying for God's blessing on one's country and its leaders was not enough; prayers specifically for the triumph of particular government leaders and policies were required. One was expected to condemn Jeff Davis, not merely refrain from criticizing Abe Lincoln. One was expected to advocate particular government policies, such as revenue laws, conscription, confiscation, and emancipation; mere restraint from criticism, or even apathetic indifference, was unacceptable. One had to be careful how the self-selected guardians of religious and political orthodoxy perceived one's associations with others; the preacher who went out ministering among the sinners—that is to say, Democrats—risked condemnation rather than commendation for Christian service. In this oppressive environment a person's unguarded "deep groans" could be interpreted as signifying treasonous sentiments, and the manner

standing of the complexities of the time are the poorer. But, as this essay suggests, enough nonofficial sources have survived to attest that politically motivated complaints against Democratic clergymen were frequent.

[58] "Church Trials," *Religious Telescope*, July 22, 1863.

in which one read war news to one's friends from the newspaper could be used as evidence of malicious intent toward one's country. On such evidence, men such as Blundell, Chamberlain, Errick, and others were driven from the ministry. Unrecorded others were doubtless affected by the social and psychological pressure that was brought to bear on pious Democrats who risked the loss of both social standing and a sense of spiritual security if they failed to conform to expectations. The words of a banished Democratic minister from north central Illinois captured the dilemma for church-going Protestant Democrats:

> We could not remain silent and be in peace; we could not speak without censure and vile abuse following. If we used moderation, we showed treason; if we condemned unjust arrests in private, the same were published on the house tops. Our very whispers appeared to be watched, and we suffered more from what we did not do than for what we did.[59]

One consequence of these attempts at ecclesiastical repression was the growth of reactive, spontaneous dissent among many Protestant Democrats—dissent that eventually assumed characteristics of a co-ordinated, self-conscious religious insurgency in many midwestern churches. But whether Protestant Democrats joined these "new church" movements, or silently suffered indignities in the pews of their old churches, they confronted a stark social reality: to a significant degree the identity of church and state had become intertwined in the minds of many evangelical Protestants in the North. With their church leaders proclaiming that "neutrality is *treason,* silence *crime,* and inaction *unpardonable,*" it must have seemed to many pious Democrats that the specter of church censure constantly hovered over their shoulders.[60]

This oppressive wartime climate of fear, suspicion, and innuendo is an aspect of the Civil War experience that is usually viewed in the context of military tribunals, the suspension of the writ of habeas

---

[59] John Van Buren Flack, *Life History of J. V. B. Flack, D.D.* (Excelsior Springs, Mo.: Christian Union Herald Print, 1912), 50–51.

[60] *Northwestern Christian Advocate,* October 21, 1863 (emphasis in the original). For the story of the rise of the "new church" movements in the Civil War West, see Andreasen, "As Good a Right to Pray," chapters 10–14.

corpus, and the repression of dissent by government. What an examination of Civil War church trials reminds us is that the sentiment of wartime repression permeated northern, or at least midwestern, society, extending beyond the secular realm of the state into other realms, even including the spiritual realm of the church.[61]

---

[61] Beyond churches, educational establishments are another class of social institutions that could bear scrutiny in regard to their role in repressing dissent on the northern home front (though this may be an extension of church repression, since many educational institutions of the time were religiously affiliated). Democratic newspapers reported instances like that of a young lady dismissed from school for refusing to join in singing a political song (*Chicago Times*, October 12, 1863), or discrimination against Democratic students at Kenyon College in Ohio, and Western Reserve Eclectic Institute in Hiram, Ohio (*Cincinnati Enquirer*, June 7, 1863; *Crisis*, June 17, 1863).

Economic discrimination against Democrats in business circles also warrants examination. The cousin of Illinois Secretary of State Ozias M. Hatch, for example, wrote his cousin regarding the sale of a certain parcel of prime real estate: "[T]here are only two men inclined to pay large figures, and we all very much prefer Mr. [Wm.] Galt to Chapman. I want to give no Copperhead any more foothold on the soil of this township and will be much obliged if you will make that preference in the sale"; V. P. Richmond to "Cousin Hatch," March 11, 1864, folder 4, box 3, Ozias M. Hatch Papers, Illinois State Historical Library.

10

"A White Man's State in New England": Race, Party, and Suffrage in Civil War Connecticut

Lex Renda

PHINEAS T. BARNUM had already achieved fame as a showman when he became a representative in the 1865 Connecticut legislature. Originally a Democrat, he had bolted the party in the mid-1850s and then drifted into the Republican camp. Barnum contended that he had sought a legislative seat only so that he might cast two affirmative votes: the first for the Thirteenth Amendment abolishing slavery, the second for the black suffrage amendment to the state constitution.[1]

On May 24 Barnum spoke in favor of equal suffrage. Responding to a Democrat's fear of miscegenation, he belittled with racist humor the theory that social equality would follow enfranchisement: "I perfectly agree with the gentleman in his tastes. I should not like to associate with or have my children marry with negroes, but the gentleman may wish to remember that when his sons propose to marry with negroes the black girls may have a word to say in objection to such a proposition. It is a matter of taste, and the tastes of the colored women may not be found sympathetic." Recalling how valiantly blacks had fought during the Civil War, Barnum contended that on that score alone they ought to have the right to vote. When another Democrat queried whether asses and oxen, who also had served with distinction, should be so empowered, Barnum quipped that "doubtless Gen. Grant will feel himself highly complimented when he learns

The author wishes to thank Robert W. Burg for his research assistance, and John J. Coleman, Stephen D. Kantrowitz, Virginia Sapiro, and Sylvia Schafer for their advice on this essay.

[1] Phineas T. Barnum, *Struggles and Triumphs, Or Forty Years' Recollections* (Buffalo, N.Y.: Warren, Johnson, 1873), 609–37.

that it requires no greater capacity to handle the musket, and meet armed battalions on the field, than oxen and asses possess." The showman conceded, however, that it took no greater intelligence than that of animal instinct to "vote the falsely-called 'democratic ticket.'"[2]

Barnum argued that political participation bred respect for the government, and he likened the benefits of biracial suffrage with those of mass property ownership. Still, he did not advocate universal suffrage. He considered the state constitution's existing literacy and moral character qualifications for voting salutary, and he hoped that African Americans would gain educational opportunities. Democrats argued that blacks had not the "genius for the arts" to qualify for the ballot. Barnum wondered whether the atrocities committed by Preston Brooks and the Missouri Ruffians exemplified the Democratic talent for the same, and he sarcastically mimicked the drawl of Irish-American Democrats to cast aspersions on their intelligence. At the same time that he mockingly agreed with one Democrat who counted the Irish among the thriftiest citizens of his community, Barnum asserted that whites needed to outgrow their prejudices. Far from being the brutes of Democratic caricatures, African Americans had proven their nobility by not avenging their masters during the war, something he suspected any white man would have done.[3]

Barnum's mixture of idealism and naked partisanship, racial tolerance and romantic racialism, pluralism and paternalistic ethnocentrism encompassed much of the reforming spirit of postwar reconstruction as well as its limitations. But his exchange with Democrats over the black suffrage amendment exemplified also the way postwar northern politics on the state level mirrored developments in Washington, so that Reconstruction pertained to northern as well as southern society.[4] African Americans were not numerous in the Nutmeg State; in 1860 they comprised only 1.8 percent of the state's population. But blacks endured many of the same legal, social, and economic disabilities of their southern counterparts, and Connecticut

---

[2] *Hartford Courant*, May 27, 1865.

[3] Ibid.

[4] James C. Mohr, *The Radical Republicans and Reform in New York during Reconstruction* (Ithaca, N.Y.: Cornell University Press, 1973); Harold M. Hyman, *A More Perfect Union: The Impact of the Civil War and Reconstruction on the Constitution* (New York: Alfred A. Knopf, 1973); Morton Keller, *Affairs of State: Public Life in Late Nineteenth Century America* (Cambridge, Mass.: Belknap Press, 1977).

was the only state in New England that had a racial qualification for voting.[5]

The black suffrage issue in northern state politics is an integral part of any solution to the riddle of change in the Civil War era. The consensus among historians is that the war bent—even if it did not break—northern racism. George Fredrickson has argued that the enlistment of blacks in the army and the transformation of the war's purpose into an abolitionist crusade "mitigate[d] Northern racial prejudice." James McPherson has enumerated laws passed by northern legislatures during and after the war that advanced blacks' rights in the courts, schools, and other public places. And although African Americans' voting rights did not expand during the war, by 1865 the Republicans' platforms in ten northern states committed the party to black suffrage on the state level.[6]

An examination of the politics of equal suffrage in Connecticut demonstrates both the extent of change in racial attitudes, and the barriers to change in race-based behavior.[7] It also highlights the complex relationship between party strategy, factionalism, and ideology. Before the Civil War Republican support for black suffrage was inconsistent and often driven by strategy; after the war strategic concerns merely tempered the Republicans' commitment to equal suffrage. Still, salient racism outside of the Republican party coupled with factionalism and latent racism within it arrested the development of a biracial polity.

In colonial and Revolutionary Connecticut, free blacks enjoyed the

---

[5] Edmund Fuller, *Prudance Crandall: An Incident of Racism in Nineteenth Century Connecticut* (Middletown, Conn: Wesleyan University Press, 1971); Ralph F. Weld, *Slavery in Connecticut* (New Haven, Conn.: Yale University Press, 1935); Leon F. Litwack, *North of Slavery: The Negro in the Free States, 1790–1860* (Chicago: University of Chicago Press, 1961), 60, 70, 123–31, 198–99, 226.

[6] George Fredrickson, *The Black Image in the White Mind: The Debate on the Afro-American Character and Destiny, 1817–1914* (New York: Harper & Row, 1971), 167; James M. McPherson, *The Negro's Civil War: How American Blacks Felt and Acted during the War for the Union* (New York: Ballantine Books, 1991), 245–74.

[7] Connecticut politics in the postwar era is treated in William J. Niven, "The Time of the Whirlwind: A Study in the Political, Social and Economic History of Connecticut from 1861 to 1875" (Ph.D. diss., Columbia University, 1954); Joanna D. Cowden, "Civil War and Reconstruction Politics in Connecticut, 1863–1868" (Ph.D. diss., University of Connecticut, 1975); and Lex Renda, "The Polity and the Party System: Connecticut and New Hampshire, 1840–1876" (Ph.D. diss., University of Virginia, 1991).

right to vote on the same terms as whites (in 1784 the state enacted gradual emancipation legislation, though slavery was not completely abolished until 1848). In 1814, however, in response to charges that an African American had been bribed at the polls in neighboring Massachusetts, the legislature passed a law stating that no one "shall be admitted a freeman . . . unless . . . he be a free white male person." At the convention to draft the state's first constitution in 1818 there was little debate on suffrage, but an attempt to reinstitute a race-blind standard for the right of suffrage was defeated. Because the constitution stipulated that those who already held the franchise retained it, and because the 1814 statute can be interpreted as not denying the right to vote to those blacks who had previously been admitted as freemen, historians have postulated that the constitution grandfathered out black suffrage, the theory being that only those African Americans who reached the age of twenty-one prior to the adoption of the 1814 statute had the right to vote even after 1818. If that were the case, roughly two hundred, or 8 percent, of adult black males by 1860 would still have retained the right to vote. Whether any actually voted after the ratification of the 1818 constitution, however, is problematic. There is no recorded evidence, or affirmation, of it after 1814, and in 1833 the state Supreme Court ruled that African Americans were not citizens of the state because none were freemen. Certainly white animosity, in addition to ambiguous legal obstacles, deterred the few theoretically enfranchised blacks from voting.[8]

In 1838 the state's antislavery society sponsored before the Connecticut House of Representatives a constitutional amendment to enfranchise the state's African Americans. Both Whigs and especially Democrats cast large majorities against the measure (see table 1), and representatives from the abolitionist haven of Windham County cast over one-third of the aye votes. The following year a legislative committee reported that "the colored population is . . . a distinct and inferior race" and that the equal suffrage proposal was "a scheme to

---

[8] On the politics of constitutional reform in Jeffersonian Connecticut, see Richard J. Purcell, *Connecticut in Transition: 1775–1818* (Washington, D.C: American Historical Asociation, 1918). The vote on passing the suffrage clause was 103 to 72; see also Lorenzo J. Greene, *The Negro in Colonial New England, 1620–1776* (New York: Columbia University Press, 1942), 303; and James T. Adams, "Disfranchisement of Negroes in New England," *American Historical Review* 30 (April 1925): 545.

TABLE 1

VOTING PATTERNS BY PARTY ON ROLL CALLS TO PASS BLACK SUFFRAGE
CONSTITUTIONAL AMENDMENTS IN THE CONNECTICUT HOUSE OF
REPRESENTATIVES, 1838–1869

| Year | Democrats | | | Opponents | | | Cramer V | |
	Pro	Anti	Not Voting	Pro	Anti	Not Voting	All	
1838	7	53	2	29	115	2	0.101	0.117
1844	8	58	22	30	53	14	0.278	0.274
1846	51	44	17	60	19	27	0.242	0.231
1847	71	16	11	78	35	13	0.143	0.136
1854	13	68	17	107	15	15	0.714	0.682
1855a	4	50	6	130	24	13	0.706	0.673
1855b	1	55	4	132	17	21	0.828	0.797
1856	2	93	12	77	20	14	0.785	0.731
1858	2	78	6	110	16	22	0.830	0.796
1859	0	101	9	49	63	3	0.490	0.487
1860	1	74	12	116	23	10	0.787	0.750
1861	1	64	22	43	66	39	0.422	0.364
1864	0	67	14	122	7	26	0.925	0.843
1865	0	77	1	156	0	2	1.000	0.994
1867	3	80	30	110	0	14	0.969	0.888
1868	2	68	33	102	1	31	0.964	0.822
1869c	0	101	5	126	2	4	0.982	0.964

Notes: "Pro" denotes the position favorable to black suffrage, "Anti" denotes the position opposed to black suffrage; (*a*) pertains to the stand-alone black suffrage amendment, (*b*) pertains to the black suffrage/twenty-one-year U.S. residency requirement, (*c* pertains to ratification of the Fifteenth Amendment. Cramer's *V*, ranging from 0 to 1.0, measures the strength of the relationship between party (Democrats on the one hand, their collective opponents on the other) and voting. The higher the *V*, the greater the degree of party conflict. For its derivation, see Lee F. Anderson, et al., *Legislative Roll Call Analysis* (Evanston, Ill.: Northwestern University Press, 1966). Column 1 pertains only to those representatives who voted; column 2 pertains to all representatives. By House rules, the Speaker did not vote (except to break ties); thus his nonvote is excluded from consideration. Because of the Senate's small size (twenty-one members), roll calls therein could not be meaningfully analyzed.

Source: Journal of the House of Representatives of the State of Connecticut (1838), 66; ibid. (1844), 181; ibid. (1846), 194; ibid. (1847), 202; ibid. (1854), 338; ibid. (1855), 156, 413; ibid. (1856), 231; ibid. (1858), 266; ibid. (1859), 312; ibid. (1860), 442; ibid. (1861), 459; ibid. (1864), 226; ibid. (1865), 133; ibid. (1867), 649; ibid. (1868), 677; ibid. (1869), 86. Party affiliations were taken from the weekly April issues (passim) of the *Hartford Courant*, 1838, 1844, 1846, and 1847; and William Goodwin, *Goodwin's Annual Legislative Statistics of . . . Connecticut* (Hartford and New Haven, Conn., [1854–69]).

encourage the amalgamation of the two races."[9] Not until black suffrage proponents had an organization capable of threatening the political order could the measure gain meaningful attention.

At its first state convention in September 1841, the abolitionist Liberty party adopted a platform that endorsed black suffrage. The party's share of the votes cast in gubernatorial contests rose from under 1 percent in 1841 to 3.4 percent by 1843. The state constitution required a majority of the vote cast to win a gubernatorial election; otherwise the election devolved upon the legislature. Because most of the Liberty party's early support came from traditionally Whig voters, and also because of the nearly equal strength of the Whig and Democratic parties, it behooved Whig leaders to adopt some of the Liberty party positions to prevent further defections. Opposition to Texas annexation was one position; a second, albeit more internally divisive one for the Whig party, was equal suffrage.[10]

In his annual message to the legislature in May 1844, Whig governor Roger Baldwin, who had won fame as the trial lawyer for the African mutineers in the *Amistad* case, provided lukewarm endorsement for black suffrage. Proposed constitutional amendments required approval by the annually elected legislature in two successive sessions—the first year by the House, the second year by a two-thirds majority in both the House and Senate—before submission to the electorate for ratification. The amendment lost, 38 to 111 (see table 1). More than half of the Whigs, and two-thirds of the Democrats, voted against it. To add insult to injury, the legislature responded to suffrage proponents' declarations against taxation without representation by passing a law that exempted African Americans from taxes.[11]

Even prosuffrage Whigs were reluctant to embrace that position actively, for in the event of black enfranchisement, the small number of black voters and projected accessions from the Liberty party might fail to compensate for the loss of Whigs alienated by the measure. The evenly matched party system left little room for miscalculation. In 1845 Baldwin omitted any reference to the issue, and Whigs allowed it to lay dormant. The following year, however, political cir-

[9] John J. O'Connell, "The Abolitionist Movement in Connecticut, 1830–1850" (M.A. thesis, Trinity College, 1971), 90–92; *Conn. House Journal* (1838), 66.

[10] Lex Renda, "Retrospective Voting and the Presidential Election of 1844: The Texas Issue Revisited," *Presidential Studies Quarterly* 24 (fall 1994): 837–54.

[11] *Conn. House Journal* (1844), 181.

cumstances had altered considerably. Although Democrats had won a narrow legislative majority, the unorthodox manner in which Texas was admitted into the Union, the denial of presidential patronage to anti-annexation Democrats, and administration backpedaling on promises to acquire all of the disputed Oregon Territory spurred charges that slaveholders dominated the Democratic party. About 6 percent of Democrats revolted by voting for the Liberty party. To prevent further desertions, Democrats allowed a black suffrage amendment to pass. Almost half of the Democrats, and three-fourths of participating Whigs, voted in favor of the measure (see table 1). In 1847, when the major parties were trying to outdo each other in proclaiming themselves the true opponent of the expansion of slavery into territories prospectively to be acquired as a consequence of the Mexican War, the equal suffrage amendment won tremendous bipartisan approval. Lawmakers now submitted the amendment to the people for ratification.[12]

Democratic leaders may have supported the amendment partly for the tactical reason of dividing the Whig party, from which the amendment's major party sponsors principally came. The Democratic *Hartford Times* criticized the measure, but not in a race-baiting manner, and it even granted space to prosuffrage dissenters. Although the Whig *Hartford Courant* exhorted voters not to be moved by "the vapors of prejudice," party leaders tepidly endorsed the proposal. They coupled their support with calls for colonization as the only real solution to racial divisions. If for no other reason, Whigs and Democrats wanted the issue depoliticized so that the Liberty party could not profit from it. Allowing voters to defeat black suffrage accomplished this goal nicely.[13]

The referendum was scheduled, as was traditional with proposed constitutional amendments, to take place in October, concurrent with municipal contests, not in April 1848 when the next state elections were scheduled to occur. And with neither party politicizing the amendment, turnout in the referendum was an abysmally low 29 percent, making interpretations of the amendment's defeat by a four-to-

---

[12] *Hartford Courant,* May 10, 1845; *Conn. House Journal* (1846), 194; (1847), 202.
[13] *Hartford Daily Times,* September 9, 30, October 1, 1847; *Hartford Daily Courant,* September 14, 1847; *New London Morning News,* October 4, 1847; Lawrence Brusar, "Political Antislavery in Connecticut" (Ph. D. diss., Columbia University, 1974), 72.

one margin shaky at best. Over 40 percent of Democrats and 60 percent of Whigs who had voted in the April 1847 gubernatorial contest abstained (see table 2). By contrast, the Liberty party mobilized virtually all of its voters to support the amendment. Participating Whig voters were divided; almost one-third of them favored the measure, thus revealing an intraparty cleavage that would later plague first Know-Nothings and then Republicans. In retrospect, Democratic politicians need not have been so circumspect, for the party's

TABLE 2

Estimated Relationships between Voting in the April 1847 Gubernatorial Election and the October 1847 Referendum on the Black Suffrage Constitutional Amendment

1847 Gubernatorial Election	1847 Referendum			
	In Favor	Opposed	Abstain	Electorate
Whig	4.2	9.6	21.4	35.2
Democratic	0.1	17.7	14.3	32.1
Liberty	2.5	−0.9	0.9	2.5
Abstain	−0.5	−3.9	34.6	30.2
Electorate	6.3	22.5	71.2	100.0

$N = 135$

Notes: Figures are ecological regression estimates, which track the behavior of voting blocs over time. The cell values are percentages of the October 1847 eligible electorate, and they sum (less rounding errors) to 100 percent. The methodology is explained in J. Morgan Kousser, "Ecological Regression and the Analysis of Past Politics," *Journal of Interdisciplinary History* 4 (autumn 1973): 237–62. In each pair of elections, parties and abstainers in the latter election are treated as dependent variables, and parties and abstainers in the previous election are treated as independent variables. Included with the abstainers of the previous election are those "net" additional voters ineligible to participate in the first election but qualified to participate in the second. In all ecological regression tables, data for towns that experienced common boundary changes in between elections analyzed were aggregated into single cases. To avoid the overrepresentation of small towns, each town was computationally weighted by the mean size of the electorate for the entire data set. Using percentile data, this study employs the "forced entry" method of ecological regression outlined in the Statistical Package for the Social Sciences, *SPSS^x User's Guide* (Chicago, 1986), 666. Using the table above as an illustrative example, 4.2 percent of the October 1847 electorate consisted of voters who cast ballots for the Whig party in April 1847 and in favor of the amendment in October. Such voters comprised 11.9 percent ((4.2/35.2) × 100) of April 1847 Whigs and 66.7 percent ((4.2/6.3) × 100) of all prosuffrage voters in October 1847. Negative regression estimates often occur when one subgroup in the electorate behaves in an overly uniform fashion, such as here, when abstainers in the April contest uniformly sat out the referendum; they can be interpreted as having the value of zero, with the other percentages adjusted according to the restraints of the marginal values. On the sources of voting data and the calculation of eligible voters, see note 14.

participating rank and file voted against the amendment almost to a man.[14] Whatever the real cause of the Democratic leadership's support of the referendum in the legislature, that action would prove anomalous. For the nearly a quarter century henceforth, Democratic politicians and voters consistently opposed the enfranchisement of African Americans.

Why more Whigs than Democrats favored equal suffrage, in most northern states, is a question that has not been adequately explored. Black suffrage was consistent with the Whig ideal of society's perfectibility. Also, southerners were more powerful within the Democratic than in the Whig party. Yet even southern Whigs, though not advocates of black suffrage, were more moderate on race issues than their Democratic counterparts. Whig Brahmins like Baldwin felt sufficiently secure socially not to be threatened by equal suffrage, just as many a wealthy southern Whig saw race-baiting as inconsistent with the ethos of paternalism. But wealthy Democrats—North or South— were no more racially tolerant than ordinary Democratic voters.

---

[14] Town-level election returns used in this study are deposited in the Archives of the State of Connecticut, located in the Connecticut State Library. I supplemented these returns with those listed in the *Connecticut Register* (Hartford and New Haven: Brown and Parsons, 1848–67), and the *Hartford Courant* (1847–66). The returns for the 1847 referendum are in the *Courant*, September 14, 1847. The *Connecticut Register* enumerates the town-level eligible voters for the years 1861–65. I accepted as an estimate of the number of eligible voters for 1840 the number of adult white males listed in the published federal census schedules (*Sixth Census of the United States* [Washington, D.C.: Government Printing Office, 1841], 59–64). For the 1850s, estimating the size of the electorate is more problematic. One way is to multiply the ratio of voters to polls for each town in 1861 by the number of polls in 1852 and 1855 (listed in the *Connecticut Register* and *Connecticut House Journal*, respectively). But this first method suffers from extrapolating backwards from 1861 the effects of an 1860 registration law that significantly reduced the number of eligible voters. Under this procedure over 21 percent of the state's adult white males would have been ineligible to vote in 1852—an unacceptably large share. To mitigate this effect, I used a more cautious procedure. First, I estimated the number of adult males in 1850 and 1860 by multiplying the number of white males in each town by the county ratios of adult males to males (*Seventh Census of the United States* [Washington, D.C.: Government Printing Office, 1851], 76–79; *Eighth Census of the United States* [Washington, D.C.: Government Printing Office, 1861], 36–39), and then I interpolated linearly to derive estimates for 1852 and 1855; second, I determined the number of voters for 1852 and 1855 by adding to the number of adult males for each year half of the difference between the number of adult males and the number of eligible voters that would have been derived from the first method described above. I interpolated linearly for the remaining years between 1847 and 1861.

On a philosophic level, the parties' responses to racial issues may have reflected their differing attitudes toward democracy. Democrats were more committed than Whigs to the abstract ideal of political and social equality. Although Whigs embraced popular politics, they held also to notions of meritocracy. Whig ideology reflected the cross-strains of the National Republican, neo-Federalist wing of the party, whose notion of government was hierarchical, and the Anti-Masonic wing, which espoused the postmillennial goal of improving society. Both parties' philosophies existed within a racist worldview, but it was easier for the Whig than the Democratic mind to incorporate the rights of racial minorities. To assert the equality of all people, as Daniel Walker Howe has suggested, Democrats had to deny the humanity of Native, and African, Americans. The meritocratic, hierarchical beliefs of the Whigs allowed them to assign a "rightful" place to "inferiors" without threatening the position of the "master" race (to some extent, this construct might also explain the Whigs' greater commitment to married women's property rights). Similarly, nativist Whigs saw no inconsistency in favoring both a waiting period for naturalized citizens before they could vote, so that they might first become "Americanized," and suffrage for "moral" African Americans.[15]

---

[15] The foregoing explanation is, of course, merely surmise. It is based in part on my reading of the secondary literature on the nature of the Whig and Democratic parties; see, for example, Harry L. Watson, *Liberty and Power: The Politics of Jacksonian America* (New York: Hill and Wang, 1990); Lawrence F. Kohl, *The Politics of Individualism: Parties and the American Character in the Jacksonian Era* (New York: Oxford University Press, 1989); Daniel W. Howe, *The Political Culture of the American Whigs* (Chicago: University of Chicago Press, 1979); and John Ashworth, *Agrarians and Aristocrats: Party Political Ideology in the United States, 1837–1846* (London: Royal Historical Society, 1983). It also extends to political party philosophy the notions of hierarchy and exclusion that undergirded *Herrenvolk* democracy. While the class and race-based aspects of the same were more pronounced in the South, they existed in the North as well (it is worth speculating whether Whigs would have favored black suffrage with greater vigor in 1847 had the state not already eliminated, two years earlier, the property qualification for voting). It is striking that calls for "universal" male suffrage from the 1810s through 1830s were accompanied by calls for more restrictions against voting by African Americans as well as more vituperative racist attacks on blacks' voting rights where none already existed. I also find the race-based notions of suffrage exclusion championed by the Democrats quite compatible with theories, put forth by feminist historians, of the relationship between patriarchy and the spread of liberalism and democracy; see, for example, Linda K. Kerber, *Women of the Republic: Intellect & Ideology in Revolutionary America* (Chapel Hill: University of North Carolina Press, 1980); Norma A. Basch, *In the Eyes of the Law: Women, Marriage, and Property in Nineteenth-*

Whatever the source of partisan differences on this issue, however, those differences should not be exaggerated. Support for equal suffrage in the 1840s was a minority position, even within the Whig party, and the 1847 referendum proved to be the high point of suffrage reform during the life of the second party system. As the Whig party declined in electoral strength between 1849 and 1853, its leadership became less willing to take risks. Moreover, political antislavery waned during these years as most voters accepted, despite some misgivings, the finality of the Compromise of 1850.[16]

Black suffrage as an issue arose again in the midst of the voter realignment that began in 1854. Animosity toward Catholic immigrants, revulsion against intemperance, and opposition to the pending Kansas-Nebraska bill, which opened up those territories to slavery on the basis of popular sovereignty, resulted in the victory of a new coalition nominally led by former Whigs. In that year's legislative session, Democrats scouted a proposed black suffrage amendment as a prelude to racial amalgamation, and more than two of every three of them voted against it (see table 1). Whigs argued that the right to vote would lead "to self-respect and the elevation of the colored race." Almost four of every five Whigs voted in favor of it, and the measure thus passed the first phase of the amendment process.[17] The prospects for the amendment in the following year's legislature were clouded by the triumph of the Know-Nothing, or American, party in the state elections. Know-Nothings of various antecedents comprised almost two-thirds of the members, but it was a motley crew with different policy priorities. Also pending from 1854 was a nativist-

---

Century New York (Ithaca, N.Y.: Cornell University Press, 1982); Stephanie Mc-Curry, *Masters of Small Worlds: Yeomen Households, Gender Relations, and the Political Culture of the Antebellum South Carolina Low Country* (New York: Oxford University Press, 1995), especially 228–38; and Genevieve Fraisse, *Reason's Muse: Sexual Difference and the Birth of Democracy* (Chicago: University of Chicago Press, 1994), especially 170–71, 175–76.

[16] Renda, "Polity and the Party System," 167–205, 263–75; J. Robert Lane, *A Political History of Connecticut during the Civil War* (Washington, D.C.: Catholic University Press, 1941), 1–22; Carroll John Noonan, *Nativism in Connecticut, 1820–1860* (Washington, D.C.: Catholic University Press, 1938), 140–55. Paradoxically, the second party system decomposed during this lull in the sectional conflict; see Michael F. Holt, *The Political Crisis of the 1850s* (New York: John Wiley and Sons, 1978).

[17] On the realignment of the 1850s, see Holt, *Political Crisis*, 139–82; *Conn. House Journal* (1854), 338, 460; *Conn. Public Laws* (1854), 80; *Hartford Times,* June 27, 1854.

inspired amendment that required all voters to pass a literacy test. Know-Nothing Governor William Minor endorsed both amendments. The literacy test proposal passed (and in October voters ratified it), but the equal suffrage amendment, after receiving the required majority in the Senate, stumbled in the House; in the end, it fell nine votes shy of the two-thirds threshold.[18]

Whereas at least 90 percent of each anti-Democratic faction supported imposition of the literacy test, one-fourth of Democratic-Americans voted against equal suffrage. Together with solid disapproval from straight Democrats, the opposition's disunity killed the amendment (see table 1). A Free Soil paper groaned that Know-Nothings favored "the slavery of Connecticut colored men." Know-Nothings prevented a schism by passing a new amendment that both enfranchised African Americans and imposed a twenty-one-year United States residency requirement on all voters. The vast majority of each Know-Nothing faction, including the Democratic-Americans, supported the proposal, whereas nearly every Democrat opposed it and the tiny Whig faction was equally divided, for and against. The measure now awaited action by the next legislature.[19]

When it assembled, in May 1856, the political future seemed uncertain. Know-Nothings had defeated the embryonic Republicans in the gubernatorial contest, but the former's national organization had been shattered over the slavery extension issue. Because of a successful legislative record, Know-Nothings remained the preeminent anti-Democratic party in the state, but their power depended on cooperation among anti-Democratic forces. With the sack of Lawrence, Kansas, by proslavery fanatics and Preston Brooks's caning of Massachusetts Senator Charles Sumner on May 21 and 22, Republicans almost overnight became the paramount anti-Democratic party in the state. Yet the prospect of supplanting the Know-Nothings would founder unless their constituents were brought into the fold. Republican legislators were willing to share power with Know-Nothings, but they opposed any measure that would alienate the foreign-born Protestants they had hoped to draw into the party ranks.[20]

---

[18] *Conn. House Journal* (1855), 156.

[19] *Conn. House Journal* (1855), 413; *Hartford Republican,* June 8, 1855, quoted in Robert D. Parmet, "The Know-Nothings in Connecticut" (Ph.D. diss., Columbia University, 1966), 138–39.

[20] William E. Gienapp, *The Origins of the Republican Party, 1852–1856* (New

In practical terms this meant that the omnibus constitutional amendment carried over from 1855 had no chance of passage. It lost in the House by an adverse vote of 113 to 79. All but two voting Democrats and one-third of voting Republicans rejected the measure (and over one-fourth of the Republicans abstained), as did several Whigs. Many, regardless of party affiliation, opposed the black suffrage provision, and nearly 30 percent either abstained from voting or rejected the amendment. In a sense divisions among anti-Democratic forces were academic, for they lacked the requisite two-thirds majority to adopt the amendment in any case (see table 1).[21] Still, this disunity forewarned that neither extreme nativists nor blacks' rights activists would find comfortable homes in the emerging American-Republican coalition.

Republicans carried Connecticut in the 1856 presidential election, and for the rest of the decade they tenuously controlled the state government. Their power depended on appeasing nativists without fully adopting their policies, neutralizing Democratic efforts to exploit fiscal and cultural issues, and carving out an antislavery image that could appeal to the greatest number of voters. The easiest way to do the latter was to emphasize the South's threats to northern liberties and to negate Democratic efforts to portray Republicans as racial egalitarians. To be sure, the party had some racially enlightened leaders, such as Joseph R. Hawley and Mark Howard, but these "radicals" shared power with nativists such as Senator James Dixon and party chieftain Nehemiah D. Sperry, old-line Whigs such as James Babcock, and former Democrats, like Gideon Welles, who had little concern for the plight of African Americans.[22]

The Republicans' handling of legislative issues exemplifies their skill in balancing the claims of competing party factions. Although Republicans elected a former Know-Nothing, Alexander Holley, as their governor in 1857, they squashed in committee his call for a suffrage-related amendment requiring a one-year probation period for naturalized citizens. And although Republican legislators passed

York: Oxford University Press, 1987), 254–64, 274–78; Parmet, "Know-Nothings in Connecticut," 192–99. The most thorough treatment of Connecticut's Republican party in its early years is Brusar, "Political Antislavery in Connecticut," 289–377.

[21] *Conn. House Journal* (1856), 231.

[22] Holt, *Political Crisis*, 183–217. The factional struggles within the party are discussed in Brusar, "Political Antislavery in Connecticut," 378–458.

resolutions condemning the infamous Dred Scott decision and af-
firming that African Americans were citizens of the state, they buried
in committee the issue of equal suffrage. Democrats were not dila-
tory in contrasting the bold pronouncement on citizenship with the
silence on black enfranchisement.[23] By contrast, in 1858 conditions
dictated that Republicans appease nativists and permitted them to
appease racial egalitarians. Former Know-Nothings felt snubbed at
the Republican state convention—both in terms of the platform and
in the party's nominations. They even ran separate candidates against
the Republicans and Democrats for lesser administrative posts and
some legislative seats. To ameliorate nativists, five of every six Republican legislators joined a unanimous bloc of Americans in passing the
constitutional amendment imposing a one-year probation period for
naturalized citizens. Anger over President James Buchanan's attempt
to impose slavery on unwilling Kansans emboldened many Republicans to take a stance on the issue of black suffrage. Republicans
framed another omnibus amendment, this time providing for both
equal suffrage and an English literacy requirement (the state Supreme Court had ruled that the existing literacy qualification could
be met by reading in other languages). After Republicans upended a
tactical Democratic amendment permitting women's suffrage,
the measure passed by a five-to-four margin. Ninety percent of Democrats opposed it, whereas almost 75 percent of their opponents—
including four-fifths of Republicans and half of the Americans—
favored it (see table 1).[24]

The black suffrage and English literacy test, as well as the one-year
probation, amendments advanced to the next session of the legislature, but it seemed probable to most politicians in 1858 that, even
collectively, Republicans and Americans would not have, the following year, the necessary two-thirds majority in both legislative
branches. In agreeing to nativist and black suffragist demands, Republican moderates had appeased those groups without really acqui-

---

[23] *New Haven Register,* May 9, 16, 1857; *Hartford Courant,* June 20, 1857; James
Sheldon to Alexander Holley, April 14, 1857, Alexander Holley Papers, Connecticut
Historical Society, Hartford; *Conn. Public Laws* (1857), 11; *Conn. Private Laws*
(1857), 210; *Conn. House Journal* (1857), 347; *Hartford Times,* June 27, 1857.

[24] Parmet, "Know-Nothings in Connecticut," 301–2; *Conn. Senate Journal* (1858),
25; *New Haven Register,* June 5, 1858; *Conn. House Journal* (1858), 263, 266, 350.

escing to them.[25] When the legislature of 1859 did assemble, five of every six Republicans joined the Democrats to defeat the one-year probation amendment over the protests from the now badly weakened Know-Nothing element within the party. More divisive, however, was the omnibus amendment. Although it too went down to defeat, 43 percent of Republicans in the House, along with their governor, William A. Buckingham, favored it. Across the North in early 1859, Republicans were moving to the left on racial issues in order to differentiate themselves from those northern Democrats who had revolted against the administration on the Kansas issue yet still claimed that slavery was not a moral issue. Arguably the English literacy test clause undermined Republican support for the entire amendment. When the issue reemerged in the 1860 session, this time in the form of a stand-alone black suffrage amendment, the pattern of 1858 was almost repeated: more than three-fourths of Republicans favored the measure; nearly every Democrat opposed it (see table 1). Republican lawmakers now seemed squarely in favor of equal suffrage, even though the party was not as yet ready to emblazon it onto its platform. The divisions within the national Democratic party over slavery, widespread revulsion against the corrupt Buchanan administration, and the consequent near-certainty of a Republican victory in the upcoming presidential contest also permitted Republican legislators to take an otherwise risky stand on the issue.[26]

It should not be inferred from Republican legislative actions that the majority of voters in 1860 favored black suffrage. The state's system of representation in the House was as undemocratic as any in the United States, for it gave rural communities power far disproportional to their numbers. The 1818 constitution apportioned each town the number of representatives (one or two) it had before the document went into effect, and one member for each new town created thereafter. With the phenomenal growth of Hartford, New Haven, and Bridgeport, a pronounced disparity in representation emerged. Thus, even though Republicans won a little over 50 percent of the votes cast in the April 1860 gubernatorial contest, and 51 per-

---

[25] *Hartford Times,* May 29, 1858; Noonan, *Nativism in Connecticut,* 323–24.

[26] *Conn. House Journal* (1859), 312, 314; ibid. (1860), 442; Holt, *Political Crisis,* 209–15; *Bridgeport Farmer,* June 17, 1859, June 29, 1860.

cent in the state senatorial elections, they captured over 63 percent of the seats in the House. It is ironic, indeed, that this undemocratic system of representation is what gave the equal suffrage amendment any chance at all of passage.[27]

Even supporters of black suffrage seemed resigned, in 1860, to its inevitable defeat. The *Norwich Courier,* left of the Republican center on most racial issues, bemoaned that only " 'when enterprising eels can wiggle up the sheet of Niagara Falls,' then and not until then, may we expect to see the principle of Negro suffrage navigated against the current of American common sense." And although its editor advocated equal suffrage and reasoned that no one should oppose a referendum on the issue, he saw suffrage as a weak panacea and took an essentially fatalistic and Lincolnesque view of the prospects of race relations in the United States:

> The right of suffrage would at best be a merely nominal benefit to the negro. It would accomplish nothing toward removing the prejudices against his color. . . . If he goes to the ballot-box, it is simply to vote for *white* men. He never can expect to see persons of his own color in places of trust or power. If made a voter, he would still be obliged to be a "hewer of wood and a drawer of water" to the dominant race. . . . Everything in the social position of the colored man tends to impress upon his mind a sense of his degradation, and no political privileges will release him. . . . There is one, and only one, method of bettering the condition of our colored population, and that is to induce them to emigrate to some country, where they can form a community by themselves, and thus be free from the crushing presence of a race to which they are in a state of subjection here.[28]

The outbreak of the Civil War actually retarded the advance of blacks' rights in Connecticut. Because Republicans controlled the federal and most state governments in the North, there were few

---

[27] To take the most glaring example of this inequity, in 1900 the town of Union, with a population of 428, had two members, as did the city of New Haven, with a population of 108,027. The Senate was apportioned in part on the basis of population. But since every county had at least one exclusive member, and no county could have more than three, representation in that body also heavily favored rural areas. See Peter Argersinger, "The Value of the Vote: Political Representation in the Gilded Age," *Journal of American History* 76 (June 1989): 59–90; and Christopher Collier, "New England Specter: Town and State in Connecticut History, Law, and Myth," *Connecticut Historical Society Bulletin* 60 (summer/fall, 1995): 137–92.

[28] *Norwich Courier,* June 28, 1860.

officeholders whom Republicans could criticize when responding to Democratic attacks on Republican governance. Republicans sought to deflect Democratic critiques by tying support for the Union to support of the Lincoln administration. This meant that initially the war had to be framed as a struggle to preserve the Union, not to end slavery. To make that claim credible, Republicans distanced themselves from anything resembling racial egalitarianism. This strategy was even more appealing to Connecticut Republicans because the state's Democratic party was bitterly divided over the legality of secession and the propriety of coercion in destroying the Confederacy. Thus, Republicans were unwilling, at the war's outset, to give otherwise fractured Democrats any mileage on the race issue. In the 1861 legislative session, three of every five voting Republicans joined almost every voting Democrat in rejecting the pending black suffrage amendment (see table 1). In the next session, in which Republicans had formed a tenuous alliance with War Democrats disenchanted with the pro-Confederate leadership of their party, the black suffrage issue was not even broached; nor did it arise in the May 1863 session. Military debacles in 1862, coupled with the initial backlash against the Emancipation Proclamation and the federal conscription and black military enrollment laws, led to Republican defeats or setbacks across the North in the fall of 1862. In April 1863 Connecticut Republicans escaped with a precariously narrow victory in the gubernatorial contest. These events made Republicans even more circumspect in preventing Democrats from using the race card.[29]

The Union victories at Gettysburg and Vicksburg in the summer of 1863 signaled a turning point not only in the military course of the Civil War but in Republican strategy on the race issue as well. With the war having taken a turn for the better, and public confidence in the Lincoln administration increasing, Republicans began to argue that slavery's destruction was necessary to any lasting peace and, more cautiously, that the war would elevate the black race. From a policy perspective, the first evidence of this new approach appeared in a special November 1863 session of the legislature. Republicans

---

[29] *Conn. House Journal* (1861), 459; on Democratic divisions, see John E. Talmadge, "A Peace Movement in Civil War Connecticut," *New England Quarterly* 37 (September 1964): 308–17. Examples of very different Democratic reactions to the call to arms are found in the *Hartford Daily Post,* April 15, 1861; and *Hartford Times,* April 20, 27, 1861.

passed a law enrolling African Americans in the militia, despite the Democrats' characterization of it as "the most disgraceful bill ever introduced into the Connecticut legislature." By war's end at least 1,784 African Americans, the equivalent of roughly 99 percent of the state's military-age black males, had fought for Connecticut.[30]

Believing that the bravery of black soldiers on the battlefield and the heightening antislavery spirit of the times had softened the electorate's racism, Republicans, in the 1864 session, now resurrected the constitutional amendment enfranchising African Americans. The House consisted of 81 Democrats, 46 straight Republicans, and 109 members, mostly Republicans in reality, who had been elected on "Union" tickets. Democrats tried to divide their opponents by proposing a clause that would eliminate the existing literacy qualification, but Republicans upended the motion on a voice vote before passing the equal suffrage amendment by a vote of 122 to 74. All but seven voting Unionists joined a unanimous bloc of Republicans in supporting the measure (although one-fifth of the former abstained) against a unanimous Democratic opposition (see table 1). The amendment now awaited action by the next legislature.[31]

In the April 1865 elections, with the war at an imminent end, Connecticut Republicans won one of their greatest victories ever. Incumbent Governor Buckingham secured an eighth annual term with 58 percent of the votes cast, the largest share won by any candidate in a statewide race since the elections of 1832 and one that would not be exceeded for another thirty-one years. Republicans and Unionists swept the congressional and state senatorial elections, and they garnered 67 percent of the seats in the state House of Representatives. If they stayed unified, the black suffrage amendment would finally pass and be submitted to the voters.

When the legislature assembled, the black suffrage issue quickly

---

[30] *Conn. House Journal* (November 1863), 70; *Hartford Times,* November 14, 1863; *Hartford Daily Courant,* November 13, 14, 1863; Joe H. Mays, *Black Americans and Their Contributions toward Union Victory in the American Civil War, 1861–1865* (Lanham, Md.: University Press of America, 1984), 128. These are the numbers accredited to Connecticut, not necessarily those African Americans from Connecticut, for states recruited out-of-state to help fulfill their draft quotas. The best book on Connecticut during the war, and one that also treats the role of Connecticut blacks, is John Niven, *Connecticut for the Union: The Role of the State in the Civil War* (New Haven, Conn.: Yale University Press, 1965).

[31] *Conn. House Journal* (1864), 226.

moved to the forefront of the agenda. For one thing, Democrats grudgingly accepted as inevitable the ratification of the Thirteenth Amendment, and the House ratified it by a voice vote. In addition, some national Republican politicians advocated black suffrage as a condition southern states had to meet for the restoration of normal political rights, and the restriction of the ballot to whites in the North, outside of New England, proved embarrassing. Exuberance over impending abolitionism and idealism counted as well, in explaining both the Republican leadership's support for equal suffrage and the calculated belief that their constituents would also favor it. Undoubtedly, the fact that the literacy qualification would apply to African Americans as it did to white voters also played a role. In his annual message to the legislature, Buckingham argued:

> In a republic the elective franchise may safely be granted to all virtuous and intelligent male citizens of proper age. We are now battling for the inalienable rights of man without regard to race or color. In this struggle the colored men, hitherto degraded and oppressed, have, in every section of the country, been on the side of the Government, and are now in our armies by thousands, fighting for freedom under the protection of law. Let us inspire the colored man with self-respect, and encourage him to struggle and hope for a more elevated destiny, by granting him the boon so long withheld.[32]

Radical Republican journals, such as the *Hartford Press* and the *Norwich Bulletin*, had endorsed black suffrage during the 1864 session. Conservative and moderate sheets now joined them. The *Hartford Courant* considered the suffrage amendment to the state constitution in keeping with our principles"; the *Litchfield Enquirer* argued against permitting "our groundless prejudices to overcome our reason and sense of justice"; and the *Stamford Advocate*, while conceding black inferiority, maintained that superiority of mind had never been a prerequisite for voting and prayed that Connecticut would through "liberal legislation prove that she will not be left behind in the great onward march of Progress." Confidence borne of two successive strong victories in the state contests of 1864 and 1865 made an ideal seem politically practical and helped it win the support of even timid Republican politicians. In 1865 conservative Republicans, who privately opposed the measure, publicly supported it.[33]

---

[32] *Conn. Senate Journal* (1865), 32.

[33] *Hartford Courant,* May 27, 1865; *Litchfield Enquirer,* June 1, 1865; and *Stamford Advocate,* June 2, 1865.

Advocates of the amendment depended on uniform support from House Republicans and Unionists, who together comprised just one member more than the two-thirds necessary to pass the amendment. The Democratic press rallied the party in opposition to the amendment. The *Hartford Times* averred that "to make the negro politically and as a consequence socially the equal of the white is an outrage that could only be conceived by fanatics of the destructive school." The Democratic minority report invoked the Dred Scott decision in an effort to deny black citizenship and maintained that "Negroes have shown as yet no capacity to compete with the white race in the march of civilization." It contended that the enfranchisement of African Americans "would merely make them the instruments of partizan intrigues; and the introduction of this new and degraded element in our political contests will be only the creation of an agent of demoralization." Nonetheless, the amendment passed the House, 156 to 77. One Democrat and two Unionists abstained; otherwise the measure passed by a perfect party vote (see table 1). The Senate then unanimously concurred with the House.[34]

Throughout the summer both parties politicized the pending October referendum on the amendment. The Republican *Hartford Courant,* which a decade earlier had spoke of preserving territories from "the pestilential presence of the black man," in 1865 reasoned that "a man's color can have nothing to do with the exercise of the faculties of his mind. It is a false distinction, full of mischief, and belongs properly to an age of ignorance and prejudice rather than to the nineteenth century. It is contrary to the spirit of our institutions, making a practical oligarchy out of a nominal republic." Republicans denied the charge of social egalitarianism, reminded voters of the paucity of blacks in the state, and reiterated their adherence to the literacy qualification. The *Litchfield Enquirer* reassured its readers that adoption of the amendment "certainly will not give every idiotic

---

[34] *Hartford Times,* May, 20, 27, June 3, 10, 17, 1865. On June 27, 1865, the state Supreme Court, in an advisory opinion, upheld the citizenship of blacks; see Niven, "Time of the Whirlwind," 234–35; *Conn. House Journal* (1865), 133. Initially the amendment passed by a vote of 154 to 77—with precisely two-thirds of the votes cast. Doubts about whether the requisite majority had been satisfied led Speaker Ezekiel Foster to cast an affirmative vote over the howls of protest from the Democratic members (by House rules, the Speaker did not vote except to break or cause ties). The legislators averted a legal squabble only after one Unionist who had abstained received permission to vote in favor of the amendment.

or ignorant negro the same privilege with intelligent and sane whites," and that just "because a man votes at the same polls with you, you are not under any obligation to borrow a hundred dollars of him, or to marry his daughter, or to recognize his 'social equality' with you in any other way." Its editor emphasized that "the real objection of our democratic neighbors to the project of negro suffrage . . . is that he would not vote their ticket." The *Stamford Advocate* equated support for the amendment with that of the Union cause during the war. To counteract Democratic racist appeals, the *Hartford Press* made dire predictions of racial conflict in the event the amendment lost: "May we not apprehend greater danger from the race if it is set apart, thrust into ignorance and semi-barbarism and kept there, than if it were elevated to the height of its capacity. . . . The only national peril to be apprehended is from making them an alien, dissatisfied and brutal element in the country."[35] Democrats retorted that "it is to the credit of the Democrats of the House that every man of them, with a single exception, stood firm for the doctrines of the framers of the government." The *New Haven Register* accused Republicans of hypocrisy and cowardice in demanding black enfranchisement, which required the approval of voters, but not an end to other forms of racial discrimination that the legislature could remedy by its own action. Black inferiority predominated as the conventional wisdom. Hence, the burden of proving otherwise fell upon suffrage advocates, and given their own ambivalence, they became easy prey for Democratic racist assaults.[36]

The amendment lost with 44.8 percent of the votes cast. The turnout rate of 61 percent, respectable as referenda normally went, still fell far below that of the spring election. Only Windham, the strongest Republican county, gave a majority for the amendment. In the

---

[35] James A. Rawley, *Race and Politics: "Bleeding Kansas" and the Coming of the Civil War* (Philadelphia: Lippincott, 1969), 150; *Hartford Courant,* September 23, 1865; *Litchfield Enquirer,* August 17 (quotation), September 7, 28, 1865; *Stamford Advocate,* September 29, 1865; *Hartford Evening Press,* September 9, 1865, as quoted in Cowden, "Civil War and Reconstruction Politics," 232; *Norwich Morning Bulletin,* September 29, 1865.

[36] Determined to make rejection of the amendment a test of party strength, the Democratic state committee even took the unusual step, for a referendum campaign, of circulating an address to the electorate; *Hartford Times,* May 27, September 16, 1865; *New Haven Daily Register,* June 3, 1865, as quoted in Cowden, "Civil War and Reconstruction Politics," 241; and see ibid., 230–43, for a good discussion of Democratic exploitation of voters' racial anxieties.

aggregate it won support from 48 percent of participating voters in the mostly rural counties of Windham, Litchfield, New London, and Tolland, but only 43 percent of the aggregate vote in Fairfield, New Haven, Hartford, and Middlesex Counties, that is, the locales in the New York–New Haven–Hartford metropolitan corridor or in the commercially oriented Connecticut River valley. Even in heavily Republican New London County, where a different referendum on a purely local issue produced heavy voter participation and effected a higher turnout rate there on the suffrage referendum than elsewhere, opponents defeated the amendment.[37]

Comparisons with voting in the spring (see table 3) reveal that virtually no Democrats favored the amendment, and only one in twenty-five Republicans voted against it. Still, almost one-third of Republicans felt sufficiently cross-pressured between supporting their party and rejecting racial equality to sit out the referendum. Republican voters abstained at almost four times the rate of Democrats. Of course, Republicans had won an abnormally high share of the votes cast in the spring contest. Yet comparisons with voting in the 1864 presidential contest (see table 4), in which the strenuous efforts of both parties produced a voter turnout rate of over 88 percent, show only a slightly different pattern, as upwards of a little

TABLE 3

ESTIMATED RELATIONSHIPS BETWEEN VOTING IN THE APRIL 1865 GUBERNATORIAL ELECTION AND THE OCTOBER 1865 REFERENDUM ON THE BLACK SUFFRAGE CONSTITUTIONAL AMENDMENT

1865 Gubernatorial Election	1865 Referendum			
	In Favor	Opposed	Abstain	Electorate
Republican	27.3	1.7	13.5	42.5
Democratic	0.1	28.5	2.8	31.4
Abstain	−0.1	3.5	22.7	26.1
Electorate	27.3	33.7	39.0	100.0

N = 162

---

[37] Returns for the referendum are listed in the *Connecticut Register for 1866* (New Haven, Conn.: Brown and Parsons, 1866). The local issue contested in New London County was whether to make Norwich the sole shire town.

TABLE 4

ESTIMATED RELATIONSHIPS BETWEEN VOTING IN THE NOVEMBER 1864
PRESIDENTIAL ELECTION AND THE OCTOBER 1865 REFERENDUM ON
THE BLACK SUFFRAGE CONSTITUTIONAL AMENDMENT

1864 Presidential Election	1865 Referendum			
	In Favor	Opposed	Abstain	Electorate
Republican	26.6	−2.3	20.5	44.8
Democratic	2.0	37.4	3.0	42.4
Abstain	−1.3	−1.4	15.5	12.8
Electorate	27.3	33.7	39.0	100.0
$N = 162$				

under 5 percent of McClellan's voters favored the amendment. No matter which electorate is used as a benchmark for comparison, roughly nine out of ten Democrats opposed equal suffrage, and at least one-third of Republicans failed to support it.

It is tempting to say that opposition to equal suffrage was greatest in those places where African Americans were most numerous. Hence, a negative reference group argument might run, black suffrage won more support in the upper North than in the border North and Connecticut. But the black share of the population in every northern state was minuscule, and on the local level in Connecticut there was no correlation between voting (whichever way) in the referendum on the one hand, and either the percentage of the population consisting of African Americans, the black growth rate in the 1860s, or the number of African Americans per square mile, on the other (see table 5). Even collectively, these three variables explain less than 3 percent of the variance in voting either for or against equal suffrage.[38]

---

[38] The number of African Americans in Connecticut in 1860 and 1870 was taken from the *Eighth Census*, 36–39; and the *Ninth Census*, 93–95. I interpolated linearly to derive an estimate for 1865. Black population density was derived by dividing the estimated number of African Americans in 1865, for each town, by the number of taxable acres (converted to square miles) listed in the 1855 Grand List (*Conn. House Journal*, 1856). The small correlation between the percentage of voters who abstained and these racial variables also suggests that the referendum did not exhibit the "canceling out" effects of Republicans strenuously advocating suffrage where they expected to gain black votes and Democratic efforts to profit from a backlash

TABLE 5
PEARSON CORRELATIONS BETWEEN RACE VARIABLES AND
VOTING IN THE 1865 REFERENDUM

Variable	Percentage in Favor	Percentage Opposed	Percentage Abstain
Percentage African American	−0.106%	+0.170%	−0.095%
Black Growth Rate	+0.161	−0.148	+0.035
Black Population Density	+0.035	+0.146	−0.169
N = 154			

Note: For definitions of, and sources for, the variables, see note 38.

Of somewhat greater importance was a long-running factional division within the Republican party. One way to measure its impact is to track the behavior in the referendum of voters from the 1856 gubernatorial election (when Americans were more powerful than the nascent Republican party) and from the 1858 Comptroller election (when die-hard nativists revolted against the Republican party into which they had been absorbed). In retrospect, the Republicans and Americans in these elections can be seen as members of the same party, for the overwhelming majority of those who voted for the Republican or American (as well as the Whig) candidates in the 1856 gubernatorial contest voted for Republican John C. Frémont in that year's presidential election, and nearly all the American revolters of 1858 voted Republican in 1859.[39] As tables 6 and 7 show, upwards of four-fifths of 1856 Republicans and 63 percent of 1858 Republicans voted in favor of black suffrage, compared with only about 45 percent of 1856 Americans and 53 percent of 1858 Americans.

The New Haven Palladium angrily faulted "those treacherous Republicans, who, in city and county, struck hands with the copperheads to perpetuate the mean prejudice of race and caste." By contrast, Democrats rejoiced. "A White Man's State in New En-

in such places. Had that been the case, one would expect a higher than average turnout rate in such communities.

[39] Ecological regression analysis reveals that 82 percent of Americans, 100 percent of Whigs, and virtually all Republicans (the actual figure exceeds 100 percent) in the 1856 gubernatorial contest voted for Frémont in the 1856 presidential contest, and indeed about 97 percent of 1856 American voters would support the Republican ticket in 1857. Of American voters in the 1858 Comptroller race, an estimated 91 percent supported the Republican gubernatorial ticket in 1859.

TABLE 6

ESTIMATED RELATIONSHIPS BETWEEN VOTING IN THE APRIL 1856
GUBERNATORIAL ELECTION AND THE OCTOBER 1865 REFERENDUM ON
THE BLACK SUFFRAGE CONSTITUTIONAL AMENDMENT

1856 Gubernatorial Election	1865 Referendum			
	In Favor	Opposed	Abstain	Electorate
Republican	5.4	−2.1	3.4	6.7
Democratic	2.4	29.3	1.1	32.8
American	11.7	−1.8	16.2	26.1
Whig	0.4	0.1	0.8	1.3
Abstain	7.4	8.2	17.5	33.1
Electorate	27.3	33.7	39.0	100.0

$N = 145$

TABLE 7

ESTIMATED RELATIONSHIPS BETWEEN VOTING IN THE APRIL 1858
COMPTROLLER ELECTION AND THE OCTOBER 1865 REFERENDUM ON
THE BLACK SUFFRAGE CONSTITUTIONAL AMENDMENT

1858 Comptroller Election	1865 Referendum			
	In Favor	Opposed	Abstain	Electorate
Republican	20.0	−6.1	17.8	31.7
Democratic	−1.5	32.6	2.7	33.8
American	2.7	−0.1	2.5	5.1
Abstain	6.1	7.3	16.0	29.4
Electorate	27.3	33.7	39.0	100.0

$N = 145$

gland," the *Hartford Times*'s headline beamed. Democrats argued that the amendment's defeat had shattered radical schemes in both Connecticut and Washington. The Republicans' failed attempt to grant African Americans the ballot would provide Democrats with powerful ammunition in the 1866 elections.[40]

In the winter of 1866 President Andrew Johnson and congressional

---

[40] *New Haven Daily Palladium,* October 3, 1865, as quoted in Niven, "Time of

Republicans drifted toward irreconcilable positions on the issue of Reconstruction. Johnson adopted a policy by which the southern states could reestablish their places within the Union by swearing loyalty to the same, repudiating their Confederate war debts, and abolishing slavery. Although requiring the disfranchisement of Confederate political and military leaders, he routinely pardoned all but the most important figures. Interpreting federal power narrowly and at best apathetic about the plight of African Americans, Johnson opposed the imposition of black suffrage upon the states. Taking their cue from the President, federal military governors in the South permitted the creation of governments that left blacks unenfranchised, reenfranchised Confederate leaders, and passed into law "black codes" that denied African Americans many basic civil rights. Although they varied in their commitment to black equality, nearly all congressional Republicans agreed that the new southern governments had to guarantee African Americans fundamental civil and economic freedoms, and that former Confederate leaders were not entitled to seats in Congress.[41]

Republicans in the 1866 campaign labored under severe handicaps. The schism between them and Johnson served as a catalyst in damaging the unity conservatives and radicals had forged during the war. In addition, Johnson vetoed the civil rights bill (meant to overturn the black codes) just one week before Nutmeggers went to the polls, and it made a mockery of Republican assurances that the President remained loyal to the party. Moreover, Republicans chose for their standard bearer Joseph R. Hawley, one of the most committed radicals in the state, and Democrats made the Republican task more difficult by nominating for governor former Congressman James English, a moderate who had supported the war effort and had voted to pass the Thirteenth Amendment. Finally, the voters' repudiation of black suffrage created an embarrassing point of friction between the

the Whirlwind," 235; *Stamford Advocate*, October 6, 1865; *Hartford Times*, October 7, 1865.

[41] Perhaps the best treatment of the subject is William R. Brock, *An American Crisis: Congress and Reconstruction 1865–1867* (New York: St. Martin's Press, 1963); see also Michael Les Benedict, *A Compromise of Principle: Congressional Republicans and Reconstruction 1863–1869* (New York: W. W. Norton, 1974); Benedict, *The Impeachment and Trial of Andrew Johnson* (New York: W. W. Norton, 1973); and Patrick W. Riddleberger, *1866: The Critical Year Revisited* (Carbondale: Southern Illinois University Press, 1979).

party and Johnson that could not easily be camouflaged. To be sure, Johnson had not opposed black suffrage outright, but his willingness to leave the matter in the hands of southern whites had the same effect. Just as Connecticut's voters had been allowed to reject black suffrage, Democrats reasoned, so too should southern whites.

The Republican platform, written by New Haven customs collector and former Know-Nothing James F. Babcock, pledged Johnson the party's "hearty support for his labors for a just, complete restoration of the Union," expressed confidence in Congress's ability to settle "questions appropriately pertaining to the legislative department," and prayed for the "destruction of slavery in fact as well as name and the enactment of appropriate laws to assure to every class of citizens the full enjoyment of" their constitutional rights.[42] The party line, therefore, resembled a tightrope, and the Republicans' balancing act became more harrowing as the campaign developed. As Johnson and Congress divided, so too did the party leadership. Babcock and Navy Secretary Gideon Welles gravitated toward Johnson's corner. Both men had privately opposed the equal suffrage amendment on a states' rights basis, and Welles hoped that its defeat would check the radicals' designs in Washington. Other former Democrats who had joined the Republicans belatedly, such as former Congressman James T. Pratt, also sided with Johnson. In the Senate Connecticut's James Dixon, another former Know-Nothing, emerged as Johnson's foremost ostensibly Republican supporter. As early as October he had written the President that "the People desire justice to the Negro but they are tired of the perpetual reiteration of his claims upon their attention to the exclusion of all other interests. Moreover, as you will see by the recent vote of Connecticut on the question of extending suffrage to the colored population, there are grave doubts as to his fitness to govern the country, even *here*." Dixon opposed congressional Reconstruction policies; Connecticut's other Republican Senator, Lafayette Foster, and all four congressmen meanwhile supported them.[43]

---

[42] *Hartford Daily Courant*, February 15, 1866.

[43] These factional rifts are detailed in Niven, "Time of the Whirlwind," 233–91. See also Cowden, "Civil War and Reconstruction Politics," 167–71; Gideon Welles to E. T. Welles, November 20, 1863, Gideon Welles to A. A. Croffut, September 22, 1865, Gideon Welles to Charles D. Warner, September 22, 1865, Gideon Welles Papers, Library of Congress; John Niven, *Gideon Welles, Lincoln's Secretary of the Navy* (New York: Oxford University Press, 1973), 467–70; James Dixon to Andrew

Republicans differed in their attitude toward the platform. The radical *Meriden Record* insisted that "to be unionist in these times is to be radical" and that the electorate had a right to know "whether in voting for General Hawley they are endorsing Johnson or sustaining our noble Congress." Dixon's organ, the *Courant,* had supported the equal suffrage amendment, but in January it reversed its position on suffrage, presumably as the issue pertained to either Connecticut or federal politics: "So long as the great questions of loyalty are settled, we have no occasion to enquire into the state of public feeling upon Negro suffrage any more than upon the increase of the tariff." In February editor Abel Clark lashed out against a proposal for universal manhood suffrage. Reaffirming his support for a literacy qualification and implicitly endorsing Massachusetts's requirement of a two-year probation period for naturalized citizens, he warned that, especially in the South, "unqualified suffrage would be a curse. . . . It is hard to conceive of a measure fraught with more peril than the admission of every citizen to the privilege of suffrage."[44]

Democrats tried to inflame the Republicans' intraparty schism. The *New Haven Register* jeered that "the Radicals embrace at least three fourths of the party, hate Andrew Johnson . . . but do not dare break openly with him." *Times* editor Alfred E. Burr demanded that Hawley explain what he considered to be the appropriate legislative matters to which the Republican platform referred. Burr extolled the President when he rebuffed a delegation of blacks who had requested his support for equal suffrage. When Congress voted to enfranchise blacks in the District of Columbia, Burr intoned that "the whole Connecticut delegation, in the face of the recent and overwhelming repudiation of negro suffrage by their own State at home, vote for *forcing* the obnoxious measure upon another community— and a community, too, more unanimously opposed to it than are the people of Connecticut." He described the Freedmen's Bureau bill as

---

Johnson, October 8, 16, 1865, Andrew Johnson Papers, Library of Congress; Nelson R. Burr, "United States Senator James Dixon: 1814–1873, Episcopalian Anti-slavery Statesman," *Historical Magazine of the Protestant Episcopal Church* 50 (March 1981): 63–68; and *Congressional Globe* 39, no. 1: 943, 1809, 1861. For the radicals' perspective, see Mark Howard to Joseph R. Hawley, January 28, 1865, William Faxon to Joseph R. Hawley, January 6, 1865, Joseph R. Hawley Papers, Library of Congress.

[44] Niven, "Time of the Whirlwind," 245–46; *Hartford Courant,* January 27, 1866; *Hartford Daily Courant,* February 8, 1866.

"a plan to establish *a vast Government Almshouse for Negroes*," and he celebrated the veto of the civil rights bill, legislation meant to create "a Central Despotism at Washington, to crush out the liberties of the people and enforce the odious scheme of Negro Equality." Republicans tried to offset these attacks by denouncing their opponents' "disloyalty" during the war, but the ferocious Democratic assaults took their toll.[45]

Hawley barely won the election with just 50.3 percent of the votes cast, and Republicans narrowly clung to a majority of state Senate seats. Democrats continued, unabated, with their racist assaults for the next two years, often contrasting the Republicans' concern for the plight of African Americans to their alleged indifference to white workers suffering the effects of the postwar recession. In 1867 English became the first Democrat to win the governorship in fourteen years, and he would be reelected in 1868. Although it is not clear that the suffrage issue was most responsible for the Republicans' woes (English won, in both years, with less than 51 percent of the votes cast), it probably had not helped the party.

Nevertheless, Republicans still controlled the legislature. After their narrow victory in 1866, they buried Hawley's call for a new suffrage amendment in committee. But while Congress was passing the Reconstruction Acts, which mandated black suffrage in the former Confederate states, radicals began to view support for black suffrage as a litmus test of party loyalty. The platform of 1867 tied black suffrage to the vitality of representative government. The *Courant*, now under Hawley's control, reasoned that "we must set the example in the North. The unfortunate vote of Connecticut upon this amendment a year ago did incalculable injury to the cause the country through." After the 1867 elections Republican Senator Orris Ferry warned Hawley that because of the Democratic resurgence, conservatives "will lay hold of the Legislature, and insist upon temporizing and a reactionary policy, and it seems to me that it is all important to keep the position of that body firm and radical." Ferry reasoned that "to that end, the proposition to strike the word white from the Con-

---

[45] *New Haven Daily Register*, February 16, 1866, as quoted in Niven, "Time of the Whirlwind," 245; *Hartford Times*, December 30, 1865, January 27, February 17, 24, March 31, 1866; see also *Danbury Times*, February 22, 1866. For the Republican counterattack, see the *Litchfield Enquirer*, March 8, 1866; *Hartford Courant*, March 10, 1866; *Stamford Advocate*, March 9, 1866.

stitution should be made again, whether we can carry it through both houses or not by a majority of each. The Party, as such, in the Assembly should evince a determination not to give back from its position in the canvass." Republicans squashed a sardonic Democratic resolution claiming that "whereas, the doctrine of State sovereignty is an exploded theory, and no longer exists except as a fossil remain in the vacant cranium of a few antiquated politicians," only the federal government could determine voter qualifications; they then passed the suffrage amendment. Only three Democrats supported the measure (see table 1). Some proponents had advocated an omnibus measure that included a repeal of the literacy qualification so as to gain Democratic support, but Republicans refused to risk a nativist backlash.[46]

Democrats made the fall 1867 municipal elections a referendum on race. They contended that the Republicans' "pet idea of forcing negro suffrage upon this State is still paramount with them, and every town they carry this fall will help them in that work." For the first time since 1854, a majority of towns fell under Democratic control. The *Times* gloated that "Connecticut again recorded her voice against negro supremacy and Radical rule." And in the 1868 state contests, Democrats warned voters to "remember that if they vote for a Radical candidate for Senator or Representative, they will vote for negro suffrage in Connecticut. . . . The Republican party, by its action last year, forced it upon the people in the present election."[47]

Democratic victories did cause a partial Republican retreat on black suffrage. They refused to endorse black suffrage in their 1868 state platform. And yet, the party continued to vote in favor of it in the legislature. Up for its second approval in 1868, the suffrage amendment stood no chance of passage. Yet in voting for the amendment, Republican legislators reestablished their commitment to black suffrage amid a presidential campaign in which their national party purposefully evaded the issue. Nearly every voting Democrat

---

[46] *Conn. Senate Journal* (1866), 30–35; *Hartford Courant*, February 2, 1867; Orris Ferry to Joseph R. Hawley, April 2, 1867, and, for earlier advice along the same lines, May 3, 1866, Hawley Papers; *Conn. House Journal* (1867), 633, 649; *Litchfield Enquirer*, May 16, 1867. To the contrary, in 1868 Republicans would pass new registration and naturalization laws in an effort to reduce the influence of the immigrant vote; *Conn. Public Laws* (1866, 1867, and 1868), 174, 182.

[47] *Hartford Times*, October 5, 12, November 30, 1867, March, 21, 28, April 4, 1868.

rejected the measure, although there was a large number of nonvotes on each side of the aisle (see table 1).[48] Republicans also sponsored, against unanimous Democratic opposition, a law that forbade racial discrimination in the public schools. The *Times* characterized Republicans as "zealous in their endeavors to wage a war against the instincts and prejudices of the people."[49]

Republicans viewed Ulysses S. Grant's victory in 1868, both in Connecticut and in the nation, as the electorate's endorsement of congressional Reconstruction, and in the short session of Congress that followed the election they passed the Fifteenth Amendment, which prohibited any state from denying the right of suffrage explic-

----

[48] The abstention by 32 percent of Democratic and 23 percent of Republican members (see table 1) is intriguing. It is tempting to attribute Democratic abstentions to either a desire to prevent a quorum (Democrats tried to prevent quora on other issues in the 1868 session) or a more Machiavellian scheme of allowing the amendment to pass so that Republicans would have to campaign for it amid the presidential race. (There is no record of the committee report on the enacting legislation, which would have specified whether the referendum was to be held in October or, as had been the case on proposed amendments in the presidential election years of 1828 and 1832, in November. In 1864, another presidential year, a referendum on an amendment allowing soldiers to vote in the field was held in August, so that the results would be known prior to the November election.) Similarly, one might suspect that tepid Republicans abstained to prevent the amendment from obtaining a two-thirds majority. The issue is further complicated by the fact that the vote occurred on the last day of the session—and in the evening no less—and many members may have simply left the capital. Two days earlier nearly all Republicans were present to override English's vetoes of nativist-inspired registration and naturalization bills. And on the morning of the day in which the black suffrage amendment came up for a vote, all but twenty-three Republicans and nineteen Democrats were present to vote on the equally partisan issue of whether to allow Catholic priests to provide services in the state reform school. One way to shed some light on this problem, however, is to compare the vote, by party, on the black suffrage amendment and the vote (occurring immediately thereafter) to authorize a constitutional convention. Democrats had, unsuccessfully, sponsored this proposal (which was up for its second approval and thus required a two-thirds majority) with the purpose of making representation in the legislature more equitable of population. Republicans opposed the measure, and neither party had any tactical reason to abstain on the roll call. Of the thirty-one Republicans who did not vote on the black suffrage amendment, twenty-four also failed to vote on the resolution authorizing a constitutional convention, implying that only seven Republicans were present and not voting on the suffrage amendment. Similarly, of the thirty-three Democrats who did not vote on the suffrage issue, thirty-one also did not vote on the convention resolution. This pattern suggests that most of the abstainers had not attended the session either for extraneous reasons or because they did not believe that either measure could pass; *Conn. House Journal* (1868), 610, 614, 659, 677, 680.

[49] *Conn. House Journal* (1868), 667; *Hartford Times,* June 27, 1868.

itly on grounds of race. However much its ratification would aid the party in the North, it would also (its proponents thought) ensure the future voting rights of southern blacks. Republicans controlled three-fourths of the state legislatures, and they held a three-fourths majority in the House of Representatives of the outgoing Fortieth Congress. As of February 1869, they had a guarantee of only one member more than even a two-thirds majority of the House in the upcoming Forty-first Congress. It seemed urgent that the Fortieth Congress adopt the Amendment. While it was being debated in Congress, Connecticut Republicans differed over how much protection the Fifteenth Amendment should offer (most Republican editors vehemently opposed the obliteration of the literacy requirement), but they agreed that it should apply equally to blacks and whites. Thus, their state platform called simply (and cryptically) for impartial suffrage. Still, Republicans stood for black suffrage—whatever the motivation, however they phrased it, and however they politicized it—and that distinguished them from their Democratic opponents.[50]

During the 1869 campaign Democrats downplayed the racial component of their opposition to black suffrage. The state convention, which renominated English by acclamation, attacked the radicals' attempt to impose the terms of suffrage upon the states as "an assumption of superiority by the creature over the creator." Burr argued that "it is a monstrous wrong for the Radicals to take advantage of majorities in Congress and the Legislatures chosen in the past and on other issues, to force negro suffrage upon the country." The Democratic *Litchfield Sentinel* asserted that "The men at Washington have usurped the rights of the people—the rights of the States. The elective franchise is but an instrument in the hands of the unscrupulous."[51]

Republicans poked fun at the Democrats' "intentional equivocation" in having "refrained from declaring their opposition to the general principles of impartial suffrage" in the party platform. But

---

[50] The delegates to the Republican state convention rejected, by a two-to-one majority, a plank specifically endorsing black suffrage in the state. For a viewpoint on the timing of the Fifteenth Amendment's passage that emphasizes more than mine the partisan goal of securing black voters for the Republican party, see William Gillette, *The Right to Vote: Politics and the Passage of the Fifteenth Amendment* (Baltimore: Johns Hopkins University Press, 1965).

[51] *Hartford Times*, December 5, 1868, January 30, 1869; *Litchfield Sentinel*, as quoted in *Litchfield Enquirer*, February 11, 1869.

viewed within the context of practical politics, Democrats could hardly be accused of temporizing. In years past they had based their opposition to black suffrage in the South on both racial prejudice and states' rights sentiment. Those for whom the former determined political behavior were already in the Democratic camp by 1869; simultaneously, the Fifteenth Amendment added a new and potent dimension to the debate over states' rights. Here was not a proposal justified on any basis of postwar settlement in the defeated South alone. The Fifteenth Amendment applied to the victors as well as the vanquished, and as Democrats repeatedly pointed out, Nutmeggers had already expressed their opinion on black suffrage. By treating the Amendment as an infringement of the principle of state sovereignty many considered unaffected by the war, by portraying the proposal as an attempt to make a "ragged affair" of Connecticut's constitution, Democrats sought to attract voters receptive to the imposition of black suffrage on the rebellious South, but against its imposition on a loyal northern state against its will. The *Times* summed it up: a vote for Republican legislative candidates is a "vote for negro suffrage." Yet "it is more than a question of Negro Suffrage! It is a question in reality *whether our good old State shall be permitted any longer to manage her own affairs.*"[52]

Conversely, Republicans countered the Democratic strategy by shifting discussion away from the issue's constitutional dimensions and toward their opponent's obsessive racism. In an editorial entitled "Democracy vs. The Nigger," the *Bridgeport Standard* denounced Democratic race-baiting. When the Windham County Democratic convention adopted a resolution pledging to "resist negro suffrage by every means," the *Courant* observed that the "Democracy without the nigger is worse than a skillet without a handle," and it bemoaned that "bigotry, prejudice, and oppression have lingered longer and fought harder in Connecticut than in any other New England state." The *Willimantic Journal* claimed that the Democrats' racism appealed mainly to barroom drunkards; and the *Stamford Advocate* reasoned that Democrats opposed the Amendment only because "it is inevitable of putting an end to the everlasting cry of 'nigger' in our State and national politics." To the extent that Republicans con-

---

[52] Gillette, *Right to Vote*, 121; *Stamford Advocate*, February 12, 1869; *Hartford Times*, February 13, 27, March 27, 1869.

fronted the constitutional issue, they justified the Amendment on the impartiality of its application and its conformity to the lawful process for ratification. The *Courant* also regarded it as the "logical conclusion of the work of the war, establishing liberty and equal rights. . . . It is the only defensible position that can be taken by a professedly democratic people." The *Norwich Courier* endorsed the principle of "fair play for men with colored skins as well as to those who are nominally white" and considered the Amendment acceptable to "every believer in justice and impartiality." Finally, Republicans emphasized Grant's endorsement of ratification, thereby harnessing the new president's popularity.[53]

Republicans recaptured the governorship with 50.2 percent of the votes cast, and in the ensuing legislative session all but two Republicans voted to ratify the Fifteenth Amendment. Not a single House Democrat voted in favor (see table 1). After the Amendment became inscribed in the federal Constitution, some Democrats began to court Connecticut's black vote. But not until 1876, when a number of amendments proposed by a constitutional convention were submitted to the electorate, did voters finally (and symbolically) remove the word "white" from the state constitution.[54]

It has been suggested that although voters rejected black suffrage in 1865, the greater support the measure received over that in 1847 demonstrates that Connecticut whites were moving toward an acceptance of black political equality.[55] Certainly Republicans advocated black suffrage with greater vigor between 1864 and 1869 than either they or their Whig predecessors had before the Civil War. Indeed, whether based on principle, the necessity of distinguishing themselves from Democrats on issues, the calculated belief that blacks, if enfranchised, would help ensure party victories in a competitive state, or the desire to be seen as consistent with the national party, Connecticut Republicans endorsed black suffrage in the late 1860s despite considerable evidence that it may have been to their short-

---

[53] *Bridgeport Daily Standard,* April 7, 1869; *Hartford Daily Courant,* February 27, April 2, 1869; ibid., April 1, 1869, as quoted in Gillette, *Right to Vote,* 122; *Willimantic Journal,* as quoted in *Hartford Daily Courant,* March 29, 1869; *Stamford Advocate,* March 5 1869; *Norwich Courier,* March 4, 1869.

[54] *Conn. House Journal* (1869); Gillette, *Right to Vote,* 123–30.

[55] Eric Foner, *Reconstruction: America's Unfinished Revolution, 1863–1877* (New York: Harper & Row, 1988), 223.

term political disadvantage. One might make the generalization that whereas, before the war, Whig and Republican leaders favored black suffrage when circumstance and party strategy permitted it, after 1863 Republicans ideologically favored black suffrage, and strategic concerns played only a secondary role. And yet the nagging question remains: why could not the Republicans, fresh from a stunning electoral victory and the moral claims of triumph and divine purpose in the recently ended war, command a majority in favor of black suffrage in 1865? Did the Civil War really have an impact on race relations?

A comparison of Connecticut's experience with that of Iowa, one of only two states whose voters enfranchised African Americans, sheds light on this problem. In 1857 Iowa Republicans distanced themselves from a black suffrage amendment, and it gained only 15 percent of the votes cast in a referendum. In 1868 Republicans actively campaigned in favor of the same amendment, making it a party issue, and it passed with 57 percent of the votes cast. Robert Dykstra argues that the Iowa experience comports with the theory that racism, though widespread in America, has also been shallow. Most people are neither implacable racists nor enlightened egalitarians. Instead, their behavior is conformist, and because parties were important instruments of socialization in the nineteenth century, the decision of Republicans to advocate black suffrage actively in 1868 energized voters in a way that they were not in 1857. The role of opinion makers, coupled with the effects of the black military experience in the war and the lack of any economic investment in racism in Iowa, was significant to the referendum's outcome.[56]

Dykstra's point is well taken. Yet although earnest Republican advocacy *was* necessary to the success of any black suffrage amendment, crucial as well was the nature of the elections contested concurrently with the referenda. In 1857 only county offices were at stake in Iowa, and only one-fourth of Frémont's voters favored black suffrage. In 1868 voters decided on the amendment at the same time that they were electing a president, and 86 percent of the state's 1867 Republican electorate cast ballots for *both* Ulysses S. Grant and black

---

[56] Robert R. Dykstra, *Bright Radical Star: Black Freedom and White Supremacy on the Hawkeye Frontier* (Cambridge, Mass.: Harvard University Press, 1993), 171–92, 216–37, 262–67.

suffrage.[57] Connecticut's referendum in 1865, like Iowa's in 1857, took place amid purely local elections in which partisanship, though certainly present, was not consistently as strong a force as it was in statewide elections.[58] In both Iowa in 1857 and Connecticut in 1865, suffrage had greater issue saliency for racists (whether of the hard-core or casual varieties) than it did for egalitarians. Only 21 percent of Iowa's and 9 percent of Connecticut's Democrats abstained in those referenda, compared with 62 percent of Iowa's and 32 percent of Connecticut's Republicans.[59] To be sure, the Democratic party was stronger in Connecticut than in Iowa, but if the same share (86 percent) of Connecticut's April 1865 Republican voters had favored suffrage as had Iowa's 1867 Republican voters in 1868, then the amendment would have passed, with 52 percent of the votes cast.

Leadership and the timing of referenda then were both crucial to the potential success of the black suffrage movement in the Nutmeg State. Voters may have been more accepting of black equality than before the war. But those who wanted to keep Connecticut the only "white man's state in New England" needed less institutional push and less electoral incentive to participate in the referendum than those who wanted to end the bane of racism. The dynamics of the three criteria here—relative strength of the Democratic party, effort on the part of Republican leaders, and importance of concurrent elections—differed from state to state in the North.[60] But in only two

[57] Ibid., 185, 229. The figure of 86 percent, derived from the table on page 229, is based on the assumption that all who voted for equal suffrage also voted for Grant, an assumption that seems reasonable since Dykstra reports a negative estimate of 1867 Democrats voting for Grant. (Dykstra does not directly regress the vote on equal suffrage with the vote in the presidential contest.) Upwards of 98 percent of 1867 Republicans voted for Grant, and the other 2 percent abstained.

[58] Moreover, in Connecticut, unlike Iowa in 1868, either ballots were cast separately on the amendment, or, if the question of "yes" or "no" was permitted to be placed on party ballots, the decision to include on party ballots the referendum voting options undoubtedly varied from one locale to another. The 1818 Constitution specified that proposed amendments be voted upon at town meetings warned for that purpose. The language of the resolution authorizing the referendum on black suffrage stipulated that the presiding officer at the town meetings call electors' names and that the latter were then to deposit their ballots, with the words "yes" or "no" written or printed on them. It is not clear whether such ballots would have been accepted if they listed, as well, party candidates for local offices; Conn. Public Laws (1865), 94–98.

[59] See table 3; and Dykstra, Bright Radical Star, 185, 229.

[60] A referendum that possibly falls in between the examples of Iowa in 1857 and Connecticut in 1865 on the one hand and Iowa in 1868 on the other is that which

states, Minnesota and Iowa, did voters accept black suffrage on their own, and they did so while voting in the 1868 presidential election. As a stand-alone measure as in Connecticut, and even with Republican exhortations on its behalf, equal suffrage for African Americans— even for those who could satisfy a literacy requirement—could not command a majority.

---

occurred in Wisconsin in 1865. That referendum, in which a black suffrage amendment was defeated, 56 percent to 44 percent, was held concurrently with a gubernatorial election. Yet although the political office was important, Republicans did not make ratification of the amendment a party issue. Between 70 percent and 76 percent of Republican voters favored the amendment; see Michael J. McManus, *Political Abolitionism in Wisconsin, 1840–1861* (Kent, Ohio: Kent State University Press, 1998), 209; Foner, *Reconstruction*, 223.

11

The Confiscation Acts:
The North Strikes Back

John Syrett

SAMUEL GRIDLEY HOWE and other abolitionists believed that with the firing on Fort Sumter, "God has opened the way" for the emancipation of the slaves and the subjugation of the "Slave power."[1] This was, to be sure, a view shared only by a small minority when the Civil War began on April 12. Most in the North hoped, with President Abraham Lincoln, that the war would soon be over and the Union restored with little pain and suffering. Although hundreds of thousands quickly volunteered to fight, few in the North welcomed the war, and probably even fewer predicted that it would end with the abolition of the peculiar institution and the destruction of the Old South.

Many factors contributed to this dramatic transformation of the war. These included the First and Second Confiscation Acts, introduced by Senator Lyman Trumbull of Illinois, and passed by Congress in August 1861 and July 1862.[2] The forces that led to their introduction and passage illustrate how the struggle evolved from an effort to restore the Union to the abolition of slavery and the arming

---

[1] Samuel Gridley Howe to Charles Sumner, April 16, 1861, series 2, reel 4 (hereinafter 2:4), Charles Sumner Papers, Lamont Library, Harvard University; Phillip Shaw Paludan, "A People's Contest": The Union and the Civil War 1861–1865, 2d ed. (Lawrence: University Press of Kansas, 1996), 6; James H. Moorhead, American Apocalypse: Yankee Protestants and the Civil War 1860–1869 (New Haven, Conn.: Yale University Press, 1978), 97–98.

[2] John Syrett, "The Confiscation Acts: Efforts at Reconstruction during the Civil War" (Ph.D. diss., University of Wisconsin, 1971); Duke Frederick, "The Second Confiscation Act: A Chapter of Civil War Politics" (Ph.D. diss., University of Chicago, 1966); James G. Randall, The Confiscation of Property during the Civil War (Indianapolis: Mutual Printing and Lithographing, 1913); James G. Randall, Constitutional Problems under Lincoln, rev. ed. (Urbana: University of Illinois Press, 1964).

of exslaves. Advocates of confiscation wanted to emancipate the slaves, punish those who waged war against the North, and lay the foundation for Reconstruction, whereas opponents argued the acts were excessive and unconstitutional. The failure of these measures to realize their sponsors' goals illustrates how confused and moderate Congress was in its efforts to reform the South during the war. Moreover, the interaction of the military, the public, Congress, escaped slaves, and Lincoln in the passage of the confiscation acts demonstrates how difficult it was to win the war, restore the Union, and simultaneously provide a remedy for the American dilemma of race. While the confiscation acts helped push Lincoln to embrace emancipation, of themselves they did not achieve their intended aims.[3]

Following Sumter, Lincoln emphasized, to both North and South, that the Union would try to "avoid any devastation, any destruction of, or interference with, property, or any disturbance of peaceful citizens in any part of the country."[4] This conciliatory policy underscored the widespread belief that most southerners would not follow the leaders of secession and that support for the Union still existed in the South. It was also meant to reassure the border states, particularly Kentucky, that they should remain loyal. There were some, however, and not just abolitionists, who worried that peace might come before "that arrogance and starch" was "taken out of all traitors," as one constituent wrote Trumbull. On the eve of Sumter an Ohio man even advocated a "war of Extermination" against "the white population of South Carolina[,] Georgia[,] Alabama and Florida" and that freed slaves be given the confiscated estates of rebels.[5] Such appeals for a war wider than Lincoln contemplated remained in the background,

---

[3] See Herman Belz, *Abraham Lincoln, Constitutionalism, and Equal Rights in the Civil War Era* (New York: Fordham University Press, 1998); and Michael Les Benedict, "Equality and Expediency in the Reconstruction Era: A Review Essay," *Civil War History* 23 (December 1977): 322–35, for discussions of the problems surrounding the change from emancipation to equal rights.

[4] Roy Basler et al., eds., *The Collected Works of Abraham Lincoln*, 9 vols. (New Brunswick, N.J.: Rutgers University Press, 1953–55), 4:331–32; Phillip Shaw Paludan, *The Presidency of Abraham Lincoln* (Lawrence: University Press of Kansas, 1994), 70; Paludan, *"A People's Contest,"* 15–18.

[5] K. K. Jones to Lyman Trumbull, April 25, 1861, Lyman Trumbull Papers, Library of Congress; J. D. Easton to Senator John Sherman, April 11, 1861, John Sherman Papers, Library of Congress; Mark Grimsley, *The Hard Hand of War: Union Military Policy toward Southern Civilians 1861–1865* (Cambridge: Cambridge University Press, 1996), 8–9.

however, as the North prepared for what it assumed would be a relatively swift victory.

Problems arose, however, when the Union forces encountered
slavery in the Confederacy. How to handle fugitive slaves entering
federal lines caused the first major problem. General Benjamin F.
Butler of Massachusetts, a volatile Democrat politician, created a
controversy at Fortress Monroe, Virginia, in late May, when, according to Butler, three slaves "delivered themselves up to" his pickets.
Rather than return them, which was the policy for dealing with fugitive slaves, Butler kept the "property," put them to work for the
Union, and sent a receipt to the owner. Three days later he began
employing these "able-bodied persons" who came into Union lines.
By the end of May, Secretary of War Simon Cameron, and presumably Lincoln, had given his approval to this "contraband" policy. This
policy rested on the assumption that such fugitive slaves would otherwise be aiding the rebellion. As such, it anticipated the First Confiscation Act. While many saw Butler's move as radical, others realized
that describing the fugitives as "property" meant the policy was, in
fact, consistent with the Dred Scott decision, which Republicans had
vigorously opposed.[6]

Butler's decisions raised crucial questions. Should the North allow
the Confederacy to use slaves to aid the rebellion? If not, how should
it handle fugitives? What should the Union forces do when slaves,
such as women and children, unable to work for the rebels, entered
their lines? What status did they acquire once inside Union lines? By
late July over nine hundred contrabands had arrived at Fortress Mon-

---

[6] Benjamin F. Butler, *Private and Official Correspondence of Gen. Benjamin F.
Butler during the Period of the Civil War,* 5 vols. (Norwood, Mass.: Plimpton Press,
1917), 1:104–8, 114, 116–17; *War of the Rebellion: A Compilation of the Official
Records of the Union and Confederate Armies,* 70 vols. in 128 (Washington, D.C.:
Government Printing Office, 1880–1901), series 1, vol. 2, 648–52, 52–54 (hereinafter cited as *Official Records*); Louis S. Gerteis, "Salmon P. Chase, Radicalism, and
the Politics of Emancipation, 1861–1864," *Journal of American History* 60 (June
1973): 45; Frank Freidel, *Francis Lieber: Nineteenth-Century Liberal* (Baton Rouge:
Louisiana State University Press, 1947), 327; Gilroy G. Clinton to Sumner, June 5,
1861, 2:22, Sumner Papers; Don E. Fehrenbacher, *The Dred Scott Case: Its Significance in American Law and Politics* (New York: Oxford University Press, 1978), 4–5.
Butler did not use the word *contraband* in any of his communications on the event
or policy. [Edward L. Pierce], "The Contrabands at Fortress Monroe," *Atlantic
Monthly* 8 (November 1861): 627, may have been the first to use the word *contraband.*

roe and had also captured the North's attention.[7] But the administration made no effort to offer a policy despite Cameron's promise to Butler at the end of May that the "question of their final disposition will be reserved for further determination." In fact, generals were allowed to respond as they saw fit; some turned fugitives away while others returned them to owners, especially loyal owners. General George McClellan even promised to "crush any attempt at insurrection on their [slaves'] part."[8]

Lincoln's decision not to call Congress into session until July 4 prevented it from responding to the issue that Butler and other generals increasingly confronted. Nor did the President allude to the "contraband" question in his first message to Congress on that date; he did not even mention slavery. Instead, he saw "much reason to believe that the Union men are the majority in many, if not" all of the seceded states. And he believed, "after the rebellion shall have been suppressed," that he "would probably" have "no different understanding" of the federal powers over states than before Sumter. Reconstruction, in short, would doubtless be swift and leave slavery intact. On July 9 the House passed a nonbinding resolution in which they denied it was the duty of Union soldiers to "capture and return fugitive slaves." It also began consideration of Trumbull's first confiscation bill, introduced on July 15.[9]

It is unclear what prompted the Illinois senator to offer his measure, but he was not the first to suggest the idea. Confiscation of Loyalist property had occurred in the Revolution, of course, and the Confederate Congress, in late May, had authorized the confiscation of debts due to northerners. Doubtless Butler's actions at Fortress Monroe also played a part. As well, Secretary of the Treasury Salmon P. Chase and at least two other senators had spoken of confiscation

---

[7] Ira Berlin et al., eds., *Freedom: A Documentary History of Emancipation 1861–1867*, series 1, vol. 1, *The Destruction of Slavery* (Cambridge: Cambridge University Press, 1985), 15; Ira Berlin et al., eds., *Freedom: A Documentary History of Emancipation 1861–1867*, series 1, vol. 2, *The Wartime Genesis of Free Labor: The Upper South* (Cambridge: Cambridge University Press, 1993), 86–87; Louis S. Gerteis, *From Contraband to Freedom: Federal Policy toward Southern Blacks, 1861–1865* (Westport, Conn.: Greenwood Press, 1973), 16–17.

[8] Butler, *Correspondence*, 1:119; Peter J. Parish, *The American Civil War* (New York: Holmes and Meier, 1975), 234; *Official Records*, series 1, vol. 1, 47–48; series 2, vol. 1, 753 (quotation).

[9] Basler et al., eds., *Collected Works of Lincoln*, 4:437, 439; *Official Records*, series 2, vol. 1, 759.

as a means to produce revenue to pay for the war. Whatever the inspiration, Trumbull's original bill authorized the President to seize the "property" of any person who used it to aid the "insurrection." Eight days later, following the disaster at Bull Run, he amended the bill to include the confiscation of any "person" used to aid the rebellion. In the interval he had heard reports of slaveowners lending or hiring their slaves to the Confederate army. It is noteworthy that Trumbull's original purpose was to confiscate property, not slaves. The Senate accepted this change and the bill as a whole. Only border state senators voted against the measure. The House, however, limited Trumbull's amendment so that only slaves used in the service of the Confederate military would be liable to seizure. The House then passed the bill, sixty to forty-eight. The Senate concurred with this change; Trumbull, oddly enough, thought the change was not that important. The Senate vote was twenty-four to eleven. The House discussed the bill a bit more than did the Senate, but neither spent much time on the first act, particularly when compared to the lengthy debates that occurred over the second act. One Republican senator opposed it; only border state Republicans in the House did so. It passed on August 3, and the President signed it shortly thereafter.[10]

Senate conservatives expressed alarm at the supposed breadth of Trumbull's bill. John Breckinridge, a Democrat from Kentucky, thought such a measure would lead "to a general confiscation of all property, and a loosing of all bonds." In a superb understatement James Pearce of Maryland predicted such a law would irritate the South; nor, he warned, would those in charge of the South's court system implement it. To create other courts for implementation would be unconstitutional, he claimed.[11] In the House John Crittenden, Unionist from Kentucky, said Congress could not legislate on the matter. War conferred no new powers on the government, he

---

[10] Syrett, "Confiscation Acts," 1–22; Randall, *Constitutional Problems,* 275; Berlin et al., eds., *Destruction of Slavery,* 332; Ralph J. Roske, *His Own Counsel: The Life and Times of Lyman Trumbull* (Reno: University of Nevada Press, 1979), 75–76 (the most recent biography of Trumbull); James Doolittle, "A Statesman's Letters of the Civil War Period," *Journal of Illinois State Historical Society* 2 (July 1909): 45. See James Willard Hurst, *The Law of Treason in the United States* (Westport, Conn.: Greenwood Press, 1970), 80–85, 104–6, for the Revolution and confiscation. See *Statutes at Large of the United States,* 12:319, for the first act.

[11] *Congressional Globe,* 37th Cong., 1 sess., 219, 431, 434 (hereinafter *Cong. Globe,* 37:1). The final Senate vote for the bill was forty-two to eleven.

argued. In addition, the previous Congress had agreed, in resolutions bearing his name, not to interfere with slavery in the states. Moreover, he claimed, the bill violated the Constitution by providing forfeiture beyond the life of the offender, an issue that would plague the second act too. Only Thaddeus Stevens of Pennsylvania attempted to refute the arguments against the bill. If constitutions contradicted the laws of war, said Stevens, they should be ignored. Nor could Crittenden and others use the Constitution to protect those who had left the Union: "Sir, these rebels, who have disregarded and set at defiance that instrument, are, by every rule of municipal and international law, estopped from pleading it against our action." But, in the end, Stevens cared little how one rationalized the use of confiscation. He wanted results, declaring "if their whole country must be laid waste, and made a desert, in order to save this Union from destruction so let it be." Along with most who supported the second act, Stevens saw the first as a military measure, not as a means to abolition. In conclusion he warned the South that if the war continued, the North would arm their slaves against them.[12] Few other members of Congress had yet to reach such conclusions.

The limited reach of the first act illustrates how cautious Congress was in the summer of 1861. Even after the Union military disaster of Bull Run in late July had demonstrated how difficult it would be to crush the rebellion, Congress did not go very far either to punish those loyal to the Confederacy or to strike at slavery. Slaves used in military labor or service in support of the rebellion did not go free under the first act; those claiming their services—the owners— simply forfeited their claim to them. Thus, the first act confiscated slaves only if directly employed in the rebellion. The only liberty granted them was not to remain slaves of rebels; Congress did not indicate how this would be carried out. Any property liable to confiscation under the first act had to be proceeded against in the "district or circuit court," which omitted almost all property inside the Confederacy.[13] Some outside of Congress realized how narrow the blow

---

[12] Ibid., 411–12, 414–15. See Hans L. Trefousse, *Thaddeus Stevens: Nineteenth-Century Egalitarian* (Chapel Hill: University of North Carolina Press, 1997), 111–12, the most recent biography of Stevens.

[13] Heather Cox Richardson, *The Greatest Nation of the Earth: Republican Economic Policies during the Civil War* (Cambridge, Mass.: Harvard University Press, 1997), 213–14; Charles Eliot Norton, "The Advantages of Defeat," *Atlantic Monthly* 8 (September 1861): 360; George F. Williams to Sumner and Richard Henry Dana,

made against slavery was and urged more. As many noted during the first two years of the war, Congress lagged behind the public's wish to strike directly at both the Confederacy and slavery.

"Antislavery men will soon be after you with ballots," John B. Wood scolded Trumbull from Kansas. Why would not Congress "use all of the means which the law of nations" allowed "to cripple" the Confederacy? "Slavery must be abolished if we are to have a permanent peace," he concluded. Thomas G. Shearman of New York also rebuked Trumbull for the narrow constitutional footing of the bill, noting that secession had reduced the former states to territories "governable by Congress." "I trust the next session will find Congress prepared to take even broader ground" and thus abolish slavery. From Philadelphia M. J. Thomas exploded at Senator John Sherman: "Can it be that nobody wishes to abolish Slavery, that great overshadowing crime of our nation, unless 'forced' so to do?" N. J. Marble, one of hundreds who wrote to request an appointment in the military, also urged Senator Ben Wade of Ohio to "present a bill to congress at its next session . . . to abolish slavery in all the states and territories." There were also many in the North who agreed with an anonymous correspondent to Trumbull who urged abolition by confiscation but linked it to colonization.[14] This plea for colonization reflected widespread racism in the North among Republicans, not to mention Democrats. Even so, those writing congressmen were alarmed at how timid Congress seemed to be. It is ironic, then, that some antislavery men were much more optimistic. Charles Sumner wrote to Wendell Phillips in early August about the demise of slavery: "Be tranquil. . . . The battle & retreat [of Bull Run] have done much for the slave. . . . I told the Prest. that our defeat was the worst event and the best event . . . the best as it made the extinction of slavery

---

Jr., to Sumner, both on July 29, 1861, 1:23, Sumner Papers; Herman Belz, "Protection of Personal Liberty in Republican Emancipation Legislation of 1862," *Journal of Southern History* 42 (August 1976): 387–89; Patricia M. L. Lucie, "Confiscation: Constitutional Crossroads," *Civil War History* 23 (December 1977): 321–23; *Statutes at Large*, 12:319.

[14] William Reddick to Trumbull, July 25, 1861, Thomas G. Sherman to Trumbull, July 30, 1861, John B. Wood to Trumbull, August 26, 1861, Anonymous to Trumbull, July 18, 1861, Trumbull Papers; John Jay to Sumner, July 28, 1861, 2:23, Sumner Papers; Samuel Clark to Sherman, July 30, 1861, Sherman Papers; J. H. Jordan to William Pitt Fessenden, William Pitt Fessenden Papers, Library of Congress; N. J. Marble to Benjamin F. Wade, August 19, 1861, Benjamin F. Wade Papers, Library of Congress.

inevitable." In late August Thomas Wentworth Higginson was "satisfied that we are gravitating towards a bolder antislavery policy. The desideratum is to approach a policy of emancipation by stages so clear & irresistible as to retain for that end an united public sentiment."[15] Only Congress and the President had to catch up to Republican thinking.

In late August a direct attack upon slavery and for confiscation came from the military in Missouri. On August 30 General John C. Frémont, the Republican presidential nominee in 1856, declared martial law throughout the state, confiscated the property of rebels, and freed their slaves. The reasons for this dramatic move were complex and the aftermath important for the course of the war. Missouri was probably the most violently divided state over the Civil War at this time. Guerilla bands operated in some parts, and many residents openly sympathized with the Confederacy. Governor Hamilton R. Gamble, for example, announced in early August that no "scheme" or "conduct" that interfered with slavery in the state would be allowed. At first Frémont had enjoyed the support of Frank Blair, Jr., the most powerful Unionist politician in the state, whose brother Montgomery was the Postmaster General in Lincoln's Cabinet. But military reverses, mismanagement, jealousy, and poor judgment led the Blairs to believe Frémont should be replaced. Frémont certainly felt considerable pressure in August and went so far as to close down several St. Louis newspapers, including one that supported the North. Perhaps to bring order from military and political confusion, Frémont, without consulting Lincoln or Cameron, impetuously made his proclamation. The pivotal part said that the "property, real and personal," of all who took up arms against the United States "is declared to be confiscated to public use, and their slaves . . . are hereby

[15] Sumner to Phillips, August 3, 1861, 2:75, Sumner Papers; James M. McPherson, *The Struggle for Equality: Abolitionists and the Negro in the Civil War and Reconstruction* (Princeton: Princeton University Press, 1964), 72 (Higginson quotation). See George M. Fredrickson, *The Black Image in the White Mind: The Debate on Afro-American Character and Destiny, 1817–1914* (New York: Harper & Row, 1971); V. Jacque Voegeli, *Free but Not Equal: The Midwest and the Negro during the Civil War* (Chicago: University of Chicago Press, 1967); Paludan, *"A People's Contest"*; Forrest G. Wood, *Black Scare: The Racist Response to Emancipation and Reconstruction* (Berkeley: University of California Press, 1968); and C. Vann Woodward, "Seeds of Failure in Radical Race Policy," 163–83, in C. Vann Woodward, *American Counterpoint: Slavery and Racism in the North South Dialogue* (Boston: Little Brown, 1971), for racism in the North.

declared freemen."[16] Frémont's proclamation, if implemented, would have gone well beyond the First Confiscation Act, and it anticipated the second act, passed in July 1862.

Reactions to this sweeping declaration were revealing. Many northerners, and not just New Englanders and abolitionists, were delighted. Secretary Cameron, before talking with Lincoln, expressed his approval. The Republican press throughout the North applauded the general's proclamation, as did many conservatives. Both the *Missouri Democrat* and the *Missouri Republican* endorsed Frémont's freeing of the slaves. Even James Gordon Bennett's *New York Herald*, often sympathetic to the South, hailed the decision; so too did the Democratic Philadelphia *Public Ledger.* Abolitionists, naturally, were jubilant. Harriet Beecher Stowe proclaimed: "The hour has come, and the man!" William Lloyd Garrison thought it was "the beginning of the end," and Gerrit Smith wrote a public letter to Lincoln to applaud the general. Even Governor John Andrew of Massachusetts broke his self-imposed silence on the slavery question to say that Frémont gave "an impetus of the grandest character to the whole cause" of emancipation. Not surprisingly, the border states were upset. Salmon P. Chase, Secretary of the Treasury, received two alarmed reports. From Louisville, Joshua Speed, an old friend of Lincoln's from Springfield, said that the Union men opposed the proclamation since it went "beyond the power conferred by the [Confiscation] Act of Congress." He and others had argued all over the state that "this was [not] to be a war upon slavery." He implored Chase to urge a reconsideration of the issue and "for God sake don[']t allow us to be turned over to the enemy." From Frankfort, Garrett Davis, an important Unionist, noted it "caused me despondency for the first time for Ky." Newspapers throughout Kentucky also attacked the proclamation.[17] Lincoln, too, was worried about the effect of Frémont's proclamation.

---

[16] *Official Records,* series 1, vol. 3, 466–67. See Andrew Rolle, *John Charles Frémont: Character as Destiny* (Norman: University of Oklahoma Press, 1991), 204–7; Allan Nevins, *Frémont: Pathmaker of the West* (New York: Longmans, Green, 1955), 497–500; and Elbert B. Smith, *Francis Preston Blair* (New York: Free Press, 1980), 294–97, for the background.

[17] William E. Parrish, *The Turbulent Partnership: Missouri for the Union, 1861–1865* (Columbia: University of Missouri Press, 1963), 61; Smith, *Blair,* 298; William Dusinberre, *Civil War Issues in Philadelphia, 1856–1865* (Philadelphia: University of Pennsylvania Press, 1965), 131; J. R. Fry to Sumner, October 8, 1861, 2:23, Sum-

The President wrote a polite letter to the ambitious and mercurial general two days after the proclamation's publication in the East. He asked that Frémont "modify" his proclamation to conform to the First Confiscation Act, a copy of which he included. The threat to confiscate "property" and liberate the "slaves of traitorous owners, will alarm our Southern Union friends," Lincoln observed, "and turn them against us—perhaps ruin our rather fair prospect of Kentucky." He closed by noting he wrote "in a spirit of caution and not censure." A special messenger was dispatched with the letter for speedy delivery to the general. Frémont, however, did not accept the President's advice. His reply admitted that he had acted "without consultation or advice with anyone," relying on "my best judgment to serve the country" and Lincoln. But if the President did not approve of "the liberation of the slaves, I have to ask that you will openly direct me to make a correction." For Frémont to change his proclamation on slavery would "imply that I myself thought it was wrong," which he did not. "I acted with full deliberation, upon the certain conviction that it was a measure right and necessary, and I think so still." Jessie Frémont, a strenuous defender of her husband, delivered the letter in person to Lincoln on September 10, the night she arrived from St. Louis. Their memories differed on what each said, but she was probably correct in believing the President had already made up his mind.[18]

The next day Lincoln amended Frémont's proclamation to conform to the First Confiscation Act, thereby setting off a howl of protest throughout the North. He began by conceding that Frémont, "upon the ground" in Missouri, was in the best position to determine

ner Papers; Wendy Hammond Venet, *Neither Ballots nor Bullets: Women Abolitionists and the Civil War* (Charlottesville: University Press of Virginia, 1991), 76 (Howe quotation); Nevins, *Frémont,* 504–5; McPherson, *Struggle for Equality,* 72–73 (Garrison quotation); Henry G. Pearson, *The Life and Times of John Andrew: Governor of Massachusetts, 1861–1862,* 2 vols. (Boston: Houghton Mifflin, 1904), 1:249; Speed to Chase, September 2, 1861, Davis to Chase, September 3, 1861, in John Niven, ed., *The Salmon P. Chase Papers,* 5 vols. (Kent, Ohio: Kent State University Press, 1996–98), 3:92–95; Victor Howard, *Black Liberation in Kentucky: Emancipation and Freedom, 1862–1884* (Lexington: University Press of Kentucky, 1983), 6–7; Wilson Porter Shortridge, "Kentucky Neutrality in 1861," *Mississippi Valley Historical Review* 9 (March 1923): 295–301.

[18] Lincoln to Frémont, September 2, 1861, in Basler et al., eds., *Collected Works of Lincoln,* 4:504; Frémont to Lincoln, September 8, 1861, *Official Records,* series 1, vol. 3, 469–70, 477–78; Smith, *Blair,* 300–301.

if martial law was required. However, the "particular clause" relating "to the confiscation of property, and the liberation of slaves, appeared" to Lincoln "objectionable, in its non-conformity" to the first act. So he "cheerfully" accepted Frémont's invitation to modify it. The following day Lincoln informed Jessie Frémont that he had answered her husband's letter but did not divulge its contents. He did, nonetheless, enter his "protest against being understood as acting in any hostility towards him."[19] Most northerners believed the President's decision was deplorable for reasons of principle alone. Only Democrats and border state Unionists were pleased.

The protest against Lincoln's letter to Frémont was loud and extreme. For many, Lincoln's decision revealed the central place that slavery now occupied in the battle to defeat the Confederacy. In that light the Frémont episode certainly assisted the antislavery cause. It made clear that the public, through Congress, would have to play a central role, as would the slaves themselves. As Sumner wisely observed to Wendell Phillips, "The London *Times* is right. We cannot subdue the rebels. But their strength [slavery] will give us the victory at last." To Francis Lieber, soon to write an important work on the rules of war, Sumner wrote that "slavery shall only be touched by Act of Congress & not through Martial Law. This weakens our armies." Others agreed with Sumner that Congress now had to take the lead, since Lincoln was incapable of seeing the will of the public. A Brooklyn resident wrote to Michigan Senator Zachariah Chandler that "Congress must complete the work it has begun. . . . There has been a great change within sixty days upon that confiscation or more properly stated emancipation act." Senator Wade of Ohio shared the low opinion of Lincoln. Like others, he noted that Lincoln's decision had been "universally condemned and execrated in the north," and he thought this "tenderness to the slave holders of old Kentucky has done more to demoralize us than all things else." Two weeks later Wade despaired of ever "putting down this rebellion through the instrumentality of this Administration."[20]

---

[19] Lincoln to Frémont, September 11, 1861, Lincoln to Mrs. John C. Frémont, September 12, 1861, in Basler et al., eds., *Collected Works of Lincoln*, 4:517–19.

[20] Sumner to Phillips, September 17, 1861, 2:75, Sumner to Lieber, September 17, 1861, Moncure Conway to Sumner, September 17, 1861, Daniel R. Goodloe to Sumner, September 19, 1861, James Chestney to Sumner, October 1, 1861, 1:64, Sumner Papers; William E. Danbliday to Zachariah Chandler, September 16, 1861, Wade to Chandler, September 23, 1861, Wade to Chandler, October 8, 1862, Zacha-

There were many, particularly in the border states, who thought Lincoln had acted properly. And they were right; the time was not ripe for emancipation, not through the military without authority from Congress. However, some of Lincoln's closest allies, even in Illinois, remained upset, unable to appreciate his logic. Joseph Medill, editor of the *Chicago Tribune,* claimed the reaction in Chicago was more severe than over the news of Bull Run. The penalty for the rebellion of a slaveholder should be "the confiscation and liberation of his slaves: This strikes at the root of the disease." If his revocation was meant to "placate" those in Kentucky, Medill predicted it would have the opposite effect. Men "ask each other, 'what are we fighting for[?]'" "Our Democrats are in agony as much as our Republicans," he concluded. More significantly, Senator Orville Hickman Browning, a good friend of Lincoln, objected. Lincoln replied to his friend at some length, noting that it astonished him that Browning "should object to my adhering to a law [the first act], which you" supported. On the question of principle, had Frémont's proclamation been "within the range of military law," and not "purely political," Lincoln would have approved. But no such seizure should last beyond the military need; that "must be settled according to law" made by Congress. Indeed, he believed Congress might "pass a law . . . just such as Fremont proclaimed," one he "might" vote for if he were a member of Congress. However, he objected to Frémont's request that the President "exercise the permanent legislative functions" of government. As for policy, he realized that Frémont's proclamation was popular "in some quarters," but it threatened Kentucky, which was crucial. "I think to lose Kentucky is nearly the same as to lose the whole game." If Kentucky went, he doubted Missouri and Maryland would stay. That would make "the job on our hands . . . too large for us."[21] Lincoln understood that Congress might consider a more

riah Chandler Papers, Library of Congress; McPherson, *Struggle for Equality,* 72; Victor B. Howard, *Religion and the Radical Republican Movement, 1860–1870* (Lexington: University Press of Kentucky, 1990), 12–13.

[21] E. Merton Coulter, *The Civil War and Readjustment in Kentucky* (Chapel Hill: University of North Carolina Press, 1926), 112–13; Howard, *Black Liberation,* 7; Berlin et al., eds., *Destruction of Slavery,* 17, 397–98; Medill to Chase, September 15, 1861, in Niven, ed., *Chase Papers,* 3:97–98; Lincoln to Browning, September 22, 1861, in Basler et al., eds., *Collected Works of Lincoln,* 4:531–33; George Sinkler, *The Racial Attitudes of American Presidents from Lincoln to Theodore Roosevelt* (Garden City, N.Y.: Doubleday, 1971), 54.

vigorous confiscation law and appreciated the growing sentiment for
an attack upon slavery, but he doubted the public was ready to accept
emancipation. In effect, he challenged the "lawmakers" to act first.
It was a wise strategy in the fall of 1861, since most generals refused
to embrace even a vigorous policy on fugitive slaves.

The First Confiscation Act, after all, had been a weak blow against
slavery and the Confederacy by those who now applauded Frémont
and attacked Lincoln. The clamor only increased when, in late October, Lincoln relieved the Pathfinder of command in Missouri. Critics
eager to link Lincoln's decision in early September with the removal
did so, but the connection was tenuous. It overlooked the many problems that informed people, including Trumbull, admitted the general's leadership had tolerated or spawned. Lincoln realized that
removing Frémont might create a political martyr and renew criticism of his revocation of the general's proclamation in September,
but he had no choice. At the same time, Frémont's removal doubtless
led other generals to be more cautious about confiscating property
and receiving fugitive slaves.[22]

The military's advance made it clear that most generals felt they
should or could do little under the first act. In part this reflected the
ambiguous instructions the War Department sent to General Butler
just after the act passed. In late July he had asked Secretary Cameron
for guidance in handling the nine hundred fugitive slaves inside his
lines. Cameron replied that the first act "discharged" from service
those "persons" employed against the United States and that the military should not recognize any claim to their services by disloyal masters. However, the act did not cover "persons escaping from the
service of loyal masters." Nonetheless, Butler should receive both
class of fugitives "into the service of the United States" and keep "a

[22] Paludan, *Presidency of Abraham Lincoln,* 87–88; McPherson, *Struggle for
Equality,* 73–74; Trumbull to Lincoln, October 1, 1861, reel 26, Robert Todd Lincoln Papers, Library of Congress; James G. Randall, *Lincoln the President: Springfield to Gettysburg* (New York: Dodd, Mead, 1945), 22–25; David W. Blight,
"Frederick Douglass and the American Apocalypse," *Civil War History* 31 (December 1985): 317n; Parrish, *Turbulent Partnership,* 72–75; William B. Hesseltine, *Lincoln and the War Governors* (New York: Knopf, 1948), 230; Norman L. Peterson,
Freedom and Franchise: The Political Career of B. Gratz Brown (Columbia: University of Missouri Press, 1965), 108; Smith, *Blair,* 303–4; Chase to Richard Smith,
November 11, 1861, in Niven, ed., *Chase Papers,* 3:107–8; John Niven, *Salmon P.
Chase: A Biography* (New York: Oxford University Press, 1995), 281.

record" of all slaves who entered his lines. When peace returned, "Congress will doubtless properly provide for all the persons thus received into" the Union's service, from loyal or disloyal masters. The letter closed with an admonition that no troops should interfere with "the servants of peaceful citizens," "encourage" them to leave their service, or "prevent" their return "to the service from which" they may have escaped. General John E. Wool, who succeeded Butler in August, interpreted this policy in a generous light, welcoming fugitives into his lines. Many Virginia slaves took advantage of this changed climate to move to Union lines, particularly in Maryland, which greatly troubled slaveowners there. Later that fall, however, other generals like John A. Dix, William T. Sherman, Don Carlos Buell, and George McClellan displayed more caution in receiving fugitive slaves.[23]

They pursued a more conciliatory policy; this meant promises of safety for property and the return of fugitive slaves. In late July Dix received command of a department, which included Maryland's Eastern Shore and Virginia. Confederate sympathy there worried him. In mid-November Dix wrote Lincoln that residents of those areas "had got it into their heads that we want to steal and emancipate their negroes; and by giving them the strongest assurances" this was not so, he hoped they would not bend toward the Confederacy. The officer implementing the orders would have "a copy" of the first act, and "I have instructed him to enforce its provisions as far as practicable." Dix's proclamation went further than this, however. It said that Union troops "will invade no rights of person or property" unless attacked. "On the contrary, your laws, your institutions, your usages will be scrupulously respected." Indeed, Dix gave orders "not to permit any such persons [slaves] to come within their lines." The orders were apparently well executed.[24] This was certainly a less ag-

---

[23] Cameron to Butler, August 8, 1861, in Butler, *Correspondence*, 1:201–3; *Official Records*, series 2, vol. 1, 761–62, 764–65, 770–71, 773–74; Berlin et al., eds., *Destruction of Slavery*, 62–64; Barbara Jeanne Fields, *Slavery and Freedom on the Middle Ground: Maryland during the Nineteenth Century* (New Haven, Conn.: Yale University Press, 1985), 108.

[24] Grimsley, *Hard Hand of War*, 54–55; Susie M. Ames, "Federal Policy toward the Eastern Shore of Virginia in 1861," *Virginia Magazine of History and Biography* 69 (October 1961): 432–59; *Official Records*, series 2, vol. 2, 139–40, series 1, vol. 5, 428–32, 641–42.

gressive approach than Cameron had authorized or Trumbull had expected, but it reflected Lincoln's wishes.

After the Frémont revocation, generals in Kentucky followed policies that protected all citizens and their property, regardless of past sympathies. Lincoln appointed Brigadier General Robert Anderson, native son and hero of Fort Sumter, who proclaimed in late September that henceforth any residents who did not aid the Confederacy would be protected. When Anderson had to quit after a few weeks, his successor William T. Sherman followed much the same policy. He informed an officer that troops should adhere to Kentucky laws; fugitive slaves therefore would "be delivered up on claim of the owner or agent," without apparent regard to the first act. To another subordinate, Sherman said it was "better to keep the negroes out of your camp altogether, unless you brought them along with the regiment." In November McClellan replaced Sherman with Don Carlos Buell and instructed him that "we shall most readily suppress this rebellion . . . by religiously respecting the constitutional rights of all." His loathing of abolitionists predisposed Buell to this opinion. McClellan further asserted that the President agreed that "we are fighting only to preserve the integrity of the Union," which meant the "domestic institutions" in Kentucky would "receive at our hands every constitutional protection." General Henry Halleck, whose authority stretched into western Kentucky, also denied entry into Union lines to all fugitive slaves.[25]

It is unlikely that many fugitive slaves knew of these orders. In any case, they came to the Union lines in significant numbers. Most were males, and most came to escape slavery. If refused entry, many camped nearby. Some soldiers admitted them despite orders. When masters came to retrieve slaves, the military generally tried to assist in their retrieval, as in Kentucky and Florida. But it was a complicated process, particularly if masters claimed to be loyal, and the slaves reported they had been required to labor for the Confederacy. It is impossible to know how many slaves approaching Union lines knew about the first act, but clearly some did and others learned

[25] Grimsley, *Hard Hand of War,* 62–63; Berlin et al., eds., *Destruction of Slavery,* 64, 469; *Official Records,* series 1, vol. 4, 302, 337; series 2, vol. 1, 774, 776–77; Howard, *Black Liberation,* 8; Coulter, *The Civil War and Readjustment,* 156–57; Stephen D. Engle, "Don Carlos Buell: Military Philosophy and Command Problems in the West," *Civil War History* 41 (June 1995): 94.

about it once contact had been made. The complexities of the slave issue certainly became more apparent when Union troops advanced beyond the border states.[26]

In November Union troops occupied islands on the South Carolina coast around Port Royal Sound. Orders from the War Department required them to safeguard property rights and "avoid all interference with" slavery and other "local institutions." They soon discovered the masters had fled while their slaves, having refused to accompany them, remained. They were, at least for the moment, exslaves. As Union control broadened, troops came into contact with more abandoned slaves whose masters had clearly been sympathetic to the Confederacy. General Thomas W. Sherman had been authorized to employ in service "any persons, whether fugitives from labor or not," but he showed no inclination to do so. Others were not so reluctant. At the same time Union officers in Florida accepted owners' claims they had been loyal and sometimes paid them what fugitives in service to the Union earned. Some even helped owners capture fugitives. As was true in the border states, a patchwork policy toward fugitives emerged in South Carolina and Florida by late 1861.[27]

Secretary Cameron November's report went far beyond these varied policies on fugitives in the field. Without consulting the President, the Secretary argued that exslaves be used by the government to fight for the Union. To leave Confederates "in peaceful and secure possession of slave property" was, said Cameron, "madness." Instead, the North should emancipate rebels' slaves, use them in various ways to help the Union, and arm some to fight against their former masters. Before its distribution Lincoln learned of the recommendation and had it altered, although members of Congress soon learned of

---

[26] See Ira Berlin et al., eds., *Slaves No More: Three Essays on Emancipation and the Civil War* (Cambridge: Cambridge University Press, 1992), 21–30; Ira Berlin, "Who Freed the Slaves? Emancipation and Its Meaning," in *Union and Emancipation: Essays on Politics and Race in the Civil War Era*, eds. David W. Blight and Brooks D. Simpson (Kent, Ohio: Kent State University Press, 1997), 108–14; Berlin et al., eds., *Destruction of Slavery*, 63–64, for discussions of how slaves' entry into Union lines pushed the debate on emancipation forward.

[27] *Official Records*, series 1, vol. 6, 186–88, 192, 200, 205; Berlin et al., eds., *Destruction of Slavery*, 20, 104–5; Berlin et al., eds., *Slaves No More*, 27; Berlin et al., eds., *Wartime Genesis*, 368–69; David H. Donald, *Charles Sumner and the Rights of Man* (New York: Da Capo Press, 1996), 48.

the change. Naturally the border states were angry at Cameron's public proposal. The Kentucky legislature later urged that he be dismissed from the Cabinet. While Cameron's proposals would not be realized until late the following summer, they did reflect a northern sentiment for a more vigorous war policy.[28]

This interest was certainly evident in the correspondence to senators in the months following Frémont's proclamation and before Congress reconvened in early December. Although writers had doubts about arming exslaves and others urged compensated emancipation, most wondered if Lincoln and his Cabinet would ever adopt emancipation as a war measure. As L.V. Barney from Akron remarked on the Frémont revocation, "If this Administration is really in earnest" to suppress the rebellion, "they take a curious way of show[ing] it." Almost all echoed the reformer Orestes Brownson, who wrote that it was "impossible to save both the integrity of the Nation & Southern slavery." W. H. Henderson of Illinois believed the "question is—shall the union endure or shall slavery. . . . If this be correct whatever is necessary to save the union let him do—1st abolish slavery." Or as Rudolph Schleiden, a diplomat, said, "abolition is not the object of the war, but simply one of its agencies." It may be that only the converted wrote, but the near unanimity on the need to destroy slavery is arresting. When the government sanctioned the return of fugitive slaves, F. D. Parish observed from Sandusky, Ohio, that it seemed eager "to preserve the 'peculiar institution,' unhurt." If so, "I trust in God, we will not allow them to succeed." The plural here referred to the public and Congress, who had to lead in destroying slavery. William Kendrick prayed that Congress would pass "new laws to back up our President—compel him to follow after. . . . The people go in advance." Henry Hart from New York inquired if he "and other gentlemen" should begin "a movement to promote"

---

[28] See *Official Records*, series 3, vol. 1, 698–708, for Cameron's altered report and Edward McPherson, *The Political History of the United States during the Great Rebellion, 1860–1865*, 2d ed. (Washington: Philip and Solomons, 1865) for the original version, which New York newspapers published in early January 1862. See also Berlin et al., *Destruction of Slavery*, 20–21; Erwin S. Bradley, *Simon Cameron: Lincoln's Secretary of War* (Philadelphia: University of Pennsylvania Press, 1966), 202–5; Coulter, *The Civil War and Readjustment*, 156; Niven, *Chase*, 282–84; James M. McPherson, *Ordeal by Fire: The Civil War and Reconstruction*, 2d ed. (New York: McGraw Hill, 1992), 268. Lincoln removed Cameron from the Cabinet in early 1862 and appointed him ambassador to Russia.

emancipation, although others suggested "that a change in public sentiment was going so rapidly" on the issue that such an effort might "retard & repress" it.[29]

Certainly Senators Sumner, Trumbull, and Sherman heard that it was time to strike more boldly at slavery. Virtually all correspondents argued the tide was turning. H. Catlin, who ran a newspaper in Erie, Pennsylvania, saw a trend where "absolute loyalty is antislavery and tend[s] to radical action, while the pro-slavery people tend toward compromise and a dishonorable peace." Numerous recruiters in Ohio wrote Senator Sherman that it was increasingly difficult to find troops. "I have the flag out and the music in full blast," G. E. Winters reported, "but all this does not seem to stir up the sluggish blood of those who ought to go." If the reports of Frémont's removal were accurate, said John Dalzel from Lima, "it will operate against us in this county for our People swear by Fremont." To Trumbull's suggestion that a more sweeping confiscation proposal be introduced, Senator James Grimes of Iowa expressed strong support in late October. Long an advocate of "a law to confiscate all the property of rebels," he now wanted the "issue to be fairly + fully made" before Congress. Sumner and Thaddeus Stevens agreed. "All things now tend to an attack on slavery," Sumner wrote in early November. Even a "majority of the cabinet is for this course," he claimed. For his part, Stevens introduced a resolution on December 2, the first day of Congress, to emancipate the slaves.[30] In his annual message to Congress the following day Lincoln suggested members eager for sterner messages should put their rhetoric into legislation.

Much of Lincoln's message discussed foreign affairs, the work of various departments, and the country's finances. A third of the way

---

[29] Birney to Wade, November 1, 1861, Wade Papers; Brownson to Sumner, October 23, 1861, Kendrick to Sumner, October 5, 1861, Hart to Sumner, October 18, 1861, 1:23, Schleiden to Sumner, November 3, 1861, 2:75, Sumner Papers; W. H. Henderson to Trumbull, November 20, 1861, Trumbull Papers; Parish to Sherman, November 5, 1861, Sherman Papers.

[30] Dalzel to Sherman, October 4, 1861, G. E. Winters to Sherman, October 10, 1861, Sherman Papers; Catlin to Sumner, October 24, 1861, 1:23, Sumner to Martin F. Tupper, November 11, 1861, 2:75, Sumner Papers; Grimes to Trumbull, October 24, 1861, Trumbull Papers; Trefousse, *Thaddeus Stevens,* 116; Stevens to Gerrit Smith, December 14, 1861, Thaddeus Stevens Papers, Library of Congress; J. E. Field to Representative Henry L. Dawes, December 1, 1861, in Herman Belz, *Reconstructing the Union: Theory and Policy during the Civil War* (Ithaca, N.Y.: Cornell University Press, 1969), 43n.

through he suggested that it was time to recognize Haiti and Liberia, but not without the "approbation" of Congress. His first mention of the First Confiscation Act was to suggest that slaves released from servitude be "deemed free" and then be colonized, a project he and others, including Trumbull, would revisit. As for the war itself, he had tried to prevent it from degenerating "into a violent and remorseless revolutionary struggle." Those questions "not of vital military importance," he said, had been left "to the more deliberate action of the legislature." As for legislation, he had, of course, "adhered" to the first act, and if "a new law upon the same subject shall be proposed, its propriety will be duly considered." Here was the challenge to legislators with reservations about the administration's policy toward the South and slavery. However, Lincoln believed nothing had changed the "principles or general purposes," articulated in his inaugural and July 4 message to Congress, upon which the North had gone to war. Moreover, his policies had secured Kentucky, Maryland, Missouri, and even western Virginia for the Union. With some success in Virginia, South Carolina, and elsewhere, Lincoln concluded, "These things demonstrate that the cause of the Union is advancing steadily and certainly southward."[31] Lincoln knew full well that one could draw a different conclusion from these facts, but he was right to argue that a change in the war's goals could be achieved only if Congress had a clear understanding of its own mind and the public's wishes. Lincoln doubted they did.

On December 5, 1861, Trumbull effectively accepted the challenge and introduced the Second Confiscation Act in the Senate. Several other Republicans followed suit with their own confiscation bills, while some members of the party urged caution. Senator Timo-

---

[31] "Annual Message to Congress," in Basler et al., eds., *Collected Works of Lincoln*, 4:35–53. See Gabor S. Boritt, "The Voyage of the Colony of Linconia: The Sixteenth President, Black Colonization, and the Defense Mechanism of Avoidance," *The Historian* 37 (August 1975): 619–32; Stephen B. Oates, "'The Man of Our Redemption': Abraham Lincoln and the Emancipation of the Slaves," *Presidential Studies* 9 (winter 1979): 15–25; Otto H. Olsen, "Abraham Lincoln as Revolutionary," *Civil War History* 24 (September 1978): 213–24; Jason H. Silverman, "'In Isles beyond the Main': Abraham Lincoln's Philosophy on Black Colonization," *Lincoln Herald* 80 (fall 1978): 115–22; Michael Vorenberg, "Abraham Lincoln and the Politics of Black Colonization," *Journal of the Abraham Lincoln Association* 14, no. 2 (1993): 23–45; Arthur Zilversmit, "Lincoln and the Problem of Race: A Decade of Interpretation," *Papers of the Abraham Lincoln Association* 2 (1980): 22–45, for discussions of Lincoln on race and colonization.

thy Howe of Wisconsin noted an angry exchange during a Senate caucus on December 9 between "timid, hesitating and unresolved" conservatives and "turbulent, passionate and reckless" radicals over confiscation. During the following seven months Congress debated at length the various issues inherent in confiscation and finally passed a law in July. However, they were forced to limit the act to forestall a veto by Lincoln. Strong opinions on a variety of important issues emerged, including how to define the hostilities, Lincoln's powers, congressional control over the military, colonization, the punishment given the rebels, length of property forfeiture, and the basis for the South's restoration. These disagreements demonstrated that the majority of Republicans were not radical on the central issues of race and Reconstruction. As well, the debates exposed the confusion and hesitation Congress felt in trying to confiscate property, abolish slavery, punish the South, and plan Reconstruction simultaneously and in the midst of a poorly defined conflict. The second act was badly designed, which accounts in part for its failure to realize the revenue many had anticipated or feared. The debates and compromises also make clear why exslaves received no land following the peace. At the same time, the very nature of the war itself changed during these seven months, in part because of the confiscation debates themselves.[32]

Trumbull's original bill was sweeping. It provided "for the absolute and complete forfeiture forever . . . of every species of property, real and personal . . . belonging to persons beyond the jurisdiction of the United States . . . who . . . shall take up arms against the United States, or in any wise aid or abet the rebellion." In short, the property of those guilty of treason was liable to confiscation anywhere in the United States. The military would confiscate within rebel areas, whereas courts would prosecute in Union areas, including the North.

---

[32] Howe to Grace Howe, December 31, 1861, in Donald, *Sumner and the Rights of Man,* 60–61; Allan G. Bogue, *The Congressmen's Civil War* (Cambridge: Cambridge University Press, 1989), 123. See Frederick, "The Second Confiscation Act," and Leonard P. Curry, *Blueprint for Modern America: Nonmilitary Legislation of the First Civil War Congress* (Nashville: Vanderbilt University Press, 1968), chapter 4, for descriptions of the act's legislative history; Belz, *Reconstructing the Union,* for discussion of Congress during the war; Allan G. Bogue, *The Earnest Men: Republicans of the Civil War* (Ithaca, N.Y.: Cornell University Press, 1981), 119–35, 307–11, for voting analysis on the second act; and Syrett, "Confiscation Acts," chapter 2, for the issues in the debates on the second act.

Colonization, on foreign soil procured by the President, would be provided for exslaves of rebels or supporters of the rebellion made free under the act. Proceeds from the act would be "for the benefit of loyal citizens" whose property had been "despoiled" by the "rebellion" and would also help pay for the war itself. Whereas the first act removed from slavery only those slaves used in support of the rebellion, Trumbull's second act potentially reached all slaves who might "in any wise aid or abet the rebellion." Unlike the first act, the new bill also authorized the military to assist in confiscation proceedings in areas where the courts had ceased to function. Trumbull discarded the term "war" and now referred to the conflict only as a "rebellion" or "insurrection." Slaves remained property, however, in descriptions of confiscation, but became people in reference to their rights after the fighting. The legal proceedings against the property continued in rem in the second bill, a term that had not been used in the first act; now the owner's presence would not be required for the forfeiture. And finally, the new bill forfeited real and personal property beyond the life of the person judged guilty of treason if that person was beyond the reach of the normal judicial process. Trumbull explained that those in the North tried for treason would have only personal property forfeited for life. Many, including Lincoln, believed this violated the Constitution's prohibition against bills of attainder.[33] The Senate referred all the confiscation bills to the Judiciary Committee, chaired by Trumbull. The other four Republicans members were moderates on the issue.

In mid-January the committee reported back a version of Trumbull's bill that reflected reservations on several key issues. Only a bare majority had allowed it to be reported from the committee in the first place. Absent now was the distinction between real and personal property, and no mention was made of confiscation beyond the traitor's life, although Trumbull claimed the penalty remained. A provision to allow the return of fugitive slaves to those able to prove loyalty to Union was added. However, the military was not allowed to adjudicate this issue, and it was not made clear what happened if master and slave differed on the issue of allegiance. Moreover, the new bill

---

[33] *Cong. Globe*, 37:2, 18–19, 334. Trumbull's proposed bill was more inclusive than the other bills. See ibid., 49–50, 176, for the other proposals. Mark M. Krug, *Lyman Trumbull: Conservative Radical* (New York: A. S. Barnes, 1965), 200–201; Roske, *Trumbull*, 82–83.

gave Lincoln the discretion, as "the military necessities" required, to use civil or military officers for confiscation of property "beyond the reach of civil process in the ordinary course of judicial proceedings by reason" of the rebellion. In effect, then, the new bill turned over confiscation in the South to the President to use as he saw fit.[34]

Advocates of vigorous confiscation later regretted this concession to the President. Furthermore, the bill did not solve the problem of referring to slaves as property, which left them within the Dred Scott decision. Trumbull insisted the bill meant to confiscate the property of those beyond the reach of normal legal process, thus in rem proceedings, from admiralty and revenue practices, not in personam. In rem proceedings were therefore constitutional, he said. At the same time, however, the rebels were enemies and not protected by the Constitution. As a people at war we "may treat them as traitors, and we may treat them as enemies, and we have the right of both, belligerent and sovereign," he concluded. Moreover, since the bill acted upon the property of traitors, it did "not corrupt the blood of the party" and thus was not a bill of attainder. Therefore, the forfeiture could extend beyond the lives of those found guilty of treason. Trumbull clearly wanted it both ways, insisting Congress had the power under both the laws of war and the Constitution.[35]

Democrats certainly could not accept such broad aims for the conflict. Although most supported a vigorous military policy to subdue the rebellion, only a few Democrats agreed that anything other than restoration of the Union should concern Congress, the military, or the President. As they said repeatedly, the war should preserve "the Constitution as it is and the Union as it was." For Democrats the Constitution's powers did not change or enlarge in time of war; confiscation, as with other measures related to slavery or Reconstruction, was beyond Congress's powers. If confiscation and abolition were unthinkable in peace, they were no less so during this conflict, which was not even a war, according to Representative William Allen of

---

[34] *Cong. Globe*, 37:2, 334, 942. Republicans Lafayette S. Foster (Conn.), John C. Ten Eyck (N.J.), Ira Harris (N.Y.), and Edgar Cowan (Penn.) were on the Judiciary Committee, along with Democrats James Bayard (Del.) and Lazarus Powell (Ken.). The Republicans were against vigorous confiscation, as were the Democrats, of course. See Syrett, "Confiscation Acts," 24–25; Bogue, *Earnest Men*, 98, 132–33, 220.

[35] *Cong. Globe*, 37:2, 942–44; Bogue, *Earnest Men*, 220–21; Harold Hyman and William Wiecek, *Equal Justice under Law: Constitutional Development, 1832–1872* (New York: Harper and Row, 1982), 251–52.

Ohio. The militia had simply been summoned to suppress an insurrection; the Constitution's war powers could not be invoked on behalf
of confiscation. Since the Constitution did not admit of secession,
said Representative William Holman, also of Ohio, Congress could
not enlarge its powers to end the rebellion. On the other hand, he
added, if "you recognize these States out of the Union, you can pass
the laws," but he realized most Republicans would not accept that
position.[36]

Admitting secession's legality was equally treacherous for Democrats. If secession was constitutional, it implied the Union's power
over defeated Confederate states, which all but guaranteed slavery's
abolition with restoration. Even so, most Democrats admitted the
reality of secession, even if illegal. They maintained, though, that only
a few southerners had willingly joined the Confederacy. Many agreed
with Senator Willard Saulsbury of Delaware that the de facto governments in the Confederacy forced most rebels to serve; therefore confiscation would unfairly discriminate if it were pursued during the
conflict. Better to punish the disloyal leaders after the war, he said.
If the Union wanted to punish rebels during the war, then recognize
that the leaders had committed crimes "which may be dealt with in
detail under the names of murder, theft, arson" or "comprehended
under the name of treason," argued Senator Joseph Wright of Indiana. Traitors deserved the Constitution's protection, nonetheless, and
that meant no corruption of blood beyond their death. Whereas the
"act of secession itself is perfectly harmless," claimed Senator John
Henderson of Missouri, taking up arms against the federal government was treason and should be punished. Representative Hendrick
Wright of Pennsylvania thought confiscation by itself too mild a penalty for the leaders; they "deserve death or exile." Widespread confiscation should not occur, Democrats concluded, simply because Jeff
Davis and other leaders had committed treason. As a distinct minority, however, the Democrats' protests over confiscation had little im-

---

[36] Jean H. Baker, "A Loyal Opposition: Northern Democrats in the Thirty-seventh
Congress," *Civil War History* 25 (June 1979): 139–55; Jean H. Baker, *Affairs of
Party: The Political Culture of Northern Democrats in the Mid–Nineteenth Century*
(Ithaca, N.Y.: Cornell University Press, 1983), 152; Paludan, *"A People's Contest,"*
90, 92; Earl J. Hess, *Liberty, Virtue, and Progress: Northerners and Their War for
the Union* (New York: Fordham University Press, 1997), 82, 86, 88; *Cong. Globe*,
37:2, pt. 4, Appendix, 122 (Allen), 151 (Holman).

pact on the second act compared to the discussions and divisions among the Republicans.[37]

Republican differences over the Second Confiscation Act demonstrate that the radicals did not control the Thirty-seventh Congress, at least not on confiscation. If the likes of Senators Sumner, Wade, and Trumbull and Representatives Stevens, Ashley, and Julian had had a coherent plan and had orchestrated wartime measures, it would not have taken seven months to produce the second act. In fact, there was more discussion on confiscation than on any other measure before that Congress. From the start the Judiciary Committee circumscribed Trumbull's original proposal. Thereafter Republicans in both houses, even though confiscation supporters, expressed the moderate position of the party in both words and legislative compromises. In July a confused law that reflected limited Republican goals emerged, a law that subsequently failed to achieve much confiscation. At the same time the bill encouraged many, mostly exslaves, to expect land reform, scared others about the potential of confiscation and Reconstruction, and pushed Lincoln to a more direct assault upon slavery.[38]

For true believers in confiscation like Sumner and Trumbull, Congress's power was wide indeed. Certainly most who wrote the two senators argued Congress should now assert itself in the war since Lincoln appeared too conciliatory to the South and unwilling to fight vigorously. The Massachusetts Senator declared "there can be noth-

---

[37] *Cong. Globe,* 37:2, 2299, 2898, 2900 (Saulsbury), 1573–74 (Henderson), 1769 (Wright); Syrett, "Confiscation Acts," 27–60. See Richard O. Curry, "Congressional Democrats: 1861–1863," *Civil War History* 12 (September 1966): 213–29; Richard O. Curry, "The Civil War and Reconstruction, 1861–1877: A Critical Overview of Recent Trends and Interpretations," *Civil War History* 24 (September 1974): 215–38, for appraisals of Democrats and Republicans on the central issues in the Civil War.

[38] See Michael Les Benedict, *A Compromise of Principle: Congressional Republicans and Reconstruction, 1863–1869* (New York: W. W. Norton, 1974); Michael Les Benedict, "Preserving the Constitution: The Conservative Basis of Radical Reconstruction," *Journal of American History* 23 (December 1974): 65–90; Herman Belz, "The New Orthodoxy in Reconstruction Historiography," *Reviews in American History* 1 (March 1973): 106–12; Herman Belz, *Emancipation and Equal Rights in the Civil War Era* (New York: W. W. Norton, 1978); and Curry, "Civil War and Reconstruction," for reassessments of the radicals' power and radicalism. See Robert F. Horowitz, *The Great Impeacher: A Political Biography of James M. Ashley* (New York: Brooklyn College Press, 1979); Patrick A. Riddleberger, *George Washington Julian, Radical Republican: A Study in Nineteenth-Century Politics and Reform* (Bloomington: Indiana Historical Bureau, 1966); and Hans L. Trefousse, *Benjamin Franklin Wade: Radical Republican from Ohio* (New York: Twayne, 1963) for biographies of Ashley, Julian, and Wade.

ing essential to its [the war's] success, which is not positively within the province of Congress. There is not one of the rights of war which Congress may not invoke." Congress, argued Trumbull, could employ whatever it thought "necessary and proper for the attainment of the end of the war, which is the suppression of rebellion." Trumbull maintained there "is not a syllable in the Constitution conferring on the President war powers." Congress could instruct the President to do as it wished. The President, as Commander in Chief of the armies and navies, Trumbull said, could "only govern and regulate them as Congress" instructed. The Constitution clearly stated that Congress "shall have the power to make rules for the government and regulation of the land and naval forces."[39]

Conservative Republicans who opposed vigorous confiscation argued that Congress could not interfere with slavery, even in time of war, nor intrude on the President's authority as Commander in Chief. Senators Edgar Cowan of Pennsylvania and Browning of Illinois were adamant in this view. Both presumed that Lincoln knew best when and how much to confiscate. Browning argued that only the President could exercise those "extraordinary powers" called forth by war; they could not be used for social reform. For Congress to interfere in the conduct of the war, he said, would admit that it could also "adjudicate a case at law or control the decisions of a court." The separation of functions had to be maintained, he believed, even in war. Cowan at one point mocked those advocating congressional confiscation: "It [the second act] is, then, law or no law, at his discretion, which is just the same as saying his discretion is the law." In Cowan's view, Lincoln could have initiated confiscation before the first act became law. Many Republicans accepted executive confiscation, at least in Lincoln's hands, confident that he would exercise it with a swift and peaceful reunion in mind. Senators James Doolittle of Wisconsin

---

[39] See Orestes Brownson to Sumner, December 2, 1861, 1:23, William Lloyd Garrison to Sumner, December 20, 1861, Charles W. Slack to Sumner, December 27, 1861, Johnson H. Jordon to Sumner, January 14, 1862, Frederick S. Cabot to Sumner, February 10, 1862, 1:24, Sumner Papers; George Banell to Trumbull, December 23, 1861, John Russell to Trumbull, December 31, 1861, W. F. Fyfe to Trumbull, January 5, 1862, Trumbull Papers, for a representative sample of letters in support of Congress's power to act. *Cong. Globe,* 37:2, 2193 (Sumner), 2325, 1560 (emphasis in the original), 1559, 1561–62 (Trumbull).

and Lafayette Foster of Connecticut, for example, both supported executive emancipation if carried out from military necessity.[40]

Trumbull's bill authorized congressional emancipation, but only indirectly. All agreed that Congress did not have this power before Sumter. His legislation, he explained, required masters who supported the rebellion to choose whether their slaves went free or not. Congress, by its war powers, could create a penalty for certain behavior in order to restore the Union. If the masters' support of the Confederacy continued after the act passed, their slaves would be freed through confiscation. Emancipation would therefore occur only following a "voluntary act" of the "rebel master" to continue war upon the United States. "I am not aware that the Republican party ever pledged itself not to allow the owners of slaves to make them free," he said. By Trumbull's logic, masters could retain their slaves by swearing an oath to support the Union before the act passed. Perhaps as a sop to worried colleagues, Trumbull even predicted his bill would confiscate the property of only one in ten rebels.[41] Trumbull's move against slavery in such a backhanded manner indicates the hesitation most Republicans felt in contemplating abolition.

There were, to be sure, Republicans who took Congress's power over confiscation for granted. Representative Charles Sedgwick of New York believed that, so "far as the war power is concerned, Congress has an absolute despotism. They have the power to pass any law which they think best calculated to carry the war to a successful conclusion. They are absolute and sovereign." Sumner said the rebellious states had destroyed their status as states; Congress could do as it wished. "Call it suicide, if you will, or suspended animation, or abeyance, they have nevertheless ceased to exist," he declared. State treason, Representative Thomas Eliot of Massachusetts said, described what secessionist states had done. As such, Congress had the duty "to make such fit enactments as will declare a forfeiture of its powers and functions as a State, and provide for its political recon-

---

[40] *Cong. Globe,* 37:2, 1050–53, 1880 (Cowan), 1136 (Browning), 1942 (Foster), pt. 4 Appendix, 137 (Doolittle); Bogue, *Earnest Men,* 220–21. Bogue argues that Browning, Cowan, Doolittle, and Foster were moderates. Glenn M. Linden, "'Radicals' and Economic Policies: The Senate, 1861–1873," *Journal of Southern History* 32 (May 1966): 192–93, believes all were either "Non-radical" or "Unaligned."

[41] *Cong. Globe,* 37:2, 1559, 1561–62 (Trumbull).

struction." Another representative, Alfred Ely of New York, claimed seceded states became territories, thereby destroying their claims under the Constitution. These theories were part of the Reconstruction debates that began during the war, but they were a minority view in the deliberations over confiscation.[42]

Most Republicans took the middle ground: for confiscation but leaning toward executive control, for punishing rebels but worried about retribution's effect on reunion, for emancipation but also for colonization, and worried lest confiscation last beyond the lives of rebels. Senator Sherman, a moderate, believed in confiscation for "the prominent actors" in the rebellion and amnesty for "the great mass of citizens" in the Confederacy. Representative Roscoe Conkling of New York agreed. Although "extravagant or passionate" legislation might be cathartic, a cautious application of confiscation would be more "practical." To punish "all who are legally guilty of treason," claimed Representative Eliakim Walton of Vermont, would be neither just nor good for reconciliation, since many southerners had been led astray by a few. As the war and the confiscation debates continued into the spring and summer, however, such discrimination found less support. While most could not agree with Representative Dwight Loomis of Connecticut that in "the case of rebels in arms, every one is an actual enemy," many came to believe that more than just the leaders should be punished. As the willingness to punish rebels grew, so did the view that the President should have broad pardoning power to assist a swift reunion. Representative Albert Porter of Indiana even said it should extend to those who failed to abandon their sympathy for the Confederacy. To defend such leniency, Cowan and others invoked the law of nations as a bar against harsh confiscation. But most believed the sovereignty of the Union allowed the North to ignore such laws, if necessary. "Nobody supposes we would do it," Trumbull concluded, "but we are talking of power."[43]

Whereas advocates of a vigorous confiscation policy hoped that

[42] *Cong. Globe*, 37:2, 2325 (Sedgwick), 2189 (Sumner), 2234 (Eliot, emphasis in the original); Donald, *Sumner and the Rights of Man*, 60–67. See Belz, *Reconstructing the Union*, 10–13, 56, 64, 69–70, for a discussion of state suicide and territorialization. Professor Joel Parker of Harvard sought to refute Sumner's thesis on territorialization in the *North American Review* 94 (April 1862): 435–63.

[43] *Cong. Globe*, 37:2, 1813 (Sherman), 1819 (Conkling), 1768–69 (Walton), 1767 (Porter), pt. 4, Appendix, 181 (Loomis), 2961 (Trumbull); Randall, *Confiscation of Property*, 17–18; Bogue, *Earnest Men*, 224; Syrett, "Confiscation Acts," 27–60.

Reconstruction of the South would be one of the results of the second act, moderates were just as eager to prevent significant change in the South, other than perhaps emancipation, as a consequence of the war. Representative John Killinger of Pennsylvania well expressed the moderate wish for a vigorous war with a painless restoration. "I would reduce them to vassalage. Lay waste to their fields with fire and sword, and annihilate every living thing within their limits," he proclaimed in support of executive confiscation. But the "moment that peace is restored law and order will take the place of military force," he said, and the ex-Confederate states will "be restored to their original rights and dignities." Representatives like Henry Grider from Kentucky hoped that confiscation would not harm slavery, but by early 1862 most moderates appeared to realize this was all but inevitable. As William Cutler, a representative from Ohio, noted, the status of slavery before and during the war had dramatically changed. "You may as well ask me to regard with like complacency the quiet house cur sleeping at my feet, and the same animal raging the streets as a slabbering mad dog," he observed. By then, however, radicals hoped that confiscation would do more than just end slavery. Just days after the confiscation bill appeared in the Senate, Sumner wrote Wendell Phillips that "the great end approaches. It cannot be postponed. . . . [W]e have before us, as I assumed . . . the grand question of the reconstruction of southern society. Pray give me the benefit of your counsel," he asked.[44]

The radicals' plans for the South were grand indeed. Confiscation of the planters' property would eliminate that class and turn the South into a land of small farmers, they said. To Senator Justin Morrill of Vermont, the "old struggle of a class for power and prestige" was "repeating itself in our history." The solution, said Senator David Wilmot of Pennsylvania, was to take the planters' property, land, and slaves. This would crush the rebellion and punish the class that fomented it. "Property is power," he concluded. If not ruined, Representative Ely predicted, the planter class would remember its loss; it would erupt again like "a political volcano, liable at any moment to belch forth smoke and fire and devastating lava." "It is only by the confiscation of the property of those who shall persist in rebellion,"

---

[44] *Cong. Globe*, 37:2, pt. 4, Appendix, 233–34 (Killinger), pt. 4, Appendix, 117 (Cutler); Sumner to Phillips, December 8, 1861, 2:75, Sumner Papers.

claimed Ely, "that society can be organized upon a loyal basis at the South." Confiscation would cause suffering for many, admitted Representative Aaron Sargent of California, but it was better to give land to the southern poor, he argued, than to keep the South under constant military control. Confiscation's result, Sumner confidently predicted, would be to create small estates peopled by poor whites and northern soldiers in the South, who, "changing their swords into plowshares, will fill the land with northern industry and northern principles." Significantly, exslaves were not yet part of the radicals' dream. That would come later. Even so, the radicals' presumption was impressive. As Justin Morrill concluded, the South needed only "the privileges of free institutions, free schools, homesteads, even handed justice, and equality of rights" to realize its sovereignty.[45]

To achieve this revolution, however, confiscation beyond the lives of the rebels had to be realized, and this proved to be the most contentious issue in the confiscation debates. After about two months, outright opponents of confiscation fell silent since it was apparent that some bill would be enacted. The discussion then turned to legal issues, including the controversial in rem proceedings. This touched the core issues, other than slavery: how to describe the conflict, executive versus congressional power, the amount of punishment given rebels, and the means of restoration. Supporters of in rem tried various arguments to assuage the moderates' claims that such proceedings violated the Constitution. Practicality was one reason. Punishing traitors in peace time was one thing, said Representative Eliot, but we "all know that in time of war we cannot try a traitor." Even traitors who owned property in the North were beyond reach. Nor would

---

[45] *Cong. Globe*, 37:2, 1077 (Morrill), 2996 (Wilmot), pt. 4 Appendix, 194–95 (Ely), pt. 4, Appendix, 177 (Sargent), 2196 (Sumner), 1077 (Morrill, emphasis in original); Syrett, "Confiscation Acts," 23–81. See Kenneth S. Greenberg, "The Civil War and the Redistribution of Land: Adams County, Mississippi, 1860–1870," *Agricultural History* 52 (April 1978): 292–307; A. Jane Townes, "The Effect of Emancipation on Large Landholdings, Nelson and Goochland Counties, Virginia," *Journal of Southern History* 45 (August 1979): 403–12; Jonathan M. Wiener, "Planter Persistence and Social Change: Alabama, 1850–1870," *Journal of Interdisciplinary History* 6 (autumn 1976): 235–60; Jonathan Wiener, "Class Structure and Economic Development in the American South, 1865–1955," *American Historical Review* 84 (October 1979): 970–92; Steven Hahn, *The Roots of Southern Populism: Yeoman Farmers and the Transformation of the Georgia Upcountry, 1850–1890* (New York: Oxford University Press, 1983), for the argument that the planter class survived the Civil War and Reconstruction.

southern juries convict traitors from their own states. To expect this would "be the very climax of absurdity," said Representative Elijah Babbit from Pennsylvania. Moderates said the Constitution required that traitors be tried after the war, but advocates of broad confiscation feared too many might have been pardoned by then. Instead, as Representative John Noell, a radical Democrat from Missouri said, in rem proceedings were "founded upon public necessity and public convenience," similar to revenue cases where the perpetrators were often beyond the jurisdiction of the United States. This would allow, said Trumbull, "all the property belonging of these rebels, as fast as we can get possession of it," to be "appropriated" for the government's use. Exslaves, of course, had already been put to work for the North, but moderates doubted that other rebel property could be sold soon enough to add to the North's treasury.[46]

The very idea of in rem proceedings greatly troubled moderates. They believed in rem proceedings were simply a way to ignore the Constitution, and they were probably correct. As Senator Jacob Collamer of Vermont observed, there was a "vast deal of hocus pocus in it," and it violated due process of law. After all, he said, the Constitution clearly prohibited bills of attainder, taking property without due process, conviction without a jury, and punishment twice for the same crime. Yet the confiscation bill would permit all this to occur. The property owner would be absent with in rem proceedings, there would be no jury, he could be tried for treason after the war, and the forfeiture would extend beyond his life. In addition, those pushing for broad confiscation were treating rebels inconsistently, both as citizens and as belligerents. If they were citizens, then the Constitution applied. If they were enemies, then confiscation was a military matter, best executed by Lincoln and the army.[47]

Many of confiscation's enthusiasts routinely described rebels as enemies yet claimed they were to be treated as citizens who became traitors. However, trials for treason would occur only after the war, by which time their property would have been confiscated and be-

---

[46] *Cong. Globe*, 37:2, pt. 4, Appendix, 2357 (Eliot), 167 (Babbit), 2239 (Noell), 942–43 (Trumbull). Noell was the only Democrat to support broad confiscation on the floor; he opposed emancipation through confiscation, however.

[47] *Cong. Globe*, 37:2, 1808–9 (Collamer); Bogue, *Earnest Men*, 224–25; Allan Nevins, *The War for the Union*, vol. 2, *War Becomes Revolution, 1862–1863* (New York: Scribner's, 1960), 203.

yond their lifetimes. The Constitution's prohibition against bills of attainder, claimed Trumbull, had no relation to his bill. Confiscation was intended only to "reach the property of such rebels or traitors as are beyond the reach of judicial process, and can neither be arrested, tried, or convicted for treason or any other offense." It would be absurd to apply this prohibition to those who could be tried for treason only after the war. In fact, Representative Noell declared, the bill "waives the crime of treason and undertakes to punish in another form and for another offense altogether different" from that in the attainder clause. Noell, along with Ely, even believed that confiscation penalized the rebel "in the thing seized and confiscated, not in person."[48]

Opponents of in rem proceedings naturally scoffed at the notion that property could be considered guilty under the confiscation bill. Representative Eliot had argued that only "guilty property, made use of to destroy the Government" was to be confiscated. But Representative Benjamin Thomas from Massachusetts saw no "guilty property" in the South that compared with prize, booty, contraband of war, or property used for war. "It is private property outside the conflict of arms," Thomas declared, "forfeited not because it is the instrument of offense, but as penalty for the crimes of the owner." Except for slaves used to aid the Confederacy, Thomas had a point, unless one accepted that plantations, the other principal object of confiscation, aided the rebellion. As Senator Cowan remarked, before in rem proceedings could be instituted, "the property itself must have been a guilty instrument" and manifested the evidence upon which the proceedings rested. But proponents of broad confiscation ignored such critiques; they wanted to punish the rebels and initiate Reconstruction before the war ended and before requests for mercy and reconciliation began. Collamer was right; arguments for in rem revealed some sophistry.[49]

Trumbull and his colleagues faced a conundrum—how to reconcile their goals for confiscation with the Constitution most of them re-

---

[48] *Cong. Globe,* 37:2, 1558, 1813 (Trumbull), 2238 (Noell).

[49] *Cong. Globe,* 37:2, pt. 4, Appendix, 220 (Thomas), 2962 (Cowan); Syrett, "Confiscation Acts," 74–75. Not all enthusiasts of confiscation worried that much about the Constitution; see Donald, *Sumner and the Rights of Man,* 62–63. Thaddeus Stevens was also less anchored to the Constitution than others; see Trefousse, *Thaddeus Stevens.*

vered. They believed Lincoln was unwilling or unable to act boldly against the South. No less obvious to them was the need to end slavery, which they saw as the curse of the nation and the cause of the war. Allowing the planter class to survive, even without slaves, almost guaranteed that the sections would remain at odds after the war and that exslaves would be at the mercy of the South, although the latter issue bothered legislators very little. So the South had to be changed, and the process had to begin before the war ended and peace and harmony clouded the issues. Vigorous confiscation appeared to be the answer; the exigencies of the war would resolve whatever constitutional doubts might arise. But there were many who spoke in favor of confiscation, and they did not all sing from the same hymn book, particularly when legal issues were involved. When doubts arose about its constitutionality, radicals like Representative Samuel Blair of Pennsylvania simply argued that confiscation was a congressional military measure, like the blockade of southern ports or enforcement of the nonintercourse act. And it was nothing but "brazen impudence" for the rebels, or those who argued in their behalf, to seek the benefits of the Constitution that they had repudiated by war. If that was an insufficient argument, Senator Jacob Howard claimed that the due process clause of the Fifth Amendment did not apply to war legislation. Too much concern for due process in the midst of war was absurd anyway, he added.[50]

Citizens who supported confiscation also saw it primarily as a military measure. Some viewed it as a means to punish the South or its leaders, but very few understood that it might form the basis of Reconstruction. At the same time, a few urged that the confiscated land be given to Union soldiers, but most suggested that proceeds from the property be used to defray the war's cost. Many linked confiscation to emancipation on the premise that slavery had caused the rebellion and now had to be abolished; in war Congress could ignore the sanctity of slavery. Only a small number, however, worried about the fate of freed slaves; most urged that colonization be pursued. At the same time almost no one expressed doubt that broad and lasting

---

[50] *Cong. Globe,* 37:2, 2299–3000 (Blair), 1719 (Howard). A Sumner correspondent echoed Blair's comments. Referring to Collamer's speech, W. G. Snethen wrote, "the rebellion could not have received a more efficient support from any quarter, than that speech gives it"; Snethen to Sumner, April 24, 1862, 1:25, Sumner Papers.

confiscation was constitutional, and no one suggested that the Constitution be ignored.

The confiscation bill's appearance in December 1861 encouraged many to believe the North might finally move against the South. "There is in that Bill the first streak of morning light that we have seen since the war commenced," John Russell wrote from Illinois. D. E. Clay thought the bill would "smother disloyalty" in the free states and "have a salutary effect in putting down the Rebellion in the slave states and eradicating the cause of it." At last, some said of the bill, something was being done. "Oh that our rulers, civil [and] military, would see & feel," said H. B. Stanton from New York, "how the people ache to have them begin the work of striking the rebellion in its vulnerable point," which was slavery. "Pray urge thro this Confiscation bill & give heart to the country," he wrote. From Ohio Justin Hamilton, a recruiter, wrote he was "anxiously watching the movements of the Administration and Congress" for some action. While he understood the need to be "prudent," he could not "see how, we, are to avoid Confiscating the Slaves and Rebels, and when confiscated" advocated putting the freed slaves in Florida, perhaps. The people were "quite dissatisfied" with the administration's effort "to put down this accursed rebellion," reported Silas Potts, also from Ohio. The government should "capture at every opportunity any property, or means" used by those "who have taken up arms" or who are in any "manner either directly or indirectly assisting this infernal proslavery war," Potts added. In fact, many worried that the administration was too sympathetic to slavery.[51]

Only a minority who followed the confiscation debates realized that Trumbull's bill would take the rebels' plantations as well as their slaves. Like moderates in Congress who doubted that property could be considered guilty, most in the public did not appreciate the implications of taking the real property of rebels forever. For most, confiscation was a just punishment for those who instigated the rebellion

---

[51] Russell to Trumbull, December 17, 1861, Clay to Trumbull, December 17, 1861, Stanton to Trumbull, January 18, 1862, Trumbull Papers; Hamilton to Sherman, Dec. 26, 1861, Sherman Papers. Many wrote Sherman about the recruiting problems that would develop if the government did not fight more aggressively; see Potts to Wade, January 3, 1862, Wade Papers. Thomas O'Reilly wrote Sumner from St. Louis to complain that there were no Republican generals; see O'Reilly to Sumner, December 5, 1861, 1:24, Sumner Papers.

or a way to end slavery, not a means to reform the South or assist exslaves. Whether radicals in Congress might have discussed this more fully to promote greater public understanding is impossible to determine. Certainly the lack of attention paid during the war to using confiscated land as a basis for Reconstruction helps explain why there was so little support for the idea once the fighting ended.[52]

Some did understand that the exslaves would need help after the war and that Union soldiers might well decide to settle in the South if given land there. Charles A. Dana, formerly at the *New York Herald,* endorsed the idea of giving "large bounties of captured lands to the soldiers to induce them" to settle in the South after the war. So, too, an anonymous correspondent recommended to Trumbull that South Carolina be set aside for exslaves after the war to provide a place "where they can cultivate the soil and enjoy the benefit of schools," away from whites, presumably. Several others also thought that exslaves could use abandoned lands principally to provide crops to the government. But only W. G. Smith of Cincinnati specifically urged that parcels of confiscated land be leased to exslaves, for fifty years, to encourage "negroes to industry and enterprise." A constituent urged Senator Sherman to place exslaves "in possession of the confiscated Estates" and give them government protection, but the Senator decidedly opposed harsh confiscation.[53]

Instead, almost all who favored broad confiscation and discussed the aftermath of slavery urged colonization for exslaves. Coloniza-

---

[52] See Eric Foner, *Reconstruction: America's Unfinished Revolution 1863–1877* (New York: Harper & Row, 1988), for the most recent discussion of this issue. Eric Foner, "Thaddeus Stevens, Confiscation, and Reconstruction," in *The Hofstadter Aegis: A Memorial,* ed. Eric McKitrick and Stanley Elkins (New York: Knopf, 1974), 153–83. See Belz, "The New Orthodoxy," 106–12, for the argument that distributing confiscated land after the Civil War had little support and may not have worked even if tried. See William C. Harris, *With Charity for All: Lincoln and the Restoration of the Union* (Lexington: University Press of Kentucky, 1997), for the most recent evaluation of Lincoln and Reconstruction.

[53] Lewis Tappan to Sumner, January 16, 1862, Charles Carroll to Sumner, February 23, 1862, 1:24, Dana to Sumner, April 7, 1862, 1:25, Sumner Papers; Anonymous to Trumbull, April 11, 1862, Trumbull Papers (the letter was written on the stationery of the Agency of the Illinois Mutual Fire Insurance Company); Elias Lee to Stevens, March 19, 1862, Stevens Papers and George S. Boutwell to Sumner, February 11, 1862, 1:24, Sumner Papers (Lee was Stevens's cousin; Boutwell was a politician from Massachusetts); Sam Gaither to Wade, February 27, 1862, N. H. Bewley to Wade, May 1, 1862, W. G. Smith to Wade, March 1862, Wade Papers; J. D. Easton to Sherman, April 11, 1862, Sherman Papers.

tion's appeal to the public, not to mention Lincoln and many in Congress, has been well documented. Trumbull's bill included a provision to encourage freed slaves to colonize. Even Thaddeus Stevens, with Sumner perhaps the strongest advocate for emancipation and equality in Congress, supported colonization.[54] William Lloyd Garrison found colonization "an absurd and preposterous scheme," but many others, for instance, Orestes Brownson, another notable reformer, supported it. He did so "as a concession to the prejudices of my countrymen." It may be that Brownson and others used this as a cover for their own racism. Whatever the reality, Lincoln and others employed a similar rationale. Some urged colonization in the South for exslaves out of fear they would move North; no one was naïve enough to suggest they would be welcome there after the war. As an alternative, Uriah Boston wanted "them sent directly to Africa," for it was the "natural and God created home for all Africans." Most who endorsed colonization agreed with Thomas Lippincott that no one should be forced into it, especially when they were "dragged hither in chains. Justice would cry out against it."[55]

In a war far from won, northerners gave little thought to the fate of exslaves once the fighting ended, except that many wanted to keep them out of the North. However, treatment accorded fugitive slaves and contrabands troubled some who suggested ways, although not adopted, to ameliorate the transition to freedom. Although their solutions may seem limited or naïve by our standards, they at least considered the matter. The striking fact is that more did not do so and, more importantly, that the issue was not addressed in the second act. John Jay, grandson of the famous Federalist, for example, hoped the confiscation bill would provide a commissioner to help blacks as the Union armies moved southward. Some free black "citizens" in the North suggested to both Trumbull and Sumner that "agents" be appointed to inquire "into the feelings and wants of the Contrabands" to secure their "future good." Secretary of War Edwin Stanton, Cameron's successor, felt that "Colored refugees from rebel service and

---

[54] Stevens to Salmon P. Chase, August 25, 1862, Stevens Papers. See note 31 for recent works on colonization.

[55] Garrison to Sumner, December 20, 1861, 1:24, Brownson to Sumner, April 11, 1862, 1:25, Sumner Papers; D. E. Clay [?] to Trumbull, December 17, 1861, Boston to Trumbull, December 23, 1861, Thomas Lippincott to Trumbull, January 28, 1862, Trumbull Papers.

how to provide for them is perhaps a ["the most" was crossed out] difficult question pressing upon this Government." He thought a solution might be found at a "convention of Gentlemen whose exalted personal character, humanitarian behavior and freedom from party objections would give conclusive weight to whatever their judgement, after careful examination on the subject would recommend."[56] But advocates of emancipation by confiscation failed to heed these few entreaties. Little wonder, then, that no groundswell arose after the war to assist blacks in the South. Radicals had offered scant leadership on the issue during the war when they had the chance.

Whereas congressmen spoke about how confiscation could transform the South, most outside of Congress viewed it solely as a means to end slavery. And, with a few notable exceptions, they believed it was constitutional. Francis Lieber, a student of the rules of war, spoke for many when he said that those "who commenced this rebellion ought to have reflected upon this [abolition]. It is now too late to talk, in the midst of war, of rights made or guaranteed by municipal or constitutional law." Joseph Medill of the *Chicago Tribune* agreed that the rebels could claim no constitutional protection: "Those who obey the Constitution can discern its safeguards; those who trample upon it and make war upon it cannot." Some grew angry at the "sensitiveness," as G. S. Rynard expressed it, of some Republicans to confiscation and emancipation. The people, he claimed, wanted the government to "go to the very edge of the Constitution in confiscation" to make the rebels pay for "their monstrous rebellion." In fact, there was only one correspondent who argued with confiscation's advocates in the Senate over the Constitution. Dr. Johnson H. Jordan, of Cincinnati and Pittsburgh, told Senators Sherman, Sumner, and Trumbull a number of times that the Constitution would not permit emancipation through confiscation. As he explained to Sumner, before the latter introduced his state suicide proposal, Congress could not liberate the slaves by confiscation if it treated the seceded states

---

[56] Jay to Sumner, January 4, 1862, William Powell et al. to Sumner, January 17, 1862, 1:24, Sumner Papers; Peter Grignon et al. to Trumbull, January 27, 1862 (quotation), Trumbull Papers; Stanton to Horace Binney, February 16, 1862, Edwin M. Stanton Papers, Library of Congress. See Willie Lee Rose, *Rehearsal for Reconstruction: The Port Royal Experiment* (Indianapolis: Bobbs-Merrill, 1964), for an example of how one theater of the war handled exslaves; and Stanton to General Rufus Saxton, June 16, 1862, Stanton Papers, for general guidelines on what to do with exslaves.

as part of the Union. Slavery remained a state matter until Congress admitted the reality of secession and treated the states as territories; only then could it emancipate through confiscation. But almost no one else, other than Democratic editors and Professor Joel Parker in the *North American Review,* challenged confiscation's advocates in such a manner.[57] In the end they had only to wrestle on what shape the bill would finally take with their own Republican colleagues.

The Senate discussed the confiscation bill until the beginning of May. Moderates tried to temper the bill's radical features and defeated efforts to pass it. They forced the creation of a select committee to incorporate their proposals with the Judiciary Committee bill. In mid-May the new committee reported back a bill that satisfied all but radicals and conservatives. The key provisions were that rebels convicted of treason would suffer death or five years in prison, a fine, and emancipation of their slaves. Those convicted of aiding the rebellion would forfeit slaves and property for life. The President could "seize and sequester" the property of certain classes of rebels. He could also free the slaves of those who did not resume allegiance within sixty days of a proclamation, pardon rebels, and colonize ex-slaves.[58] The moderates had been largely successful; this bill bore slight resemblance to Trumbull's original proposal.

The House, meanwhile, created its own bill. Following three months of discussion, the Judiciary Committee rejected all confiscation measures under consideration. The House then chose a fairly radical select committee to consider the matter again. It reported back two measures. The first confiscated all property belonging to

---

[57] Lieber to Sumner, December 19, 1861, 2:75, Jordan to Sumner, January 14, 1862, 1:24, Sumner Papers; Donald, *Sumner and the Rights of Man,* 54. Sumner introduced his state suicide thesis on February 11, 1862. Medill to Trumbull, July 4, 1862, Jordan to Trumbull, December 28, 1861; Jordan to Trumbull, February 20, 1862, Trumbull Papers; G. S. Rynard [?] to Wade, June 27, 1862, Wade Papers; Jordan to Sherman, December 22, 1861; Jordan to Sherman, January 1, 1862, Sherman Papers; Joel Parker, "Constitutional Law," *North American Review* 94 (April 1862): 435–63; Edward L. Gambill, *Conservative Ordeal: Northern Democrats and Reconstruction, 1865–1868* (Ames: Iowa State University Press, 1981), 10–15; Baker, *Affairs of Party,* 323–45.

[58] Frederick, "The Second Confiscation Act," 136–50; *Cong. Globe,* 37:2, 1895. Trumbull declined to serve on the committee because he did not have "much confidence in anything growing out of it." See *Cong. Globe,* 37:2, 1991, 2878–79 (for text of the bill); Syrett, "Confiscation Acts," 81–82; Roske, *Trumbull,* 83–88; Bogue, *Earnest Men,* 227–34.

prominent rebels in six classes, authorized the President to seize all property of rebels who did not resume allegiance within sixty days of a proclamation, and subjected all property confiscated to in rem proceedings. The second bill freed all slaves of persons who aided the rebellion. If a person could prove he had not "in any way aided, assisted, or countenanced" the rebellion, he could keep his slaves. Subsequently, the House passed the confiscation bill, eighty-two to sixty-eight, and defeated the emancipation bill, seventy-four to seventy-eight.[59]

The Senate and House rejected each other's bills. Each then chose colleagues for a conference committee; the senators were moderates and the representatives a bit more radical. The committee's new bill pleased most moderates, many radicals, and few conservatives. It provided that a convicted traitor would suffer death or five years in prison, a $10,000 fine, and emancipation of slaves. Fines would come from the sale of the traitor's property. Those convicted of aiding the rebellion would be imprisoned for ten years or fined $10,000. The President was instructed to seize all property of six classes of rebels and seize all the property of any who did not cease aiding the rebellion within sixty days of a proclamation. In rem proceedings would be used for all confiscated property, and all slaves entering Union lines would be freed. Finally, the President was authorized to colonize willing exslaves and pardon any rebel.[60]

This last version was a modest victory for moderate Republicans. They obtained treason as a basis of punishment, confiscation for only six classes of rebels, broad authority for the President, including the pardoning power, and the opportunity for rebels to resume allegiance to the North and thus avoid punishment. While the radicals obtained in rem proceedings and the liberation of slaves in Union-controlled areas, two central issues for them, they failed to get an explicit provision for forfeiture beyond the lives of those convicted, and the bill authorized the President to implement the act. The House passed

---

[59] Frederick, "The Second Confiscation Act," 156–69; *Cong. Globe,* 37:2 1767, 1770, 2361–63 (for text of House bills and votes); Richardson, *The Greatest Nation of the Earth,* 221–25. All but two of the eighty-two were Republicans. Twenty Republicans voted against the emancipation bill; Syrett, "Confiscation Acts," 82.

[60] *Cong. Globe,* 37:2, 3006, 3106–7, 3166, 3184–85. See pt. 4, Appendix, 412–13 for a full text of the final bill. See also Herman Belz, *A New Birth of Freedom: The Republican Party and Negro Rights, 1861–1866* (Westport, Conn.: Greenwood Press, 1976), 9–12.

the conference bill eighty-two to forty-one. Bradley Granger of Michigan and Joseph Segar of Wisconsin were the only Republicans to oppose it. The bill passed the Senate by twenty-seven votes to twelve, with only Republicans Browning and Cowan voting with the minority.[61] The Second Confiscation Act, entitled a bill to "suppress insurrection, to punish treason and rebellion, to seize and confiscate property of rebels, and for other purposes," now needed only the President's signature to become law.

Congress realized that Lincoln favored less severe measures to subdue the South and emancipate the slaves. In early March 1862 he had asked Congress for money to implement gradual abolition so that "the more Northern shall, by such initiation, make it certain to the more Southern" that they would never "join the latter in their proposed confederacy." That realization would, he believed, persuade the rebels they could not achieve "independence," and the rebellion would "substantially" end. Lincoln thought this was "one of the most efficient means of self-preservation" the North could pursue and stressed that the "general government sets up no claim of a right . . . to interfere with slavery within" the states. Congress ignored the border state representatives' objections and subsequently agreed to his request for funds. In late March as Congress contemplated the abolition of slavery in the District of Columbia, Lincoln observed to Horace Greeley that he did not oppose abolition in the capital in principle; he just worried "as to the time and manner of doing it." When Congress subsequently passed the bill, Lincoln noted his concern was only "one of expediency, arising in view of all the circumstances." In other words, he wondered if it were necessary to move so quickly, even if toward a noble end.[62]

Lincoln's concern became clear on May 19, 1862, when he revoked Major General David Hunter's proclamation freeing the slaves in Georgia, Florida, and South Carolina, the area of his command. In early April Hunter had requested from the War Department permission to arm fifty thousand "loyal men," presumably blacks. In mid-April Hunter declared all slaves owned by rebels in Fort Pulaski and

---

[61] *Cong. Globe*, 37:2, 3267–68 for the House vote on July 11, 1862, and 3274–76 for the Senate vote on July 12, 1862.

[62] Basler et al., eds., *Collected Works of Lincoln*, 5:144–46 (Message), 169 (Greeley), 192 (Message); Paludan, *Presidency of Abraham Lincoln*, 125–29; Fields, *Slavery and Freedom*, 110–11.

Cockspur Island, Georgia, free. This drew little attention in the North and no rebuke, perhaps because it involved few slaves. Less than a month later, Hunter far exceeded his April declaration and even Frémont's proclamation. Having earlier instituted martial law in the Department of the South, on May 9 Hunter proclaimed that "Slavery and martial law in a free country are altogether incompatible"; the slaves in these three states "are therefore declared forever free." He also conscripted all able-bodied black men between the ages of eighteen and forty-five. Reactions to Hunter's proclamation were not surprising; abolitionists thought it marvelous, while the more cautious believed it was too radical.[63]

Lincoln's view was all that counted, however. His proclamation of May 19 revoking Hunter's order was intended for the border states, not the North. Lincoln made clear that Hunter had not consulted the administration before issuing the declaration. More importantly, Lincoln reserved to himself alone, as Commander in Chief, the question of whether to declare free the slaves as a "necessity indispensable to the maintenance" of the government. Having disposed of Hunter, he then returned to his message on gradual abolition and Congress's support for this method in March. "I do not argue. I beseech you," he told the border states, "to make the arguments for yourselves. You can not if you would be blind to the signs of the times." Gradual abolition "would come gently as the dews of heaven, not rending or wrecking anything" truly held dear. If they did not accept gradual change, more dramatic alterations would be imposed, he predicted. But Lincoln's offer in the revocation of Hunter's proclamation had no appeal to the influential citizens in the border states.[64]

---

[63] Edward A. Miller, Jr., *Lincoln's Abolitionist General: The Biography of David Hunter* (Columbia: University of South Carolina Press, 1997), 96–104; *Official Records,* series 1, vol. 14, 333 (April 13, 1862); series 3, vol. 2, 42–43 (May 9, 1862); Ira Berlin et al., eds., *Freedom: A Documentary History of Emancipation, 1861–1867,* series 2, *The Black Military Experience* (Cambridge: Cambridge University Press, 1982), 38–39; A. S. Bundy to Wade, May 20, 1862, Wade Papers; John Murray Forbes to Sumner, May 16, 1862, George S. Boutwell to Sumner, May 19, 1862, 1:25, Sumner Papers; Sumner to Wendell Phillips, May 22, 1862, in Beverly Wilson Palmer, ed., *The Selected Letters of Charles Sumner,* 2 vols. (Boston: Northeastern University Press, 1990), 1:113.

[64] Basler et al., eds., *Collected Works of Lincoln,* 5:222–23; Paludan, *Presidency of Abraham Lincoln,* 130–31; Chase to Major General David Hunter, May 20, 1862, Chase to Greeley, May 21, 1862, in Niven, ed., *Chase Papers,* 3:202–3.

This did not deter Lincoln from renewing his appeal on the day that Congress approved the Second Confiscation Act. On July 12, 1862, he wrote the border state representatives, observing that had they accepted gradual emancipation, "the war would now be substantially ended." Nothing less would be possible now. The chance to return to the status quo ante bellum had certainly passed. "If the war continue long, as it must, if the object be not sooner attained, the institution in your states will be extinguished by mere friction and abrasion—by the mere incidents of war." But "substantial compensation" and colonization were still available if they would agree "at once to emancipate gradually." His repudiation of Hunter's proclamation "gave dissatisfaction, if not offense, to many" whose support the Union needed; the "pressure, in this direction, is still upon me, and is increasing." So, he concluded, "consider this proposition," since they, "more than any others," had the opportunity "to bring" the country "speedy relief." Two days later, in a meeting with Lincoln, these same representatives rejected the offer once again.[65] Lincoln was running out of alternatives to emancipation by broader means.

At the same time Lincoln conferred with Senator William Pitt Fessenden of Maine about the confiscation bill. Aware the President objected to parts of the law, some moderate senators asked Fessenden to discover what they might do to avert a veto, since no time remained for a revised bill. Lincoln urged two changes: the confiscation of slaves should be only prospective, and no forfeiture of real property should go beyond the lives of the offenders. The House agreed, by a voice vote, to a resolution that confiscation of slaves would be prospective. In the Senate some objected to the President's methods, while Trumbull argued against preventing forfeiture beyond the lives of those who aided the rebellion, as distinct from traitors. But these protests were of no avail; the Senate accepted both of the President's requests, twenty-five to fifteen. The House accepted the Senate's amendment to the joint resolution, eighty-three to twenty-one, the next day.[66] These concessions substantially weakened

[65] Basler et al., eds., *Collected Works of Lincoln,* 5:317–19.

[66] *Statutes at Large,* 12:589–92 (Second Confiscation Act); 627 (Joint Resolution); Francis Fessenden, *The Life and Public Services of William Pitt Fessenden,* 2 vols. (Boston: Houghton Mifflin, 1907), 1:272–75; Roske, *Trumbull,* 89; Nevins, *War for the Union,* 145–46; *Cong. Globe,* 37:2, 3370, 3374–75, 3383, 3400; Syrett, "Confiscation Acts," 84–86.

the second act, which moderates had already modified a good deal. The joint resolution allowed rebels to retain slaves even if they declared allegiance to the Union only a day before the bill became law. More significantly, no forfeiture of real estate would occur beyond the lifetime of any person convicted under the act, even those who lost their property through in rem proceedings during the war. This removed any real chance that confiscation could produce a reconstructed South or that exslaves might obtain land, with their freedom.

Lincoln signed the second act into law on July 17, 1862, but he remained troubled by the bill and so sent his veto message, prepared before the joint resolution passed, to Congress. By sending his veto message Lincoln made clear his dislike of confiscation and illustrated how problematic he found the bill to be. In the message Lincoln expressed no objection to punishing persons for treason; they would receive due process and could be pardoned. Nor did he oppose the emancipation of slaves through confiscation, although he strongly believed Congress had no power to free them until title of their ownership had been transferred to that body. He thought that the military already had the power to "seize and use whatever of real or personal property may be necessary or convenient" during the war, including slaves. He believed, though, that the confiscation contemplated was too sweeping. "The severest justice may not always be the best policy," he explained. "The principle of seizing, and appropriating the property of persons embraced within these sections is certainly not very objectionable; but a justly discriminating application of it, would be very difficult, and, to a great extent, impossible." His chief concerns, however, were forfeitures beyond the lives of the offenders and in rem proceedings. Although he recognized that "no formal attainder" occurred by in rem proceedings, "I still think the greater punishment can not be constitutionally inflicted, in a different form, for the same offense." He preferred that "a reasonable time should be provided" the owners of confiscable property "to appear and have personal hearings." In sum, he wanted confiscation only for military purposes during the war and trials for treason after, with emancipation left to the executive.[67] Still, Lincoln approved the bill, whatever its failings, because it reflected the growing sentiment within Con-

---

[67] Basler et al., eds., *Collected Works of Lincoln,* 5:328–31; Syrett, "Confiscation Acts," 86–87.

gress and the public that more be done to end the rebellion, abolish slavery, and punish the rebellion's leaders.

During the next two weeks Lincoln acknowledged the importance of the second act in a number of ways. On July 13 he told Secretary of State William Seward and Secretary of the Navy Gideon Welles that he had decided to free the slaves. Nine days later the Cabinet heard the first draft of the preliminary Emancipation Proclamation. The first paragraph, issued three days later as a proclamation to the public, invoked the second act and its sixth section, warning "all persons . . . to cease participating in, aiding, countenancing, or abetting the existing rebellion" against the United States. The Emancipation Proclamation would be announced on January 1, 1863. On July 22 he also wrote a memorandum authorizing the recruitment of "free negroes," slaves of disloyal owners, and slaves of loyal owners with their owners' consent. An executive order to military commanders the same day authorized seizure and "use of any property, real or personal" for military purposes and the employment as "laborers . . . persons of African descent" with wages. It required an account "from whom, both property, and such person shall have come" as the basis for future compensation. Three days later Lincoln issued a proclamation, which repeated the first paragraph of the preliminary emancipation.[68]

The second act's passage in July clearly played a major part in that momentous summer when the focus of the war changed, as historian Mark Grimsley notes, from conciliation to hard war. To be sure, a number of pressures encouraged Lincoln to emancipate the slaves, use them as laborers and soldiers, and be more aggressive toward the South. By early July the clamor from abolitionists and McClellan's failure to move against Richmond increased demands in the North for more action. McClellan's inaction, for instance, might not have been interpreted as such had the confiscation debates not stretched over six months. It is clear, at least, that the prospect of confiscation was in the air. On July 7 McClellan himself offered Lincoln unsolicited advice not to include confiscation of property or abolition as part

[68] Paludan, *Presidency of Abraham Lincoln*, 146–47; David Herbert Donald, *Lincoln* (New York: Simon and Schuster, 1995), 364–65; Basler et al., eds., *Collected Works of Lincoln*, 5:336–37 (Emancipation Proclamation—First Draft), 338 (Memorandum on Recruiting Negroes), 341 (Proclamation of the Act to Suppress Insurrection); Stanton notes in the Cabinet, July 22, 1862, Executive Order, July 22, 1862, Stanton Papers.

of the war effort.[69] And yet there can also be no doubt that the second act was a confused piece of legislation and that Lincoln, however much he had been pushed by it, showed no inclination to implement it, as his intended veto message implied. The irony is that the law, not well crafted and not vigorously implemented, attracted so much attention at the time and produced so many hopes and fears about what it might accomplish.

There are a number of reasons why the Second Confiscation Act was an imperfect instrument. Congress's expanded role during the war was new and unexpected. Perhaps because of this increased responsibility, the original intent of legislation was not always realized. After all, the Thirty-seventh Congress had passed the largest number of laws up to that time, double the previous record. One contemporary also believed that too many lawyers, in the Senate at least, had a hand in drafting the confiscation bill. Legislation with as many contributors as the second act was likely to contain inconsistencies. Moderates and radicals were forced to compromise to pass the law, and that meant practicality suffered. It is also evident that, despite Congress's efforts to change the South, federalism, as Daniel J. Elazar has argued, came through the Civil War "substantially as it was before the war began." Most legislators remained wedded to the antebellum understanding of state's rights and the role of the central government. As well, racism was widespread and certainly influenced certain pieces of legislation like the second act. As Herman Belz has shown, there was little interest in emancipation for the sake of the slaves; freeing the slaves was a military measure. In the end, whatever the rhetoric, most Republicans also retained notions of property, like Lincoln's, that prevented them from embracing sweeping confiscation.[70] The result was a law that was not very effective.

While the idea of confiscation certainly had encouraged hopes of

---

[69] Grimsley, *Hard Hand of War*, 67–69; Daniel E. Sutherland, "Abraham Lincoln, John Pope, and the Origins of Total War," *Journal of Military History* 56 (October 1992): 567–86; Donald, *Lincoln*, 364; James G. Randall, "Some Legal Aspects of the Confiscation Acts of the Civil War," *American Historical Review* 18 (October 1912): 81; Randall, *Constitutional Problems*, 279n; Stephen W. Sears, *George B. McClellan: The Young Napoleon* (New York: Ticknor and Fields, 1988), 226–29; McClellan to Lincoln, July 7, 1862, in Stephen W. Sears, ed., *The Civil War Papers of George B. McClellan: Selected Correspondence, 1860–1865* (New York: Ticknor and Fields, 1989), 344–45. This advice came in the famous Harrison's Landing letter.

[70] Joseph Logsdon, *Horace White: Nineteenth-Century Liberal* (Westport, Conn.:

emancipation, the law itself made it difficult to free slaves. Under the act slaves of rebels became free only when they came under the military's control. The assumption was that emancipation would advance with the army. But slaves could only be freed individually, or by groups, when a federal court found their owners to be rebels. The military had no power to adjudicate the matter. Doubts even arose about whether the military had the power to transfer slaves to federal courts for such proceedings. This bill would have required, therefore, hundreds of thousands of trials of individual masters. Furthermore, it did not affect slaves owned by nonrebels or those who could prove they had given no aid to the rebellion or those who swore allegiance to the North. It also omitted a method to resolve the issue if slaves claimed freedom under the act while the masters insisted on their loyalty to the Union, a conflict that seemed likely to arise. The debates indicated that some had wanted to prevent reenslavement if slaves and owners differed in testimony, but the law did not include such a provision. If slaves were confiscable as property through in rem proceedings, the second act reinforced the Dred Scott decision. As well, the law's declaration that slaves successfully confiscated were "forever free" violated the attainder clause of the Constitution. Either Congress could ignore this clause, because of the exigencies of war, or it could not. Both views could not be endorsed in the same act. In sum, if the second act moved Lincoln to realize the North's desire for emancipation, it persuaded him that a more effective means to that end, such as emancipation by executive proclamation, had to be found.[71]

Greenwood Press, 1971), 89; Wallace D. Farnham, "'The Weakened Spring of Government': A Study in Nineteenth-Century American History," *American Historical Review* 68 (April 1963): 662–80; Daniel J. Elazar, "Civil War and the Preservation of American Federalism," *Publius* 1:1 (1971): 39–58; Paludan, *Presidency of Abraham Lincoln*, 108–9; Hyman and Wiecek, *Equal Justice*, 266–67; Harold Hyman, *A More Perfect Union: The Impact of the Civil War and Reconstruction on the Constitution* (New York: Knopf, 1973), 178–81; William B. Scott, *In Pursuit of Happiness: American Conceptions of Property from the Seventeenth to the Twentieth Century* (Bloomington: Indiana University Press, 1977); David R. Wrone, "Abraham Lincoln's Idea of Property," *Science and Society* 33, no. 1 (1969): 54–70; Steven Joseph Ross, "Freed Soil, Freed Labor, Freed Men: John Eaton and the Davis Bend Experiment," *Journal of Southern History* 44 (May 1978): 214–16; Morton J. Horowitz, *The Transformation of American Law, 1780–1860* (Cambridge, Mass.: Harvard University Press, 1977); Gaines M. Foster, "The Limitations of Federal Health Care for Freedmen, 1862–1868," *Journal of Southern History* 48 (August 1982): 349–72; Belz, *Abraham Lincoln, Constitutionalism*, 111–12.

[71] Paludan, *Presidency of Abraham Lincoln*, 146; Lucie, "Confiscation," 312–20; Hyman and Wiecek, *Equal Justice*, 251–53; Randall, *Constitutional Problems*, 357–63.

The second act's purpose was never clear. It was a war measure intended to help defeat the South, yet by requiring that all offenders be tried in federal courts, with due process observed, the law prevented extensive enforcement during the war. Unlike with prize cases, where Congress passed legislation to assist the courts once the vessels had been captured, no provisions were made to simplify the confiscation process. As a result prize cases realized over $10 million whereas confiscation achieved less than $130,000. For confiscation it was virtually impossible for federal courts to operate in the South while the fighting continued. Had the federal courts been able to operate in the South before the fighting ended, it is doubtful that juries would have been eager to convict neighbors. As a consequence, even had Lincoln vigorously enforced the law, it could not have been used to help defeat the South, other than by intimidating rebels who might have shifted allegiance from the Confederacy to the Union. Congress needed to make the law more practical in its application. The second act was also meant to reconstruct the South, but in that it was equally inadequate. The moderates' insistence that no forfeiture extend beyond the lives of the offenders, be they guilty of lesser crimes than treason or not, meant that no property would be available for distribution until long after the war ended. Trumbull, among others, had argued that the war powers in the Constitution gave Congress authority to punish, through in rem proceedings, during the war those criminals who would not fall under the protection of the attainder clause for treason. But the majority refused to accept this reasoning, partly because they feared what it would achieve. As a result, the law extended protection of the Constitution to rebels while ignoring the ways in which the war might have created extraordinary powers. And, of course, the pardoning power given the President made such distribution of property even during the lives of the offenders less than likely, except perhaps for that of the leaders of the rebellion. The Second Confiscation Act was most notable then for the discussions it generated and the pressures they reflected, the fears that arose, and the way the confiscation debate provoked support for emancipation by different means.[72]

---

[72] Lucie, "Confiscation," 307–9; Belz, *Emancipation and Equal Rights,* 33–38; Randall, *Confiscation of Property,* 15. See Robert J. Plowman, "An Untapped Source: Civil War Prize Case Files," *Prologue* 21 (fall 1989): 197–204; Virginia Jeans Laas, "'Sleepless Sentinels': The North Atlantic Blockade Squadron, 1862–1864," *Civil War History* 31 (March 1985): 24–38; and Stuart L. Bernarth, *Squall Across the Atlantic: American Civil War Prize Cases and Diplomacy* (Berkeley: University of California Press, 1970), for the prize cases.

12

Modernization and the Federal System: The Example of Kentucky and Its War Claims against the United States Government

Kyle S. Sinisi

IN RECENT YEARS historians have written provocatively about the origins of modern American government. While there is ample disagreement as to the precise dates and meanings of modernization, it is safe to conclude that contemporary scholarship, following the lead of Richard Bensel and Stephen Skowronek, has located the beginnings of national governing modernity in the Civil War and early Gilded Age. Other historians have applied the principle of modernity, if not the terminology, to their studies of subnational politics. Theda Skocpol, Ballard Campbell, and Morton Keller, for example, have challenged the long-held notion that state governance in the early Gilded Age was either minimalist or laissez-faire. According to this revisionism, shortly after the war a reform impulse grew in the states that eventually touched upon issues as varied as social welfare, public schooling, and commercial regulation.[1]

---

[1] Richard F. Bensel, *Yankee Leviathan: The Origins of Central State Authority in America, 1859–1877* (Cambridge: Cambridge University Press, 1990); Stephen Skowronek, *Building a New American State: The Expansion of Central State Authority, 1877–1920* (Cambridge: Cambridge University Press, 1982); Theda Skocpol, *Protecting Soldiers and Mothers: The Political Origins of Social Policy in the United States* (Cambridge, Mass.: Belknap Press, 1992); Ballard Campbell, *The Growth of American Government: Governance from the Cleveland Era to the Present* (Bloomington: Indiana University Press, 1995); Morton Keller, *Affairs of State: Public Life in Late-Nineteenth-Century America* (Cambridge, Mass.: Harvard University Press, 1977). For an extended summation and analysis of these trends, see R. Hall Williams, "The Politics of the Gilded Age," in *American Political History: Essays on*

In the study of federalism, the search for modernization presents at least one explicit question. Just how modern did the administration of federalism, or intergovernmental relations, become in the aftermath of a war that, to most recent scholarship, eroded old bureaucratic structures and instilled governments with a new sense of policy activism? A preliminary answer can be found in one of the few administrative issues that demanded and received the attention of both the states and national government—state war claims against the United States.

The financial importance of the war claims cannot be overstated. In 1866 a congressional committee estimated that the loyal states had spent over $460,000,000 on behalf of the northern war effort. Included in the total cost were payments for militia and all costs associated with the raising of volunteer units prior to their mustering into the Union army. Early in the war Congress accepted the responsibility for a portion of these expenses in an indemnification act of July 21, 1861. This bill quickly became the key piece of legislation covering reimbursement for the next thirty years.[2]

Not surprisingly, the states with the biggest, or most controversial, claims were those that either suffered Confederate attacks or lived in constant fear of invasion. Thus, emergency mobilizations of militia in Kansas, Missouri, Kentucky, Indiana, and Pennsylvania generated not only large expenditures of state dollars but also significant disputes about Washington's ultimate responsibility for those expenditures. The resulting scramble for claims disclosed the simple fact that administering federalism was not included in the modernization phenomena that seemed to spread over other aspects of American governance. Indeed, a test case of one state, Kentucky, reveals an intergovernmental system remarkably unaffected by the war.

Kentucky's claims experience was typical in three important areas.

---

the State of the Discipline, ed. John F. Marszalek and Wilson D. Miscamble (Notre Dame, Ind.: University of Notre Dame Press, 1997), 108–42, and Lawrence C. Dodd and Calvin Jillson, eds., The Dynamics of American Politics: Approaches and Interpretations (Boulder: Westview Press, 1994).

[2] The amount is reported by the Select Committee on the War Debt of the Loyal States in U.S. Congress, House Report, 39th Cong., 1st sess. (1866), House Document no. 16 (serial 1272), 1. A more recent estimate of state and local expenses is approximately $300,000,000. However, the categories of expenditure that constitute this figure are vague. See Benjamin U. Ratchford, American State Debts (Durham, N.C.: Duke University Press, 1941), 6.

First, its claims covered all possible scenarios of wartime expenditures. Kentucky, like most loyal states, presented claims for supplies, services, and bonded interest. It also filed claims for a variety of military forces, whether militia or volunteers waiting to be federalized. Second, Kentucky did not deviate from long accepted administrative procedures in its intergovernmental dealings. Before it had presented its last claim, the Bluegrass State had used all of the then traditional methods to gain reimbursement, including claims agents, congressmen, and even militia officers. Third, and most important, Kentucky's claims experience resembled most states in that it was beholden to local affairs and circumstances. What exactly this meant varied from state to state. For some, the effect of localism translated into the personal and partisan disputes that often occurred between governors and their legislatures. For other states, it translated into simple administrative distractions represented by Indian uprisings and corruption scandals. In Kentucky's situation partisan squabbles with Washington colored most everything associated with the drive for reimbursement. To most Kentuckians reimbursement would come far too slowly and only after what seemed an unnecessary administrative battle with the government.

Kentucky traced its claims difficulties to the partisan politics of the war. Early controversies over troop recruitment led to problems associated with a large Union military presence in the state. Increasingly Democratic in their sympathies and voting behavior, many loyal Kentuckians soon believed the state an occupied territory of the Republican-led national government. The suspension of habeas corpus, the arrest or banishment of political candidates, the intimidation of Democratic voters, and the debate and passage of the Thirteenth Amendment all readily disillusioned even the most ardent of Unionists in the state. Further Republican talk of racial equality, the Freedmen's Bureau, and limiting the civil liberties of ex-Confederates ruined any chance of creating a political or governing environment sympathetic to Washington. Kentucky's intergovernmental relations were thus, in the words of the historian E. Merton Coulter, characterized "by mutual distrusts, suspicions, and misunderstandings."[3]

---

[3] The writing on Kentucky's difficulties with the Union government is voluminous. See particularly William B. Hesseltine, *Lincoln and the War Governors* (New York: Alfred A. Knopf, 1948; reprint, Gloucester: Peter Smith, 1972), 209–11, 244–46; Thomas L. Connelly, "New-Confederatism or Power Vacuum: Post-war Kentucky

The political and social rift with the United States government was deep. But it had developed slowly, and it did not stop over ninety thousand Kentuckians from serving in the northern armies. The rift also did not stop the flow of Union money during the war to help pay for Kentucky's costs in raising and equipping these men. By the end of 1861 the United States government had created any number of vehicles to funnel money to different regions, states, and even communities. Of those vehicles none was as efficient as the cash advance. In the fall of 1861 Secretary of the Treasury Salmon P. Chase offered cash advances to the states based upon estimations of how much the states spent on behalf of the war effort and could, therefore, eventually be reimbursed. Kentucky tapped readily into this supply of money. In May 1862 the state received $315,000. The next month it gained $436,000. In 1864 Kentucky collected an additional $300,000. By any measure, the state had been very successful. It had garnered a total wartime advance of $1,051,000 when the average total advance for the loyal states had been $352,938.[4]

Nevertheless, Kentucky's wartime success in extracting money from the government never went far beyond the cash advance. Not even the intervention of Joshua Speed—Abraham Lincoln's personal friend and emissary to Kentucky—aided reimbursement under the terms of the congressional indemnification act of July 21, 1861. Cash advances were a wartime expedient with few documentary strings attached. Actual indemnification of expenses was another matter, and here Speed ran into the wall of a Treasury bureaucracy that did not make any accommodations for the explosion of war-related business, save for incremental increases in clerical help.[5]

Politics Reappraised," *Register of the Kentucky Historical Society* 64 (October 1966): 257–69; Betty Gibson, " 'Reconstruction' and 'Readjustment': Some Comparisons and Contrasts," *Filson Club History Quarterly* 35 (April 1961): 167–73; E. Merton Coulter, *The Civil War and Readjustment in Kentucky* (Chapel Hill: University of North Carolina Press, 1926), 189–214 (quotation on page 189).

[4] Figures for Kentucky's advances can be found in a number of areas, but see particularly C. D. Pennebaker to Thomas Bramlette, October 18, 1865, Governor's Papers, Thomas Bramlette, Militia Correspondence, folder 105, box 5, Kentucky State Archives, Frankfort. Figures for the advances of other states can be found in U.S Congress, *Senate Report*, 50th Cong., 1st sess. (1888), no. 1286 (serial 2524), 54–62. Nevada, West Virginia, and Virginia were excluded from computations, as these states contributed and claimed an insignificant amount of manpower and material to the Union war effort.

[5] Magoffin to Speed, February 28, 1862; Third Auditor to Speed, March 29, De-

In the administrative struggle to follow, Kentucky was in a position little different from other loyal states. Fearing an unregulated attack upon its vaults both during and after the war, the Treasury rigorously investigated each state's claim for reimbursement. Although it had great latitude to approve claims in accordance with the wartime legislation authorizing reimbursement, the Treasury consistently resisted the urge to loosen its grip on public dollars. Beginning with Chase, a succession of Treasury secretaries demanded careful documentation in support of each claim and showed little willingness to form new administrative precedents that would increase the flow of money to the states. In some states, such as Massachusetts and Connecticut, there was general acceptance of this situation. In other states, such as Missouri, there was scorn for a bureaucratic system deemed not up to its task of determining good or bad claims. But in Kentucky there was a popular sense that the Bluegrass State had been singled out for political retribution.[6]

The decline of Kentucky's intergovernmental relations did not always seem inevitable. Indeed, following the ouster of the pro-Confederate Governor Beriah Magoffin in August 1862, the future looked bright. The new governor, James F. Robinson, was a noted Union man, and, when he did not seek reelection in November 1863, he was succeeded by Thomas F. Bramlette—a man no less devoted to Lincoln and the Union. Evidencing this, Lincoln's administration went to great lengths to ensure Bramlette's election by declaring martial law, removing rival candidates from the ballot, and intimidating dissenting voters. Bramlette's love of the Union never waned, but his goodwill toward Lincoln's administration evaporated quickly. Content with the intervention that helped make him governor, Bramlette rebelled when that intervention continued after his inaugura-

---

cember 22, 1862; Third Auditor to L. B. Temple (President of the Military Board), August 4, September 27, 1862, vol. 1, Letter Books, Third Auditor; Speed to Third Auditor, May 3, 29, 1862, vol. 1, Letters Received; Speed to Third Auditor, May 26 and 29, 1862, vol. 4, Letters Received, Third Auditor, Accounting Offices of the Department of the Treasury, Record Group 217, National Archives, Washington, D.C. (hereinafter cited as RG 217).

[6] One example of Missouri's attitude toward the government's handling of the claims can be found in George C. Bingham to William Hardin, March 13, 1876, Governor Hardin's Papers, folder 15221, microfilm reel 151, Missouri State Archives, Jefferson City; and Bingham to James S. Rollins, March 16, 1876, Rollins Papers, folder 124, microfilm reel 6, Western Historical Manuscripts Collection, Columbia, Mo.

tion. Over Bramlette's objections, the Lincoln administration turned slaves into soldiers and arrested state officers critical of the policy. When the government later denied Bramlette's attempt to raise state troops, the governor moved decidedly toward those who had opposed Lincoln from the outset of the war.[7]

The shaky status of the state's war claims easily accelerated many Unionists' growing antipathy toward Lincoln and the Republicans. Despite the cash advances, the Treasury had not adjusted any of Kentucky's actual claims by the beginning of 1864. There was also little indication that the government would, in the near future, move on any of the state's claims. This hesitancy was of particular concern to Bramlette and the legislature on a series of claims emanating from John Hunt Morgan's invasion of 1863. Kentucky's dissatisfaction grew with news that both Indiana and Ohio, which had also suffered Morgan's invasion, had succeeded in introducing special indemnification legislation in Congress. Resolving that Kentucky was "as loyal as any state within the Union," the legislature demanded equal treatment in Washington.[8]

Kentucky's indignation was misplaced. Indiana and Ohio had merely proposed legislation that the government reimburse its costs. There was no indication that Congress would approve any such legislation. More importantly, Kentucky was hardly alone in having its claims unexamined. At the time of its resolution demanding equal treatment, only three other states had received indemnification. Regardless, these more general circumstances mattered little. Few Kentuckians knew the status of all state claims, and they were not predisposed to search hard for explanations. The national government was responsible for a host of perceived infamies forced on the state, and a claims conspiracy only made sense.[9]

Over the next few years the perception of Republican discrimination seemed beyond dispute. In August 1865 Kentuckians overwhelmingly rejected the Republican party in legislative elections.

---

[7] Coulter, *The Civil War and Readjustment in Kentucky*, 170–79.

[8] Information on the Morgan claims can be found in Third Auditor to Brig. Gen. W. S. Ketchum, May 29, 1863, vol. 1, Letter Books, Third Auditor, RG 217; and Resolution of January 20, 1864, *Acts of the General Assembly of the Commonwealth of Kentucky, 1863–1864* (hereinafter referred to as *Kentucky Acts*).

[9] U.S. Congress, *Senate Report*, 50th Cong., 1st sess. (1888), Senate Document no. 1286, (serial 1286), 54–62.

The newly installed legislature, with the approval of Governor Bramlette, then repealed all wartime acts that restricted the civil liberties of Confederate sympathizers. Shortly thereafter, a portion of Kentucky's claim hit an administrative roadblock. Although the Treasury approved a claim for $34,000 in militia expenses, an auditor forwarded the claim to the War Department for verification that the expenditures had occurred under actual service to the United States. This was a routine procedure, but Kentucky's military and political leadership was outraged. To State Quartermaster General George Monroe, the transfer of the claims was a "foolish delay," noting further that "this treatment is perfectly outrageous, and I am almost forced to believe . . . that the action of our recent Legislature in certain respects has caused them to pursue this course toward Kentucky." State Agent Charles Pennebaker, a former soldier hired to present the claim in Washington and lobby both Congress and the Treasury, concluded that all officials involved in the auditing process were disposed "to postpone Kentucky to other states." Governor Bramlette asserted that the government rejected Kentucky's claims for "no good reason," and that the state must trust "to an abatement of any unjust prejudice." Among the state's newspapers, the pro-Democratic *Frankfort Tri-Weekly Kentucky Yeoman* was especially prone to see discrimination. Sectional bias, after all, was easy to find in what it called a "Sham Congress" only too ready to shower money upon northern states while denying the claims of loyal Kentuckians. The paper's editor ultimately concluded that all of the state's claims were being held hostage to Kentucky's next election in the fall of 1866, which many observers believed would be the Republican party's last real opportunity to influence state politics.[10]

Although the above statements were no doubt deeply believed, they also reflected the pressure that Kentucky placed upon its officials to produce results. Quartermaster Monroe believed public cen-

---

[10] Hambleton Tapp and James C. Klotter, *Kentucky: Decades of Discord, 1865–1900* (Frankfort: Kentucky State Historical Society, 1977), 12–13; Monroe to Bramlette, March 6, 1866, Governor's Papers, Thomas Bramlette, Militia Correspondence, folder 106, box 5, Kentucky State Archives; Report of the Quartermaster General, December 1, 1866, Document no. 9, *Kentucky Documents, 1866*, vol. 2, 4–7; *Report of the State Agent for Kentucky, at Washington, made to the Governor, January 1, 1867,* Legislative Document no. 8, 3; Governor's Message, January 4, 1867, *Kentucky House Journal, 1867,* 16; *Frankfort Tri-Weekly Kentucky Yeoman,* April 14 and July 26, 1866.

sure likely if some progress was not made. Likewise, by December 1866 Agent Pennebaker had been employed for three years without having completely settled any of the state's claims. Legislative authorization for his job expired in February 1867, so the necessity of finding some explanations was probably even more apparent to him. Governor Bramlette, a moderate in a conservative state, pondered a senatorial run in 1867. The benefits of castigating the national government could not have escaped him, especially after the state Democratic party produced a platform in the summer of 1866 that denounced Washington's usurpations in Kentucky and the South.[11]

There was no doubt that 1866 had been marked by unexpected delay in the handling of a small portion of the state's claim, but progress had occurred that belied the complaints of state officials. The progress happened on three fronts. First, beginning in May, Kentucky's congressional delegation successfully produced legislation that authorized the Treasury to audit claims for state troops called into action in May 1862. Second, the third auditor, whose office examined all state claims, recommended that Kentucky receive a $500,000 advance on its yet to be approved claims. Third, by December Pennebaker managed to get over $1,800,000 in claims approved for reimbursement.[12]

Despite the financial windfall, Kentucky's leaders focused instead upon the remainder of the state's outstanding claims, which amounted to approximately $1,500,000. The concern was not merely the emotional by-product of tension with Washington. There was a financial necessity that weighed heavily on the minds of Kentucky's leadership. By the end of 1866, the state paid almost $90,000 per year in interest on its war debt. Administrative delay over any part of the state's claims thus increased Kentucky's total debt and its ability

---

[11] For Monroe's belief in impending rebuke, see his Report of the Quartermaster General, December 1, 1866, Document no. 9, *Kentucky Documents, 1866,* vol. 2, 4–7. For the party platform, see Tapp and Klotter, *Kentucky: Decades of Discord,* 15.

[12] Kentucky's claims legislation can be tracked in the *Congressional Globe,* 39th Cong., 1st sess., 2612, 2888–89, 2927, 3440; 39th Cong., 2nd sess., 971, 976, 1116; and *United States Statutes-at-Large* (1867), 14:565. Recommendation for the advance seen in Report of the Quartermaster General, December 1, 1866, Document no. 9, *Kentucky Documents, 1866,* vol. 2, 4–7. Figure for Pennebaker's approved claims found in *Report of the State Agent for Kentucky, at Washington, made to the Governor, January 1, 1867,* Legislative Document no. 8, 7.

to locate Republican misdeeds in Washington. When indemnification did occur, as it did during 1866 and again in 1867, the tendency was still to see Republican malevolence. According to Agent Pennebaker, the only reason Kentucky received indemnification in 1867 was that few other states had business pending before the government. Hence, accounting officials had no other states deliberately to prioritize ahead of Kentucky. In a similar fashion, Kentucky's new Democratic governor, John W. Stevenson, closed out 1867 noting not so much Kentucky's success with reimbursement, but rather the "technical and specious objections [that] are interposed at Washington to the payment of [or claims], so sacredly due."[13]

While Kentucky's leaders began to point repeatedly and insistently at Republican treachery, many of the state's claims problems started at home. Like many states, Kentucky had considerable difficulty in organizing its claims amid a popular clamor for bureaucratic—and fiscal—retrenchment, which muted any chance of bureaucratic growth or modernization. Throughout the United States, the explosion of wartime spending and executive power met with a widespread cry for either more efficient or reduced governmental structures. When a state such as Kentucky appointed a state agent, a staple of prewar intergovernmental operations, it often did so while providing limited clerical help and funding. Consequently, it did not take long for Agent Pennebaker to become buried in the minutiae of ledgers, vouchers, muster rolls, and pay warrants. A lawyer by trade, Pennebaker lacked experience with claims and Kentucky's financial and militia bureaucracies.

The problem of Pennebaker's inexperience was magnified by the sheer volume of the claims he controlled. In addition to over $3,000,000 worth of state claims, Pennebaker found himself with the responsibility of coordinating and representing the claims of individual Kentuckians against the United States government. This other duty placed Pennebaker in charge of individuals' claims for property damage, back pay, enlistment bounties, and pensions. The legislature's appointment of a state official to mediate its citizens' problems

---

[13] Pennebaker's charge found in Report of the State Agent for Kentucky, January 1, 1869, Document 15, *Kentucky Documents, 1868*, vol. 2, 6. Interest figure found in Report of the Kentucky State Agent, January 1, 1868, Document no.18, *Kentucky Documents, 1867*, vol. 2, 15–16. Quotation taken from Stevenson message to State Assembly, December 3, 1867, *House Journal, 1867–1868*, 12.

with Washington was not a startling innovation in running the federal system. A small number of other states had similar arrangements, yet, more importantly and as a practical matter, the claims of individuals overwhelmed an agent already struggling to master the state's claims. Between April and December of 1864 alone, Pennebaker received approximately three thousand letters, which then produced over a thousand individual claims.[14]

The situation did not get better in 1865, and the agent requested help. In numerous letters and reports, Pennebaker documented the need. When not tracking down errant military payrolls in the field, his office routine left little time to eat or sleep. Between 9:00 A.M. and 3:00 P.M. daily, Pennebaker made the rounds of the administrative departments in Washington. He spent the daylight hours before and after those rounds catering to the demands of the crowds of soldiers and officials who came to the office. Only at night was he able to answer the thousands of letters and claims that came from Kentucky. In a job that required a great deal of personal contact, Pennebaker was reduced to providing general information and blank claims forms for publication in the state's newspapers. Short of giving up, Pennebaker concluded that he needed a raise and two new clerks.[15]

The state legislature did listen to its agent. Pennebaker got his raise and one new clerk. Better yet, the state appointed three agents who would assist, and report to, Pennebaker. Unfortunately for Pennebaker and the state, these administrative alterations did not anticipate congressional legislation in 1866 that allowed greater numbers of individuals to press pension and bounty claims in Washington. As a result, over fifteen thousand letters containing 2,476 claims flooded the state agent's office in 1867. Pennebaker soon found himself in the unenviable position of having to use his own money to hire an additional clerk and purchase office stationery.[16]

[14] Pennebaker to Bramlette, December 15, 1864, Governor's Papers, Bramlette, Militia Correspondence, file 101, box 5; and *Kentucky House Journal, 1865*, 129–33.

[15] Pennebaker to Bramlette, December 15, 1864, Governor's Papers, Bramlette, Militia Correspondence, file 101, box 5; and *Kentucky House Journal, 1865*, 129–33. The newspapers remained Pennebaker's best means of getting out information and advice for as long as he handled individual claims. See *Frankfort Tri-Weekly Kentucky Yeoman*, January 9, 1866, and *Frankfort Commonwealth*, January 20, 1866.

[16] Pay, clerk, and other financial matters described in *Kentucky Acts, 1865*, vol. 1, 59–61, and notation in Executive Journal, Thomas Bramlette, Governor's Papers,

By 1869 Pennebaker began to fall out of favor with both the governor and the legislature. At least two reasons explain this turn in his fortunes. First, Pennebaker had produced fewer and fewer results since 1866. Frequently sick, Pennebaker managed to push through the auditor's office in 1869 only $14,000 in claims out of a possible total claim of $1,300,000. His work in Washington languished, while most collection, documentation, and presentation duties fell into the hands of either the state adjutant or the quartermaster general, a situation that both officers noted prominently. Governor Stevenson was made painfully aware of the reality of Pennebaker's absence when in July both he and the state quartermaster general had to travel to Washington to review the state's claims. A second problem contributing to the demise of Pennebaker was Stevenson's growing sense that the agent had failed through simple inefficiency and a clash of personalities. According to reports, Pennebaker had become an annoyance in the Treasury's offices, leading some clerks to delay Kentucky's claims as a basic matter of spite.[17]

The combination of these two problems and a precipitous decline in the number of claims petitions from individuals led the state legislature to eliminate the position of state agent in March 1870. Although the legislature left it open to the governor to appoint a new agent paid by commission, Governor Stevenson refused. Citing fiscal concerns, the governor rejected the idea that an agent was necessary. Instead, Stevenson turned to State Quartermaster General Fayette Hewitt, who had succeeded George Monroe in 1867. Hewitt had not only investigated Pennebaker's difficulties, but had also volunteered to handle the claims himself. A militia officer already employed by the state, Hewitt satisfied Stevenson that he was well able to break

---

microfilm 993702, Kentucky State Archives. The Kentucky system is described in the *Frankfort Commonwealth*, July 14, September 29, and November 5, 1865. Other information in this paragraph can be found in Pennebaker to Bramlette, Report of the State Agent, January 1, 1867, Legislative Doc. no. 8, 4 and Report of the State Agent, January 1, 1868, Document no. 18, *Kentucky Documents, 1867*, vol. 2, 1–12.

[17] Report of the Adjutant General for Kentucky, November 30, 1868, Document no. 4, *Kentucky Documents, 1868*, vol. 1, passim; Report of the Quartermaster for Kentucky, December 1, 1869, Document no. 12, *Kentucky Documents, 1869*, vol. 2, 5–9; Governor Stevenson's message, December 6, 1869, in *Kentucky House Journal, 1869–1870*, 12–14. For reports of Pennebaker's inefficiency and personality clashes, see Hewitt to Stevenson, April 12, 1870, and April 16, 1870, vol. 29, Stevenson Family Papers, Library of Congress; H. P. Helm to Benjamin Bristow, November 22, 1870, Bristow Papers, Library of Congress.

down all intergovernmental barriers and gain indemnification without any salary enhancements.[18]

Hewitt's appointment came at a critical time. Administratively, time was running out for Kentucky, and all other states, to receive reimbursement under the claims act of July 21, 1861. Effective June 30, 1871, all claims not allowed by the Treasury would have to get special congressional legislation authorizing the payment of claims. This was an extra administrative hurdle that few states wanted to incur. Political problems intruded as well when Kentucky's frosty relations with the Republican Congress worsened. Reconstruction politics served as a persistent irritant to the conservative state and the Republican-led Congress. Threats of martial law could even be heard from Washington.[19]

Over the next five years the claims issue could not be severed from such rhetoric, especially given the background of Quartermaster General Fayette Hewitt, who succeeded George Monroe in 1867. The new recipient of all claims responsibility for Kentucky, Hewitt was a meticulous man who dabbled in the law. He reveled in the mental gymnastics of the claims and, later in his career, the auditing of state finances. Although important to the unfolding claims activity, these attributes mattered less than Hewitt's fiery personality and his previous service with the Confederacy. At the outset of the Civil War, Hewitt played an important role in the establishment of the Confederacy's postal system. Desiring military action, Hewitt left the postal service in December 1861 for the first of a number of staff positions in the Confederate army. For the next two years he bounced around a number of unit commands before finally settling in as the adjutant of the Kentucky, or "Orphan," Brigade. According to all available accounts, Hewitt was a distinguished officer. Brave in battle and skilled in administration, Hewitt was an ideal staff officer with a passionate love of Kentucky and the Confederate cause.[20]

Of those within the Kentucky government, there would be no man

---

[18] On qualifications of Hewitt, and reason for not using an agent, see Stevenson's message, January 5, 1871, *Kentucky House Journal, 1871*, 13–14.

[19] *United States Statutes-at-Large* (1870), 16:250.

[20] W. H. Perrin et al. eds., *Kentucky: A History of the State*, 5th ed. (Louisville: F. A. Battle, 1887), 744–45; William C. Davis, *The Orphan Brigade: The Kentucky Confederates Who Couldn't Go Home* (Garden City, N.Y.: Doubleday, 1980), passim.

as predisposed as Hewitt to believe that Washington acted unjustly toward the state. Better yet, he was convinced that the government applied its rules without consideration of any special circumstances. To Hewitt this meant that although the rules were "proper and just" when used for the northern states, they harmed Kentucky because of its unique situation as a border state.[21]

The irony of Hewitt as a former Confederate officer pursuing the Union claims of Kentucky could not have been lost on two other key figures. First, Hewitt had ultimately to deal with the Secretary of the Treasury, George Boutwell. A Massachusetts politician intimately tied to the prewar antislavery movement and wartime radical politics, Boutwell would be a natural suspect in any perceived attempt to harm Kentucky's financial interests. Second, Hewitt had also to deal with the government's new chief legal officer, Solicitor General Benjamin Bristow. As Hewitt steered the claims into litigious waters during the 1870s, he met the adverse opinions of Bristow. The Solicitor was in no different a position than Secretary Boutwell. A Kentuckian, Bristow had been a vocal wartime supporter of the Republicans and, thus, effectively barred from holding any important office in the state during the Gilded Age. Like some other prominent Kentucky Republicans, such as John Marshall Harlan, Bristow found new political life in Washington through Republican patronage. It would be no great stretch of the imagination for Hewitt, and most like-minded Kentuckians, to see Bristow as a Republican conspirator ready to undermine and embarrass the Democratic party's efforts to secure reimbursement.

Despite his misgivings about Washington's willingness to cooperate with Kentucky, Hewitt threw himself into his duties, trying to beat the June 30, 1871, deadline after which all claims required congressional legislation. By the end of 1870, and despite the long sickness of one clerk in the auditor's office, he pushed through claims amounting to approximately $174,000. His work was a significant improvement over that seen in Pennebaker's last year as agent, but over $1,193,761 in claims remained outstanding. With the June 30 deadline fast approaching, Hewitt worked exclusively on one particu-

---

[21] Report of the Quartermaster of Kentucky, December 1, 1869, Document no.12, *Kentucky Documents, 1869*, vol. 2, 5–9, contains Hewitt's beliefs and quotation concerning the state's claims.

lar class of claims valued at close to $600,000. This particular set of claims was popularly known as the Tenth Installment and covered the state's mobilization of militia in 1864 and 1865. Governor Bramlette called out the troops to secure a state and region left, apparently, defenseless by William T. Sherman's march to Atlanta and Savannah. Hewitt's subsequent efforts at indemnification proved to be Herculean, involving considerable time and the coordination of resources within the legislature, state military offices, and the Treasury.[22]

Hewitt made his deadline—or so it seemed. By the middle of June 1871, he had shepherded the claim through the standard administrative screenings in the Treasury and War Departments. Only one hurdle remained, and that was to have Secretary of the Treasury Boutwell provide his signature, allowing Hewitt to draw pay warrants. This was a problem. Boutwell had been out of Washington for most of June, and the acting Secretary of the Treasury wanted no part of signing such a large pay warrant, especially one jammed through the Treasury's clerks at the last moment. Unwilling to issue the warrants, the acting Secretary did the next best thing. Late in the evening of June 30, he signed the warrants and informed Hewitt that the signature was legal only if Boutwell approved when he returned to Washington. Unfortunately for Hewitt and Kentucky, Boutwell returned to the Treasury's offices in the middle of July and refused to sign the warrants.[23]

To Boutwell, the decision was easy. In a governing era dominated by patronage-driven turnovers in personnel, administrative precedence was the glue that held the executive agencies together, and Boutwell believed that all precedence was against Kentucky. He noted that there were a variety of problems with the claim, but, most important, the claims did not comport with the Treasury's accepted procedures and published rules for reimbursement. Although Hewitt

---

[22] Report of the Kentucky Quartermaster, January 2, 1871, Document no. 6, *Kentucky Documents, 1870*, 5–9. Governor Stevenson's message, January 5, 1871, *Kentucky House Journal, 1871*, 13–14, has information on total claims still due the state. "An Act to expedite the collection of the War Claims of the State of Kentucky," March 22, 1871, *Kentucky Acts, 1871*, vol. 1, 88–89, reveals the extent to which Kentucky tried to coordinate its resources in the final countdown to June 30.

[23] Report of the Kentucky Quartermaster, December 1, 1871, Document no. 8, *Kentucky Documents*, 1871, vol. 1, 3–20; *Commonwealth of Kentucky vs. Boutwell*, 13 Wallace 526 (1871).

had assembled the appropriate vouchers, muster rolls, and receipts that were required under the rules, Boutwell believed that the claims failed due to a simple lack of authorization for the state to call out its militia and hence spend reimbursable money.

Since the implementation of the claims process under the legislation of July 21, 1861, proper authorization to call out state troops had been controversial. Fearing the assemblage of hordes of state troops subsidized but not controlled by the government, Treasury Secretary Chase in 1861 had limited the government's fiscal responsibility only to those troops called out at the behest of either the President or the Secretary of War. This provision caused a stir in the border states where Confederate activity—both real and imagined—made emergency troop call-ups a frequent fact of life. It was this condition that had led Fayette Hewitt to proclaim that the border states, and Kentucky in particular, occupied a "unique situation" for war reimbursement. Nevertheless, and despite protest, Congress seemed to codify Chase's reading of the indemnification act of July 21, 1861, when it forced Missouri to seek special indemnification legislation for claims that Chase deemed outside his rules. Although Hewitt continued to protest Chase's rules throughout 1871, he also thought the authorization controversy irrelevant to the Tenth Installment. On two separate administrative screenings, Secretary of War William Belknap had deemed Kentucky's expenditures valid. According to Belknap, it was legally impossible for any Kentucky troops called out in 1864 and 1865 to not be in the service of the national government. Quite simply, Kentucky was under martial law.[24]

George Boutwell did not see the situation this way. He ignored Belknap's interpretation and authority to meddle in claims' disputes. For Boutwell, the incredible part of Kentucky's claim was not so much its illegitimacy, but the obtuseness of Hewitt for presenting it in the first place. The rules, after all, had been prepared and "made known to the country before any considerable expenses were incurred by the several states, and long before the expenses" of Kentucky's current claim. Boutwell went on to add that his last-minute intervention was merely a part of his accepted duties: every Secre-

---

[24] Report of the Kentucky Quartermaster, December 1, 1871, Document no. 8, *Kentucky Documents, 1871*, vol. 1, 27–32.

tary, "as I am informed, has practically recognized it to be his duty to pass upon all claims."[25]

Hewitt's, and Kentucky's, reaction to this decision was predictable. Boutwell was seen less as a bureaucrat following precedent and more as a radical Republican Massachusetts crony of President Ulysses S. Grant. Accordingly, outrage bubbled over at this most recent example of governmental arrogance and Republican conspiracy. According to one editorial, "as long as Kentucky is a nullity in National politics . . . so long will she be a target for the shafts of Radical malice." The same editorial went on to proclaim: "the fact is, Kentucky is the victim of a gigantic diddling operation which is none the less contemptible for being puritanically elaborate." Few Kentuckians would have argued with the newspaper's conclusion that "the present political complexion of the State weighs with the Secretary more than its [actual] record in the War."[26]

Quartermaster Hewitt was not content to let the issue die. Convinced that Boutwell's actions were "unwarranted by law or practice," Hewitt orchestrated a legal effort to force the Secretary to authorize reimbursement. Late in 1871 Kentucky then became the first state to bring a Civil War claims dispute into the federal court system. Although Hewitt prepared most of Kentucky's arguments well—attacking not only the ability of one department secretary to override the decision of another but also the legality of a department secretary making administrative rules for congressional enactments—the Supreme Court refused to order Boutwell to reimburse Kentucky.[27]

There was no small irony in Hewitt's persistent attack upon the Treasury. Kentucky, like all states, still had an alternative once the Treasury had rejected a claim. The state could then ask Congress for special legislation that would allow the Treasury to audit and reimburse any given claim. Hewitt generally disliked this procedure, believing Congress no less recalcitrant than the Treasury. However, he could not have been more wrong. In 1872 he helped Kentucky's congressional delegation, and Senator John W. Stevenson in particular,

---

[25] Report of the Kentucky Quartermaster, December 1, 1871, Document no. 8, *Kentucky Documents*, 1871, vol. 1, 27–32.

[26] Quotations taken from the *Lexington Observer and Reporter*, August 9, 1871.

[27] *Commonwealth of Kentucky v. Boutwell*, 13 Wallace 526 (1871).

draft legislation that authorized reimbursement of the $600,000 stopped by Boutwell. Although lobbying congressmen was an acceptable and expected part of a claim handler's job, the abrasive Hewitt wisely backed off, letting Stevenson guide the bill through the halls of Congress. The bill thus became law with little opposition. Suddenly realizing the possibilities of the more sugary approach, Hewitt now wasted little time getting other, and more appropriate, claims before Boutwell's Treasury, where they were approved with little difficulty.[28]

By the time Hewitt retired in 1875, suffering no small measure of exhaustion from the multiplication of other duties, less than 9 percent of Kentucky's total claim remained outstanding. Hewitt's success had come quickly, surprising all of those who had perceived conspiracy in the upper reaches of Washington. Still, few of Kentucky's Bourbon Democrats would be quite ready to credit Republican Washington with any help in matter. After investigating the history of the state's reimbursement effort, the legislature concluded that all credit belonged to the indefatigable Hewitt, who had slain the Republican monster that guarded the doors of the Treasury. Many within the state proclaimed the triumph of frugality and retrenchment as Kentucky received Hewitt's services cheaply. The state paid Hewitt no commission and certainly no gratuity of $10,000 as New Jersey had provided for its agent. In the end the Frankfort *Daily Kentucky Yeoman* trumpeted the state's victory by noting that "the Sharks [agents] in Washington said that it could not be gotten through without employing them [and] giving them half" of the reimbursement. Nowhere was there any mention that the long dominant and all-consuming charge of Republican conspiracy had been wrong.[29]

For all of its partisan and misguided political rhetoric, Kentucky's claims experience typified that of the other states. Certainly, no other state asserted political victimization similar to that of Kentucky, but all states were ultimately subject to the pervasive influence of local affairs in their intergovernmental contacts. Given its limited personnel and general unwillingness to part with public money, the United States Treasury would do little to facilitate administrative dealings.

---

[28] Governor Leslie's Message, January 8, 1873, *Kentucky House Journal, 1873*, 13; *Frankfort Daily Kentucky Yeoman*, February 3, 1873.

[29] *Frankfort Daily Kentucky Yeoman*, February 18, 1873.

The department usually corresponded with the states only when approached first. More significantly, Treasury rules carefully restricted the amount of time an agent could spend in departmental offices. A state's success with its claims, therefore, depended upon its organization. If organized to the letter of the rules, the state would find money. If disorganized, the state had no chance. Just how the states and their affairs drove the operations of the federal system could be seen in a set of unfortunate examples. In Kansas, it was a perpetual Indian threat that distracted militia officials from ever prosecuting the states' claim with any efficiency. In Missouri, internal political feuding between a succession of governors, congressmen, state legislators, and claims agents about who should receive credit for any reimbursement inevitably short-circuited the claims effort. Perhaps worse, corruption charges buffeted a state claims commission in 1875 that then hampered any future attempt to get money from Washington. Although local affairs often undermined intergovernmental administration, the impact was not always negative. Where political, economic, and administrative distractions were minimal in places such as Connecticut and Massachusetts, war indemnification occurred with little difficulty.[30]

Finally, these locally molded efforts were part of an intergovernmental system of operation that had been remarkably untouched, or modernized, by the war. The states appointed officials to handle the matter much as they had done before the war. Agents on term contracts and preexisting militia officers ushered the claims to Washington, where they met a Treasury Department that had been cut back at the conclusion of the war and would not grow again until 1890s. In an administrative world where eight clerks toiled in the third auditor's office with few divisions of labor and even fewer meritocratic promotions, state emissaries discovered that unbending precedents governed all decisions. Precedents effectively guided short-term patronage appointees, who often brought little or no experience to the office. Commonly held precedents also easily capped what most fed-

[30] For a more detailed discussion of the Civil War claims of Massachusetts, Missouri, and Kansas, see Kyle S. Sinisi, "Civil War Claims and American Federalism, 1861–1880" (Ph.D. diss., Kansas State University, 1997), 68, 77–168, 253–323. Information on Connecticut can be found in the annual messages of the Governors of Connecticut collected in the successive volumes of the *Legislative Documents of Connecticut*, running 1862–70.

eral public officials feared most: a policy innovation or exception that would unlock the doors of the Treasury. In a political culture that would come to value state governmental development to handle matters commonly held to be state affairs, the Gilded Age was not the era to alter how the states and Washington did business with each other.[31]

---

[31] Clerical life in the Treasury can be glimpsed in Cindy S. Aron, *Ladies and Gentlemen of the Civil Service: Middle-Class Workers in Victorian America* (New York: Oxford University Press, 1987), passim, but especially 78–79, 81.

AFTERWORD

J. Matthew Gallman

I FIRST BEGAN THINKING about the North during the Civil War nearly two decades ago. At the time there was little scholarship on the topic, and the notion of a collection of essays on the northern home front would have been nearly unthinkable. I turned to Emerson David Fite's seventy-year-old *Social and Industrial Conditions in the North during the Civil War*[1] for the factual lay of the land, and found methodological inspiration in the pioneering community studies on colonial America[2] and in the innovative quantitative work of the New Social Historians. The latter had much to say about broad patterns of development in mid-nineteenth-century America, but surprisingly little about the bloody conflict at its center.[3]

By the time Maris Vinovskis asked the profession "Have Social Historians Lost the Civil War?" in 1989, several young scholars were already exploring aspects of the northern home front. The following

---

[1] Emerson David Fite, *Social and Industrial Conditions in the North during the Civil War* (New York: Macmillan, 1910). Fite's classic does not appear in many footnotes and bibliographies these days—it is largely superseded by Phillip Shaw Paludan's superb *"A People's Contest": The Union and the Civil War, 1861–1865* (New York: Harper & Row, 1988)—but Fite is still a valuable resource. (Recently I was pleased to see it for sale in the small National Park Service bookstore at Harpers Ferry.)

[2] I am thinking of John Demos, *A Little Commonwealth: Family Life in Plymouth Colony* (New York: Oxford University Press, 1970); Kenneth A. Lockridge, *A New England Town: The First Hundred Years* (New York: W. W. Norton, 1970); Philip J. Greven, Jr., *Four Generations: Population, Land, and Family in Colonial Andover, Massachusetts* (Ithaca, N.Y.: Cornell University Press, 1970); and particularly Robert A. Gross, *The Minutemen and Their World* (New York: Hill & Wang, 1976).

[3] The noteworthy exceptions among the early-nineteenth-century community studies include Michael Frisch, *Town into City: Springfield, Massachusetts, and the Meaning of Community, 1840–1880* (Cambridge, Mass.: Harvard University Press, 1972); and Don Harrison Doyle, *The Social Order of a Frontier Community: Jacksonville, Illinois, 1825–70* (Urbana: University of Illinois Press, 1978).

year Vinovskis collected some of that early work in *Toward a Social History of the American Civil War.*[4] Before long, references to life in the wartime North began cropping up with more regularity in textbooks, encyclopedias, and edited collections on the Civil War.[5] Now, twelve years after the publication of *Toward a Social History of the American Civil War,* Paul A. Cimbala and Randall M. Miller have assembled this excellent collection of essays on the Civil War North and added it to Fordham University Press's rapidly growing new series on "The North's Civil War." It seems a propitious time to take stock of the scholarship on the northern home front.

Although the home-front literature encompasses a multitude of topics and approaches, three distinct sets of questions define the field of study. Certainly the most traditional questions concern how the civilian world functioned most literally as an additional "front" in the Civil War. How did events at home help shape the war's military history and help the Union achieve victory? This is a story with many components. A combination of governmental, voluntaristic, and market forces combined to recruit and equip a massive Union army, effectively mobilizing the North's superior resources. Vast armies of volunteers formed local aid societies and national commissions dedicated to supporting the armies both in the field and at home. Meanwhile, Republican leaders, editors, orators, ministers, cartoonists, and all manner of public men and women promoted patriotism through four years of carnage.

On the other hand, the North was neither demographically homogeneous nor politically unified. Once the early war fervor died down, internal divisions threatened to undermine the northern war effort before the Union army could turn the tide on the battlefield. The

---

[4] Maris A. Vinovskis, "Have Social Historians Lost the Civil War? Some Preliminary Demographic Speculations," *Journal of American History* 76 (June 1989): 34–58; and Vinovskis, ed., *Toward a Social History of the American Civil War: Exploratory Essays* (Cambridge: Cambridge University Press, 1990).

[5] For any excellent example of this evolving Civil War historiography, compare the treatment of the northern home front in David Herbert Donald, Jean Harvey Baker, and Michael F. Holt, *The Civil War and Reconstruction* (New York: W. W. Norton, 2001) with earlier editions of *The Civil War and Reconstruction,* originally authored by James G. Randall in 1937, and substantially revised as Randall and Donald, *The Civil War and Reconstruction* (1961). For an example of the steady incorporation of home front scholarship into a leading survey of American urban history, see the various editions of Howard P. Chudacoff and Judith E. Smith, *The Evolution of American Urban Society,* 5th ed. (Englewood Cliffs, N.J.: Prentice-Hall, 1999).

traditional home front narrative included some reference to the New York City draft riots and such street-level discord, and historians have long recognized that Abraham Lincoln navigated through treacherous political waters, encountering both dissenting voices within his own Republican party and a rising tide of opposition—both loyal and disloyal—from the ranks of the northern Democrats. But it is only through a more careful analysis of such internal debates that we can fully understand how popular support for the war was contingent on specific events and decisions. Such topics also open important points of comparison with recent work on the Confederacy, where scholars have emphasized the possible role of internal divisions in undermining the Confederate war effort.[6]

Other home front scholarship pays only modest attention to specific military and political developments, emphasizing instead a second set of questions concerning the war's impact on life at home. For these scholars, the war years become almost a laboratory for examining a society under stress. How did the Civil War affect everyday experiences in the North? How did life change for the region's rank and file? What adjustments did they make in their normal routines? What did those communities that were safely isolated from the war's carnage learn about the grim realities of war, and how did they learn it? To what extent did wartime demands also create new opportunities for women? Did the military experiences of African Americans change race relations at home? Perhaps the chief insight emerging from this diverse scholarship is simply that the social history of nineteenth-century America is better understood by examining the war years, rather than by seeing them as a terrible anomaly best left to Civil War specialists.

The studies of the war years themselves build to a third set of questions: What was the war's enduring impact on the North? The governing assumption of this query is that such a bloody civil war must have left the North transformed, even if not so much as the defeated South. But what were those changes? Did the conflict's massive mobilization leave a reshaped economy? Did this war for union change the individual's relationship with the state and with

---

[6] See Gary Gallagher's discussion of these issues in *The Confederate War: How Popular Will, Nationalism, and Military Strategy Could Not Stave Off Defeat* (Cambridge, Mass.: Harvard University Press 1997).

the larger society? How did participation in the war effort affect the political and social status of African Americans? Of white women? Such questions have been recently joined by reconsiderations of the importance of the Civil War's memory and commemoration in American culture. Certainly in my community of Gettysburg, Pennsylvania, the lines between the war years and the conflict's commemoration seem to blur, much like the lines between where the battlefield ends and the community begins.

The twelve essays in this collection reflect a diversity of questions and approaches, although such a small number cannot begin to map out the entire terrain of recent home front scholarship. Several contributions represent innovative analyses of economic and political topics, thus employing new investigations of the home front to rethink the familiar wartime chronology. These include Melinda Lawson's reconsideration of Jay Cooke and the Civil War bond drives, Michael Green's analysis of Republican ideology, Adam Smith's discussion of political partisanship, and John Syrett's reexamination of the Confiscation Acts. In some senses, the most traditional essay yields some of the freshest argument. Both Peter Parish and Bryon Andreasen have introduced religious institutions into a political narrative that has commonly remained quite secular: Parish finds northern clergymen actively supporting the war effort, and Andreasen mines fascinating material on wartime church trials as a means of suppressing dissent.

Other authors focus more specifically on how the war was experienced at home. Alice Fahs and Earl Hess examine understudied sources on wartime popular culture: sentimental popular literature and print journalism. Both essays suggest the important gap—a chasm, really—between the war as it was lived on the battlefield and the fighting as it was portrayed in the public media. The essays by Lex Renda and Rachel Seidman suggest two very different approaches to the study of hitherto underexamined groups. Renda's quantitative analysis asks how African Americans—and particularly black male suffrage—became a political issue for northern white voters; Seidman's innovative study of several groups of women demonstrates the broad wartime challenge to received notions of gender dependency. Seidman's essay hints at the war's importance for the status of women in the postwar years, and Renda's study takes his analysis well into

Reconstruction. Kyle Sinisi picks up his narrative after the war, with an examination of the role of war claims in shaping the postwar political world.

It is perhaps significant that several of these essays are portions of larger studies that extend well beyond the war years, indicating the ways in which research on the Civil War home front has become more thoroughly integrated into the larger literature on nineteenth-century America.

As a group, they make an interesting comparison with the Vinovskis collection. Those seven essays also included one analysis of contact between the home front and the battlefield, a study of political developments during the war years, and two essays on postwar public policy. But over half of those earlier essays—including Vinovskis's own contribution—hinged on substantial quantitative analysis, generally emphasizing demographic issues, whereas only Lex Renda's essay in the current volume is built upon quantitative data. Certainly the cliometrician has not abandoned Civil War studies, but today's new methodologies commonly focus more on innovative use of literary sources. The Vinovskis collection was also distinctive in that four of the seven essays emerged from community studies—two of cities and two of small towns—and a fifth essay compared experiences in three communities. In contrast, the essays by Sinisi, Renda, and Smith focus on research spanning a single state, several others concentrate on a large region within the Union, and the majority of the authors either focus on a particular individual or cast a wide geographic net to address a specific question.

As we look to the future, what might we expect from new scholarship on the northern home front? Certainly one important item on the agenda should be continuing progress in integrating the various scholarly subfields into a cohesive Civil War narrative; and another ought to be an expanded consideration of the importance of the war years in the broad sweep of nineteenth-century social history. And, of course, various specific home front topics are ripe for more analysis and synthesis. The recent flurry of work on northern women suggests that it is time for some broader interpretive studies comparable to the competing perspectives on Confederate women. Numerous aspects of the African American experience in the North remain surprisingly underexplored, particularly in light of recent discussions of

African American agency in ending southern slavery. The two essays on religious institutions hint at the exciting possibilities for future scholarship on religion during the Civil War.

The agenda for the future should also include continuing investigation into the internal divisions within the North. We know something of how the various regions differed in political, economic, and ethnic terms, but there is room for more fully integrated home front studies of large geographic regions, bridging the gap between the city and community studies on the one hand and the national surveys on the other. We also have ample evidence of political discord—and occasional violent dissent—within specific communities and regions. But how fully did those conflicts weave their way into the fabric of northern society? We agree, for instance, that Abraham Lincoln might well have lost the election of 1864 had events taken a slightly different course. We also know that even modest-sized communities supported two or more competing newspapers that engaged in spirited partisan debate from early on in the conflict. How do we reconcile this evidence of internal friction with other portions of the home front narrative that seem to point toward a broad patriotic consensus? One answer to that conundrum is that the most spirited conflicts were often over means rather than ends. And certainly other points of friction reflected antebellum conflicts—over race, ethnicity, and class—merely reframed into a wartime context. Still, scholarly overviews too often speak of a unified northern political world without acknowledging the compelling evidence to the contrary.

As a final agenda item, I would like to make a pitch for further consideration of that third set of questions emphasizing the enduring legacy of the Civil War. In my own early work I argued for the presence of underrecognized continuities that persisted amid a world of rapid wartime change.[7] Too often social historians of the Civil War seemed to assert, or at least imply, war-related transformations that could not really be supported by research that neglected either antebellum or postwar patterns. As scholarship moves forward, I hope that Civil War historians will remain attentive to seeds of change in the antebellum decades, as well as evidence of postwar retrench-

---

[7] Gallman, *Mastering Wartime: A Social History of Philadelphia during the Civil War* (Cambridge: Cambridge University Press, 1990); Gallman, *The North Fights the Civil War: The Home Front* (Chicago: Ivan R. Dee, 1994).

ment. Those who paint with a broader brush argue for the war's role in the growth of industrial capitalism and the rise of the modern state. I have no quarrel with the direction of that analysis, even where I might quibble over matters of degree. On the other hand, perhaps there is room to reframe the question in order to explore the war's larger legacies. Certainly the recent work on memory is an exciting new arena for investigation.[8] Another approach would be to follow the experiences of particular cohorts whose experiences—both during and after the war—deviated from the aggregate norms. Certainly there is more to be learned about the postwar integration of war veterans into northern society and culture. And what of the particular experiences of African American veterans of the U.S.C.T.? It also may be that aggregate analyses mask important differences between age cohorts. For instance, how might our understanding of the war's enduring impact on gender roles, political ideology, attitudes toward the national government, or a host of other topics change if we were to restrict our analysis to men and women who were born around 1845, and thus came to early political awareness in the midst of the Civil War? In short, there remains ample room to explore the myriad ways in which northerners experienced the American Civil War.

---

[8] See David W. Blight, *Race and Reunion: The Civil War in American Memory* (Cambridge, Mass.: Harvard University Press, 2001).

ABOUT THE CONTRIBUTORS

EDITORS

Paul A. Cimbala, professor of history at Fordham University in the Bronx, received his Ph.D. from Emory University. He is the author of *Under the Guardianship of the Nation: The Freedmen's Bureau and the Reconstruction of Georgia, 1865–1870,* winner of the Georgia Historical Society's Malcolm and Muriel Barrow Bell Award, and the forthcoming *The Freedmen's Bureau: A Short History.* He and Randall M. Miller edited *Union Soldiers and the Northern Home Front: Wartime Experiences, Postwar Adjustments, The Freedmen's Bureau and Reconstruction: Reconsiderations, Against the Tide: Women Reformers in American Society,* and *American Reform and Reformers: A Biographical Dictionary.* He also edited (with Robert F. Himmelberg) *Historians and Race: Autobiography and the Writing of History.* He is working on two monographs, one dealing with the Veterans Reserve Corps during the Civil War and Reconstruction and the other dealing with African American musicians and their transition from slavery to freedom in the nineteenth-century South. He is editor of two Fordham University Press book series, *The North's Civil War* and *Reconstructing America.*

Randall M. Miller, professor of history and William Dirk Warren '50 Sesquicentennial Chair at Saint Joseph's University, received his Ph.D. from the Ohio State University. He has published numerous books, including the award-winning *"Dear Master": Letters of a Slave Family,* (with John David Smith) the award-winning *Dictionary of Afro-American Slavery,* (with Harry S. Stout and Charles Reagan Wilson) *Religion and the American Civil War,* and (with Robert Engs) *The Birth of the Grand Old Party: The Republicans' First Generation.* His latest book project is a study of immigrants in the American South. He is coeditor of the University Press of Florida book series *Southern Dissent,* and editor of two Greenwood Press series,

Historic Guides to the Twentieth Century and *Major Issues in American History.*

CONTRIBUTORS

Bryon C. Andreasen is a research historian for the Illinois Historic Preservation Agency, where he is an assistant to the Illinois State Historian. He earned his Ph.D. from the University of Illinois at Urbana-Champaign, where he wrote a dissertation about Copperhead Christians on the northern home front. He also holds a law degree from Cornell University.

Michael F. Conlin is an assistant professor of history at Eastern Washington University. He received his Ph.D. from the University of Illinois at Urbana-Champaign, where he wrote a dissertation titled "Science under Siege: Joseph Henry's Smithsonian, 1846–1865." He is presently at work on a study of "patriotic culture" in nineteenth-century America.

Alice Fahs received her Ph.D. from New York University. She teaches at the University of California, Irvine, and serves on the editorial advisory board of *Civil War History*. She is the author of *The Imagined Civil War: Popular Literature of the North and South, 1861–1865*.

J. Matthew Gallman is Henry R. Luce Professor of the Civil War Era at Gettysburg College. Among his books are *Mastering Wartime: A Social History of Philadelphia during the Civil War, The North Fights the Civil War: The Home Front,* and *Receiving Erin's Children: Philadelphia, Liverpool, and the Irish Famine Migration, 1845–1855*. He is currently working on a biographical study of Anna E. Dickinson, the celebrated wartime orator.

Michael S. Green received his Ph.D. from Columbia University and is a professor of history at Community College of Southern Nevada. He is coeditor of *Nevada: Readings and Perspectives* and coauthor of *A Liberal Conscience: Ralph Denton, Nevadan*. His forthcoming book is *Freedom, Union, and Power: Lincoln and His Party in the Civil War.*

Earl J. Hess teaches at Lincoln Memorial University, where he is the director of the History Program. He received his doctorate in American Studies from Purdue University. He is the author, coauthor, and editor of numerous books about the Civil War, including *Liberty, Virtue, and Progress: Northerners and Their War for the Union, Pea Ridge: Civil War Campaign in the West,* and *The Union Soldier in Battle: Enduring the Ordeal of Combat.* His most recent books are *Pickett's Charge: The Last Attack at Gettysburg* and *Lee's Tar Heels: The Pettigrew-Kirkland-McRae Brigade.*

Melinda Lawson is a visiting assistant professor at Union College. She received her doctorate from Columbia University and is the author of *Patriot Fires: Forging a New American Nationalism in the Civil War North.* Her next project is a study of images of the nation in the New Deal era.

Peter J. Parish is Mellon Senior Research Fellow in American History at the University of Cambridge and Professor Emeritus of American History at the University of London. From 1983 to 1992 he was Director of the Institute of United States Studies at the University of London. His publications include *Slavery: The Many Faces of a Southern Institution, The Divided Union: The Story of the Civil War,* and *Slavery: History and Historians.* He is completing a collection of essays on the Civil War and a study of the historical reputation of Abraham Lincoln.

Lex Renda is an associate professor of history at the University of Wisconsin–Milwaukee. He earned his Ph.D. at the University of Virginia and is the author of *Running on the Record: Civil War Era Politics in New Hampshire.* He is currently writing a book about the abolition of debtors' prisons in the United States.

Rachel Filene Seidman is the author of *The Civil War: A History in Documents.* She earned her Ph.D. at Yale University and is at work on a study of the public reading culture in early Saint Paul, Minnesota.

Kyle S. Sinisi is an assistant professor of history at The Citadel. He received his Ph.D. from Kansas State University and is at work on a book titled *Civil War Claims and American Government.*

Adam I. P. Smith is a Research Fellow at Sidney Sussex College, Cambridge. He was a visiting fellow at Harvard and completed his Ph.D. at Cambridge University. He is currently completing a book on politics in the North during the Civil War.

John Syrett, prior to his retirement, was Professor of History at Trent University in Peterborough, Ontario. He received his Ph.D. from the University of Wisconsin. He has published several articles on American politics during the 1920s and 1930s, concentrating on New York, Virginia, and Maine, with the most recent being a study of Maine's 1924 gubernatorial election and the Ku Klux Klan. He is presently completing the book *The Confiscation Acts: Efforts at Reconstruction in the Civil War.*

INDEX